Despite much attention to the wisdom literature of the Old Testament in recent years, there is still great uncertainty about the nature of wisdom in relation to the thought world of the ancient near east in general and about its impact on the rest of the Old Testament. In this volume, these issues are systematically advanced, surveyed and evaluated by an international group of specialists. In addition to full coverage of the wisdom books and other literature most frequently thought to have been influenced by them, thematic studies also introduce the principal comparative sources among Israel's neighbours and discuss the place of wisdom in Israelite religion, theology and society. Each essay includes a useful survey of relevant recent studies, and the many fresh insights offered by the contributors will make this volume indispensable to students and scholars alike.

Wisdom in ancient Israel

Professor J. A. Emerton
(Reproduced by courtesy of the Syndics of the Cambridge University Library)

Wisdom in ancient Israel

Essays in honour of J. A. Emerton

Edited by

John Day, Robert P. Gordon and H. G. M. Williamson

CAMBRIDGE
UNIVERSITY PRESS

Published by the Press Syndicate of the University of Cambridge
The Pitt Building, Trumpington Street, Cambridge CB2 1RP
40 West 20th Street, New York, NY 10011–4211, USA
10 Stamford Road, Oakleigh, Melbourne 3166, Australia

First published 1995
Reprinted 1996
First paperback edition 1998

Printed in Great Britain at the University Press, Cambridge

A catalogue record for this book is available from the British Library

Library of Congress cataloguing in publication data

Wisdom in ancient Israel / edited by John Day, Robert P. Gordon, and
H. G. M. Williamson.
     p.   cm.
Includes bibliographical references and index.
ISBN 0 521 42013 X (hardback)
1. Wisdom literature – Criticism, interpretation, etc.   I. Day, John, 1948–
II. Gordon, R. P.   III. Williamson, H. G. M. (Hugh Godfrey Maturin),
1947–   .
BS1455.W56   1995
223'.06 – dc20   94–32951   CIP

ISBN 0 521 42013 X (hardback)
ISBN 0 521 62489 4 (paperback)

Contents

Abbreviations

AbB	*Altbabylonische Briefe*
ABL	R. F. Harper (ed.), *Assyrian and Babylonian Letters* (London and Chicago, 1892–1914)
AEL	M. Lichtheim, *Ancient Egyptian Literature* (3 vols., Los Angeles, 1973, 1976, 1980)
AJSL	*American Journal of Semitic Languages and Literatures*
ANET	J. B. Pritchard (ed.), *Ancient Near Eastern Texts Relating to the Old Testament* (3rd edn, Princeton, 1969)
AnSt	*Anatolian Studies*
ARAB	D. D. Luckenbill, *Ancient Records of Assyria and Babylonia* (Chicago, 1926–27)
ASTI	*Annual of the Swedish Theological Institute*
AV	Authorized Version
BA	*Biblical Archaeologist*
BAR	*Biblical Archaeology Review*
BASOR	*Bulletin of the American Schools of Oriental Research*
BDB	F. Brown, S. R. Driver and C. A. Briggs, *A Hebrew and English Lexicon of the Old Testament* (Oxford, 1906)
BJRL	*Bulletin of the John Rylands Library*
BN	*Biblische Notizen*
BO	*Bibliotheca Orientalis*
BWL	W. G. Lambert, *Babylonian Wisdom Literature* (Oxford, 1960)
CAD	*Chicago Assyrian Dictionary*
CBQ	*Catholic Biblical Quarterly*
Enc. Brit.	*Encyclopaedia Britannica*
ET	*Expository Times*
E. tr.	English translation
EvT	*Evangelische Theologie*
FGH	F. Jacoby, *Die Fragmente der griechischen Historiker* (Berlin and Leiden, 1923–58)
FS	Festschrift
GK	E. Kautzsch and A. E. Cowley (eds.), *Gesenius' Hebrew*

	Grammar (2nd English edn, Oxford, 1910)
HE	*Historia Ecclesiastica*
HS	*Hebrew Studies*
HTR	*Harvard Theological Review*
HUCA	*Hebrew Union College Annual*
ICC	International Critical Commentary
IEJ	*Israel Exploration Journal*
IOS	*Israel Oriental Studies*
JAAR	*Journal of the American Academy of Religion*
JANES	*Journal of the Ancient Near Eastern Society of Columbia University*
JAOS	*Journal of the American Oriental Society*
JB	Jerusalem Bible
JBL	*Journal of Biblical Literature*
JCS	*Journal of Cuneiform Studies*
JEA	*Journal of Egyptian Archaeology*
JJS	*Journal of Jewish Studies*
JNES	*Journal of Near Eastern Studies*
JPSV	Jewish Publication Society Version
JQR	*Jewish Quarterly Review*
JRAS	*Journal of the Royal Asiatic Society*
JSOT	*Journal for the Study of the Old Testament*
JSP	*Journal for the Study of the Pseudepigrapha*
JSS	*Journal of Semitic Studies*
JTS	*Journal of Theological Studies*
KAR	E. Ebeling, *Keilschrifttexte aus Assur religiösen Inhalts* (Leipzig, 1911–27)
KTU	M. Dietrich, O. Loretz and J. Sanmartín, *Die keilalphabetischen Texte aus Ugarit* (Neukirchen-Vluyn, 1976)
LAS	S. Parpola, *Letters from Assyrian Scholars to the Kings Esarhaddon and Assurbanipal* (Neukirchen-Vluyn, 1970, 1983)
LXX	Septuagint
M.	Mishnah
MT	Masoretic Text
NAB	New American Bible
NEB	New English Bible
NF	Neue Folge
NJB	New Jerusalem Bible
NRSV	New Revised Standard Version
ns	New series
NTS	*New Testament Studies*
OB	Old Babylonian

obv.	obverse
OLZ	*Orientalistische Litteratur-Zeitung*
OTS	*Oudtestamentische Studiën*
PBS	*Publications of the Babylonian Section, University Museum, University of Pennsylvania*
PE	*Praeparatio Evangelica*
PEQ	*Palestine Exploration Quarterly*
RA	*Revue d'Assyriologie*
RB	*Revue Biblique*
REB	Revised English Bible
rev.	reverse
RMA	R. C. Thompson, *The Reports of the Magicians and Astrologers of Nineveh and Babylon* (London, 1910)
RQ	*Revue de Qumran*
RS	Ras Shamra
RSR	*Recherches de Science Religieuse*
RSV	Revised Standard Version
SAA	*State Archives of Assyria*
SDB	*Supplément au Dictionnaire de la Bible*
SEL	*Studi Epigrafici e Linguistici*
SJT	*Scottish Journal of Theology*
SVT	*Supplements to Vetus Testamentum*
TDOT	G. J. Botterweck and H. Ringgren (eds.), *Theological Dictionary of the Old Testament* (Grand Rapids, 1974–)
ThLZ	*Theologische Literaturzeitung*
ThT	*Theologisch Tijdschrift*
ThWAT	G. J. Botterweck and H. Ringgren (eds.), *Theologisches Wörterbuch zum Alten Testament* (Stuttgart, 1970–)
ThZ	*Theologische Zeitschrift*
Tos.	*Tosephta*
UF	*Ugarit-Forschungen*
VT	*Vetus Testamentum*
VuF	*Verkündigung und Forschung*
WuD	*Wort und Dienst*
ZA	*Zeitschrift für Assyriologie*
ZAW	*Zeitschrift für die alttestamentliche Wissenschaft*
ZDPV	*Zeitschrift des deutschen Palästina-Vereins*
ZNW	*Zeitschrift für die neutestamentliche Wissenschaft*
ZThK	*Zeitschrift für Theologie und Kirche*

Introduction

John Day, Robert P. Gordon and H. G. M. Williamson

The rehabilitation of Israelite wisdom has been one of the more significant developments in Old Testament scholarship in the last third of the twentieth century. For too long wisdom had been a casualty of the long-running quest for a theological centre in the Old Testament which had seen a variety of potential unifying themes proposed and wisdom almost invariably marginalized in the accompanying discussion. Since the wisdom texts paid little attention to cult and even less to covenant it was virtually inevitable that, as long as the quest persisted in this form, wisdom would be on the sidelines. But the Old Testament contains wisdom literature as part of its witness to the religion, not to say the faith, of ancient Israel, and its importance cannot simply be assessed in proportion to its compatibility with some overarching statement of what Old Testament theology is about. Wisdom's lot is now, in any case, a happier one with the advent of less reductionistic and more pluriform approaches to the description of Old Testament theology. Whatever its special emphases, wisdom as the foremost expression of Israelite intellectual endeavour is, in its more usual manifestations, predicated on a belief in the orderly governance of the world by God. Its character is thus misstated if it is presented merely as a secular alternative to the religious outlook of the rest of the Hebrew scriptures. Current interest in the subject has been deepened by an increased scholarly appreciation of the importance of wisdom thinking and literature among Israel's neighbours, notably in Egypt and Mesopotamia. The strongly ethical flavour of much of this writing, far from arguing for the downgrading of Old Testament wisdom as representing the lowest common denominator in near eastern religious thought, is recognized as offering a basic repertoire of religious insight and ethical consciousness upon which even the prophets of Israel might construct their call to high moral endeavour and enlightened social conscience. So the importance of Israelite wisdom is not to be measured solely in accordance with wisdom's place in the Old Testament canon. In the course of this volume it will be suggested that wisdom insights have affected both the shaping of the Hebrew canon and the reading strategy recommended in certain parts of it.

1

And it will also be a major function of the volume to help determine the extent to which wisdom has been active, now more in the way of a leavening agent, in the narrative, prophetic, psalmic and apocalyptic traditions that are represented in the Old Testament.

This collection of essays, for all that it is entitled *Wisdom in ancient Israel*, happily begins, for the reason already stated, with an acknowledgement of the common stock of wisdom insights shared by Israel with her neighbours in Egypt, Mesopotamia and Syria. Wisdom literature, as John Ray reminds us, was one of the earliest products of the Egyptian scribal tradition, and one of its prime purposes was instruction in the art of being successful in public affairs. However, this survey of wisdom through the several epochs of ancient Egyptian history shows it to have been much more than utilitarianism in service of the 'upwardly mobile'. A strong religious interest is sometimes apparent, for Egyptian scribes 'were trained in an atmosphere of acute religiosity', and there is also evidence of a Socratic-type seeking after knowledge for its own sake. The golden era of the New Kingdom, with its imperial expansion and consequent influx of wealth, witnessed a burgeoning of wisdom writing, most famously in the Instruction of Amenemope, which considers questions of fate and moral responsibility and comes especially close to the Old Testament wisdom of Proverbs, to which, indeed, it seems to have made literary contribution. But in the end Ray resists the temptation to generalize about the course of Egyptian wisdom as if it were headed towards some spiritual or religious telos – a sort of '*via crucis* along the Nile' – and this partly because participation in a wisdom tradition means more borrowing from within the tradition and less firsthand experience and observation than we might imagine.

With a single known exception, the main Babylonian words for 'wisdom' do not have the particular Hebraic sense of 'wise conduct before God', so that at first sight the potential for comparison between Israelite and Babylonian wisdom may appear limited. W. G. Lambert overcomes this slight impediment by focussing on Babylonian writings that exhibit broader characteristics of the Hebrew wisdom literature. The intellectual dimension of wisdom is judged to offer the best basis for comparison, and is represented on the Babylonian side by *Ludlul bēl nēmeqi*, the Theodicy and the Dialogue of Pessimism, each of which is briefly described and assessed in the course of the essay. Lambert also supplements the textual evidence of his corpus of *Babylonian Wisdom Literature*, published in 1960, with further information and with translations of Emar and Sumerian editions of a text which shows that the 'vanity of vanities' theme bequeathed by Qoheleth to world literature was already present in Mesopotamian wisdom texts prior to 1600 BC. With 'creative recensions' this text continued to be

copied and transmitted until at least the seventh century BC. 'Thus
Ecclesiastes was presenting an old theme in an Israelite garb.' This newer
evidence will obviously have to be taken into account when the case for
Qoheleth's having been influenced by Greek philosophy is being considered.

The figure of Ahiqar does not appear in the Old Testament, though he is
found in the apocryphal book of Tobit and is represented in a number of
other ancient sources written in a variety of languages, including an
Aramaic text from Elephantine. The 'Words of Ahiqar' consists of two
parts, the framework story and the 'Sayings of Ahiqar'. Greenfield finds
evidence to suggest that both originated during the reign of the seventh-
century Assyrian king Esarhaddon whom, as the tradition has it, Ahiqar
served as chief counsellor. 'Ahiqar' is a polytheistic work, but it has the
high moral tone characteristic of much of the near eastern wisdom
literature. Greenfield suggests that the polytheistic element must have been
abandoned at an early stage for Ahiqar to figure as he does in Tobit. Later
versions of the story are also generally free of polytheistic features. The
presentation of Ahiqar in Tobit could be said to be emblematic of the
treatment of wisdom generally in Israelite hands, for Ahiqar figures as an
Israelite, a member of the tribe of Naphtali who served in the courts of
Sennacherib and Esarhaddon.

The affinity of Israelite wisdom with that of ancient Egypt in particular
has been apparent since the discovery that the Instruction of Amenemope
closely parallels a section in the book of Proverbs. Whilst in no way denying
this, John Day is concerned to highlight the Semitic influences that have
also helped shape the biblical wisdom traditions. The biblical Job, for
example, is an Edomite. It was probably the very internationalism of
wisdom that made possible the writing of an Israelite book centred on Job
in the period 500–300 BC, when Jewish hatred of the Edomites burned
quite intensely. Job, at any rate, leans towards the Semitic side; there is no
Egyptian counterpart with which comparison may be made. As a specific
instance of foreign Semitic influence on biblical wisdom Day cites the
apparent dependence by Qoheleth upon the epic of Gilgamesh at Eccles. ix
7–9. And, whereas it is a commonplace to assume that the Israelite court
was modelled on its Egyptian counterpart, and by this means came under
the influence of Egyptian wisdom, Day argues that David, the founder of
the Judean court, is more likely to have been influenced by Canaanite
practice and so also by Canaanite wisdom. A number of features in the
book of Proverbs (e.g. the righteous/wicked contrast, graded numerical
sayings, and the personification of wisdom) also suggest that some of its
sayings have been influenced by Semitic wisdom.

Ernest Nicholson's study of theodicy in Job is conducted against the
background of Israelite belief in a direct relationship between the 'fear of

God' and human reward and prosperity. The Satan's question, 'Does Job fear God for nought?' (Job i 9), far from casting cynical aspersion on Job, reflects the common Israelite conviction that God 'rewards the righteous and punishes those who offend his righteousness'. The dialogues of the book of Job, argues Nicholson, respond to Job's statement at the climax of the prologue, in which he turns his back on the old reward-retribution theodicy (Job ii 10), for, simply by implying that there is no need for a theodicy, Job makes theodicy an issue. Thereafter in the dialogues various theodicies are aired but are rejected by Job because he believes that no defence of God's ways in the world can make him look just. Then do the divine speeches at the end of the book attempt a theodicy? Nicholson suggests that they do to the extent that God asserts both his mastery over the creation and his continuing commitment to uphold his creation in the face of the chaotic forces that are contained by his power but not destroyed. Such a faith 'contains at least the seed of a theology of redemption in the sense that if evil is somehow inherent in the creative process, so too is the overcoming of evil'.

Qoheleth also wrestles with troubling contradictions between traditional wisdom teaching and his own observations of life. He is pictured by Otto Kaiser as a scribe who doubled as a teacher, probably working in Jerusalem in the mid-third century BC, in a period of considerable intellectual and religious uncertainty. In Ecclesiastes he has recorded some of his classroom discussions. Only in i 3–iii 15 is there evidence of a carefully planned composition, so it is here, and especially in the concluding section iii 10–15, that Kaiser finds the essential thought of Qoheleth. The message is that humans are committed to unremitting planning and activity, and yet are not in control of their own destiny. They are at the mercy of time and chance, and, as the ultimate perversity, good people may suffer as though they had been wicked, while the ungodly may prosper in their ungodliness. So the book of Ecclesiastes is 'a ghost at the banquet among the other books of the Bible'. The work of Qoheleth has been supplemented by two epilogists (principally in xii 8–11 and xii 12–14) who are reckoned not to have done justice to his central insights. Qoheleth's own advice is of the *carpe diem* variety, to enjoy the present, especially one's youthful present (xi 9–xii 7), and to consider death to the extent that it may concentrate one's mind upon present opportunities.

Some scholars have detected the influence of wisdom circles outside the select 'wisdom canon' of Proverbs, Ecclesiastes and (possibly) Job, perhaps most conspicuously in the Old Testament narrative traditions (e.g. the Joseph story, the 'Succession Narrative', Esther). Robert Gordon finds little to commend in any of the arguments for the existence of a sub-genre of wisdom narrative and so gives his attention to the main Old Testament narratives in which wisdom is prominent as a theme, namely, the account of the tabernacle, the 'Succession Narrative' in 2 Sam. ix–1 Kings ii, and the account of Solomon's reign in 1 Kings ii–xi. The last-named comes in for special treatment as being ideologically less wisdom-orientated than it is commonly assumed to be. A comparison with the account of the tabernacle in Exod. xxxv–xl shows how secularized the Solomonic tradition is, and how, in particular, it makes less of the idea of wisdom as divinely-given than does the Exodus narrative. Wisdom, it is suggested, is even treated negatively, or at least very ambiguously, in 1 Kings ii–iii when the subject of political revenge is in question: the same Solomon who was advised by his ailing father to deal out death to his enemies in accordance with his 'wisdom' (ii 6, 9) is afterwards commended by God for asking for wisdom and not for the lives of his enemies (iii 11–12).

The role of wisdom in the Solomonic traditions in 1 Kings is also the subject of André Lemaire's essay. Lemaire's starting-point is the scant regard paid by some scholars to the biblical depiction of Solomon as the patron of Israelite wisdom, and the surprising omission of 1 Kings iii–xi from some scholarly listings of wisdom-influenced narratives in the Old Testament. His own discussion pursues a strongly historical line of inquiry. Comparisons are made between the biblical account of Solomon's reign and West Semitic royal inscriptions of the ninth and eighth centuries BC in order to show the extent to which 1 Kings iii–xi is rooted in royal near eastern ideology. In a flanking movement on the biblical side Lemaire argues that the theme of Solomonic wisdom cannot be attributed to Deuteronomistic redaction, since the Deuteronomistic summaries of reigns habitually speak of a king's strength, not his wisdom. The preferred solution is to date the original account of Solomon (cf. 1 Kings xi 41) to the reign of Rehoboam and a time when the highlighting of Solomon's political wisdom 'was intended as an implicit criticism of Rehoboam's pretentious attitude at the Shechem assembly which, by refusing to follow the advice of his father's counsellors, was the primary cause of the revolt of Israel against the house of David'.

Johannes Fichtner's 1949 essay, in which he sought to demonstrate the presence of wisdom elements in the work of Isaiah of Jerusalem, opened up discussion of the relationship generally between prophecy and wisdom. The wisdom matrix envisaged in the case of Amos, who is the subject of J. A. Soggin's contribution to this volume, is not the courtly wisdom that has mainly featured so far, but a 'clan wisdom' that developed away from the court and the cities of Israel and that was fostered, as the term itself implies, in the context of home and family. Amos, from Tekoa, presents himself as a very plausible subject not just because of his rural origins but also because of certain ostensibly wisdom features in his oracles. Soggin sets out to check the hypothesis of Amos's wisdom connections which, though it has enjoyed distinguished advocacy, has commanded something less than universal assent. The negative verdict on the wisdom criteria according to which Amos has been included among 'the wise' seems conclusive enough, but Soggin avoids generalizing statements about the prophets and wisdom for lack of clinching arguments, and offers instead a series of options, one or more of which may provide the answer to the larger issue.

An undoubtedly wisdom perspective on the book of Hosea is commended to the reader by its closing verse. The question that Andrew Macintosh sagely poses is whether the clear terminological links between the verse and the substance of the book may indicate awareness of, and openness to, the wisdom tradition on the part of Hosea. Indications of such awareness are found: Hosea 'was greatly interested in the connexion between thought and action and, above all, was convinced that wrong perceptions of reality, of the way things were, would lead inevitably to the demise and ruin of his people and nation'. But his use of wisdom language is free and unfettered by allegiance to any wisdom school or tradition. When Hosea uses words and themes characteristic of the wisdom tradition it is not as if he is representing some authoritative source which, as a member of a wisdom fraternity, he is obliged to reproduce unvaried and unaltered. He is free to yoke the language of wisdom with the metaphors of prophecy, and the realities that they represent, in order to underline the urgency of his message, as is well illustrated by xiii 13, despite its difficulty.

Isaiah, where it all started as regards prophecy and wisdom, looks as if it could also be where it all ends as we read Hugh Williamson's account of recent Isaiah scholarship and of the trends in wisdom studies that make it ever more difficult to speak of a discrete wisdom tradition within Israelite society. But a redefining of the issue makes further exploration possible and worthwhile, for it is shown that both Isaiah and his audience shared a common epistemological basis in that they assumed natural standards of behaviour the recognition of which was not dependent upon any special revelation. This was a viewpoint particularly congenial to the writers of Israel's wisdom literature. It was partly on this basis that Isaiah sought to convince the royal advisers – the 'wise men' of xxix 14 – who influenced the policy decisions of Hezekiah in his relations with the Assyrians. At the same time, the prophetic element that Isaiah introduced into his analysis of Judah's situation brought him into conflict with the royal counsellors. For Isaiah personally there was the vision of the Lord 'high and lifted up', with its implications of God's supremacy over, and orderly superintendence of, the created order. 'It was this towards which the wisdom writers (however defined) in Isaiah's day were struggling, giving him a strong point of contact with them in many respects, but ultimately his prophetic vision outstripped theirs and so also brought him into conflict with them.'

As with Isaiah, the wise against whom Jeremiah polemicized included the statesmen who advised the Judaean kings, especially in relation to the threat posed by the Babylonians under Nebuchadnezzar. As William McKane notes, the claim by the wise that the wellbeing of Judah depended upon their intellectual discernment and judgement was strongly opposed by the pre-exilic prophets. At the same time, there are occasions when the statesmen speak in Jeremiah's favour, as in ch. xxvi, which McKane regards as at least fairly representing the attitude of the statesmen to someone who claimed to speak in the name of the Lord, and again, to a limited extent, in ch. xxxvi, though actual agreement with the prophet's point of view cannot be assumed in either case. In point of fact, an absolute distinction between 'word' and 'counsel' is not one that McKane finds helpful. The transmutation required to convey a divinely-given insight in appropriate human language, when the prophet concerned is deeply immersed in current political realities, imparts a counsel-like character to the oracular word. There is even one occasion, recorded in ch. xxix, when the advice of Jeremiah may be assumed to have coincided with official policy vis-à-vis the Babylonians. The prophetic word and the counsel of the wise did proceed from different sources, but, as in Williamson's discussion of Isaiah, it is noted that the acknowledgement of 'international customary law', as expressing a concept of common humanity and commonly agreed standards, at least had the potential to bring prophet and wise man closer together. 'In our terms', says McKane, 'this suggests that counsel is not necessarily inimical to morality or to the prophetic word.'

'Wisdom psalm' is a familiar genre term in both psalms and wisdom scholarship, but the entity 'wisdom psalm' is not universally recognized nor are those who do acknowledge its existence agreed as to which psalms merit the description. In asking the question, 'What is a wisdom psalm?', Norman Whybray understandably goes back to first principles. Since liturgical texts may be said to have a didactic function, an absolute distinction between wisdom and other psalms is regarded as mistaken. Two factors contribute to the existence in the psalter of psalms that are more in the nature of reflection than of worship and cultic observance: the development of regular private devotions inspiring the composition of new psalms, and the creation of a 'psalm-book' arranged so as to be read consecutively by private individuals. Part of the editorial work will have involved the writing of new psalms for inclusion in the new psalter, and these will have included those for instructional or devotional purposes, which are at any rate unlikely to have originated in the context of temple worship. A few are 'wisdom psalms' in the sense that certain features in them have affinity with the wisdom writings, but the use of the term is deemed not to be helpful when it is applied to a wider range of psalms of a more broadly reflective or didactic character.

When the relationship between wisdom and apocalyptic – here represented by Daniel, the primary Old Testament example – comes under scrutiny, the discussion-point for Brian Mastin is necessarily whether apocalyptic had its roots in wisdom thinking, as was first suggested by L. Noack in 1857 and argued more recently by Gerhard von Rad. A conclusion in such broad terms is resisted, but evidence of a link between apocalyptic and mantic wisdom is visible in both the narrative and the visionary halves of the book of Daniel, whose authors shared many of the presuppositions of mantic wisdom. Yet the fundamental beliefs of the learned men responsible for the book of Daniel 'were not compromised by the fact that the religious synthesis which prevailed in the circles to which they belonged was more favourable to divination than either the Deuteronomists or Second Isaiah had been'. Mastin is careful to leave room for other currents of influence, including the prophetic, in the development of Israelite apocalyptic. This relative late-comer in the history of Jewish religious thought was heir to accumulated biblical traditions as well as to such elements of Canaanite mythology as had been domesticated in Judaism by the time the apocalyptic literature began to be written.

Ben Sira, author of Ecclesiasticus, was one of the last of the traditional wisdom writers. Thanks to information provided by his grandson in the preface that he wrote for his Greek translation of his grandfather's work, the original version can be dated to the early second century BC, just before the onset of the Hellenistic reforms. The political and social circumstances of Ben Sira's own time are therefore especially significant for the understanding of what he wrote. Surrounded by a sea of Hellenism he may have been, but John Snaith insists that Ben Sira was no reactionary against every Hellenistic innovation. He shows his awareness of Greek literature and is clearly dependent on Egyptian wisdom writings for some of his ideas and expressions, yet at the same time his basic loyalty to Judaism finds expression in his warnings against philosophical speculation, with its tendency to weaken commitment to Torah. This loyalty is also evident in the way in which true wisdom is equated with Torah and the way of wisdom with the observance of Torah. In his 'In Praise of the Fathers' in Ecclus xliv 1–xlix 16 Ben Sira's purpose was to remind loyal Jews of their spiritual and cultural heritage and to show them how they could remain loyal to God even while integrating Greek ways with their Jewish faith.

Whereas Ecclesiasticus is quite generously supplied with information relating to origin and background, the Wisdom of Solomon is not so forthcoming. Though almost certainly of Jewish origin, its earliest attestations are in Christian writings. William Horbury therefore concerns himself with the important questions of date, status, authorship and authority. The book was probably compiled in Egypt and had assumed its present Greek form by the early first century BC. As regards status and authority, some knowledge of the development of the Old Testament canon on both the Jewish and Christian sides is helpful, though accessible only after skilfully conducted passage through a number of relevant issues. It is suggested that Wisdom's place in the church – 'a leading position in the class of non-canonical but acceptable books' – may reflect its status among Jews at the end of the Second Temple period. Wisdom makes few concessions either to Greek literary tastes or, on the question of future hope and immortality, to 'Epicurean' tendencies such as are found even in Ecclesiastes and Ecclesiasticus. The Solomonic authorship was questioned early in both Jewish and Christian circles, but the book was valued by Jews as containing inspired prophecy and by Christians as including prophecies concerning the sufferings of Christ and as being specially suitable for study by catechumens.

The link between wisdom in its more specialist and intellectual forms and school education is easily forged, but the Old Testament evidence for the existence of schools is slight and easily summarized. Graham Davies seeks to improve the situation with two 'persuasive indirect arguments'. The first is the existence of scribal training schools in other ancient near eastern countries, with the likelihood of such in Israel in view of Israel's similar need of trained administrators, and the second builds on the possible analogy between the book of Proverbs and certain non-Israelite writings such as the Egyptian 'Instructions' which are known to have functioned as school text-books. The paucity of epigraphic evidence for the existence of scribal schools in Israel compared with the more copious information coming out of Egypt and Mesopotamia may be owing in part to the perishable material used for writing by Palestinian scribes, while the largely accidental nature of archaeological discovery is another possible factor – the more so when there are so few inscriptions of any sort emerging from Jerusalem, where scribal arts must have flourished most of all. But the epigraphic evidence is significant, and growing, and Davies draws attention particularly to some inscriptions, probably the practice exercises of trainee scribes, from a Judaean outpost at Kadesh-barnea. If scribal skills were being sharpened and employed there, the likelihood of formal school training in the main cities and administrative centres is strong.

Some Old Testament literary types at least look as if they should stand in a special relationship to wisdom writing. In particular, fable, parable and allegory, the subject of Kevin Cathcart's essay, have been seen as 'wisdom literary types' (G. Fohrer) or, in the cases of fable, and allegory, as 'forms in which knowledge is expressed' (G. von Rad). As with imagery and metaphor generally, these have not received as much attention from Old Testament scholars as they deserve. Given the determinative role of religion in the formation and preservation of the traditions that make up the Old Testament, it is hardly surprising that fable especially has not been given much prominence in the Old Testament itself. It is, nevertheless, represented. On the other hand, it may be cause for legitimate surprise that the Hebrew wisdom literature, which is to a considerable extent fathered on Solomon who 'discoursed about animals and birds, and reptiles and fish' (1 Kings v 13 [iv 33]), has no fables and few allegories. And fables, like parables (in and out of the Old Testament), may in any case easily disintegrate into allegory. These and similar issues are discussed by Cathcart in his introduction to a survey of those Old Testament fables, parables and allegories in which trees, animals and birds appear in an acting capacity.

There is no personification in the Old Testament that can compare with that of wisdom, according to Roland Murphy. For though justice and peace may kiss, and alcohol may be a rowdy, 'only Wisdom is given a voice that resembles the Lord's (Prov. viii 35, "whoever finds me finds life")'. Nevertheless, wisdom personified is an enigmatic figure (personification, hypostasis or person?), and a variety of claims are made on her behalf. Murphy elects, therefore, to examine the significance of personified wisdom in the contexts of the books in which she features. In Proverbs she stands for the fulness of life open to those who follow in her way, and, since this is in contrast with the fate of those who go after Dame Folly, the issue becomes one of life and death and of fidelity to God or infidelity. Here wisdom 'has assumed the burden of the covenant, fidelity to the Lord, in language reflecting the old struggle so mercilessly bared in the book of Hosea and elsewhere'. In Ecclus xxiv, on the other hand, we have a theology of presence according to which it was wisdom that came down and became concretized in Torah (and not *vice versa*), while Wisdom vii–ix presents her as 'spirit, all-pervasive, an artisan in creation, the divine consort' and 'a divine gift who is also a saviour'. Small wonder, then, that Murphy claims that, from a 'literary-theological' standpoint, personified wisdom is unequalled in the Old Testament. Personified wisdom, moreover, helped wisdom in general to survive the 'crisis of wisdom' reflected in Job and Ecclesiastes and to live on in Ben Sira and the Wisdom of Solomon.

Because 'Lady Wisdom' has divine attributes in several Old Testament and apocryphal texts a number of scholars have thought to detect a goddess behind the figure, or have argued that the bestowal of divine characteristics upon wisdom is an attempt to legitimize the worship in Israel and Judah of an 'established' goddess such as Asherah. Wisdom personified is approached from another angle by Judith Hadley who argues that it functions as a literary device intended to compensate for the eradication of the worship of goddesses in Israel. This apparent apotheosis of wisdom took place as a reaction to the displacement (or assimilation) of the goddess figure and sought to secure a place for the feminine where it needed to be expressed in the context of the divine. Extra-biblical evidence of the association of Yahweh with goddess consorts in the pre-exilic period is found at Kuntillet 'Ajrud (Asherah) and Elephantine (Anat). 'Now, here in the Wisdom literature, can be seen a female figure of Lady Wisdom with seemingly divine attributes, but still very much "under the thumb" of Yahweh, which may be an attempt at satisfying this apparent need for the feminine to be represented in the deity.'

Many of the forms and meanings of wisdom as they are found in the Old Testament also appear in the Dead Sea Scrolls, which shows that the Qumran community participated in a common Jewish wisdom tradition. Parts of the most important texts are, accordingly, presented in translation, and with brief comments, by A. S. van der Woude in order to establish how far the Qumran material conforms to, and to what extent it differs from, the religious thought-world of its time. What emerges clearly is that the relevant texts lack unambiguous Qumranic traits or references to the Qumran community (e.g. 4Q184, 4Q424, 11QPs[a] 154) and may even be demonstrably pre-Qumranic in origin (e.g. 4Q185). Van der Woude therefore concludes that the Qumran community itself did not compose wisdom literature, 'although its members certainly handed down writings of this kind and held them in esteem'. A possible explanation suggested by van der Woude is that, in the view of the community, true wisdom came with the 'Teacher of Righteousness' and it was this that most interested his followers. But their respect for traditional wisdom teaching is seen in the fact that they copied the sapiential literature that was handed down to them, and that they made room for its terminology even in their non-sapiential writings.

Wisdom, as Rudolf Smend observes in his overview of the subject in nineteenth-century scholarship, has been less of a preoccupation of German scholars in the present century than in the nineteenth. Slightly more discouraging is his observation that, often unawares, the recent debate has repeated much of the ground covered a century and more ago. Smend's own efforts are trained mainly on the book of Proverbs and its treatment at the hands of its nineteenth-century interpreters. Thus in discussing the date of the book he can trace a trajectory of opinion from J. G. Eichhorn's early dating and substantial Solomonic attribution through to T. K. Cheyne's assertion that 'in its present form the Book of Proverbs is a source of information, not for the pre-Exilic, but for various parts of the post-Exilic period'. One obvious handicap affecting nineteenth-century study of wisdom was the lack of comparative material from outside Israel. Scholars of the period were aware, partly from the Bible itself, that biblical wisdom belonged within a larger sapiential framework, but they did not have available the Egyptian and Mesopotamian texts that have helped to give new life to the subject in more recent times. It was perhaps natural, then, that the more classical-sounding term 'philosophy' was commonly used to describe the wisdom that is presented in the Old Testament, and that wisdom was consequently often regarded as speculative in character.

The statement in Prov. ix 1 that wisdom 'has built her house' reads almost like wry commentary on the way in which wisdom has apparently struck out on its own in the Old Testament, having little to do with the theology surrounding the other 'house', in Jerusalem, that is so strongly associated with Solomon in biblical tradition. It is very appropriate, then, that the concluding essay in this volume should address the issue of wisdom in relation to Old Testament theology. Ronald Clements writes approvingly of the renewed emphasis on wisdom, once regarded as 'an aberrant offshoot of the mainstream of Israelite–Jewish religious life'. This reassessment, it is noted, should not encourage the thought that wisdom was valued uniformly in Old Testament times; it appears to have flourished for a time and then to have lost influence, 'leaving its mark only on the fringes of the canonical literature'. Yet at a crucial time in Jewish history wisdom helped to express basic Jewish attitudes and values and so shape a response to the challenges faced by Jews living in a predominantly Gentile world. Wisdom did achieve a lowly enough place in the Old Testament canon, but, as Clements shows, it also contrived to play a part in the structuring and shaping of that same canon. And, with its commitment to timeless truths that transcend historical particularity and cultural specificity, wisdom always has the potential to rise from the lowlier canonical foothills in order to convey truth about God and the world of his making.

This volume is intended to serve the dual purpose of presenting a suitable tribute to an outstanding scholar in the fields of Hebrew and Old Testament and of providing a survey of the important topic of wisdom in the Old Testament, the Apocrypha and the ancient near east, in which contributors would also have opportunity to advance aspects of the subject beyond its present limits. It is a topic on which John Emerton himself has made several significant contributions, most importantly in his edition of the Peshiṭta of the Wisdom of Solomon, which laid the foundation for the work of the international Peshiṭta project (*The Old Testament in Syriac: Peshiṭta Version*) based in Leiden, and also in his several articles on the text of Proverbs and his essay on wisdom in the volume *Tradition and Interpretation*, produced by the Society for Old Testament Study. In addition, he has deployed his formidable scholarship in writing on a wide range of other subjects relating to the language and literature of the Old and New Testaments, as well as in his contributions on the Ugaritic literature and on Semitic philology in general. Inevitably, not every conceivable topic within wisdom has been included in this volume, nor has it been possible to involve everyone who might have wished to be associated with it. We know, however, that the honorand's many friends, colleagues and former students throughout the world – many of them, as contributors to *Vetus Testamentum* and its supplement series, the beneficiaries of his selfless editorial labours on their behalf – will want to join us in wishing both him and Norma, herself a distinguished scholar in the history of science, many more years of enjoyable and productive scholarship.

Part 1

The ancient near eastern setting

1   Egyptian wisdom literature

J. D. Ray

Pharaoh was the incarnation of the sun-god, and the light of his presence illuminated the Nile Valley. Such was his splendour that neighbouring states found it impossible to ignore his influence, and this was particularly true of the land of Palestine. Palestine was poor, fragmented and anarchic, while Egypt for most of its history was the opposite: agriculturally wealthy and possessing great natural resources, artistically sophisticated, militarily powerful, and the first state in history to enjoy centralized government. The Old Testament is full of the shadows cast by Pharaoh's sun, and the result – a mixture of admiration, distrust, envy and emulation, often at the same time – shows through in its pages, from the nostalgia of the Children of Israel in Sinai to the denunciations of Ezekiel and Jeremiah. Part of the fascination of the Joseph story for its Jewish audience must have been that it showed a poor Hebrew beating the most cultured society of the ancient near east at its own game, and there must have been many who wished that they could do the same. However, Egypt's position in the biblical world was more complex than this: its wealth and sophistication made it a target for immigration at most periods, and this was frequently seen as a problem by the Egyptians themselves. Feelings of cultural superiority kept the Egyptians, or certainly their government, from appreciating foreign innovations, and the technological and intellectual history of the country is one of acute fits and starts, as the Egyptians realized the need for a new process or idea and rushed to catch up. The innovation was often disguised as something purely Egyptian from the outset, and pride was satisfied.

In spite of its aloofness, Egypt shared in the general culture of the near east. Vicissitudes of fate and the elements were common, and this tended to give rise to pithy observations on the realities of existence. The gap between rich and poor was large, perhaps increasingly so as society developed, and this too must have produced its share of speculation on the reasons for such inequalities. There was a similar dichotomy between powerful and powerless. All the literate societies of the area needed to train an administrative class, and all probably approached the problem in much the same way: complex writing-systems required long training, with emphasis on rote-learning and reverence for the past, and the combination of tradition, didacticism, and repeatable sentiment encouraged the use of proverbs and rules for successful or ethical behaviour. Schools for this purpose were often attached to temples. This in turn led to the production of full-scale manuals of behaviour, the genre which modern scholars term wisdom literature. To the Egyptians these compositions were known by the collective name of *sb3yt*, 'instruction', or more simply 'teaching' (the root meaning is closer to 'enlightenment'). This concept, however, extended beyond a single type of literature, and probably included huge numbers of proverbs or ethical observations, many of which are lost, but some of which are probably preserved in individual letters or in the funerary compositions which we group under the general title of *The Book of the Dead*. In addition, the influence of an ethical and didactic tradition can be seen in other literary works, some of which come close to being works of *sb3yt*, and which may even have been thought of as such by their audiences. A few of these will be mentioned in this chapter, if only as a reminder that modern classifications are not the only, or necessarily the best, way of approaching the ancient world.[1]

Wisdom literature was probably among the first creations of the Egyptian scribe, but we need to wait until well into the Old Kingdom (*c.* 2300 BC) before the preservation of texts on papyrus allows us to observe it. The earliest at present seems to be the fragmentary Instruction of Prince Ḥardedef,[2] which is named after an historical character, a son of Cheops, the builder of the Great Pyramid. However, this title is probably a case of pseudepigraphy, as with most ancient didactic writings. Ḥardedef, like others, became famous as one of the traditional sages, and it may be that this reputation caused later works of literature to be ascribed to him in addition to genuine ones that he had written himself; the details are unfortunately lost to us. A similar composition of roughly the same date is the Instruction addressed by an unknown sage to one Kagemni, who is said to have been promoted to the office of *vizîr* under king Sneferu on the

---

[1] Translations of the main works of Egyptian wisdom literature can be found in the volumes by Miriam Lichtheim, *Ancient Egyptian Literature,* 1 (Los Angeles, 1973), 2 (California, 1976), and 3 (California, 1980). These are abbreviated as *AEL*. In general, I have followed Lichtheim in the passages quoted, although with small alterations. A basic anthology in translation is included in R. O. Faulkner, E. Wente and W. K. Simpson, *The Literature of Ancient Egypt* (New Haven, 1972), pp. 159–265. A useful general survey is contained in the article by J. Leclant in *Les Sagesses du Proche-Orient ancien* (Colloque de Strasbourg 17–19 May 1962; Paris, 1963), pp. 5–26 with bibliography; a later version appears in *Sagesses et religion* (Colloque de Strasbourg October 1976 = *Bibliothèque des Centres d'Etudes supérieures specialisés;* Paris, 1979), pp. 7–19. There is much comparative material in E. Hornung and O. Keel (eds.), *Studien zu altägyptischen Lebenslehren* (Fribourg and Göttingen, 1979).

[2] The surviving Old Kingdom wisdom texts can be studied in *AEL* 1, pp. 58–80.

strength of the wisdom contained within it. This is a delightful combination of pseudepigraphon and advertisement, and it reminds us that the primary purpose of texts of this sort was to act as a manual for worldly success. This notion can be seen in its fullest form in the Wisdom of Ptaḥḥotep, which is shown to be an Old Kingdom composition by the language in which it is written. However, the text survives in copies from much later periods, and seems to have passed into a second, revised edition during the New Kingdom, some thousand years after its original composition. The work clearly achieved something close to canonical status, and it deserves to be studied more closely.[3] As is usual in texts of this sort, the aged sage is shown passing on his accumulated wisdom to his son. The result is at first sight a disconcerting mixture of serious moral insight and trivial rules of social behaviour that remind one of being told not to eat peas with a knife, and the latter rules in particular have led some Egyptologists to disparage the entire composition as little more than a rulebook for the upwardly mobile petty official. This is probably to miss the point, although it is obvious that few lengthy texts that have been compiled from a variety of sources are likely to maintain a consistent standard of moral intensity. Ptaḥḥotep, like other similar texts, appears to be written in verse form, although the exact metre and the rules of composition are obscured by the vowellessness of the script. The opening stanza contains the following well-known injunction to intellectual modesty:

> Do not be proud of your knowledge,
> Consult the ignorant as well as the wise;
> The limits of art are not reached,
> No artist's skills are perfect;
> Good speech is more hidden than the greenstone,
> Yet it is found among maids at the grindstones.[4]

This theme, of humility without complacency and ambition without snobbery, is the leitmotif for much that follows. The numerous social examples in which the text delights are best viewed in the light of the problem of what constitutes an abstract definition. This can be seen at its most acute in the Socratic dialogues of Plato. As is well known, Socrates in these dialogues takes a keen pleasure in discomfiting the intellectually grand and complacent by asking questions such as 'What is virtue?' The poor victim invariably replies with an example, whereupon Socrates springs the trap, saying that he was not looking for examples; he was asking for a definition, which is why he went to someone universally thought to be wise. Indeed, the problem of defining categories has preoccupied philosophers ever since, some concluding, with Wittgenstein, that there is

[3] *AEL* 1, pp. 61–80.   [4] After Lichtheim, *AEL* 1, p. 63.

no definition, only an algebraic sum of examples. The unknown author of Ptaḥḥotep would probably have sided with Socrates' victims, at least when it came to method; put more simply, he sets out to define virtue by how it reveals itself in practice. This description can serve as a rule of thumb for other wisdom texts from ancient Egypt. On the other hand, Egyptian scribes were trained in an atmosphere of acute religiosity, and would probably have agreed with Plato in seeing any example of virtuous behaviour as partaking of a divine prototype. In Egyptian terms this would be the concept of *Ma'at*, a notion which incorporates ideas such as truth, harmony and justice, and which could be personified as a goddess, the daughter of the sun-god himself.[5]

The Old Kingdom (Dynasties III–VI) was the first centralized state in history, and there is sufficient evidence that its collapse, however it came about, was regarded by later generations, and probably by contemporaries, as a traumatic event. In the Middle Kingdom, the period from Dynasty XI which follows, this lesson is remembered, and a chiller wind blows through the Egyptian state. The divine charisma of the Old Kingdom Pharaohs now needed to be supplemented by practical politics, and persuasion or eloquence (*mdt* or *mdt nfrt*) increasingly came to be seen as an arm of government. A more realistic translation of this concept might be propaganda.[6] In its artistic excellence, tight control of thought, and political cohesion designed to prevent fragmentation and breakdown, the Middle Kingdom of Egypt has several points in common with the other Middle Kingdom, that of early imperial China. This comparison is not entirely fanciful.

Eloquence and instruction are of course complementary, and it is not surprising to see motifs and impressions derived from wisdom literature extended during the Middle Kingdom to other classes of writing. One of the earliest is the powerful composition known as the Instruction for Merikare', which takes the form of an open letter to the heir-apparent of one of the Ninth- or Tenth-dynasty kings from his ageing predecessor.[7] On one level this can be seen as a simple political manual, giving advice on how to hold the kingdom together. However, it is unprecedented in Egyptian literature because of the degree of self-criticism which the king reveals, and the stress he lays upon divine judgement for misdeeds, even those done by Pharaohs. Here wisdom is linked explicitly with eschatology, a theme which will recur in later texts:

---

[5] The best recent study of this concept is by J. Assmann, *Ma'at: Gerechtigkeit und Unsterblichkeit im alten Ägypten* (Munich, 1990).

[6] The standard work on the use of propaganda in Egyptian government at this period is still that by G. Posener, *Littérature et politique dans l'Egypte de la XIIe dynastie* (Paris, 1956). A thoughtful selection of Middle Kingdom texts can be found in R. B. Parkinson, *Voices from Ancient Egypt* (London, 1991).   [7] *AEL* 1, pp. 97–109. See also *ANET*, pp. 414–18.

There was retribution for what I had done,
For it is evil to destroy,
Useless to restore what one has damaged ...
To every action there is a response.
While generation succeeds generation,
The god who knows characters is hidden;
One cannot oppose the lord of authority;
He reaches all that the eye can see.[8]

The profundity and unorthodox tone of Merikare' can be paralleled in another text which may be contemporary, the dialogue between a disillusioned man and his soul which is generally known by its German name, the *Lebensmüde*.[9] The moral of this tightly argued tale is that life of a sort, even with misery and imperfections, is preferable to no life at all. It survives only in one manuscript, and some of the gods mentioned in the text are distinctly unusual. The *Lebensmüde* represents an extreme adaptation of the instruction genre to fictional narrative, and the evidence of survival suggests that it was not entirely to orthodox taste.

Another application of *sb3yt* to wider questions is seen in the propaganda texts which seek to define the nature of good government. A fragmentary tale, Neferkare' and the General Sisene, gives a salacious (and probably fictitious) account of the court of Pepi II at the end of the Old Kingdom, and has as its sub-text the message that the previous system collapsed because of moral depravity, thus pointing the contrast with the present régime.[10] Similar ideas are explored in Papyrus Westcar, a series of tales about magicians reminiscent of the *Thousand and One Nights*; here the Pharaoh Cheops is shown as arbitrary and overbearing – features which are in conflict with the idea of *Ma'at*.[11]

A parallel theme is explored in the Tale of the Eloquent Peasant, in which a poor countryman is robbed by an unjust official, but succeeds by natural eloquence in capturing the attention of the court and securing justice. In one of his speeches the metaphor of the ship of state appears for the first time, although the ship is so overloaded as to be in danger of sinking. Though not wisdom texts in the strict sense, these works deserve to be included as showing an extension of the theme and purpose of *sb3yt* into ethics and political life. An even closer combination of wisdom and propaganda can be seen in the Instruction of Amenemhet I, where a disillusioned ruler describes an assassination attempt on himself, and concludes with cynicism that friendship and kingship are incompatible.[12]

[8] After Lichtheim, *AEL* 1, p. 105.
[9] *AEL* 1, pp. 163–9; Faulkner, Wente and Simpson, *The Literature of Ancient Egypt*, pp. 201–9.
[10] Parkinson, *Voices from Ancient Egypt*, pp. 54–6.
[11] For the tales of Papyrus Westcar see *AEL* 1, pp. 215–22, and Faulkner, Wente and Simpson, *The Literature of Ancient Egypt*, pp. 15–30.
[12] *AEL* 1, pp. 135–9; Parkinson, *Voices from Ancient Egypt*, pp. 48–52.

On the social side, some so-called instructions are designed to poke fun at various trades, in an attempt to persuade reluctant schoolboys into the scribal profession.

A further extension of *sb3yt* can be seen in the group of pessimistic texts, common in the Middle Kingdom, which are known collectively as Admonitions.[13] These adhere to a common pattern: a sage or other reactionary figure bemoans the decadence of society, and paints a verbal picture of moral decay, the collapse of institutions and the economy, and a general return to savagery and barbarism. These descriptions are sometimes so vivid that they have tempted commentators into seeing them as literal descriptions, either of the anarchy which is supposed to have accompanied the First or Second Intermediate Period, or (in extreme cases) as an eye-witness account of the Plagues of Egypt and the Exodus. This seems unnecessary. Texts of this sort make better sense against a background of some comfort and security, when it is easier to indulge in melancholy at arm's length. The Elizabethan love of dirges is a similar phenomenon, as are the present-day songs of unrequited love, teenage angst, jealousy and murder which continue to give pleasure to millions.

The Middle Kingdom also produced its share of conventional wisdom. The standard text, and the most popular if later manuscripts are any indication, is a rather lifeless compendium known as *Kemyt* or 'completion'.[14] It is not only modern societies which feel at home with the mediocre. It is perhaps symptomatic here that one of the most orthodox Middle Kingdom wisdom texts, the Complaints of Khakheperra-sonbe, devotes much of its space to the fact that language is exhausted, and that new metaphors are hard to find.[15] The Middle Kingdom is often described as Egypt's classic age, but one has the impression that wisdom literature was not at the centre of its achievement. The situation alters when we come to the New Kingdom (Dynasties XVIII–XX). This period, characterized by imperial expansion into Africa and the near east and a corresponding influx of wealth, brings new themes into play throughout Egyptian literature: the growth of the grandiose and the exotic, a tendency to universalism in thought and ethics, and a developing preoccupation with fate and the problems raised by its existence. Consciousness of background produces an effect which can almost be described as romantic. The New Kingdom continued to edit and re-edit the wisdom texts of the past, but also contributed much of its own, notably the two remarkable Instructions

[13] *AEL* 1, pp. 139–45 (the Prophecies of Neferti, which are adapted to a political end and given a happy conclusion) and pp. 149–63 (the Admonitions of Ipuwer).

[14] For a new translation of part of this text see A. N. Dakin, *Sesto Congresso Internazionale di Egittologia: Atti* (Rome, 1992), pp. 465–71.

[15] *AEL* 1, pp. 145–9.

ascribed to Ani and Amenemope. The Instruction of Ani is known from an increasing number of copies, and it is now possible to have a clearer picture of its scope and intentions.[16] In essence, it is a collection of conventional themes: respect for motherhood and religion, avoidance of alien or unfaithful women, honesty in transactions (greatly emphasized), restraint in the face of aggression, and reticence before strangers. However, a novel tone is introduced in an epilogue, in which the sage's son and heir replies that he finds his father's words tortuous and impractical. The father succeeds in rebutting this adolescent rebellion, but only with difficulty. This epilogue reminds us of the New Kingdom love of the dramatic, and it comes close to being a self-parody. This may even be the intention of the author, although it is difficult to be sure of this, since the end of the text is still obscure.

The Wisdom of Amenemope is in a different class, and it has long been recognized as one of the masterpieces of near eastern literature.[17] The text is known from several copies, the principal one being BM 10474, and the date of composition is probably Ramesside (*c.* 1250–1100 BC). The depth of its thought is matched by the vividness of its poetry, and its organization into thirty stanzas is clearly deliberate, thirty being the number which epitomized justice in ancient Egypt. The author is introduced as an official from the city of Akhmîm, a place which will recur later in this chapter, and which was famous for its intellectual tradition.[18] The almost pictorial quality of the text's imagery is well caught in the following passage:

> The trodden furrow worn down by time,
> He who disguises it in the fields,
> When he has snared it by false oaths,
> He will be caught by the might of the Moon.   (vii 16–19)[19]

Underlying the philosophy of Amenemope is the question of fate, a characteristic New Kingdom preoccupation, and the notion of moral responsibility. The relationship between these concepts is a perplexing one, and Amenemope's contribution to the debate is to characterize two types of human behaviour. One, the 'silent man', discerns divine purpose and accommodates himself to it. In such a way he avoids pitfalls in this life, and is found pleasing to the gods. The other, the heated or rash man, is in conflict not only with external conditions and their dispensation but also, in the last resort, with himself. This contrast is of course implicit in earlier

---

[16] *AEL* 2, pp. 135–46. An additional fragment has since come to light in the Egypt Exploration Society's excavations in the New Kingdom necropolis at Saqqâra.
[17] *AEL* 2, pp. 146–63; Faulkner, Wente and Simpson, *The Literature of Ancient Egypt*, pp. 241–65 and literature cited.
[18] The intellectual tradition of Akhmîm is discussed in H.-J. Thissen, *Der verkommene Harfenspieler* (Sommerhausen, 1992), pp. 80–3.   [19] After Lichtheim, *AEL* 2, p. 151.

works, notably Ptaḥḥotep, but in Amenemope it is made into the centre of the teaching. In stanza 4 this distinction is extended beyond everyday ethics into the realm of theodicy and eschatology, a realm well explored in Egyptian religious thought. The metaphor is clear, and does not need to be explained either by the ancient author or a modern commentator:

> As for the heated man in the temple,
> He is like a tree growing in a wasteland (?);
> A moment lasts its growth of leaves,
> Its end comes in the woodshed;
> It is floated far from its place,
> And the flame is its burial-shroud.
> The truly silent, who keeps apart,
> Is like a tree grown in a meadow.
> It is green, it doubles its yield,
> It stands in front of its lord.
> Its fruit is sweet, its shade delights,
> And it reaches its end in the garden.   (iv 1–12)[20]

The imagery and intensity of Amenemope is frequently compared with that of the Old Testament, and particular relationships are sometimes claimed, notably with Prov. xxii 17–xxiv 22. The discussion of this sometimes has a circular quality about it, in the absence of precise knowledge about the date of the text and the mechanism of transmission into Hebrew. An alternative possibility, that of a Semitic prototype, seems to have been refuted, at least for the time being.[21] However, there are equally clear links between Egyptian and biblical poetry (the Song of Songs and the Egyptian lyric cycles) and between the Hymn to the Aten and Ps. civ. There are also striking, but unexplained, resemblances between Ramesside love poetry and Alexandrian literature in Greek, written a millennium later. In such a context, a link between Amenemope and Proverbs does not seem out of the question. Indeed, Hebrew and Egyptian wisdom literature from the late New Kingdom onwards can be shown, *ceteris paribus*, to share a similar vocabulary, and even to be constructed on parallel lines.[22]

Another interesting feature of Amenemope is something which, although not new, is moved deliberately into the foreground: the use of the expression *p3 nṯr*, which is variably translated 'the god', 'god', or 'God'. This is controversial, not least because the Egyptians were not monotheistic in the sense normally understood by the word.[23] However, there was a clear

---

[20] Adapted from *AEL* 2, pp. 150–1.
[21] R. J. Williams, 'The Alleged Semitic Original of the *Wisdom of Amenemope*', *JEA* 47 (1961), pp. 100–6.
[22] This is made clear in the study by Nili Shupak, *Where Can Wisdom Be Found? The Sage's Language in the Bible and in Ancient Egyptian Literature* (Fribourg and Göttingen, 1993).
[23] See in particular J. Vergote, 'La notion de dieu dans les livres de sagesse égyptiens', in *Les Sagesses du Proche-Orient ancien*, pp. 151–90.

henotheistic tendency in Egyptian religion, and it is possible that outright monotheism would have been recognized as a legitimate interpretation of that religion, at least in some circles. The monotheism would need to be inclusive, recognizing the validity of traditional gods and expressions, rather than exclusive (which was the mistake made by Akhenaten); but with this provision, it would probably have been admitted. The most sensible conclusion seems to be that the phrase *p3 ntr* was intended, like many religious concepts, to be understood on more than one level: it could embrace the notion of a local god, an unnamed major divinity, a collective noun for the entire pantheon, or an unrealized supreme principle, depending on circumstances and on the audience involved. Whatever the exact nuance, the power of the expression is clear from the following passage:

> Do not lie down in fear of tomorrow:
> 'Comes day, how will tomorrow be?'
> Man knows not how tomorrow will be;
> God (*p3 ntr*) is ever in his perfection,
> Man is ever in his failure.   (xviii 1–5)[24]

The Third Intermediate Period which follows the New Kingdom has left us no works of wisdom that we can identify, but the situation changes noticeably when we turn to the Late Period (Dynasties XXVI–XXX). This is even more marked in the Hellenistic era, following the incorporation of the country into the empire of Alexander. During the seven centuries between Dynasty XXV and the coming of the Romans, Egypt was always aware of the threat of foreign conquest, and the literature of these dynasties has a cosmopolitan aspect to it. Influences from Aramaic, Iranian, Akkadian and from the literature of the Greek world can be detected, and Egypt contributed to these cultures in its turn. In such an international context, it is not surprising to find that the didactic themes which are common to most of the near east are also reflected in Egyptian.[25] Demotic, the final stage of the Egyptian script, has yielded fragments of a considerable number of works, and there is no doubt that more remains to be discovered. There are substantial texts in the Louvre, and a wisdom text in Brooklyn is also known.[26] Other extracts survive on ostraca. However, it is more helpful to concentrate on the two outstanding works which have survived, and on the issues which they raise.

The Wisdom of Ankhsheshonqy is known from a lengthy demotic

---

[24] After *AEL* 2, p. 157.

[25] Many of the questions raised by this body of literature are discussed in Miriam Lichtheim, *Late Egyptian Wisdom Literature in the International Context* (Fribourg and Göttingen, 1983).

[26] An idea of the wealth of texts still unpublished can be seen in R. J. Williams, 'Some fragmentary demotic wisdom texts', in J. H. Johnson and E. Wente (eds.), *Studies in Honor of George R. Hughes* (Chicago, 1976), pp. 263–71. The Brooklyn papyrus is described by G. Posener and J. Ste Fare Garnot in *Les Sagesses du Proche-Orient ancien*, pp. 153–7.

papyrus in the British Museum, a manuscript which seems to date from the end of the Ptolemaic period.[27] The wisdom that it contains is preceded by a literary introduction which owes much to the Aramaic text known as the Wisdom of Ahiqar. Ankhsheshonqy is a priest of the sun-god Pre' who is visiting an old friend, the chief physician of Pharaoh. He is informed about a plot on Pharaoh's life, which comes to nothing; however, Ankhsheshonqy is arrested along with the conspirators for failing to reveal the plot – a case of choosing to betray one's country rather than one's friends. In prison and disillusioned, he writes the moral of the story on potsherds, which are to be smuggled out for the instruction of his son. He begins with a series of laments about the state of the nation, ending with verse 13: 'When Pre' is angry with a land, he makes its washerman the chief of police.' (One wonders what he would make of some contemporary politicians.) What follows takes the form of an anthology of sayings, grouped loosely by tone or format. Some of these sentiments are doubtless established proverbs, while others may well be deliberate variations or comments upon such proverbs. Study shows that an Aramaic version of the Wisdom of Ahiqar must be the prototype for some of these sayings, but others should probably be sought in Greek sources, or even in Hellenistic philosophy. There is something reminiscent of Stoicism in parts of Ankhsheshonqy.

Although many of the sayings are cynical or disillusioned, it must be admitted that the world they illustrate is hardly that of a respected priest going through a moral dilemma. Instead, they take us into a society where everything has its price, and it is a price which needs to be paid. It is that of the near eastern peasant, faced with the forces of nature, living his life at or near subsistence level, and finding almost no-one to trust. Accompanying this is a strong trait of misogyny, which is by no means unique to this text, but which is used here to point up the prevailing mood of grim self-reliance. There have been attempts to compare Ankhsheshonqy with Hesiod, the sour farmer of Askra in Boeotia; although a detailed comparison cannot be maintained, the underlying thinking is much the same. These two characters would have understood each other readily enough.

Although the sayings in the text are arranged apparently at random, certain themes emerge, and testify to extreme skill on the part of the compiler. These are the ubiquity of change and the vicissitudes that go with it, and the fact that actions have consequences. This can often be brought out by the use of contrasts and paradoxes (ix 16: 'Do not say "It is summer"; there is winter too'; xv 11–12: 'When a man smells of myrrh his wife is a cat before him. When a man is suffering his wife is a lioness before him'). Other than this, there is no strongly articulated moral order, and the

[27] AEL 3, pp. 159–84; Lichtheim, *Late Egyptian Wisdom Literature in the International Context*, pp. 13–92.

concept of *Ma'at* is strangely absent. This is in line with Hellenistic notions of fortune and decay, and it reflects some of the problems of the world which followed Alexander.

These dilemmas are dealt with more fully in the wisdom text whose ancient name is uncertain, but which goes under the title Papyrus Insinger.[28] The principal manuscript, which probably dates from the first century AD, is now in Leiden, but other extracts are known, and the work clearly achieved some circulation. It comes from Akhmîm, the city which we have already observed in connection with Amenemope. It is arranged in twenty-five paragraphs or 'instructions' (the first five are lost), and this is reminiscent of, though not identical with, the thirty chapters into which Amenemope is divided. Another feature which it has in common with the earlier text is a dual analysis of human behaviour as positive or negative, but, instead of the silent man and his heated counterpart, these are now characterized as the wise man and the fool, a contrast which is familiar from biblical texts.[29] Many of the paragraphs end with a refrain, normally a variant on the words, 'The fate and the fortune that come, it is God (*p3 ntr*) who makes them come.' The workings of fate are seen as dependent upon this agency, and this is the only thing in the universe which is possessed of constancy. The parallels between Insinger and Qoheleth have often been noted, and a start has been made in comparing the text with the Jewish wisdom of Ben Sira and even Greek writers such as Theognis.[30]

The parallels between Insinger and Amenemope are clear enough, but it is important also to stress the differences. Both are obsessed with fate and responsibility, but whereas Amenemope describes the right course as extremely difficult but nevertheless compatible with divine will, in Insinger there is an almost complete rift between moral behaviour and divine providence. There is also a dichotomy between ethical actions and character. In several passages Insinger comes close to asserting that moral rightness is something which should be followed without thought of reward or gain, and almost as an act of defiance in the face of inscrutable fortune. The following passages may make this clear:

> There is a trace of the inferior man in the character of the godly man.
> He is not a great man who is chosen because of his city (?),
> Nor is he an inferior man who leaves the way because of foolishness.
> The heart and the character, like their owner, are in the hand of God.
> Fate and fortune go and come when he commands them.   (xv 2–6)[31]

---

[28] *AEL* 3, pp. 184–217; Lichtheim, *Late Egyptian Wisdom Literature in the International Context*, pp. 107–234. The text is sometimes known by the name Phibis given at the end of the manuscript, but this may be that of the owner rather than the author.

[29] Shupak, *Where Can Wisdom Be Found?*, pp. 78–216 (chs. 3–5).

[30] J. T. Sanders, *Ben Sira and Demotic Wisdom* (Chico, 1983).

[31] After *AEL* 3, p. 197.

Many are the small things that are worthy of respect.
Few are the great things that are worthy of admiration.
There is one who fears blame, yet commits a great crime,
There is one who shouts out of scorn, yet he gives service.
He who guards himself is not a wise or respectful man,
Nor is he to whom harm comes a deceitful fool.
The fate and the fortune that come, it is God who determines them.

(xxv 7–13)[32]

Insinger explores with profundity many of the perplexing questions of fate, responsibility and ethical duty. The style is sometimes elliptical and convoluted, but the images are vivid and thoughtful. It is a text which deserves to be known by students of the near east.

In conclusion, it is tempting to draw a line through Egyptian history by surveying the wisdom texts which have survived, from the pragmatic rules of Ptaḥḥotep, through the disillusionment of some Middle Kingdom teaching, to the synthesis of moral behaviour and divine will which is seen in Amenemope, and finally to the divorce between ethics and providence which is argued in parts of Insinger. This can be seen in some respects as a spiritual progress. It might then be tempting to apply this picture to the whole of Egyptian culture, a sort of *via crucis* along the Nile. This would surely be going too far. Authors of Instructions, like painters, probably copied and learnt from others of their kind, rather than turning constantly back to direct observation of the world. Egyptian wisdom literature is valuable enough, without generalizations of this sort. It has earned its place in Pharaoh's sun, and in our admiration.

The miscellanies and students' exercises from the Ramesside period abound with eulogies of distinguished teachers and scholars. Some of these take the form of hopeful pupils promising to build a villa for their mentor, and to fill its garden with a variety of obscure herbs and vegetables. In the case of the present author's honouring John Emerton this course would be impractical, nor would he and Norma necessarily be impressed if I were to try. It is simpler and more appropriate to conclude with the following wishes from a New Kingdom scribe to a revered teacher:

'Good sir, may you endure and have victuals with you every day, you being cheerful, flourishing daily, and praised a million times. May joy and delight cleave fast to you, and your limbs proclaim health; you shall feel younger every day, and no harm shall draw nigh you. A year will come when one will recall your virtue and find not the like of you, your eye being bright every day and your step firm. May you multiply happy years, your months in prosperity, your days in life and dominion, your hours in health, and your gods pleased with you.'[33]

[32] After *AEL* 3, p. 205.
[33] P. Anastasi III 4, 4–8; R. A. Caminos, *Late-Egyptian Miscellanies* (Oxford, 1954), p. 85 (slightly adapted).

This short essay is offered to John Emerton, as a small return for his friendship and encouragement over sixteen years in Cambridge, and in the belief that he will excuse the touch of polytheism in the last words of our Egyptian scribe with his unfailing tolerance and humour.

2 Some new Babylonian wisdom literature

W. G. Lambert

It is now over thirty years since the present writer, following a suggestion of the late Sidney Smith, produced a corpus of *Babylonian Wisdom Literature* (Oxford, 1960). The time is now ripe to survey some additions that have since come to light, both published and unpublished, and to consider some of the ideological issues which have been debated since. The corpus was basically a text edition, and touched only very lightly on the thought-content and on comparisons with other literatures, such as biblical Hebrew texts. The demarcation from Sumerian was mainly practical. Such texts in that language which might be called 'wisdom' were often of uncertain meaning in key parts, and the writer had no access to the large amount of unpublished material from Nippur. Also, not all texts compared with Hebrew wisdom literature are really of the same category. Thus what the late S. N. Kramer called 'Man and his God'[1] and compared with Job should not, in the present writer's opinion, be considered wisdom because this Sumerian sufferer confesses his sins while asking for release from his sufferings.

The Hebrew term 'wisdom' and other derivatives of the root can refer to skill of any kind (note the case of Bezalel), but there also existed a specialized use of the term, for 'piety' in effect, so that in this sense *ḥokmâ* embraces the whole conduct of life in service to God. In the modern world the term has often been used to refer to the Hebrew books which are especially devoted to inculcating right living and to reflecting on its implications. The various Babylonian terms for 'wise' and 'wisdom' can likewise be used for any kind of skill. Thus the Babylonian *ummânu* (borrowed once in the Old Testament: Song of Songs vii 2) can refer to both the manual skills of the cabinet-maker and goldsmith, and to the intellectual talent of temple scribes. Further, these terms do not, save for a single passage overlooked in 1960, ever allude to the sermonizing and the thought-world of this special use of the Hebrew *ḥokmâ*. Thus the procedure

---

[1] S. N. Kramer, '"Man and his God": A Sumerian variation on the "Job" motif', in *Wisdom in Israel and in the Ancient Near East* (*SVT* 3, 1955), pp. 170–82.

must be to note the characteristics of Hebrew wisdom literature and to study material of similar type in Babylonian. In this technical sense the Hebrew term covers not the strictly practical problems of life, such as how to be a good farmer, but rather more general matters of principle such as the need to work hard to succeed.

Of course, religious attitudes are merged in this Hebrew *ḥokmâ*: duties to God are emphasized, and the idea that God rewards those who seek him is constantly implied even when not explicitly stated. From this dual base of common-sense admonitions and religiously derived principles *ḥokmâ* became a philosophy of life. This world-view, however, created intellectual difficulties when performance of religious duties seemed to go unrewarded, or, worse, to result in personal disaster. Questions about the generally assumed cosmic justice were raised and attempts were made to answer them. Discussions of this kind are often far removed from the homely advice of many proverbs and represent the more intellectual side of wisdom. In the Old Testament, Proverbs contains most wisdom of the popular kind, the sort of thing that most people in society would carry in their heads, and which would be passed down from generation to generation, and which was often international, freely moving across ancient cultural barriers. Job is the opposite: a highly intellectual and literary composition, while Qoheleth shares in both types.

The solitary example of the Babylonian word *nēmequ*, 'wisdom', in the sense of the Hebrew *ḥokmâ*, a philosophy of life, occurs in the incantation series Šurpu II 173: 'Šiduri ... goddess of wisdom' (^{d}*ši-du-ri* ... ^{d}*ištar*(15) *né-me-qî*).[2] This minor deity is best known from the Babylonian Gilgamesh Epic, where Gilgamesh meets her during his travels in his quest for eternal life. She discourages him from such futile ambition and offers him instead this philosophy of life:

> As for you, Gilgamesh, let your belly be full,
> Day and night ever rejoice,
> Every day have pleasure,
> Day and night dance and make merry,
> Let your garments be clean,
> Wash your head, bathe in water,
> Look at the little one who holds your hand,
> Let your spouse have constant pleasure in your bosom.
> This is the task(?) [of mankind],
> Whereby a living person [...]   OB X.iii[3]

The long-noticed resemblance of this passage to Eccles. ix 7–9 (however explained: the Babylonian tablet is not later than *c*. 1600 BC) supports the view that Šurpu II 173 alludes specifically to this advice to Gilgamesh and is

[2] E. Reiner, *Šurpu* (Graz, 1958), p. 18.   [3] *ANET*, p. 90.

thus the only so far known use of *nēmequ* in the sense of the Hebrew *ḥokmâ* as a literary and ideological type.

The more intellectual forms of wisdom offer the best basis for a comparison between Babylonian and Hebrew texts. For the former there are still only three major works, 'I will praise the Lord of wisdom' (*Ludlul bēl nēmeqi*), the Theodicy, and the Dialogue of Pessimism.[4] They vary in form, the first being a monologue, the second a simple dialogue, and the third a satirical dialogue. They also vary in tone. The first is orthodoxly pious, though it comes near to challenging the orthodox outlook. The second debates the orthodox view more robustly and reaches a conclusion which, if pursued logically, would have demolished that common attitude, but the argument ends with the reaching of the conclusion. The third is openly agnostic and impious.

'The Lord of wisdom' in the opening phrase of the first text, which served as its title, is Marduk, whose wisdom was expertise in magic spells to ward off evil demons. This long poetic monologue describes how a once prosperous public figure lost his post, wealth, family, friends and health, for no reason that he could fathom, and was then in reverse order given back by Marduk what he had lost. Marduk is discreetly blamed for the unexplained disasters. The story indeed parallels that of Job, though in other ways the two texts are different. Job begins and ends with narrative, but is mainly dialogue between Job and his three friends, culminating (at least now) with speeches of another man and with intervention by God. *Ludlul* begins and ends with praise of Marduk, and the opening hymn, recovered in full since *BWL* appeared, consists mainly of couplets with always the same theme: severity, *then* goodness, e.g.:

> Whose fury surrounds him like the blast of a tornado,
> Yet whose breeze is as pleasant as a morning zephyr,
> His anger is irresistible, his rage a hurricane,
> But his heart is merciful, his mind forgiving...   I 5–8[5]

This theme provides, of course, the framework of the whole text, which begins with a prosperous, successful man, who first succumbs to Marduk's severity, but then regains all he lost thanks to Marduk's goodness. This motif is, in fact, much older than the text, which, as explained below, cannot be earlier than *c.* 1300 BC. There is a Sumerian personal name Mir-šà-kušu₄, attested first under the Third Dynasty of Ur (*c.* 2100–2000 BC), meaning 'savage-relenting'. Theoretically it could refer to the character of its human bearer, but more probably it refers to the bearer's

---

[4] See the editions in *BWL*.

[5] *BWL*, p. 343; D. J. Wiseman, 'A New Text of the Babylonian Poem of the Righteous Sufferer', *AnSt* 30 (1980), pp. 102ff.; W. L. Moran, 'Notes on the Hymn to Marduk in *Ludlul bēl nēmeqi*', *JAOS* 103 (1983), pp. 255ff.

personal god: first savage, but later relenting, since the god can hardly be both at once. In the Middle Babylonian Epic of Creation, Enūma Eliš VI 137,[6] this very name appears as the fourth of Marduk's fifty names, and in the Middle Babylonian god list An = Anum II 181 it occurs as the eighth of a variant list of fifty names of Marduk, in each case also literally translated into Akkadian as *eziz u muštāl* 'savage then relenting'. Here, then, is clear evidence that this doctrine of *Ludlul bēl nēmeqi* is more than 700 years older than this text, and was commonly applied to Marduk in the period in which *Ludlul* was composed.

Thus it can only be in the answers to the traditional problem of the god's character that *Ludlul* offers anything original. Of course, we do not know what previous answers to the problem may have been given in earlier, but now lost, texts. The writer does dare to blame Marduk discreetly for his accumulated disasters (III 1ff.), and so puts the question why a righteous man should suffer the penalties properly meant for the wicked (II 12–33). But beyond wondering whether humans have misunderstood divine requirements (II 34–8) no reply is put forward. As in Job, no clear answer to the problem raised is given. Recovery of what was lost is the traditional answer transmitted through the story in both *Ludlul* and Job. When further questions are put the answers are tentative and inconclusive.

Already in *BWL* it was pointed out that, unlike Job, there is no attempt to project the events back into a distant past, but personal names from the Cassite period – the most likely period of composition – are used. The sufferer's name, Šubši-mešrê-Šakkan, also appears in a fragment of an historical epic about Cassite times (*BWL*, pp. 296–7), perhaps for the same man. More precise evidence is now available. O. R. Gurney, in publishing Cassite-period documents from Ur, observed the occurrence of a Šubši-mašrê-Šakkan entitled 'governor' ([lú]*gar kur*) in a legal document dated to the 16th year of king Nazimuruttaš (*c.* 1324–1298 BC) and sealed by this governor, and asked whether this might be the hero of *Ludlul*.[7] The present writer had already noted that in the fourth year of the same king of Babylon a tablet from Nippur recorded a ration of grain issued to 'the messenger of [m]*šub-ši-ma*[*š-ra-a*]-[d]*šakkan*' (*PBS* II/2 20 31). Also a fragment of a literary Babylonian text from Assur, *KAR* 116, has since been certainly identified by the present writer as a piece of *Ludlul*, thanks to unpublished overlapping duplicates, and this names [[m]*na-zi*]-*muru-taš* [. . .]. While the context of this line is too damaged to be understood, the same king is likely to be meant because early in the story 'the king' (there unnamed) became angry with Šubši-mešrê-Šakkan (I 55–6). Towards the end of the text (where *KAR* 116 belongs) the king must obviously restore Šubši-mešrê-

---

[6] J. Bottéro and S. N. Kramer, *Lorsque les dieux faisaient l'homme* (Paris, 1989), p. 644.

[7] O. R. Gurney, 'Šubši-mešrê-Šakkan', *RA* 80 (1986), p. 190.

Šakkan to his lost post. The name of the hero of *Ludlul* is extremely rare. All known occurrences have been quoted save for the one passage in *Ludlul*, III 43. The evidence strongly supports the conclusion that this man was an historical figure under Nazimuruttaš, important enough as an official in the fourth year of the king to have a messenger of his fed at state expense, and attested as a provincial governor in the sixteenth year. Against such a background of an apparently historical figure, one naturally asks whether this official did in fact experience personal disasters of the kind described. There is, of course, no evidence on this point, but it is surely likely that an historical figure chosen to be the speaker in this long monologue would be chosen because something of the kind had actually happened to him. Job, be it repeated, is different in using a patriarchal figure as its hero, alluding to a distant past, for which, at the best, there could only have been oral tradition.

In Babylonian terms, the thought of *Ludlul* is orthodox and pious. The author probes the reasons for Marduk's anger with great delicacy and avoids openly accusing Marduk of injustice. The orthodoxy is confirmed by the continuation of the basic motif in the text in much later times. The very first expression of Marduk's changing moods occurs in Tablet I, lines 2 and 4:

> *e-ziz mu-ši mu-(up)-pa-(áš)-šìr ur-r[u]*
> who is savage in the night, but relaxes by day

A Babylonian scribe, Ašarēdu the elder, sent an astrological report to the Assyrian king Esarhaddon (681–669 BC), and then added a personal note, introduced, it seems, by a literary citation or literary allusions: 'The sage, the wise, merciful Bel, warrior Marduk, became angry in the night, but relaxed at dawn (*ina mūši i-zu-uz-ma ina še-e-ri it-tap-šar*). You, king of the world, are the image of Marduk. When you became angry with your servants we bore the anger of the king our lord. Then we experienced the reconciliation of the king...' (*SAA* 8, 333 4-rev. 6). The wording is not close enough to *Ludlul* to be sure that a conscious allusion to it occurs, though this is possible, but the similarity of thought is not in doubt. The same thought occurs in another personal name, in Babylonian language and attested in late Cassite times and under the Late Babylonian empire: *ez-u-pašir*, 'savage then relaxing'. Thus it is possible in the case of Babylon to observe how the thought of the more intellectual and sophisticated wisdom texts did arise from more popular environments, and how it could be used by scholars in their personal lives.

The Theodicy, though a dialogue between a 'just sufferer' and an orthodox friend, is much more remote from the thought of Job. After vigorous sparring at the beginning between the sufferer, pressing both his righteousness and his suffering, and the friend, endlessly repeating that piety pays, a series of points is made which at least tackles the subject seriously. The first is that the gains of the wicked are shortlived: retribution from the gods soon follows (lines 45–66). This point is, of course, also asserted in Job and in wisdom Psalms; but in the Theodicy the sufferer evidently attacked this answer in the following sections (now incomplete) because, when the text resumes, the friend has been forced to retreat somewhat from his previous dogma that piety pays, and now admits that the pious may not be well off, but at least they never go hungry, and that the personal god can quickly make up what the pious have lost over a period (235–42). This the sufferer appears to accept. Next, the privileges of the first-born are cited by the sufferer as an example of cosmic injustice. (As always, the customs of society are assumed to be of divine origin.) To this the friend answers that the first-born is physically weaker and so his privileges are offset (243–64), a reply in which the sufferer appears to acquiesce. But he now plays his trump. Powerful but wicked men, he argues, constantly oppress the pious poor. This time the friend fully accepts the point and goes on to explain it: that the human race has a perverse streak because the gods created them this way: 'With lies, and not truth, they endowed them for ever.' So it is, he continues, that the rich and powerful grind down the poor. So agreement has at last been reached, and by implication the sufferer has gone though his life of misery because the gods implanted a criminal bent in the human race at the time of creation. Such an explanation was not of course possible for an orthodox Yahwist. In Gen. i man was created 'very good', and in Gen. ii–iii the first human pair was given free will and choice, and by disobedience to God brought evil into the world. The writer of the Theodicy, in contrast, was merely using traditional ideas. Sumero-Babylonian polytheism was a truer reflection of the world as it existed, with deities assigned to every aspect of the perceived or conjectured universe. It was believed that, as first created, man had been animal-like, and was later civilized by the express intervention of the gods. The latest expression of the idea was given by Berossus' story of the creature Oannes emerging from the Red Sea during the daytime and instructing the human race in the arts of civilization.[8] Sumerian texts talk of the *me*s, with each *me* conceived as a physical object, representing some aspect of human society as well as cosmic norms. These *me*s, something like Platonic ideas, thus regulated the whole of human society, so that canals were as much part of the physical universe as rivers. Both had been decreed through the *me*s from the beginning, and religious duty required the keeping-up of the canals. Similarly life in cities had been laid down by the

[8] F. Jacoby, *FGH* III C (Leiden, 1958), pp. 369–70.

gods in this way, so when the sufferer in the Theodicy in desperation declares that he will abandon his life in the society which he finds so unjust and live as a vagrant henceforth (133–47), the friend immediately rebukes him for such a blasphemous idea. One Sumerian myth gives a long list of the *me*s, including *lul-da* 'lying'.[9] This myth, Inanna and Enki, is known to us from copies more than half a millennium older than the composition of the Theodicy. That lying should have been given to the human race as an enjoined norm is not surprising when the gods themselves in myths also lied. In this same myth Inanna accuses Enki of dishonestly dealing with her, four times using the very term *lul-da*. Also in a long Sumerian cultic lament, Inanna deflects criticism of herself in saying, 'Whoever says, "She is a liar"', I will bring a liar into his house.'[10] Thus the doctrine of the Theodicy was in no way original; the originality, so far as our knowledge extends, was its use of this old teaching in a context where its mention implicitly cast doubt on whether the gods do maintain justice in the universe, and so on the point previously upheld in this text, namely that piety pays. Though the relevance of this old doctrine is not made explicit, it seems clear that the author meant the point to be taken, because it is the one point accepted without reservation by the friend, and once it has been asserted and accepted by both disputants, there is no further discussion. A bland section brings the text to its completion. As stated at the beginning of the consideration of the Theodicy, much of the distinctive argument could not occur in orthodox Hebrew writings due to the monotheistic concept of a holy and just god.

The Dialogue of Pessimism has been the subject of very varied opinions, taking it as anything from a piece of light entertainment to a serious philosophical tractate. The present writer's opinion has not changed, namely that the chosen literary form was meant to be entertaining while the wisdom content was intended seriously. The exchanges between master and slave are social satire anticipating such works as Theophrastus' *Characters* and Thackeray's *Book of Snobs*. However, the thought-content of each such exchange, the futility of all human endeavour, is exactly what Qoheleth emphasizes throughout, but especially in chs. i–vi: 'Vanity of vanities, all is vanity.' The two writings set out their ideas in very different ways. The Babylonian writer methodically ends each section on a negative – the activity proposed is *not* worth doing – then reinforces this in the final section, asking what is worth doing, to which 'suicide' is the reply given. The Hebrew writer merely repeats his 'vanity' theme, both verbatim and in many examples. In each case the same logical dilemma is raised. If every

---

[9] See the recent discussion of J. J. Glassner, 'Inanna et les me', in M. de J. Ellis (ed.), *Nippur at the Centennial* (Philadelphia, 1992), pp. 55–86.

[10] See Glassner, 'Inanna et les me', p. 67.

aspect of life is futile, why did the author bother to write his text? In *BWL* the writer suggested that perhaps the Babylonian author was psychologically disturbed, but if the thought-motif was a wisdom topos, then perhaps this is wrong, and both authors were developing a traditional theme, not drawing particularly on their own feelings and experiences. Here, as with the Theodicy, the Hebrew writer cannot follow the Babylonian reasoning because of the constraints of Israelite orthodox faith. He cannot assert that there is no point in making offerings to God because by withholding them one can force the god to run after one like a poodle. Nor does he take his argument to the logical conclusion and insist that suicide is the sole good in life. But it can be suspected that there is a common wisdom theme somewhere in the background of the two works.

So far as Babylon is concerned, there is actual evidence. The futility of all human endeavour is already put in the mouth of Gilgamesh in the Old Babylonian edition (*c.* 1700 BC), in the following words:

> As for mankind, their days are numbered,
> Whatever they do is wind.[11]

The background for this view is Gilgamesh's feeling dissatisfied with life because of the overshadowing threat of death and extinction. This motif is already present in the Sumerian version of the story, but only the Babylonian version offers the succinct generalization just quoted. Another similar statement occurs in a wisdom text known from a single Late Assyrian copy, but no doubt traditional Babylonian:

Mankind and their achievements alike come to an end (*BWL*, p. 108, line 10).

Also, there is an earlier parallel to the suggestion that one can make one's god one's slave. An Old Babylonian letter (not after *c.* 1600 BC) was written to the personal god in these terms:

Speak to the god, my father, 'Thus says Apil-Adad, your servant: "Why have you neglected me? Who can supply you with someone to take my place? Write to Marduk, who loves you, so that he will release my bond, then I will see your face and kiss your feet . . ."' (M. Stol, *AbB* 9, 141)

The threat implied here is that unless the worshipper gets better satisfaction from his god, he will cease to worship, no-one else will wish to take on such a god, and so offerings will be cut off. Thus the Dialogue of Pessimism is firmly rooted in earlier thought, but pushes the matters further.

The futility of life is also the theme of a collection of literary sections in

---

[11] *ANET*, p. 79 (iv 7–8).

cuneiform, so far little known.[12] The earliest attested form is Sumerian, best known from two tablets in the British Museum, both with two columns on each side, but both offering only part-lines due to damage. They date *c.* 1800–1600 BC. There are two Sumerian fragments from Nippur in Philadelphia, so far unpublished and not seen by the present writer, of about the same date or a little earlier. The next attestation of this text is at Emar (modern Meskene), on the Euphrates in Syria, and at Ugarit, in both cases *c.* 13th century BC. Ugarit has yielded three incomplete copies, all Sumerian with Babylonian translation, one a single-column tablet containing at least three sections (*Ugaritica* V, 164), the other two (*Ugaritica* V, 165–6) duplicates differing from 164 both recensionally and in format (the two languages in parallel columns, not in interlinear arrangement). The two apparently contained one section only. Emar has yielded five pieces of a single copy with the same one section, but in three parallel columns: first, Sumerian in conventional orthography, next, Sumerian in phonetic orthography, and then Babylonian. Finally the library of Ashurbanipal, king of Assyria from 669–627 BC, has yielded two fragments, K 6917 + 13679, identified and joined by R. Borger, which give the end of one section and the beginning of another, in two parallel columns, in conventional Sumerian and Babylonian.

The importance of this material lies not only in its addition to our knowledge of the 'futility' theme in ancient near eastern literature, but also in the way that it illustrates literary development such as can only be conjectured in traditional texts like Ecclesiastes. The Sumerian is certainly original, though it may have been composed by scholars who spoke Babylonian after 2000 BC. Like most Sumerian literature, it presents considerable difficulties for us. At least the British Museum tablets are well and competently written. In contrast the Ugarit and Emar copies, though derived and created as editions in Babylonia and not Syria, are full of signs of incompetence. The Syrian scribes probably did not understand Sumerian at all, and may have had limited Babylonian. The Ashurbanipal copy is excellently written, but is only a fragment.

Each section begins with the same three lines:

> Rules were formulated by Enki,
> Regulations were laid down at the command of the gods.
> From days of old there has been vanity (literally 'wind').

This reflects the Sumero-Babylonian idea that every aspect of human life was laid down by the gods when they civilized the human race in early

---

[12] The main sources are: B. Alster, 'A Sumerian Poem about Early Rulers', *Acta Sumerologica* 8 (1986), pp. 1–11; D. Arnaud, *Recherches au pays d'Aštata, Emar* VI. 4 (Paris, 1987), pp. 359–65; C. Wilcke, 'Die sumerische Königsliste und erzählte Vergangenheit', in J. von Ungern-Sternberg and H. Reinau (eds.), *Colloquium Rauricum*, Band 1, *Vergangenheit in mündlicher Überlieferung* (Stuttgart, 1988), pp. 113–40.

times, but it then adds its distinctive note, which would have warmed the heart of Qoheleth. Though only one section is more or less complete and can be given in translation: the last section of the British Museum tablets, the first preserved in *Ugaritica* V, 164, and the only section on the other Ugaritic and the Emar tablet, the sprinkling of the terms 'life', 'death' and 'lot' in the damaged sections confirms a unity of content.

Previous attempts to translate the one section are now inadequate. B. Alster was able to use only the two British Museum tablets and *Ugaritica* V, 164. D. Arnaud used all the Ugarit and Emar material, but while knowing one British Museum tablet and one Philadelphia fragment ignored them. C. Wilcke used everything except the Ashurbanipal fragment, but produced a variorum text which was based on the Emar edition, in which the substantial variants of other copies were present but virtually concealed. This composite text he then translated (stressing its provisional character), but in his discussion disregarded the recensional variants and frequently translated the Babylonian rather than the original Sumerian. However, with appropriate caution his text can be used, so we offer here first a translation of the Emar edition, restoring the gaps in it only when enough is preserved for the justification to be very probable, and not translating where the problems are at present insuperable. Then we give a translation of the earlier Sumerian edition, so far as it is preserved, again only restoring the missing part-lines when this seems reasonably assured.

Emar edition

1–3 (given above)
4 Have you never heard from the mouth of a man of yore?
5 'These kings were superior to them, and others to those.
6 Their eternal home is above their ... house.
7 Like the remote heavens, my hand has not reached (it).
8 Like the depths of hell, no one knows (it).
9 [....] the whole of life is but the twinkling of an eye.
10 The life of mankind does not [last] for ever.
11 Where is Alulu, the king who reigned for 36,000 years?
12 Where is Etana, the king who ascended to heaven?
13 Where is Gilgamesh, who sought life like Zi'usudra?
14 Where is Ḫuwawa..........?
15 Where is Enkidu .... in the land?
16 Where is Bazi? Where is Zizi?
17 Where are the great kings from days of yore to the present?
18 Have they not been conceived? Have they not been born?
19 How is life without joy superior to death?
20 Man, I will truly ... let you know your god.

21 Overthrow and drive out grief! Despise gloom!
22 As a substitute for a single day's happiness can one pass 36,000 years in days of silence?
23 Like a ... young man, Siraš is your pride and pleasure!
24 This is the true rule of mankind.'

    Unilingual Sumerian edition
 a ...].did not do/make
 b ...]..exchanged for those men
11 [Where is Alulu], the king who reigned for 36,000 years?
12 [Where is Etana], the king who ascended to heaven?
13 [Where is Gilgamesh], who sought life like Zi'usudra?
14 [Where is Ḫuwawa]..........?
15 [Where is Enkidu]........in the land?
17 [Where are the] kings, the leaders of days of old?
18 [Have they not been conceived?] Have they not been born?
 7 Like [the remote heavens] my hand has not reached (them),
 8 Like [the depths of hell] no-one knows (them).
 9 [All life] is but the twinkling of an eye.
19 How is [life without joy] superior to death?
22 [As a substitute] for a single day's happiness can one pass 36,000 years in days of silence?
 c [....] granted [life] to the gods.
 d Though one may seek life like(!) [Zi'usudra, death] is the lot of mankind.
 e [.........] of a man's house.
    (for convenience the line numbers are those of the Emar edition; lines not contained in that edition have been assigned letters)

The beginning of the one Ugaritic copy, *Ugaritica* V, 164, is broken away, but when it sets in it offers the lines: 15, 17, 18, 7, 8, 9, 19 and 22, where it ends. The other two, *Ugaritica* V, 165–6, agree with the Emar text where they are adequately preserved, namely lines 1–8 and 18–24, except that 10 appears between 18 and 20, and 19 between 22 and 23.

The earliest attested form of the text is clearly a wisdom composition reflecting on the futility of life as is apparent from great men of old, kings especially. Alulu is the first king in the Sumerian King List, assigned a 36,000-year reign in one Old Babylonian tablet and in Berossus, but 28,800 and 67,200 respectively in two other Old Babylonian copies.[13] Etana is king of the town of Kish after the flood in the Sumerian King List, which also records his ascent to heaven. Gilgamesh was king of the town of Uruk in

[13] J.J. Finkelstein, 'The Antediluvian Kings: A University of California Tablet', *JCS* 17 (1963), p. 46.

the dynasty following that of Kish in the Sumerian King List,[14] but it does not mention his search for immortality, though it is mentioned in a Babylonian omen.[15] The two following names, Ḫuwawa and Enkidu, occur in the pertinent Sumerian and Babylonian Gilgamesh epics as respectively a kind of demon Gilgamesh fought, and as his companion in arms on that occasion, but they were not kings. Bazi and Zizi, which occur without any description in the Emar recension, but not in the unilingual Sumerian copies, are apparently unknown elsewhere.

The theme seems to be that great though these men were, their achievements are now forgotten, and so were in vain. A solution to this dilemma is offered at the end: that happiness is what is worthwhile, one day of that being of greater worth than 36,000 years in the grave. The Ugaritic tablet 164 ends at that point, probably the original form of the text. The three extra lines in the unilingual Sumerian read like an addition expressing the same idea as is offered to Gilgamesh in the Babylonian epic in the lines immediately before the *carpe diem* philosophy already quoted:

> When the gods created mankind
> They assigned death to man,
> But life they kept in their own hands.

The Emar recension and the Ugaritic copies which agree with it obviously are based on something very like the unilingual Sumerian version and have inserted into it a second, more specific, idea of how to find happiness. Line 20 hints at the solution coming, which is given in lines 21 and 23, with 24 as a concluding emphasis. Siraš (also Siriš, and possibly related to the Hebrew *tîrôš*) is a beer deity of Sumerians and Babylonians. Thus in this version happiness is to be sought in drink. Alster and Arnaud took the text as a wisdom text in either form, but Wilcke dissented: 'Nein! Das ist ein Trinklied, frech und zynisch. Ein Studentenlied . . .' We agree with Alster and Arnaud, first because Wilcke ignored the shorter form lacking any allusion to alcohol, secondly because even with that addition there is no fundamental change. *Carpe diem* can include drink, and 'eat, drink and be merry' in Eccles. viii 15 hardly refers to water or fruit juice.

The importance of this text for Old Testament studies lies in its demonstration that 'vanity of vanities' was a wisdom theme in Mesopotamian wisdom texts before 1600 BC. And with creative recensions this text continued to be copied out at least until the 7th century BC. Thus Ecclesiastes was presenting an old theme in an Israelite garb. Just how the author drew on the ancient near eastern tradition is the big question. The

[14] T. Jacobsen, *The Sumerian King List* (Chicago, 1939), p. 80 and pp. 88, 90.
[15] W. G. Lambert, 'Gilgameš in Religious, Historical and Omen Texts and the Historicity of Gilgameš', in P. Garelli (ed.), *Gilgameš et sa légende* (Paris, 1960), pp. 44–5.

verbal similarity of the passage in the Babylonian Gilgamesh Epic to Eccles. ix 7–9 is well known, and now in addition line 5 of the Sumero-Babylonian text parallels i 11. The suggestion of influence on Qoheleth from Greek philosophy may have been exaggerated. But if instead one thinks of influence from this Mesopotamian tradition, then questions have to be asked. It is unlikely that the author himself read cuneiform texts. It is possible that the Mesopotamian texts were translated, whether orally or in writing, into a West Semitic language in the period of the Ugaritic and Emar copies, or in the first millennium BC into Aramaic. But so far there is no hard fact to build on. The possibilities will have to be kept in mind until more evidence comes to light.

Addenda

Another edition of the Ugarit and Emar copies of the Sumero-Akkadian 'Vanity' text appeared after the above article was completed, namely M. Dietrich, ' "Ein Leben ohne Freude . . ." ' (*Ugarit-Forschungen* 24 [1992], pp. 9–29). While knowing the Old Babylonian Sumerian copies, it does not edit them and regards the Ugarit and Emar pieces as related but distinct literary compositions. The differences, however, are less than the recensional differences between variant editions of Akkadian texts from southern Mesopotamia in the Old Babylonian period, e.g. the Gilgamesh Epic, and there is of course no proof that the Ugarit and Emar copies of the texts under discussion offer editions created in the west.

It is reported that a tablet of the Sumerian King List excavated at Tell Leilan in north-east Syria, but not yet published, contains the king Bazi.

3   The Wisdom of Ahiqar

Jonas C. Greenfield

The figure of Ahiqar has remained a source of interest to scholars in a variety of fields. The search for the real Ahiqar, the acclaimed wise scribe who served as chief counsellor to Sennacherib and Esarhaddon, was a scholarly preoccupation for many years.[1] He had a sort of independent existence since he was known from a series of texts – the earliest being the Aramaic text from Elephantine, followed by the book of Tobit, known from the Apocrypha, and the later Syriac, Armenian and Arabic texts of Ahiqar.[2] An actual royal counsellor and high court official who had been removed from his position and later returned to it remains unknown.[3] E. Reiner found the theme of the 'disgrace and rehabilitation of a minister'

[1] The recent editions of Aramaic Ahiqar are: J. M. Lindenberger, *The Aramaic Proverbs of Ahiqar* (Baltimore, 1983), hereafter, Lindenberger, *Aramaic Proverbs*; I. Kottsieper, *Die Sprache der Ahiqarsprüche* (Berlin, 1990); B. Porten, A. Yardeni, *Textbook of Aramaic Documents*, 3 (Jerusalem, 1993) pp. 24–57, hereafter Yardeni, *Textbook*. The decipherment of the Ahiqar palimpsest has required a renumbering of the proverbs, see A. Yardeni, 'Maritime Trade and Royal Accountancy in an Erased Custom Account from 475 BCE on the Ahiqar Scroll from Elephantine', forthcoming in *BASOR*. Many aspects of the Ahiqar tradition are treated in M. Küchler, *Frühjüdische Weisheitstraditionen* (Freiburg and Göttingen, 1979), pp. 319–411.

[2] J. R. Harris, F. C. Conybeare and A. S. Lewis, *The Story of Aḥiḳar* (2nd edn, Cambridge, 1913) has the Syriac, Armenian and Arabic texts as well as an Old Turkish text and translations of the Slavonic and Ethiopic texts. Only the first three are significant for research. The Syriac text that underlies the Armenian and Arabic translation often differs from the major Syriac text. The synoptic presentation of the Ahiqar material in R. H. Charles, *Apocrypha and Pseudepigrapha of the Old Testament*, II (Oxford, 1913), pp. 715–84, maintains its usefulness. Lindenberger, *Aramaic Proverbs*, pp. 310–12, provides an English translation of the Demotic fragments of the framework story originally published by T. Zauzich.

[3] W. von Soden suggested that Adad-šum-uṣur, who at one time was Esarhaddon's chief exorcist, might have been the model for this role, 'Die Unterweltsvision eines assyrischen Kronprinzen', *ZA* 43 (1936), pp. 1–31. See also A. T. Olmstead, *JAOS* 56 (1936), p. 243. For Adad-šum-uṣur see S. Parpola, *Letters from Assyrian Scholars to the Kings Esarhaddon and Assurbanipal*, Part I: Texts (Neukirchen-Vluyn, 1970 = *LAS* 1), no. 121, pp. 88–91; Part II: Commentary and Appendices (Neukirchen-Vluyn, 1983 = *LAS* 2), pp. 103–7; and for his son Urad-Gula see S. Parpola, 'The Forlorn Scholar', in F. Rochberg-Halton (ed.), *Language, Literature and History: Philological and Historical Studies presented to Erica Reiner* (New Haven, 1987), pp. 257–78. Note that there is *nothing* in the Ahiqar story to indicate that his wisdom and counsel were based on divination.

combined with that of the 'ungrateful nephew' in the 'Bilingual Proverbs', and saw this as a sort of parallel to the Ahiqar story.[4] She also emphasized that in Mesopotamia the *ummânu* was not only a learned man or craftsman but was also a high official.

At the time that Reiner noted the existence of this theme in Babylonian wisdom literature, Ahiqar achieved a degree of reality with the discovery in Uruk, in the excavations of winter 1959/60, of a Late Babylonian tablet (W20030,7) dated to the 147th year of the Seleucid era (= 165 BCE).[5] This tablet contains a list of antediluvian kings and their sages (*apkallû*) and postdiluvian kings and their scholars (*ummânu*). The postdiluvian kings run from Gilgamesh to Esarhaddon. This text informs us (p. 45, lines 19–20) that in the time of King Aššur-aḫ-iddina, one A-ba-^{d}ninnu-da-ri (= Aba-enlil-dari), (whom) the Aḫlamû (i.e., Arameans) call Aḫ-'u-qa-ri (= Aḫuqar), was the *ummânu*. As was immediately noted, Aḫuqar was the equivalent of Aḫiqar.[6] The names of the *ummânê* of Sennacherib and Esarhaddon are known to us from a variety of sources, but Ahiqar's name does not appear in any contemporary source.[7] Indeed, it has been recently claimed that the passage from the Uruk document 'is clearly fictitious and of no historical value', for Aba-^{d}ninnu-dari was the name of a scholar known from the Middle Babylonian period.[8] Yet, the listing of Ahiqar in a Late Babylonian tablet testifies to the fact that the role of Ahiqar, as known from the Aramaic version found at Elephantine, the book of Tobit, and the later Ahiqar sources, was firmly entrenched in Babylonian tradition. Nevertheless, it is interesting to note that none of the proverbs found in the Aramaic text from Elephantine has a counterpart in the various cuneiform collections of proverbs or among those quoted in Assyrian letters.[9]

In the Aramaic text from Elephantine Ahiqar is presented as the counsellor of the king and his seal-bearer, in charge of the affairs of the kingdom. The titles used are *spr mhyr wḥkym*, 'wise and skilful scribe' (1, 1);

---

[4] See E. Reiner, 'The Etiological Myth of the "Seven Sages"', *Orientalia* 30 (1961), pp. 1–11, especially p. 8, where a revised translation of the pertinent section of the Bilingual Proverbs is given. This may be based on an actual case, but in all likelihood was universal in intent. See too W. G. Lambert, *BWL*, p. 96 with reference to p. 103, lines 81–92.

[5] J. J. A. van Dijk, 'Die Inschriftenfunde', in H. J. Lenzen (ed.), *XVIII Vorläufiger Bericht . . . Ausgrabungen in Uruk-Warka* (Berlin, 1962), pp. 43–52.

[6] For typographic convenience Ahiqar is used in this study.

[7] S. Parpola, *LAS* 2, pp. xv–xxi, for these *ummânê* especially under Esarhaddon, and pp. 448–9 for the chronographic text 1, where in lines 10–13 the *ummânê* of Sennacherib and Esarhaddon are listed. However, an Assyrian proverb that has a parallel in Ahiqar (see below) is quoted in a letter attributed to Esarhaddon; and an attribute of Esarhaddon, *rēmēnu*, to be discussed below, is used of him in the Ahiqar framework story as noted by Parpola, *LAS* 2, p. 58, n. 100.

[8] Parpola, *LAS* 2, p. 450. He also notes that Aba-^{d}ninnu-dari was possibly the author of the *Counsels of Wisdom*, the 'Babylonian archetype of the Sayings of Ahiqar'; cf. also Lambert, *BWL*, pp. 96–7. Lambert, however, suggests that Ahiqar may have chosen this name consciously (oral communication).   [9] This will be discussed below.

[ṣ]byt ʿzqth zy śnḥʾryb mlk ʾtwr, 'seal-bearer of Sennacherib, king of Assyria' (1, 3);[10] *sprʾ ḥkymʾ yʿṭ ʾtwr klh*, 'wise scribe, counsellor of all Assyria' (1, 12); *sprʾ ḥkymʾ wbʿl ʿṭth ṭbth*, 'wise scribe and master of good counsel' (3, 42); *ʾbwhy zy ʾtwr klʾ zy ʿl ʿṭth snḥʾryb mlkʾ wḥyl ʾtwr [klʾ] [hw]w*, 'father of all Assyria, by whose counsel king Sennacherib and all the host of Assyria were guided' (4, 55; see 60–61). Ahiqar was childless, and therefore presented his nephew Nadin (or Nadan) to the king as his successor.[11] Nadin was unscrupulous, devised a plot against Ahiqar and claimed that he was a traitor. The king in his wrath gave orders that Ahiqar was to be executed and assigned Nabusumiskun, one of his officers, to carry it out. This proved to be Ahiqar's salvation for he had once hidden Nabusumiskun when Sennacherib had condemned him to death. Nabusumiskun agreed in turn to save Ahiqar by hiding him in his house until the king called for him; a eunuch was slain in Ahiqar's place.[12] This is the end of the narrative in the Aramaic text, and it will be necessary to turn to the later versions for the rest of the story.[13] It is important to note that there are some further columns of narrative missing before the preserved sayings of Ahiqar proper begin. We learn that Ahiqar taught Nadin but are not told how this was done. It may be assumed that the then prevalent method of copying 'wisdom texts' and learning them by rote is meant, and the sayings in the 'Words of Ahiqar' are thought to have been used for Nadin's education.[14]

From the strictly chronological point of view it is in the book of Tobit that Ahiqar is next encountered after the Elephantine texts, but it is to the Syriac text that we turn first since it adds details to the story told above. We are explicitly told that Nadin was prepared for serving in the royal court by being taught a series of proverbs and maxims and these are detailed. We are also told that he forged letters to prove that his uncle was plotting with

[10] See my 'Studies in Aramaic Lexicography I', *JAOS* 82 (1962), pp. 292–3, 297–9.

[11] Neither *ndyn* (Nadin) nor *ndn* (Nadan) occurs in the Aramaic text. The latter occurs in the major Syriac texts, but since Nadin follows a frequent type in Akkadian onomastics it has become the accepted form.

[12] Does this mean that Ahiqar was a eunuch, and therefore did not have children? The *srysʾ* is also called *ʿlym*, which means 'servant, slave' rather than 'lad', since if he were a lad he would be easily detected. In the Syriac version Ahiqar takes many ('sixty') wives hoping to have a son, but there is none of this in the Aramaic text; instead of the *srysʾ* an *ʾsyrʾ*, 'prisoner', is killed in his stead.

[13] It is worth noting here that the later versions – Tobit, Syriac, etc. – preserve many elements of the lost narrative. Thus Tobit xiv 10 mentions that Ahiqar was hidden in a small underground hiding place, a fact repeated by the Syriac version.

[14] Line 9 begins with *wḥkmth*, 'and I taught him wisdom'. We may assume that another verb such as *rbyth*, 'I raised him', or *wʾlpth*, 'I instructed him', belongs at the end of the previous line. It has been noted that some of these sayings are not apt for this role. In the Syriac version, p. 38, line 10, Ahiqar says *wkd rbʾ bry ʾlpth sprʾ wḥkmtʾ*, 'when my son grew up I taught him letters and wisdom'. On *sprʾ* ('letters') see J. C. Greenfield, '"Because He/She Did not Know Letters": Remarks on a First Millennium CE Legal Expression', *JANES* 22 (1993), pp. 39–44.

foreign rulers against Esarhaddon and the supposed correspondence is quoted in the text. In the continuation of the narrative Nadin takes over his uncle's home and disports himself with the female members of the staff. When the Egyptians learn that Ahiqar is gone they challenge the Assyrians to send someone who can build a palace between heaven and earth. Nabusumiskun reveals to the king that Ahiqar is alive; he is brought out of hiding and dispatched to Egypt, where he not only builds the palace in the sky, but also solves riddles and meets other challenges. Ahiqar returns with wealth and honour to Assyria and takes revenge on Nadin. After inflicting a severe physical beating on Nadin, he chastises him verbally with an apt set of proverbs and maxims. Nadin seems to have suffered from an overdose of moral instruction for he swells up and dies. As there are two sets of proverbs in the Syriac and subsidiary versions, some scholars have tried to divide the sayings in the Elephantine Aramaic 'Words of Ahiqar' into two such groups, but there is no criterion for this in the surviving text and it has properly not won acceptance.[15]

Ahiqar plays an important rôle at the beginning and end of the book of Tobit, a book whose date is disputed, but which probably stems from the later part of the Achaemenid period.[16] In this work, a tale of great piety and probity, Ahiqar is an Israelite from the tribe of Naphtali. He was one of the high officials at the courts of the Assyrian kings Sennacherib (704–681) and Esarhaddon (680–669), and the book of Tobit takes place during the latter's reign. Before the discovery of the Qumran Scrolls the main sources for Tobit were the various Greek recensions – Sinaiticus, Vaticanus and Alexandrinus – and the Vetus Latina. There are now a number of manuscripts of parts of the original Aramaic text from Qumran Cave 4,[17] and also a Hebrew text. It is reported that the Sinaiticus is the Greek recension closest to the Aramaic.[18] From the Sinaiticus we learn that Ahiqar was *archioinochoos kai epi tou daktuliou kai dioikētēs kai eklogistēs*, 'chief cup-bearer, keeper of the royal seal, comptroller, and treasurer' of Sennacherib and Esarhaddon. This is phrased in the Aramaic text: *rb šqh wrb ʿzqn whmrkl wšyzpn qdm ʾsrhryb* (sic) *mlk ʾtwr wʾšlṭh ʾsrhdwn tnyn lh.*[19]

[15] Ada Yardeni's new arrangement of the text also precludes this.

[16] Many scholars opt for the early Hellenistic period in the third century BCE, but there are various Iranian elements in Tobit which cannot be ignored.

[17] These Aramaic fragments were to have been published by J. T. Milik, but they have now been assigned to J. A. Fitzmyer.

[18] Variously reported in Milik's name, and so also Fitzmyer (orally).

[19] The Aramaic text was quoted by Milik, *RQ* 15 (1992), p. 386. I was able to complete the word *wšyzpn*, read by Milik *w.yzpn*, by means of a handout prepared by J. A. Fitzmyer for a Jerusalem lecture. If this reading is correct it is a *shafʿel* of *yzp*, 'to borrow', and indicates that the bearer of the title is in charge of monetary matters. The Aramaic also states that Esarhaddon made him second in command, but the Greek understood this to mean that he was returned to his place (*ek deuteras*). For *hmrkl* see my discussion of the *hmarakara* in M. A. Boyce and E. Gershevitch (eds.), *Memorial Volume for W. B. Henning* (London, 1970), pp. 180–6.

Of importance for our tale is the fact that in this book he is a relative of Tobit, and his protector in adversity. The interesting point is that among these titles we do not find any specific indication that he was a 'sage' or 'wise man'. It may not have been necessary to state this since the roles attributed to him assume that faculty. In this work it is Tobit who plays the sage with wise sayings and good advice. It is only towards the end of the work that we learn about Ahiqar's ne'er-do-well nephew and his fitting end (xi 18, lxiv 10–12). The two works are intertwined and the story of Ahiqar serves as a foil for the story of Tobit.[20] There is no indication in any of the other Ahiqar traditions that he was an Israelite.

Two folklore themes have been noted in the Ahiqar story – the 'disgrace and rehabilitation of a minister' and the 'ungrateful kinsman'. But Ahiqar, like Joseph and Daniel, had a happy ending and thus belongs also in a different category, that of the successful courtier.[21] It is plausible that the author of Ahiqar, or rather its compiler, since the story may have circulated orally for some time before being written down, used actual themes from the day. The text that we have was transcribed in Egypt towards the end of the fifth century.[22] It is a unitary whole and presented as one composition. But the 'Words of Ahiqar' actually contain two parts: the framework story and the 'sayings of Ahiqar'. The former is written in Standard Literary Aramaic, based on the dialect used in the east, while the latter is written in a form of western Aramaic.[23] The complete framework story, of which we have only a part in the Elephantine text, could have stood as an independent entity. A set of proverbs and maxims which were attributed to the sage Ahiqar were attached at some point to the 'framework story'. It helped that some of these wise sayings fused with the themes of the 'framework story', as we shall show below. The compiler of the 'Words of Ahiqar' had before him diverse material. The 'sayings' contain instructions, proverbs, fables and graded numerical sayings. There is skilful use of simile and imagery as there is of comparison and contrast.[24]

The 'framework story' is set in the days of Esarhaddon after he had succeeded his father Sennacherib on the throne. Ahiqar had served Sennacherib, and was now in the same position with Esarhaddon. The text

[20] I have dealt with this in detail in 'Ahiqar in the Book of Tobit', in M. Carrez, J. Doré and P. Grelot (eds.), *De la Tôrah au Messie. Mélanges Henri Cazelles* (Paris, 1981), pp. 329–33.
[21] S. Niditch and R. Doran, 'The Success Story of the Wise Courtier. A Formal Approach', *JBL* 96 (1977), pp. 179–93.
[22] J. Naveh, *The Development of the Aramaic Script* (Jerusalem, 1970).
[23] J. C. Greenfield, 'The Dialects of Early Aramaic', *JNES* 37 (1978), pp. 93–9; Lindenberger, *Aramaic Proverbs*, pp. 279–307; I Kottsieper, *Die Sprache der Ahiqarsprüche* (Berlin, 1990). The 'Words of Ahiqar' are virtually free of Akkadian loan-words while the 'framework story' has a number of them.
[24] W. McKane, *Proverbs* (London, 1970), provides a good analysis of the typology of the various sayings and their comparison with the book of Proverbs. See also W. G. E. Watson, 'The Ahiqar Sayings: Some Marginal Comments', *Aula Orientalis* 2 (1985), pp. 253–61.

gives no indication that the transition was not smooth. As is well known, Esarhaddon became king after his father Sennacherib was murdered, but he had, it would seem, been previously designated by his father as his successor.[25] From 'The Sin of Sargon' and 'Sennacherib's Last Will' we are aware of the possible influence of his ministers and advisers on the king, especially a king like Esarhaddon who placed great stock on the advice given him by his haruspices and exorcists.[26] In line with this he revised his father's policy towards Babylon. Sennacherib had destroyed the city of Babylon, but Esarhaddon rebuilt Babylon and showed favour to its gods. This policy may have aroused opposition among those courtiers who were members of the 'Assyria first' faction. He went one step further when he dealt with the question of succession, for he proposed his older son, Šamaš-šumu-ukin, for the throne of Babylon, and the younger, Assurbanipal, for Assyria. All this required loyalty on the part of his court and on the part of his vassals. It is from the reign of Esarhaddon that we have the recently published loyalty oath on his accession and also the important group of succession treaties made later in his rule with his 'Iranian' vassals.[27] Absolute loyalty was demanded of his courtiers. This is a subject that is important in the 'Queries to the Sun God', where a question like 'will there be a rebellion against Esarhaddon?' is asked.[28] We may assume that the slightest suspicion brought suspension, exile or even death.

The Egyptian interlude that is found in the Syriac and subsidiary versions of Ahiqar is usually taken to be a late addition since it provides the needed excuse for Ahiqar's return and also a means of displaying his wisdom and abilities. But here too the country was aptly chosen, for Egypt was a target for Assyrian control. Egypt had encouraged every rebellion in the western part of the Assyrian empire. Memphis was conquered in 671 and Tarharqa's army was routed; the princes of Lower Egypt acknowledged Esarhaddon's suzerainty and Assyrian officials were appointed to oversee Egyptian affairs. This was not only reported in Esarhaddon's annals, but was also memorialized in the well-known stele from Zenjirli which shows

---

[25] A. K. Grayson, in *Cambridge Ancient History*, 3.2 (2nd edn, Cambridge, 1991), p. 121; S. Parpola, 'The Murderer of Sennacherib', in B. Alster (ed.), *Death in Mesopotamia* (Copenhagen, 1980), pp. 171–82.

[26] See H. Tadmor, B. Landsberger and S. Parpola, 'The Sin of Sargon and Sennacherib's Last Will', *State Archives of Assyria Bulletin* 3 (1989), pp. 3–51.

[27] The 'Accession Treaty of Esarhaddon' and 'Esarhaddon's Succession Treaty' are now handily available in S. Parpola and K. Watanabe, *Neo-Assyrian Treaties and Loyalty Oaths* (Helsinki, 1988), pp. 22–3, 28–58, respectively.

[28] I. Starr, *Queries to the Sun God. Divination and Politics in Sargonid Assyria* (Helsinki, 1990), no. 139, pp. 148–50; no. 144, pp. 154–5. Starr remarks, 'By far the largest single group of queries is concerned with matters of internal security, notably the loyalty of various classes of officials and people, as well as individual appointees to office' (p. lxiii).

him holding cords which pass through the lips of Baal, king of Tyre, and Ušanaḫuru, the crown prince of Egypt. Were there tales of an Assyrian sage sent to negotiate with the Egyptians or to serve as an administrator there who overwhelmed the Egyptians by his wisdom and craft?

Another indication of the date of composition may be the reference to Esarhaddon as *raḥmān* in line 53. Ahiqar was pleading with Nabusumiskun to save his life by hiding him and said: *'srḥ'dn mlk' rḥmn hw kmnd'*, which may be translated, 'King Esarhaddon is merciful, *as is known.*'[29] Now this assumption on the part of Ahiqar was indeed apt. In *LAS* 51: 7–8 (*ABL* 78), Esarhaddon is addressed by Balasī, one of his astrologers: *šarru bēlni rēmānû šū*, 'the king, our lord, is merciful'.[30] Elsewhere (*ABL* 499: 13) the king is addressed before a petition: *šarru rēmānû atta*, 'you are a merciful king'. Parpola noted that 'as a matter of principle, mercifulness was a royal characteristic on the basis of his [*scil.* the king's] equation to Marduk'. This was best expressed in an astrological report: 'The wisest, merciful Bel (*ᵈBel rēmānû*), the warrior Marduk (*qarrad ᵈMarduk*), became angry at night, but relented in the morning. You, O king of the world, are an image of Marduk; when you were angry with your servants we suffered the anger of the king our lord; and we saw the reconciliation (*sulummû*) of the king' (*RMA* 170: 4–rev. 6).[31] The image of Esarhaddon that emerges from the framework story matches that projected from the many texts of Esarhaddon that have reached us.

There are also elements which may show that the 'sayings of Ahiqar' were compiled during the time of Esarhaddon. Among these one can refer to the use of *rḥmn* for god and king in Ahiqar, in saying 25 (line 107):[32] *mlk krḥmn 'p qlh gbh h[w] mn hw zy yqwm qdmwhy lhn zy 'l 'mh*, whose translation is, 'A king is like the Merciful; his voice also is loud: who is there that can stand before him, except one with whom is god?'[33] As noted above, Esarhaddon was the 'merciful' king. But the other side of the coin is also emphasized in the sayings – the king can be fierce and his courtiers must be careful in his presence. The comparison of the king to Shamash in saying 24 also fits this scheme since Esarhaddon, given to divination, was a devotee of

---

[29] The meaning of *kmnd'* remains problematic, but I believe that this is the most likely translation.

[30] S. Parpola, *LAS* 1, pp. 32–3. Discussion in *LAS* 2, p. 58. Parpola quotes other examples too. The reference in the next line and the following quotation are taken from there.

[31] See Hermann Hunger, *Astrological Reports to Assyrian Kings* (Helsinki, 1992), no. 333, pp. 188–9. See also *LAS* 2, p. 112, to *LAS* no. 125: 18f. Note also *ABL* 137, r. 8–9: *qātāya ana šarri bēliya addiki rēmēnû atta*. It can also be used of a commoner as in *BWL*, p. 80, line 287.

[32] This is saying 14 (line 91) according to A. Yardeni's new numbering. In this numbering the sayings that refer to the king head the collection.

[33] Following essentially H. L. Ginsberg, *ANET*, p. 429a. I have attempted to elucidate this saying in 'From *'lh rḥmn* to *ar-Raḥmān* – the Source of a Divine Epithet' in the forthcoming volume in honour of W. M. Brinner.

Shamash, *bēl dīni u bēl purussê*, 'lord of judgement and (omen) decisions'.[34] Finally, saying 110, the only one in Ahiqar in which two contrasting ethnic designations are found – Sidonian, the sea-goer, and Arab, the desert-dweller – also fits the reign of Esarhaddon, during the *pax Assyriaca*.[35]

Soon after the discovery of the Elephantine Aramaic text, it was noted by scholars that there were very few direct connections between it and the previously known Syriac text, despite an overall similarity in themes and subjects. It is now quite clear that there were different bodies of gnomic sayings attached to the figure of Ahiqar. As I have tried to demonstrate elsewhere, the author of Tobit took for granted that his audience knew the tale of Ahiqar, and his use of the Ahiqar material is closer to both the story line and the sayings of the Syriac than to the Aramaic. Also, it is with the Syriac Ahiqar that a proverb quoted in a letter of Esarhaddon (*ABL* 403, obv. 4–7) has its parallel.[36] It is with the Syriac and Armenian versions that the important Demotic wisdom collection called 'The Instruction of Ankhsheshonqy' has definite ties.[37] The few parallels with Ben Sira are also with the Syriac Ahiqar.[38] The parallels with Talmudic literature, where the name of Ahiqar is never mentioned, are with the Syriac rather than the Aramaic text.[39]

A word is in order about religion in the Aramaic version of Ahiqar.[40] It is clearly a polytheistic work and, as noted above, Shamash is the dominant god. The word *'l*, 'god', is often used, but there is no reason to take it as the divine name El, and associate it with the long since otiose head of the

---

[34] This is saying 14 (line 91) according to A. Yardeni's numbering. Shamash figures in saying 12 (Yardeni, *Textbook*, nos. 95–6, lines 187–9) for which see A. Lemaire, 'Le Proverbe araméen Ahiqar # 12', in J.-M. Durand and J.-R. Kupper (eds.), *Miscellanea Babylonica, Mélanges offerts à M. Birot* (Paris, 1985), pp. 197–200; and also in no. 77 (Yardeni, *Textbook*, no. 27, lines 107–8) for which see J. C. Greenfield, 'Two Proverbs of Ahiqar', in T. Abusch *et al.* (eds.), *Lingering over Words. Studies in Ancient Near Eastern Literature in Honor of W. L. Moran* (Atlanta, 1990), pp. 194–201.

[35] F. Israel, 'La datazione del proverbio no 110 di Ahiqar', *Semitica* 38 (1990), pp. 175–8. This is Yardeni, *Textbook*, no. 113, line 207.

[36] Scholars have pointed to parallels between the *Counsels of Wisdom*, lines 31–6, and Arabic Ahiqar (cf. *BWL*, p. 313), and between the proverb quoted in *ABL* 403, obv. 4–7, and Ahiqar Syriac, p. 125, and Arabic, p. 158; cf. *BWL*, p. 281. These are lacking in the Aramaic Ahiqar. Lambert says 'almost certainly Esarhaddon' for the writer of *ABL* 403.

[37] M. Lichtheim, *Late Egyptian Wisdom Literature in the International Context* (Freiburg, 1983), pp. 13–22, for the convincing comparisons. The comparison is made in the section on Ankhsheshonqy and Ahiqar (pp. 13–22), with references to Talmudic and other material.

[38] R. H. Charles, *Apocrypha and Pseudepigrapha of the Old Testament*, 1 (Oxford, 1913), p. 296; Lichtheim, *Late Egyptian Wisdom Literature*, p. 19.

[39] A. Yellin, *Sefer Ahiqar he-Hakam* (Jerusalem, 1937), gives the parallels in his notes. They are also listed in M. Küchler, *Frühjüdische Weisheitstraditionen*, pp. 403–10. For Syriac 13 see my remarks in 'A Mandaic Miscellany', *JAOS* 104 (1984), pp. 81–5. See also S. Niditch, 'A Test Case for Formal Variants in Proverbs', *JJS* 27 (1976), pp. 192–4.

[40] Cf. J. Lindenberger, 'The Gods of Ahiqar', *Ugarit-Forschungen* 14 (1983), pp. 105–17. I disagree with his conclusions.

Canaanite pantheon. I have suggested elsewhere that in saying 25 it refers to Hadad, and this is probably true in other sayings such as 66 (line 156).[41] There are also enigmatic references to *šmyn* and *b'l qdšn* (13, line 15). The sayings are on the whole not directed to a specific god, except for those directed to Shamash, who as 'god of justice' had a special place, and reflections of this usage are known from the Hebrew Bible. Religious colouring is present throughout, the moral tone is high, and the sentiment that man cannot achieve anything without the approval of god (*'l* or *'lhn*) is strong. The polytheistic element must have been abandoned at an early period, so that Ahiqar could become an Israelite in the book of Tobit. The later versions are almost entirely free of polytheistic elements.[42] As a curious sidelight it should be mentioned that this is one of the few works from the pagan heritage of early Syriac literature to survive.[43] Ahiqar was translated and copied in various languages into the early modern period.

Ahiqar lived on in the works of others. His fame as a wise man went beyond the Semitic world.[44] Clement of Alexandria reported that Democritus of Abdera (460–370 BCE) plagiarized from a stele of Ahiqar (Akikaros).[45] And in the form Achaikaros he is recorded by Strabo (*Geographia*, xvi, 2, 39) as being one of the ancient diviners. A work called *Akicharos* was, according to Diogenes Laertius (*Vitae*, v, 2, 50), among the works of Theophrastus (372–287 BCE).[46] The Greek 'Life of Aesop' (chs. 23–32), as is well known, borrows from the life and proverbs of Ahiqar.[47]

---

[41] See above, n. 33. For no. 66 see 'The Background and Parallel to a Proverb of Ahiqar', *Hommages à André Dupont-Sommer* (Paris, 1972), pp. 49–59. This is Yardeni, *Textbook*, 72 (line 157).

[42] But popular customs were no hindrance. Syriac Ahiqar, 10, refers to pouring wine on the tombs of the righteous, for which see my article in Abusch *et al.*, *Lingering over Words*, pp. 199–201. Also, Ahiqar wanted a son to fulfil the ancient custom of putting earth on the eyes of the dead (Syriac Ahiqar, p. 38, lines 3–4).

[43] The influence of Ahiqar can be seen in S. P. Brock, 'A Piece of Wisdom Literature in Syriac', *JSS* 13 (1968), pp. 212–17.

[44] For the current controversy among Italian scholars over the extent of Ahiqar's fame and influence, see M. J. Luzzatto, 'Grecia e Vicino Oriente: tracce della "Storia di Ahiqar" nella cultura greca tra VI e V secolo a.C.', *Quaderni di Storia* 36 (1992), pp. 5–84, and F. M. Fales, 'Storia di Ahiqar tra Oriente e Grecia: la prospettiva dall'antico Oriente', *ibid.*, 38 (1993), pp. 143–57.

[45] The passage from *Stromata* is quoted by Harris (Harris, Conybeare and Lewis, *The Story of Aḥiḳar*), pp. xli–xlii. Some sayings attributed by Shahrastani to Democritus originated in an oriental version of Ahiqar. See the remarks of F. Altheim and R. Stiehl, *Die aramäische Sprache unter den Achaimeniden*, 2 (Frankfurt, 1960), pp. 186–92.

[46] For Strabo and Diogenes Laertes see Harris (Harris, Conybeare and Lewis, *The Story of Aḥiḳar*), p. xliii, and Küchler, *Frühjüdische Weisheitstraditionen*, pp. 344–6.

[47] For documentation see Küchler, *Frühjüdische Weisheitstraditionen*, pp. 338–44, and J. M. Lindenberger in J. H. Charlesworth (ed.), *The Old Testament Pseudepigrapha*, 2 (New York, 1985), pp. 490–2. Note also N. Oettinger, 'Achikars Weisheitssprüche im Licht älterer Fabeldichtung' (pp. 3–22) and R. Kussl, 'Achikar, Tinuphis und Äsop' (pp. 23–30) in N. Holzberg (ed.), *Der Äsop-Roman. Motivgeschichte und Erzählstruktur* (Tübingen, 1992), and the extensive bibliography.

There are echoes of Ahiqar in Middle Iranian Literature.[48] Luqman, referred to and quoted in the Qur'ān (Surah 31), also has strong connections with Ahiqar and the influence of Ahiqar has been noted elsewhere in Arabic literature.[49] The 'Words of Ahiqar' remain a source of study for scholars in many fields.

Addendum

After this article was in press the important study by F. M. Fales, 'Riflessioni sull'Ahiqar di Elefantina', *Orientis Antiqui Miscellanea*, 1 (1994), pp. 39–60, came to my attention. It contains both interesting ideas and useful bibliography.

[48] C. J. Brunner, 'The Fable of the Babylonian Tree', *JNES* 39 (1980), pp. 191–202, 291–302, and F. de Blois, 'The Admonitions of Adurbad and their Relationship to the Ahiqar Legend', *JRAS* 1984, pp. 41–53.

[49] A. Frayha, *Ahiqar, Wise Man of the Ancient Near East* (Beirut, 1962, in Arabic).

Part 2

Old Testament and Apocryphal texts

4 Foreign Semitic influence on the wisdom of Israel and its appropriation in the book of Proverbs

John Day

1. Semitic influence on the wisdom of Israel generally

Ever since the discovery that the Egyptian Instruction of Amenemope has remarkable parallels with Prov. xxii 17–xxiii 11, as well as other parts of Proverbs, the kinship of Israel's wisdom with that of the ancient near east has been recognized. Interestingly, the Old Testament itself recognizes that the Egyptians were noted for their wisdom and that this was not something confined to Israel. 'Solomon's wisdom', we read, 'surpassed the wisdom of all the people of the east, and all the wisdom of Egypt' (1 Kings v 10 [iv 30]). In the light of the kinship of Israel's wisdom with that of Egypt already noted, this verse would lead one to suspect that Israel was also dependent on the wisdom of the people of the east, i.e. the Semitic people who inhabited Transjordan. Explicit acknowledgement of something like this is frankly given in Prov. xxx 1 and xxxi 1, which claim to be imparting respectively 'The words of Agur son of Jakeh of Massa' and 'The words of Lemuel, king of Massa, which his mother taught him', Massa being in north-west Arabia (Gen. xxv 14; 1 Chron. i 30).[1] Contrast the way in which Proverbs quietly appropriates the Egyptian wisdom of Amenemope without acknowledgement.[2] However, unlike the wealth of attention bestowed on Israel's indebtedness to Egyptian wisdom, less attention has been paid to Israel's dependence on Semitic wisdom. Admittedly our sources of information on this subject are much more limited, but it is worth assessing what evidence we have.

---

[1] It is widely agreed that the place-name Massa, not the word for 'oracle', is in view here, since the latter is a prophetic form which is inappropriate to the contents of Prov. xxx and xxxi. In Prov. xxx 1 we should presumably read *hammaśśā'î* or *mimmaśśā'* for *hammaśśā'*.

[2] Amazingly, the NAB does import the name of Amenemope into its translation of Prov. xxii 19, 'That your trust may be in the Lord I make known to you the words of Amen-em-ope', but this radical emendation has received no support.

That there was dependence specifically on the wisdom of the people of the east is further suggested by the book of Job, for Job is declared to be 'the greatest of all the people of the east' (Job i 3). More particularly, the hero of the book of Job is said to hail from the land of Uz (Job i 1). There have been two main views as to where Uz was. The first locates it in Syria, on the basis of Gen. x 23 and xx 21, where Uz is related to Aram, and the second places it in Edom, on the basis of Gen. xxxvi 28, where Uz is an Edomite clan, and Lam. iv 21, where we read, 'Rejoice and be glad, O daughter of Edom, dweller in the land of Uz.' The latter view is surely to be followed, since Job's 'comforter', Eliphaz, is from Teman in Edom, and the book shows familiarity with places adjacent to Edom, namely Sheba (Job i 15, vi 19) and Tema (Job vi 19) in north-west Arabia, but no corresponding places in Syria are mentioned.[3] Although Shuah, the home of Bildad the Shuhite, has sometimes been equated with the Akkadian place-name Sūḫu on the middle Euphrates, this is about 700 miles away from the southern geographical horizon suggested by the other references, and is unattested elsewhere in the Old Testament. Rather, we should connect Bildad with the southern Shuah mentioned in Gen. xxv 2, represented as the uncle of Sheba and Dedan (Gen. xxv 3).

Since the book of Job is widely agreed to date from c. 500–300 BC,[4] we thus seem to have here an Edomite as the hero of a Jewish wisdom book at the very time when the Edomites were so hated by the Jews, apparently because of their connivance in the Babylonian destruction of Jerusalem in 586 BC (cf. Ps. cxxxvii 7; Lam. iv 21; Obad. 1–21; Jer. xlix 7–22; Ezek. xxv 12–14, xxxv 1–15; Isa. xxxiv 5–17, lxiii 1–6; Mal. i 2–5; Joel iv 19 [iii 19]). One may suggest four reasons to explain how it was possible for an Edomite to be the hero of the book of Job at that time. First, Job is a wisdom book and the wise men were more internationally minded, and doubtless less likely to have 'hang-ups' about Edomites. Secondly, Job is represented as a Yahweh worshipper. Thirdly, the story is set in ancient times, when relations with Edomites were less hostile. Fourthly, the tradition that Job was an Edomite – hardly invented in the post-exilic period – was probably so strong that it could not be altered. This last point suggests that an originally Edomite tradition about Job lies behind the work. We recall that elsewhere in the Old Testament the Edomites are noted for their wisdom (Jer. xlix 7; Obad. 8; cf. Baruch iii 22–3).[5]

[3] The reference to Chaldeans in Job i 17 is not significant in this regard, since although nearer to Syria than Edom, they are known to have campaigned as far south as Arabia.

[4] Thus most commentators. A. Hurvitz, 'The Date of the Prose-Tale of Job Linguistically Considered', *HTR* 67 (1974), pp. 17–34, produces a whole series of features of the language of the prologue and epilogue which agree with post-exilic rather than pre-exilic Hebrew.

[5] See J. Day, 'How could Job be an Edomite?', in W. A. M. Beuken (ed.), *The Book of Job* (Leuven, 1994), pp. 392–9, for a much fuller treatment of this question.

In terms of its theological content – its grappling with the problem of theodicy – the book of Job also clearly belongs to the Semitic sphere rather than evidencing Egyptian influence. No comparable works from ancient Egypt are attested. A work such as the Tale of the Eloquent Peasant, which is sometimes compared, concerns social injustice rather than directly questioning the divine justice.[6] Possibly it was the ancient Egyptians' strong belief in immortality, combined with their traditional fatalism, that prevented the problem of theodicy from raising its head in the way in which it did in the Semitic world. As is well known, we possess a number of Mesopotamian works on the theme of the righteous sufferer, e.g. *Ludlul bēl nēmeqi*, 'I will praise the Lord of wisdom', and the Babylonian Theodicy, though none of these is as outspoken as the book of Job.[7] Not so well known is the fact that a work in Akkadian comparable to *Ludlul bēl nēmeqi* has turned up at Ugarit (RS 25.460).[8] That this text was found at Ugarit proves that the theme of the righteous sufferer was known very early in Canaan, so that such texts *might* have been available to the author of Job. But it would be unwise to assume dogmatically that Job was dependent on any particular known work and so, for example, to reconstruct a first edition of the book of Job without a dialogue on analogy with *Ludlul bēl nēmeqi*, as N. H. Snaith did.[9]

Another instance of a non-Israelite Semitic wise man being taken up into the Old Testament and integrated into the Yahwistic scheme of things is the figure of Daniel. Already before the discovery of the Ugaritic texts there were suspicions that the righteous Daniel referred to alongside the hoary old figures of Job and Noah in Ezek. xiv 14, 20, and the wise Daniel apparently known to the king of Tyre in the oracle against him in Ezek. xxviii 3, could hardly refer to the young Jewish exile in Babylon alluded to in our book of Daniel.[10] More naturally a non-Israelite figure of hoary antiquity was being referred to. With the discovery of the Ugaritic texts it became widely accepted that this figure had been found in the person of the Canaanite righteous judge (and possibly king) Daniel, the father of

---

[6] *ANET*, pp. 407–10.

[7] See W. G. Lambert, *Babylonian Wisdom Literature* (Oxford, 1960), pp. 21–91. For an additional work, see J. Nougayrol, 'Une version ancienne du "juste souffrant"', *RB* 59 (1952), pp. 239–50.

[8] See *Ugaritica* V (Paris, 1968), pp. 264–73. Other wisdom compositions in Akkadian from Ugarit are contained in *Ugaritica* V, pp. 273–300. See J. Gray, 'The Book of Job in the Context of Near Eastern Literature', *ZAW* 82 (1970), pp. 251–69, for discussion of the Ugaritic righteous sufferer text as well as the Mesopotamian works.

[9] N. H. Snaith, *The Book of Job* (London, 1968).

[10] See the examples cited from the history of interpretation in the generally overlooked book of B. Mariani, *Daniel: 'il patriarca sapiente' nella Bibbia, nella tradizione, nella leggenda* (Rome, 1945), pp. 44–53.

Aqhat.[11] Although not explicitly described as wise in the Ugaritic Aqhat text, he is certainly depicted as a just judge of the widows and orphans (*KTU* 1.17.V.4–8 and 1.19.I.19–25), which coheres with the reference to Daniel's righteousness in Ezek. xiv 14, 20, and we need to remember that wisdom and the administration of justice were closely associated (cf. 1 Kings iii 9, 12). It makes sense that Ezekiel's Daniel should have been a Canaanite hero when we recall that Ezekiel expects the king of Tyre to have heard of him (Ezek. xxviii 3).

Attempts in recent years to question this relationship have proved unsuccessful, for example, that of H. H. P. Dressler,[12] who claims that Ezekiel would hardly have cited a polytheist such as the Ugaritic Daniel as an example of a righteous man. However, against this it may be argued that Dressler fails to take into account the point that Daniel worshipped El – a god equated with Yahweh in the Old Testament – and that the large number of centuries between the Ugaritic texts and Ezekiel allows plenty of time for Daniel's becoming a monotheistic figure at the hands of Israel's Yahwists. We have several other examples of this process, e.g. Enoch (Enmeduranki), Noah (Utnapishtim), Balaam, and Ahiqar (on which last, see below).

One suspects that Dressler wishes Ezekiel's Daniel to be the same as the figure in our book of Daniel, but he cannot quite bring himself to say so. More explicit in equating Ezekiel's Daniel with the hero of the book of Daniel is H.-M. Wahl.[13] He concludes that this is possible by dating the traditions in Daniel i–vi early – he thinks that they existed already in something like their present form about 500 BC – and by dating Ezek. xiv 12–20 late, also to about 500 BC. But both these propositions are highly questionable, and we have already noted above why Ezekiel's Daniel is more likely to derive from the Ugaritic Daniel.

Nevertheless, it seems very likely that there was an ongoing Daniel tradition and that the depiction of Daniel in Ezekiel has influenced the figure in the book of Daniel. Just as the Daniel of Ezek. xxviii 3 is superlatively wise, so is the hero of the book of Daniel – in fact wisdom is associated with him more often than any character in the Old Testament apart from Solomon. Furthermore, the dependence of the book of Daniel on Ezekiel is widely acknowledged. Interestingly, even at a late date there is still a reflection of the original judicial role of the Ugaritic Daniel in the apocryphal book of Susannah, where Daniel used judicial wisdom to

[11] For a detailed defence of this view see J. Day, 'The Daniel of Ugarit and Ezekiel and the Hero of the Book of Daniel', *VT* 30 (1980), pp. 174–84.

[12] H. H. P. Dressler, 'The Identification of the Ugaritic Dnil with the Daniel of Ezekiel', *VT* 29 (1979), pp. 152–61.

[13] H.-M. Wahl, 'Noah, Daniel und Hiob in Ezechiel xiv 12–20 (21–3): Anmerkungen zum traditionsgeschichtlichen Hintergrund', *VT* 42 (1992), pp. 542–53.

expose the lies and attempted adultery of the two elders. (Hence the phrase 'a Daniel come to judgement' in Shakespeare's *The Merchant of Venice*, 4. 1.222.)

Another ancient near eastern Semitic wise man whom the Israelites appropriated to their own tradition, this time an Aramean, was the figure of Ahiqar. He appears several times in the apocryphal book of Tobit (i 21–2, ii 10, xi 18, xiv 10–12), and instead of remaining an Aramean we find him there actually transformed into a northern Israelite from the tribe of Naphtali, and he is stated to be Tobit's nephew, the son of his brother Anael (i 21–2; cf. i 1).[14] For the Israelitization of an originally foreign Semitic wise man, we may compare what happened to Daniel, noted above.

When we come to Ecclesiastes we find that there is still no consensus amongst scholars as to the foreign influences that affected him, especially whether and how far there was any Greek influence. One thing we may be confident of is that, whatever foreign influences there may have been, Qoheleth had very much made the ideas his own, for he clearly felt things passionately, and was not simply a slavish follower of foreign philosophies.

In so far as there was foreign Semitic influence, we may reject M. J. Dahood's proposal of Phoenician influence.[15] R. Gordis,[16] in fact, has made a very thorough rebuttal and shown how thinly based Dahood's claims were. Rather, when it comes to foreign Semitic influence on Qoheleth, there is no doubt that by far the most striking parallels are in the Babylonian Gilgamesh Epic. The remarkable parallel between Qoheleth's advice about enjoying life in Eccles. ix 7–9 and the barmaid Šiduri's exhortation to Gilgamesh on the same subject in the Old Babylonian version of the Gilgamesh Epic (X.iii.6–14) was first noted by H. Grimme[17] in 1905. Grimme argued that Ecclesiastes is dependent on Gilgamesh at this point, and this view has been followed by a number of scholars subsequently.[18] Other scholars, on the other hand, have claimed that it is unnecessary to posit direct dependence; it is claimed that similar sentiments can be found in Egyptian or Greek literature.[19] This last claim, however, is a rather superficial objection, for it fails to take into account how close the parallel really is, which is much greater than is often realized. There are, in fact, no less than six parallels between the two passages – seven if we include

[14] On Ahiqar and Tobit, cf. J. C. Greenfield, 'Ahiqar in the Book of Tobit', in M. Carrez, J. Doré and P. Grelot (eds.), *De la Tôrah au Messie. Mélanges Henri Cazelles* (Paris, 1981), pp. 329–36.

[15] M. J. Dahood, 'Canaanite-Phoenician Influence in Qoheleth', *Biblica* 33 (1952), pp. 30–52 and 191–221.

[16] R. Gordis, 'Was Koheleth a Phoenician?', *JBL* 74 (1955), pp. 103–14.

[17] H. Grimme, 'Babel und Koheleth–Jojakhin', in *OLZ* 8 (1905), cols. 432–8.

[18] E.g. G. A. Barton, *Ecclesiastes* (Edinburgh, 1908), pp. 39–40, and the more recent scholars cited below in n. 20.

[19] E.g. R. N. Whybray, *Ecclesiastes* (Grand Rapids and London, 1989), pp. 143–4.

ix 5–6 as well – and, what is more, they all occur in the same order. The dependence of Qoheleth on Gilgamesh at this point is therefore very difficult to deny.

The following illustrates the parallels:

Ecclesiastes	*Gilgamesh*
For the living know that they will die, but the dead know nothing and they have no more reward; but the memory of them is lost. Their love and their hate and their envy have already perished, and they have no more for ever any share in all that is done under the sun.	Gilgamesh, whither do you rove? The life you pursue you shall not find. When the gods created mankind, Death for mankind they set aside, Life in their own hands retaining.
Go eat your bread with enjoyment,	As for you, Gilgamesh, let your belly be full,
and drink your wine with a merry heart for God has already approved what you do.	Make merry by day and by night. Of each day make a feast of rejoicing, Day and night dance and play!
Let your garments be always white; let not oil be lacking on your head.	Let your garments be sparkling fresh, Your head be washed; bathe in water. Pay heed to the little one that holds on to your hand.
Enjoy life with the wife whom you love, all the days of your vain life which he has given you under the sun, because that is your portion in life and in your toil at which you toil under the sun.	Let your spouse delight in your bosom! For this is the task of [mankind]!

More recently, other striking parallels between Gilgamesh and Ecclesiastes have been noted by such scholars as O. Loretz, A. Shaffer, J. de Savignac and B. W. Jones.[20] Thus, both Gilgamesh and Ecclesiastes compare the shallowness of human achievement to the wind – Eccles. v 15 (16) says, 'just as they come, so shall they go; and what gain do they have from toiling for the wind', and Gilgamesh (Yale tablet IV.5) declares, 'As for mankind, numbered are their days. Whatever they achieve is but the wind.' Further, both employ the unusual image of the threefold cord – cf. Eccles. iv 9–12, 'two are better than one ... If they fall, one will lift up his

---

[20] O. Loretz, *Qohelet und der alte Orient* (Freiburg, 1964); A. Shaffer, 'The Mesopotamian Background of Qoheleth 4:9–12' (in Hebrew), *Eretz-Israel* 8 (Jerusalem, 1967), pp. 246–50 (English abstract, p. 75*), and 'New Light on the "Three-Ply Cord"' (in Hebrew), in *Eretz-Israel* 9 (Jerusalem, 1969), pp. 159–60 (English abstract, pp. 138*–9*); J. de Savignac, 'La Sagesse du Qôheleth et l'Epopée de Gilgamesh', *VT* 28 (1978), pp. 318–23; B. W. Jones, 'From Gilgamesh to Qoheleth', in W. W. Hallo, B. W. Jones and G. L. Mattingley (eds.), *The Bible in the Light of Cuneiform Literature* (Lewiston, Queenston and Lampeter, 1990), pp. 349–79.

fellow... A threefold cord is not quickly broken', with Gilgamesh and the Land of the Living (lines 106–10, also, less well preserved, in Epic 5.2.20–5), 'Two men will not die; the towed rope will not sink, A towrope of three strands cannot be cut. You help me and I will help you, (and) what of ours can anyone carry off?'

Job, Daniel and Ahiqar were all members of the ruling class, and Solomon, of course, was a king. The extent to which wisdom should be seen as a product of the court and ruling class in ancient Israel is currently disputed, but there can be little doubt that this was *one* of the contexts in which it was cultivated. Until recently it has been widely supposed that Israel's court officials were modelled on those of ancient Egypt.[21] It has been customary to speak of 'Solomonic state officials' on the understanding that their emergence was encouraged by Solomon's Egyptian contacts. However, it is noticeable that most of Israel's court officials were already in place under David (2 Sam. viii 16–18, xx 23–6; cf. 1 Kings iv 2–6), and David's stamping-ground was Canaan and Transjordan rather than Egypt. This suggests the likelihood of a Canaanite origin for Israel's court officials. The unlikelihood of an Egyptian origin is further increased when the alleged parallels are examined in detail.[22] If then we posit a Canaanite origin for Israel's court officials, and wisdom had some connection with the court, there is a likelihood of some Canaanite wisdom being appropriated when the Israelite court was established.

In connection with Solomon's wisdom we read in 1 Kings v 13 (iv 33) that 'he spoke of trees, from the cedar that is in Lebanon to the hyssop that grows out of the wall; he spoke also of beasts and of birds, and of reptiles and of fish'. It has been almost axiomatic for many scholars, since the appearance of A. Alt's article on the subject, to suppose that this passage indicates dependence on onomastic or list wisdom such as was known in Egypt and Mesopotamia.[23] It is clearly not the case that Solomon's wisdom was actually onomastic in character, for against this it may be noted that Solomon is said to have *spoken* of the trees and beasts, which does not seem appropriate for a mere catalogue of names such as we find in the Egyptian and Mesopotamian onomastica. A careful reading of Alt,[24] however, makes it clear that he believed that, in appropriating the onomastica, Solomon radically transformed them by giving them proverbial and song

[21] R. de Vaux, 'Titres et fonctionnaires égyptiens à la cour de David et de Salomon', *RB* 48 (1939), pp. 394–405; J. Begrich, 'Söfer und Mazkîr', *ZAW* 58 (1940), pp. 1–29; T. N. D. Mettinger, *Solomonic State Officials* (Lund, 1971).

[22] See now especially, S. Weeks, *Early Israelite Wisdom* (Oxford, 1994), pp. 115–29. Also U. Rütersworden, *Die Beamten der israelitischen Königszeit* (Stuttgart, 1985).

[23] A. Alt, 'Die Weisheit Salomos', *ThLZ* 76 (1951), cols. 139–44 (E. tr., 'Solomonic Wisdom', in J. L. Crenshaw (ed.), *Studies in Ancient Israelite Wisdom* [New York, 1976], pp. 102–12). The list of those who follow Alt is endless.   [24] A. Alt, col. 142 (E. tr., pp. 108–9).

form (cf. 1 Kings v 12 [iv 32]). Such a procedure, however, is nowhere else attested. In any case, if Solomon's nature wisdom was in proverbial form, why need one seek an origin for it in onomastica at all? Possibly, therefore, we should see Solomon's nature wisdom simply as animal and plant proverbs (cf. Prov. vi 6–8, xxx 15, 17–19, 24–31). Alternatively, we should see Solomon's nature wisdom as fables. The subjects covered – various kinds of beasts and trees – correspond precisely to the subject matter of fables, a genre which, we know, clearly belonged to the wisdom tradition, as we see from their inclusion in the Wisdom of Ahiqar[25] (lines 110, 118–120a, 120b–123a, 165–6, and probably 204–5). Fables also feature as a part of the Mesopotamian wisdom tradition.[26] (The Old Testament itself attests knowledge of fables in Judg. ix 7–15 and 2 Kings xiv 9.) Whether we see Solomon's nature wisdom simply as animal and plant proverbs or more particularly as fables, it has nothing to do with onomastica.[27] Moreover, Semitic rather than Egyptian influence will have been operative, since animal proverbs are rare in Egyptian wisdom prior to the late Instruction of Ankhsheshonqy, and beast fables are not clearly attested in Egypt till the Graeco-Roman period.[28]

2.   Semitic influence on Proverbs

Much work has been done on the book of Proverbs' appropriation of Egyptian wisdom. Less has been written on the distinctively Semitic contribution to the book.[29] Commentators most commonly cite the parallel between Prov. xxiii 13–14 and Ahiqar, lines 81–2. Proverbs reads, 'Do not withhold discipline from a child; if you beat him with a rod, he will not die. If you beat him with the rod you will save his life from Sheol.' Compare Ahiqar, 'Spare not your son from the rod; otherwise, can you save him [from wickedness]? If I beat you, my son, you will not die; but if I leave you alone, [you will not live].' Interestingly, the text in Proverbs follows almost

---

[25] For the Wisdom of Ahiqar see A. Cowley, *Aramaic Papyri from the Fifth Century BC* (Oxford, 1923), pp. 204–48, and J. M. Lindenberger, *The Aramaic Proverbs of Ahiqar* (Baltimore and London, 1983).

[26] See W. G. Lambert, *BWL*, pp. 150–212.

[27] M. V. Fox, 'Egyptian Onomastica and Biblical Wisdom', in *VT* 36 (1986), pp. 302–10, rejects a number of attempts to find onomastic influence on the Old Testament, but does not discuss the interpretation of 1 Kings v 13 (iv 33).

[28] Cf. R. J. Williams, 'The Fable in the Ancient Near East', in E. C. Hobbs (ed.), *A Stubborn Faith. Papers on the Old Testament and Related Subjects Presented to Honor William Andrew Irwin* (Dallas, 1956), pp. 17–18.

[29] An older study was C. I. K. Story, 'The Book of Proverbs and Northwest Semitic Literature', *JBL* 64 (1945), pp. 319–37. Two purely philological works from the Dahood school are M. J. Dahood, *Proverbs and Northwest Semitic Philology* (Rome, 1963), and W. A. van der Weiden, *Le livre des Proverbes* (Rome, 1970).

immediately after the series of citations from Amenemope (Prov. xxii 17–xxiii 11), and it is generally assumed that it is Proverbs again which is the borrower. Several of the examples in the following sections of this essay are taken from Ahiqar, a work which has been somewhat neglected in studies of Proverbs, although it is one of the very few ancient near eastern wisdom compositions that can claim to be contemporary with the Old Testament. Although the Aramaic manuscript dates from the 5th century BC, it is now generally agreed that the composition dates from the 7th century BC.[30]

Righteous/wicked contrast

The contrast between the righteous (*ṣaddîqîm*) and the wicked (*rᵉšāʿîm*) is very characteristic of the book of Proverbs, especially in the antithetic proverbs in Prov. x–xv. It has been argued by W. McKane[31] that this contrast is part of the Yahwistic redaction of the old wisdom, part of the same stratum (his group 'C' proverbs) which, in his view, introduced God-language to previously secular proverbs. A similar view has more recently been taken by F.-J. Steiert,[32] who claims that the righteous/wicked contrast is characteristically Israelite. It is true that the righteous/wicked contrast is not found in Egyptian wisdom literature, where the contrast sometimes is rather between the hothead and the silent or cool-headed man, traces of which are found in Proverbs (cf. Prov. xv 18, xvii 27, xxii 24, xxix 22). However, it should be noted that the righteous/wicked contrast is attested in the Aramaic Wisdom of Ahiqar, thus suggesting that this is an example of Israel's appropriation of the (West) Semitic tradition of wisdom. We may compare Ahiqar, line 167, which has a reference to 'righteous', while the next proverb in line 168 has a reference to 'wicked'; similarly line 171 contains the word 'wicked', while the following proverb, in line 173, has the word 'righteous'. Thus, lines 167–8 read, 'It is best to support a righteous (*[ṣ]dyq*) man; all who clash with him are laid low. [The city] of the wicked (*ršyʿn*) will be swept away in the day of the storm, and its gates will fall into ruin; for the spoil [of the wicked shall perish].' Again, lines 171–3 read, 'If a wicked man (*ršyʿ*) grasps the fringe of your garment, leave it in his hand. Then appeal to Shamash; he [will] take what is his and will give it to you. Establish me, O El, as a righteous man (*ṣdyq*) with you! To [(?)...]'

[30] See J. Lindenberger, *The Aramaic Proverbs of Ahiqar*, p. 20; I. Kottsieper, *Die Sprache der Ahiqarsprüche* (Berlin, 1990), pp. 241–6; and the essay by J. C. Greenfield in this volume.
[31] W. McKane, *Proverbs* (London, 1970), p. 420.
[32] F.-J. Steiert, *Die Weisheit Israels – ein Fremdkörper im Alten Testament?* (Freiburg, 1990), p. 86.

Graded numerical proverbs[33]

Another feature of Israelite wisdom literature, including the book of Proverbs, which is completely unattested in Egyptian wisdom, is the occurrence of sayings involving a graded numerical sequence (Prov. vi 16–19, xxx 15–31; cf. Job v 19–22, xxxiii 14–22, 29, xl 5; Eccles. xi 2; Ecclus xxiii 16, xxv 7–11, xxvi 5, 28, 1 25–6). Graded numerical sayings are frequent in the Ugaritic texts, but with one exception these are not in proverbial contexts. There is, however, one Ugaritic proverbial saying containing a graded numerical sequence, and this is noteworthy as it bears comparison with Prov. vi 16–19. It is *KTU* 1.4.III.17–21:

Truly (there are) two sacrifices Baal hates, three the rider on the clouds – a sacrifice of shame and a sacrifice of meanness and a sacrifice where handmaids debauch.

Compare Prov. vi 16–19,

There are six things which the Lord hates, seven which are an abomination to him: haughty eyes, a lying tongue, and hands that shed innocent blood, a heart that devises wicked plans, feet that make haste to run to evil, a false witness who breathes out lies, and a man who sows discord among brothers.

It is noteworthy that the Aramaic Wisdom of Ahiqar also has one numerical saying of this type, in lines 92–93*a*:

There are two things which are good, and a third which is pleasing to Shamash: one who drinks and shares it, one who masters wisdom [and observes it]; and one who hears a word but tells it not.

This suggests that the occurrence of these numerical proverbs in Proverbs and elsewhere in Jewish wisdom literature reveals dependence on the West Semitic wisdom tradition. Interestingly, all three of the proverbs cited concern a deity and what is displeasing or pleasing to him. Another interesting point is that graded numerical proverbs are one of a series of parallels between Prov. i–ix and xxx–xxxi. Other parallels between these sections, as we shall see, are animal proverbs and allusions to the mother's instruction, which also seem to have a (West) Semitic background.

Animal proverbs

We have earlier argued that Solomon's nature wisdom in 1 Kings refers either to fables, comparable to what we find in the Wisdom of Ahiqar, or to

---

[33] On graded numerical sayings, see W. M. W. Roth, 'The Numerical Sequence $x/x + 1$ in the Old Testament', *VT* 12 (1962), pp. 300–11, and *Numerical Sayings in the Old Testament* (*SVT* 13, 1963); G. Sauer, *Die Sprüche Agurs* (Stuttgart, 1963); M. Haran, 'The Graded Numerical Sequence and the Phenomenon of "Automatism" in Biblical Poetry' (*SVT* 22, 1972), pp. 238–67; H. P. Rüger, 'Die gestaffelten Zahlensprüche des Alten Testaments und aram. Achikar 92', *VT* 31 (1981), pp. 229–34.

animal and plant proverbs. Although there are no fables in the book of
Proverbs, there are a number of animal proverbs. It is to be noted that the
one animal proverb in Prov. i–ix, that about the ant in Prov. vi 6–8, is fairly
closely followed by the one graded numerical saying in Prov. i–ix, namely
Prov. vi 16–19. Again, strikingly, the only other graded numerical sayings
in Proverbs, to be found in Prov. xxx 15–31, almost all incorporate animal
sayings. It is therefore worthy of note that in the Wisdom of Ahiqar the one
graded numerical saying in lines 92–93a (the 2/3 proverb comparable to the
6/7 one in Prov. vi 16–19 noted above), is likewise closely associated with
animal sayings, for it is immediately preceded by a series of animal
proverbs in lines 85b–91. This contrasts with the rarity of animal proverbs
in the Egyptian wisdom literature prior to the late Instruction of
Ankhsheshonqy.[34] We may therefore confidently assert the Semitic
background of the animal proverbs in the book of Proverbs. This would
cohere with the heading in Prov. xxx 1, attributing the section to Agur, son
of Jakeh of Massa, though it is not entirely clear whether this heading
includes verses 15–31. In view of the ant proverbs in Prov. vi 16–19 and xxx
25, we may note that we possess a Canaanite proverb about the ant in the
letter of Lab'ayu of Shechem included among the el-Amarna letters
(252.16–19): 'If ants are smitten, they do not accept (the smiting) quietly,
but they bite the hand of the man who smites them.'[35]

My son

Throughout Proverbs we find the sage addressing his pupil with the words
'my son'. This is especially prominent in Prov. i–ix (e.g. Prov. i 8, 10, 15, ii 1,
iii 1, 11, 21, iv 1, 10, 20). It is particularly striking that this form of address is
never found in the Egyptian Instructions, with the single exception of a late
demotic work,[36] even though these Instructions are characteristically
presented as the words of advice by a father to his son. On the other hand,
the words 'my son' appear several times in the Aramaic Wisdom of Ahiqar
(lines 82, 96, 127, 129, 149). Note that in lines 127 and 129 the words 'my
son' introduce two succeeding admonitions, just as we find repeated cases
of 'my son' in the book of Proverbs (e.g. Prov. xxiii 15, 19, 26). The words

---

[34] For Ankhsheshonqy, see M. Lichtheim, *Ancient Egyptian Literature,* 3 (Berkeley, 1980),
pp. 159–84.

[35] W. F. Albright, 'An Archaic Hebrew Proverb in an Amarna Letter from Central Palestine',
BASOR 89 (1943), pp. 29–32.

[36] This is P. inv. Sorbonne 1260, line 7. On this work, which dates from about the 3rd century
BC, see M. Pezin, 'Fragment de sagesse démotique (P. inv. Sorbonne 1260)', *Enchoria* 11
(1982), pp. 59–61, and plates 7–8. The occurrence of 'my son' in the Instruction of
Amenemhet (Pap. Sallier II, 3:3–4) is not comparable, as it does not introduce words of
advice (*ANET,* p. 419).

'my son' also occur as a form of address in Babylonian (as well as Sumerian) wisdom, e.g. the Instructions of Šuruppak, line 9, and the Counsels of Wisdom, line 81, as well as in the Akkadian Counsel of Šube'awilum (or Šupe'awilum) attested at Ugarit (I.9, II.6; cf. 'son' in I.17, 19).[37] Interestingly, we also find the words 'my son' in a further piece of non-Israelite, Semitic wisdom instruction, namely as part of 'the words of Lemuel, king of Massa, which his mother taught him', in Prov. xxxi 2, 'What my son? What, son of my womb? What, son of my vows?' We clearly have here, therefore, another instance of influence from the Semitic rather than the Egyptian wisdom tradition on the book of Proverbs.

Mother's teaching

There are a number of instances in Proverbs which refer not only to the father's instruction but also to that of the mother (Prov. i 8, vi 20, xxxi 1, and possibly xxxi 26). There is, so far as I am aware, no reference to the mother's teaching in any of the Egyptian Instructions, and the isolated Mesopotamian wisdom references to it are Sumerian rather than Semitic. For example, in the Instructions of Šuruppak, lines 259–60, we read, 'The word of your mother, as if it were the word of your god, do not ignore it. A mother is (like) the sun, she gives birth to mankind.'[38] It is therefore striking that Prov. xxxi 1 explicitly designates itself as part of the foreign Semitic wisdom appropriated by Israel: 'The words of Lemuel, king of Massa, which his mother taught him.' Prov. vi 20, notably, is also part of the same chapter that contains an animal saying (Prov. vi 6–8) and a graded numerical proverb (Prov. vi 16–19), and therefore likewise plausibly reflects a Semitic background.

The fear of the Lord

In Prov. i–ix the fear of the Lord has a paradigmatic role in connection with wisdom. Its centrality is emphasized by the reference to it near the beginning in Prov. i 7, 'The fear of the Lord is the beginning of knowledge',

[37] Cf. B. Alster, *The Instructions of Suruppak* (Copenhagen, 1974), p. 35; W. G. Lambert, *BWL*, p. 103; *Ugaritica* V, pp. 280–1. For a more recent translation of Šuruppak, with philological notes, see C. Wilcke, 'Philologische Bemerkungen zum *Rat des Šuruppag* und Versuch einer neuen Übersetzung', *Zeitschrift für Assyriologie* 68 (1978), pp. 196–232, and for a new edition of Šube'awilum (or Šupe'awilum) including the Emar, Ugaritic and Hittite sources, see M. Dietrich and G. Keydana, 'Die Dialog Šūpē-amēli und seinem "Vater"', *UF* 23 (1991), pp. 33–74.

[38] B. Alster, *Studies in Sumerian Proverbs* (Copenhagen, 1975), pp. 137–8. There is a similar saying in the Sumerian Preceptive Work, rev. 5.1. Cf. J.J.A. van Dijk, *La Sagesse suméro-accadienne* (Leiden, 1953), pp. 103, 105.

as well as the allusion to it towards the end of this section in Prov. ix 10, 'The fear of the Lord is the beginning of wisdom; and the knowledge of the Holy One is insight.' (Cf. also Prov. i 29, ii 5, iii 7, viii 13, and the LXX of vii 1a.)

The centrality of the fear of the Lord, like the personification of wisdom, is one of the things which connects Prov. i–ix with the later wisdom found in the book of Ecclesiasticus. Together with the absence of references to the king (apart from the universalizing viii 15), this suggests a post-exilic date for Prov. i–ix, in contrast to Prov. x–xxix, much of which bears comparison with earlier Egyptian wisdom literature and is replete with allusions to the king, thus suggesting a pre-exilic date, at least for some of the material in these chapters. However, already within Prov. x–xxix the fear of the Lord is not absent, though it is not given such a central role in connection with wisdom (cf. Prov. x 27, xiv 2, 26–7, xv 16, 33, xvi 6, xix 23, xxii 4, xxiii 17, xxiv 21).

Now the *centrality* given to the fear of the Lord may be distinctive of Israel, but the idea that fear of the deity is a part of wisdom is attested outside Israel.[39] Although the idea of the fear of the deity is common in ancient Egypt, it is not found in Egyptian wisdom literature until the late demotic compositions, e.g. Ankhsheshonqy xiv, 10, 'Make burnt offering and libation before the god; let the fear of him be great in your heart.'

However, the idea of the fear of the deity is found a number of times in Babylonian wisdom literature (*Ludlul bēl nēmeqi*, ii.18, 25, 32, Babylonian Theodicy, line 22, Counsels of Wisdom, lines 143–7, the Shamash hymn, line 165, and Proverbs, ii.11–14).[40] Most interesting for us is Counsels of Wisdom, 143–7:

> Reverence (*palāḫu*) begets favour,
> Sacrifice prolongs life,
> And prayer atones for guilt.
> He who fears the gods (*pāliḫ ili^meš*) is not slighted by [...]
> He who fears (*pāliḫ*) the Anunnaki extends [his days].

With this last one may compare the idea found in Proverbs more than once that the fear of the Lord prolongs life (Prov. x 27, xix 23, xxii 4). It therefore appears that Proverbs appropriated the idea of the fear of the deity from Semitic wisdom, rather than from Egypt, even though it gave it a greater centrality in relation to wisdom than it had had previously.

---

[39] On the fear of the deity in ancient near eastern wisdom literature, see J. Derousseaux, *La Crainte de Dieu dans l'A.T.* (Paris, 1970), pp. 21–66; M. L. Barré, '"Fear of God" and the World View of Wisdom', *Biblical Theology Bulletin* 11 (1981), pp. 41–3.

[40] See W. G. Lambert, *BWL*, pp. 39, 41, 71, 105, 165, and 247.

The personification of Wisdom

As is well-known, wisdom is personified in Prov. i–ix as well as in later wisdom books such as Ecclus xxiv and Wisd. vii–ix. There is, however, no consensus on the origin of this personification.[41] In the past it was sometimes seen as a reflection of the Egyptian goddess Isis-Sophia,[42] but the speculation about her dates from the Hellenistic period and so is too late to have influenced the book of Proverbs.[43]

More recently, it has become quite common to see personified Wisdom as a Hebraized version of the Egyptian goddess Ma'at. Ma'at, which means 'Justice, Order, Truth', was the fundamental principle of reality underlying the Egyptian wisdom books.[44] It was also sometimes personified as a goddess, and a number of parallels between this and Prov. i–ix have been drawn, especially by C. Kayatz.[45] However, there are some serious problems with this view. First, it has to be observed that Ma'at is never personified anywhere in Egyptian wisdom literature. Secondly, when it is personified (outside the wisdom literature), Ma'at never speaks in the first person, or indeed at all, which contrasts strikingly with personified Wisdom in Prov. i–ix (cf. Prov. i 20–33, viii 1–36, ix 4–6). Thirdly, some of the alleged parallels, on closer inspection, prove to be questionable. For example, Kayatz[46] noted that the symbol of Ma'at was worn on a chain round the neck in Egypt, especially by high officials, and compared this with the references to the neck adornment referred to in Prov. i 9, iii 3, 22, and vi 21. However, in none of these verses is the pendant explicitly related to *ḥokmâ* (though arguably this is implicit). Moreover, a better claim can be made that the imagery is a free adaptation of Deut. xi 18 (cf. Deut. vi 8; note especially the close parallelism between Deut. xi 18–19 and Prov. vi 21–2), *nepeš* in Deut. xi 18 having been taken to mean 'neck' rather than 'soul' (as apparently in Prov. iii 22).

We seem driven, therefore, to seek a Semitic origin for the personification

---

[41] See the survey in C. V. Camp, *Wisdom and the Feminine in the Book of Proverbs* (Sheffield, 1985), pp. 23–46.

[42] R. Reitzenstein, *Zwei religionsgeschichtliche Fragen* (Strasbourg, 1901), pp. 104–9.

[43] Cf. H. Ringgren, *Word and Wisdom* (Lund, 1947), p. 144. This is not to deny that there might have been influence from Isis on the personification of Wisdom in Ecclus xxiv and Wisd. vii–ix. See H. Ringgren, *Word and Wisdom,* pp. 144–6, and J. M. Reese, *Hellenistic Influence on the Book of Wisdom and its Consequences* (Rome, 1970), pp. 46–9.

[44] For an up-to-date treatment of Ma'at, see J. Assmann, *Ma'at: Gerechtigkeit und Unsterblichkeit im alten Ägypten* (Munich, 1990).

[45] C. Kayatz, *Studien zu Proverbien 1–9* (Neukirchen-Vluyn, 1966), pp. 76–119; O. Keel, *Die Weisheit spielt vor Gott* (Freiburg, 1974). The parallel with Ma'at seems to have been proposed originally by H. Donner, 'Die religionsgeschichtliche Ursprünge von Prov. Sal. 8', *Zeitschrift für ägyptische Sprache* 82 (1958), pp. 8–18, but he denied any direct influence, preferring to see the dependence of Prov. viii on the personification of Wisdom in Ahiqar, which was a parallel development to that of Ma'at.

[46] C. Kayatz, *Studien zu Proverbien 1–9*, pp. 107–11.

of Wisdom. One such view was that of G. Boström,[47] who saw Wisdom as the counterpart of Dame Folly, whom he understood to be a sacred prostitute, a devotee of Ishtar/Astarte. However, this is extremely unlikely. First, wisdom literature generally is remarkably unconcerned about foreign cults. Secondly, Dame Folly's actions do not sound like cultic prostitution but rather like ordinary adultery. Compare, for example, her words 'My husband is not at home; he has gone on a long journey' (Prov. vii 19). Thirdly, Prov. i–ix seems to be post-exilic, when cultic prostitution was less in evidence in ancient Israel.

Mark Smith[48] has recently proposed that the personification of Wisdom in Proverbs derives from the goddess Asherah. In support, he notes that both are feminine divine figures, that wisdom is associated several times in Proverbs with the tree of life (cf. Prov. iii 18, xi 30, xv 4), which one might compare to the Asherah stylized tree, and that the word *'ašrê*, 'blessed', occurs in Prov. iii 13 and 18, one of the passages concerning the personification of Wisdom. In spite of its ingenuity, however, this hypothesis seems doubtful. Most importantly, it may be noted that the goddess Asherah is never associated with wisdom, whether in the Ugaritic texts, the Old Testament, or any other known source. Further, the relationship of Wisdom to Yahweh is more akin to that of a child than a wife (cf. Prov. viii 22), and the employment of the word *'ašrê* in Prov. iii 13, 18 is not so remarkable, since it occurs quite frequently in Proverbs and related wisdom literature (cf. Prov. viii 32, 34, xiv 21, xvi 20, xx 7, xxviii 14, xxix 18; Ps. cxxvii 5, cxxviii 1).

Another recent suggestion as to the origin of the personification of Wisdom is that of B. Lang,[49] who has proposed that it derives from a Canaanite goddess called Wisdom (*hokmâ*), who was patroness of the scribal schools. Unfortunately for this view, there is not a scrap of evidence that any such goddess ever existed.

An earlier view was that of W. F. Albright,[50] who believed that the personification of Wisdom was taken over from the hypostatization of the Wisdom of the Canaanite god El. However, although El is noted for his wisdom at Ugarit, we lack evidence that his wisdom was hypostatized. Further, Albright's linguistic arguments for a Canaanite textual source underlying Prov. viii–ix are widely agreed to be exaggerated.[51]

[47] G. Boström, *Proverbiastudien* (Lund, 1935).
[48] M. S. Smith, *The Early History of God* (San Francisco, 1990), pp. 94–5.
[49] B. Lang, *Wisdom and the Book of Proverbs* (New York, 1986). This is a thorough revision of *Frau Weisheit: Deutung einer biblischen Gestalt* (Düsseldorf, 1975).
[50] W. F. Albright, 'Some Canaanite-Phoenician Sources of Hebrew Wisdom', in M. Noth and D. W. Thomas (eds.), *Wisdom in Israel and in the Ancient Near East* (*SVT* 3, 1955), pp. 7–9.
[51] R. N. Whybray, *Wisdom in Proverbs* (London, 1965), pp. 84–5; J. A. Emerton, 'Wisdom', in G. W. Anderson (ed.), *Tradition and Interpretation* (Oxford, 1979), pp. 231–2.

In my view, the personification of Wisdom, like so many other features of Prov. i–ix, has its background in the (West) Semitic wisdom tradition. In the Wisdom of Ahiqar, lines 94*b*–95, we read, '[From] heaven the peoples are [fa]voured; [W]isdom i[s of] the gods. Indeed, she is precious to the gods; Her kingdom is et[er]nal. She has been established in the he[aven]s. Yea, the lord of the holy ones (or Baal *Qdšn*) has exalted her.' Here Wisdom is clearly personified.[52] We may compare Ecclus xxiv 4, where Wisdom says, 'I dwelt in high places, and my throne was in a pillar of cloud' and 1 Enoch xlii 1–2, 'Wisdom found no place where she could dwell, and her dwelling was in heaven. Wisdom went out in order to dwell among the sons of men, but did not find a dwelling. Wisdom returned to her place and took her seat in the midst of the angels.' Although it has sometimes been supposed that the personification of Yahweh's Wisdom in Proverbs took place in Israel quite independently, the parallel in Ahiqar makes it more natural to suppose that this is yet another instance in which Israel was indebted to the West Semitic wisdom tradition.

In conclusion, therefore, it may be stated that Israel's wisdom, including the book of Proverbs, was indebted to foreign Semitic influence in addition to the Egyptian influence which has more frequently been noted. Although our sources of information about Semitic wisdom are more limited than is the case with regard to Egyptian wisdom, enough is known for us to be able to deduce at least some of the influence which it exerted on the wisdom of Israel in general and the book of Proverbs in particular.

---

[52] Although the word for 'wisdom' (*ḥkmth*) has to be partially reconstructed, this reading is generally accepted.

5 The limits of theodicy as a theme of the book of Job

E. W. Nicholson

1

Generally speaking, the Satan's question to God in i 9, 'Does Job fear God for nought?', is understood as being cynical, the implication of the question being that Job sees a direct relationship between his piety and his prosperity and therefore naturally cultivates his piety. But if the question is intended as cynical, it is certainly not dismissed as such by God in the narrative, but is taken with the utmost seriousness, and there is good reason for believing that its implication was nothing more than many in ancient Israel would have regarded not merely as unobjectionable but as fully warranted. The belief appears to have been widely current that there is indeed a direct relationship between 'the fear of God' and wellbeing, as an examination of the contexts of the expressions 'fear of the Lord/fearing the Lord' indicates. The 'fear of the Lord' is not only 'the beginning of wisdom' but has for its 'reward' 'riches and honour and life' (Prov. xxii 4); it 'prolongs life' (Prov. x 27) and anyone who has it 'rests satisfied and will not be visited by harm' (Prov. xix 23); 'by the fear of the Lord one avoids evil' (Prov. xvi 6) and 'the snares of death' (Prov. xiv 27); 'those who fear him have no want' (Ps. xxxiv 10); God's 'abundant goodness' is laid up for those who fear him (Ps. xxxi 20); they are delivered from death and kept alive in famine (Ps. xxxiii 19); 'wealth and riches' are in the house of those who fear the Lord, and their 'descendants will be mighty in the land' (Ps. cxii 2, 3). In short, happiness, wellbeing, and prosperity are assured to those who fear the Lord (cf. Ps. cxxviii).

Given this commonly accepted belief, the Satan's question, 'Does Job fear God for nought?', did not necessarily require cynicism for its motivation. On the contrary, it was an obvious question for this tester of the ways of humanity to ask. And just as obviously, many in Israel, had they been asked this question, would have replied, 'No! Job does not fear

God for nought. No-one does; that's the way the world works: God, who is righteous and seeks to uphold righteousness, rewards the righteous and punishes those who offend his righteousness.' Further, it is apparent from the opening verses of the book that Job himself held such a belief, for his religious scrupulosity was such, we are told (i 5), that he would summon his sons to purify them after their feasting, and would 'busy himself' offering sacrifices on their behalf lest any of them had offended God even with a thought, thus bringing a threat of misfortune upon the family. The implication of Job's wife's advice to him (ii 9) is that she too had held such a belief, but then considered it to be no longer valid when misfortune struck so devastatingly at her righteous husband, whereupon she declared God to be worthy no more of Job's devotion.

All the more surprising, in view of this, is Job's reaction when calamity befalls him, for whilst maintaining his fidelity to God in the midst of his misery, what he twice over states (i 21, ii 10) appears to represent a negation of this reward/retribution *theologoumenon* that those who fear God are guaranteed divine blessing and safety from all ill. As God gives blessing to a righteous person, he declares, so also he may take it away from a righteous person (i 21); as wellbeing may attend the life of those who fear the Lord, so also their lot may instead be misfortune from the Lord (ii 10). The second of his two statements, which is made at the climax of the prologue in response to his wife's enticement of him to curse God, is of particular significance for the point I wish to make. Her counsel to him (ii 9) acts as a foil for his well-known declaration: knowing no more than does Job the hidden cause of his suffering, she inculpates God for the evil that has come about, and regards him as no longer worthy of Job's devotion but only of a curse. Job's dismissal of her bitter counsel as being like the chatter of 'one of the foolish women' leads us to anticipate that he will then counter her outburst not only by reaffirming his fidelity to God but also by exculpating God of the evil that has devastated his life. But though he does the former, he makes no attempt at the latter, for in reaffirming his fidelity he declares that this evil is no less from God than was the good that was his lot hitherto in life, and that as the good was accepted so must this evil also be accepted. In short, we expect a theodicy, but none is offered, since by definition a theodicy seeks to acquit God of the evil that befalls his servants.

Viewed 'from above' in the story, Job's declaration vindicates God's trust in him against the Satan's accusation. Viewed 'from below', however – that is, from a standpoint not privy to the goings-on in the heavenly court between God and the Satan – it appears as a strikingly candid admission of the stark reality that not even the righteous are guaranteed safety from the sorrows and misfortunes of life in God's world. As such, however, though it seems to acknowledge no need for a theodicy, in reality it raises the issue of theodicy. It would certainly have raised this issue for many in the post-exilic period, when the reward/retribution concept from which it so obviously departs seems to have acquired something of a doctrinaire status, as, for example, in the Chronicler's history where it is the basis of a 'divine pragmatism', as J. Wellhausen aptly put it, according to which 'Never does sin miss its punishment, and never where misfortune occurs is guilt wanting.'[1] The view I shall argue is that this issue of theodicy raised by Job's declaration at the climax of the prologue set the 'agenda' or part of the 'agenda' for the author of the dialogues that follow, whether or not this author was also the author of the prologue. Such a view accounts for one of the most pronounced features of the book: its preoccupation with theodicy, different stock positions of which its author has placed for defence or rejection upon the lips of his characters.[2]

2

Theodicy is primarily an intellectual exercise but has a strong pastoral function. For an ancient Israelite it was a comfort to know, when misfortune struck, that the fault lay in oneself and that repentance would bring forgiveness and restoration of wellbeing from a merciful God, or that such misfortune was divine 'testing' which would be followed by renewed blessing for one whose heart was proved to be true to God. That is, theodicy constructed meaning from misfortune and thus gave solace and hope to those whose life had been invaded by adversity. Without theodicy the righteous servant of God was faced with both meaninglessness and despair. It is significant, therefore, that Job's opening speech (ch. iii) after his response to his suffering in ii 10 is one of despair and of a sense of the meaninglessness of his life. Thus he curses the day of his birth (verses 1–10) and asks why he did not die in the womb (verses 11–19), for death would have been more meaningful than his life has now become, and a fate to be rejoiced at like hidden treasure for which men dig (verses 20–23). He asks why light is given to one who is in misery and whose 'way', that is, 'direction' or 'purpose of life', is 'hidden' by God and thus rendered meaningless, a chaos (verses 20, 23). The speech as a whole is marked by the contrast between day and night, light and darkness, life and death, all symbolizing the contrast between order and disorder, meaning and chaos, and in a significant allusion to the primaeval forces of chaos Job summons the allies of Leviathan, those who are inimical to the creation and thus

[1] J. Wellhausen, *Prolegomena zur Geschichte Israels* (Berlin, 1883), p. 211 (E. tr., *Prolegomena to the History of Israel* [Edinburgh, 1885], p. 203).
[2] John Barton, 'Reading the Bible as Literature: Two Questions for Biblical Critics', *Journal of Literature and Theology* 1 (1987), p. 146, has made the interesting suggestion that the book may have been intended or partly intended to provide a sort of 'sampler' of stock positions on the theme of theodicy.

'curse the day', to return the day of his own creation to the domain of primordial absence (verse 8). 'It is not the suffering or bitterness of life as such that consumes him, but the misery of meaninglessness.'[3]

Eliphaz is the first of the companions to respond to Job (chs. iv–v), and it is significant that this opening speech, the longest to be given either by him or his two friends in the dialogues, already sets out each of the theodicies, three in all, advanced by him and his two allies in their exchanges with Job. That is, it seems that Eliphaz's opening speech is intended to be in some measure programmatic. He refers first to the well-known reward/retribution concept, not as an explanation of Job's suffering – Job's integrity as a devout servant of God is not in question at this stage – but as a source of comfort and hope for him. Job is exhorted to place his confidence in his 'fear of God'; herein lies his hope, for no innocent person has ever perished, and only those who 'plough iniquity and sow trouble reap the same' (iv 7–8). As Job in times past counselled those who were stumbling in the face of adversity, so he too must now be patient. Secondly, Eliphaz claims that all human beings are by nature inherently morally flawed – since God charges even his angels with error; how much more 'those who dwell in houses of clay' (iv 18–19) – the implication being that not even Job is fully righteous in God's eyes and so cannot hope to escape God's judgement (iv 12–21). Thirdly, Eliphaz maintains that this suffering is an 'educating chastening' from God, who seeks to correct any shortcoming in his servants. This represents a tamer version of the reward/retribution theodicy, and is apparently intended to meet the case of an acknowledged servant of God such as Job who is nevertheless suffering adversity. That is, it is not that Job is a deliberately sinful man, but that, as one who serves God, he has nevertheless erred in some way and so is in need of corrective chastening. Such chastening may accordingly be received as a blessing which will result in renewed wellbeing and happiness (v 17–27).

In none of the speeches in the dialogues does any of Job's antagonists add to these three theodicies. No further mention is made of the concept of suffering as chastening, although it is taken up and argued strongly by Elihu in his monologue (xxxiii 19–28, xxxiv 31–7, xxxvi 7–13,15–16). But the remaining two theodicies are frequently returned to, not simply to be restated, however, but to be argued with increasing intensity.

3

The concept of reward/retribution receives greatest emphasis, being mentioned in virtually all of the friends' speeches (iv 7–11, viii 8–22, xi

---

[3] N. C. Habel, *The Book of Job* (London, 1985), p. 111.

13–20, xv 17–35, xviii 5–21, xx 4–29, xxii 5–20) as well as in the Elihu speeches (xxxiv 10–30), and it is this that is most vigorously contested by Job. As we have seen, in Eliphaz's opening speech this type of theodicy is employed as a source of comfort for Job, whose innocence is at this stage not questioned. But as the speeches develop the companions increasingly imply and finally assert that Job's afflictions are indeed retribution for wrongdoing. In his first contribution (ch. viii) Bildad may already be casting some doubt upon Job's innocence with his statement to Job, '*If* you are pure and upright, surely then he will rouse himself for you...' (viii 6). Zophar subsequently roundly states that God is exacting from Job less than his guilt deserves (xi 6), and Eliphaz, having begun so mildly, at the beginning of his second speech now accuses Job of iniquity (xv 4–6). The biting sarcasm with which Bildad begins his second speech in chapter xviii suggests that the description of the fate of the wicked that follows is directed pointedly at Job himself, and the unmistakable innuendo of Zophar's description of the fate of the wicked in chapter xx, for which he borrows descriptions used earlier by Job to describe his own plight, is that Job himself is one of the wicked. The climax is reached in Eliphaz's final speech in which he accuses Job of 'great wickedness' and catalogues the heinous offences and crimes which he now believes Job to have committed and for which his affliction has come upon him in retribution (xxii 5–20); only by making peace with God and ridding himself of his unrighteousness will good come again to Job (xxii 21–30).

Such is the fastidiousness with which Job's antagonists insist upon the reward/retribution concept as expressing God's just governance of the world that we must infer that it had acquired the status of revealed truth at the time of our author. And such is the passion with which Job seeks to refute his companions' insistence upon such a concept that we must see part of this author's purpose as being to expose how manifestly inadequate it is as a theodicy, indeed, how facile it is.

The devastation of Job's life notwithstanding his piety is evidence of this, and if his antagonists doubt or deny his blamelessness, there is the ample testimony of the wellbeing and security of the wicked whose plans God seems to favour (x 3), whose homes are at peace (xii 6), who reach old age, grow mighty in power, and are blessed with descendants, spending their days in prosperity and going to the grave in peace (xxi 1–16). Nor is Job prepared to allow that God should sometime store up the punishment due to the wicked for their descendants. True justice is rendered only when the wicked themselves reap their own calamity, for what do such people care about their households after they have gone in peace to the grave (xxi 19–21)?

The description of the mounting abuse with which Job's antagonists assail him, and the vehemence with which they finally accuse him of 'great wickedness' on the basis of the reward/retribution concept, must be seen as a comment by the author of the dialogues upon the cruelty to which such a concept could lead at the hands of its protagonists. Thus is the cry for pity of a blameless sufferer (cf. xix 21) swept aside, and elemental compassion itself suppressed, in the interests of the doctrinaire. More precisely, what the author has described is the classic shift on the part of Job's antagonists from theodicy to 'anthropodicy';[4] the companions endeavour to force the issue into one of Job's sinfulness and thus away from God's possible culpability. It is equally clear, however, that through his character Job this author has rejected such a shift: Job will not permit the lie necessary to sustain this form of theodicy, however deeply entrenched in tradition it may be.

4

Although the reward/retribution concept receives greatest attention in the disputations between Job and his companions, the more 'generic' theodicy according to which human beings are by birth and nature inherently morally flawed in God's eyes and therefore subject to punishment or chastisement is given prominent representation. And here too there is a noticeable heightening in the presentation of this concept in the course of the dialogues. Thus Eliphaz, who introduces this approach (iv 17–21), at first describes human creatureliness and frailty by means of such moderate imagery as 'clay' and 'dust' (verse 19). But when he returns to this theme later (xv 14–16) much more intemperate terminology is used. Human beings are now referred to as being 'abominable', 'loathsome', 'corrupt', and 'foul', with a propensity for evil, 'drinking iniquity' as naturally as one drinks water. A climax is reached in Bildad's final speech (ch. xxv) in which humanity's inherent uncleanness in God's eyes is described as being such that they are counted as no more than 'maggots' or 'worms'. 'Mortals are not merely weak, sinful creatures, they are at the bottom of the order of creation... The possibility of mortals like Job standing before God and being declared guiltless is preposterous' (Habel, *The Book of Job*, p. 370).

It is not difficult to see that such a theodicy is, so to speak, the ultimate 'fall back' position among theodicies. When all other explanations of the suffering of someone have failed in the face of the evidence of his or her innocence, the belief that the person is in any case morally flawed simply by being a human being and as such therefore subject to divine anger and chastisement is a 'catch all' position. The path down which it leads,

---

[4] For this see, for example, P. Berger, *The Social Reality of Religion* (London, 1969), pp. 53–80 (on Job see especially pp. 74–5). Cf. J. L. Crenshaw, 'The Shift from Theodicy to Anthropodicy', in J. L. Crenshaw (ed.), *Theodicy in the Old Testament* (Philadelphia and London, 1983), pp. 1–16.

however, is graphically described by the author of the dialogues in Job in
the way outlined above: such a theodicy can be sustained only at the price
of an abject abasement of the worth of humankind. In attributing such a
contemptuous view of human worth to the companions, the author may be
understood as criticizing such a concept by presenting it as something of a
desperate attempt on the part of Job's antagonists to convict him of his
unworthiness in a righteous God's eyes, and therefore of the justice of the
afflictions that have befallen him. In this the author of Job is at one with the
rest of the Old Testament, the whole atmosphere of which, as James Barr
has shown, 'works against the assumption that sin and evil were taken, as a
matter of theological principle, as something that belonged of necessity to
all human life'.[5]

Further evidence of the rejection of such an assumption is provided by vii
17–21 and x 1–17. In the latter of these, Job charges that God's present
treatment of him is in flat contradiction of his own good handiwork in
having fashioned and made him in the first place, granting him life and
bestowing 'steadfast love' upon him. It is not that the creature was in any
way inherently morally defective in the making, as the notion of 'innate
human sinfulness' claims, but that apparently the Maker has now
arbitrarily and unjustly turned with destructive intent against his handiwork.
The other passage (vii 17–21) is the well-known parody of Ps. viii 5–6. It
belongs to a chapter which has much to say about human creatureliness.
Yet nowhere is there any indication that this creatureliness involved an
innate sinfulness. On the contrary, Job's purpose in parodying the
psalmist's high teaching about humanity as God's noblest creation seems
to be to contrast such a status with God's behaviour as a relentless
fault-finder in pursuit of Job, whom he apparently treats as a burden rather
than as one destined to be crowned with 'glory and honour'. What the
author is evidently seeking to do in texts such as these is to voice through his
character Job the complaint of many that there is a jarring disjunction
between what a text such as Psalm viii declares about human worth and the
actual lot of many like Job in God's world. It is not that the creature is
flawed in the making, but that for many God's world seems to be such that
human beings are the victims of apparently arbitrary evil.

5

The third of the three theodicies mentioned by Eliphaz in his opening
address – the notion of suffering as divine disciplining – may be considered
more briefly, as, indeed, it is in the book itself. It is not mentioned again in

[5] J. Barr, 'The Authority of Scripture: The Book of Genesis and the Origin of Evil in Jewish
and Christian Tradition', in G. R. Evans (ed.), *Christian Authority. Essays in Honour of
Henry Chadwick* (Oxford, 1988), p. 68.

the dialogues, but is taken up with greater emphasis by Elihu, whose exposition of it is the fullest in the Old Testament (xxxiii 13ff., xxxiv 31ff., xxxvi 7–13, 15–16). Perhaps the reason such an explanation of Job's sufferings is not mentioned again by any of the three companions is that their increasingly outright accusation of wickedness and inherent sinfulness on Job's part simply ruled it out as inadequate. But the more likely reason is that already in Job's response to Eliphaz the author has exposed the rank implausibility of such an explanation of the suffering of one such as Job.

As indicated earlier, such an explanation of suffering was evidently intended to meet the case of an acknowledged servant of God who is nevertheless suffering adversity. Its rationale is that the sufferer is in some way blameworthy and that God, not out of anger but out of merciful solicitude, seeks by warnings or by chastisement to correct what is amiss and so to restore his servant to wellbeing and to full fellowship with himself (cf. xxxiii 14–33). Thus Eliphaz can say 'blessed is the man whom God reproves; therefore despise not the chastening of the Almighty' (v 17). But Job, in his response to Eliphaz, sees no solicitous hand of God in what has befallen him, no father-like correction. Rather, the devastation that has wreaked havoc with his life is such that it can only be the work of one who regards him as an enemy. Indeed, far from being benevolently intended chastisement, Job's afflictions are of such an unremitting nature and on such a scale as to suggest that God treats him as one with his primordial enemy 'the sea', 'the sea monster' (vii 12). Thus is the inanity of such a theodicy exposed, for Job's suffering, like that of many others, is self-evidently absurdly incongruent with the notion of 'fatherly correction'. It is little wonder that after its first mention by Eliphaz it is not again alluded to by Job's three companions, and is raised again only by the brash young Elihu, whose exposition of it, however, serves but to underline its limitations, for he has to depict the 'chastening' as bringing the sufferer virtually to destruction to achieve its desired goal (xxxiii 19–33). The 'chastening' is monstrously out of proportion to the 'error' it is intended to correct.

6

To sum up at this stage: Job's response to his wife at the climax of the prologue (ii 10) may be read as a candid statement that evil and not necessarily good can be the lot of God's servants and is to be accepted as the sovereign will of God. Understood in this way, such a declaration self-evidently considers theodicy unnecessary, since one of the main purposes of theodicy is to acquit God of the evil that may befall the righteous. But neither Job in the dialogues nor his companions accept this.

As we have seen, the companions argue a number of different theodicies in explanation of Job's suffering, each of which Job rejects, not because he submissively accepts, as in ii 10, his suffering as the sovereign will of God, but because he now believes that God misgoverns the world, cruelly permitting calamity upon a righteous man such as himself whilst allowing the wicked to prosper.

Job's oath at the climax of the dialogues (ch. xxxi) solemnly and at length underlines his innocence, and no less represents a challenge to God whom by implication it puts 'in the dock': Job is 'one with a suit against the Almighty', one who 'arraigns' God (cf. xl 2). That is, having in the dialogues rejected a number of different theodicies, Job by this oath poses anew the question of theodicy, in the sharpest form possible; indeed, God himself, it seems, is being asked to provide his own theodicy. The question remaining to be discussed is whether the divine speeches which constitute the denouement of the book attempt some sort of theodicy.

7

It is well known that sharply opposing views are held by commentators on whether these speeches make any attempt to deal with the issues raised and debated in the body of the book. Some have argued that they simply ignore Job's claims and accusations and portray instead a 'blustering deity' who crushes Job into abject and humiliating submission.[6] At the opposite extreme is the view that they solve the problem of the book, understood as the problem of the suffering of the innocent, by dissolving it. It is the principle of retribution, according to this view – the belief shared by both Job and his companions that the world is founded on justice, reward and punishment – that these speeches attack by declaring that in reality the world is 'amoral' and so a world in which it is absurd to expect a fate corresponding morally with one's deeds.[7]

A major difficulty with this latter view is that already in the dialogues Job himself has rejected the reward/retribution 'doctrine'. Indeed, as we have seen, it is this particular notion that comes in for the most sustained attack by him upon the arguments of his companions. It does not seem likely that the purpose of the divine speeches is simply to endorse what Job has already concluded and maintained, especially since these speeches, on any reading of them, also censure Job.

[6] See, for example, J. L. Crenshaw, 'The Shift from Theodicy to Anthropodicy', p. 9.
[7] This view has been argued most notably by M. Tsevat in his influential essay, 'The Meaning of the Book of Job', *HUCA* 37 (1966), pp. 73–106, and more recently by Habel, *The Book of Job* (pp. 65, 534–5). Tsevat's essay has been reprinted in his book, *The Meaning of the Book of Job and Other Biblical Studies* (New York and Dallas, 1980), pp. 1–37.

The other view mentioned above fares no better. What it amounts to is the claim that the author of these speeches, far from ignoring the issue, is declaring Job's case against God to be unanswerable, and to this end portrays God as incapable of meeting Job's accusation and instead 'blustering' with the intent of coercing Job by blind force into submission. That is, on such an understanding of these speeches, the book's claim is that God stands indicted of misgovernance of the world. The consequence of such a view for our understanding of the book as a whole is then that, having begun with a description of God's delight in the righteousness of his servant Job, at its denouement it portrays God as immoral, one for whom his servant's manifest innocence is of no account, and then anachronistically ends with a description of this same God restoring Job to wellbeing and making him an intercessor for others. Given the complex growth that the book has evidently gone through to reach its present form, such incoherence cannot perhaps be entirely ruled out. But it surely strains credulity. In my opinion Habel (*The Book of Job*, p. 533) is correct in suggesting that such an understanding of the divine speeches arises from a naive identification on the part of commentators with the hero of the book. Certainly our sympathy has been on the side of Job against the increasingly vitriolic claims of his companions impugning his innocence. But why should it be that the author necessarily intends us to believe that Job was beyond reproach any more than, say, Aeschylus intends us to believe that Prometheus was wholly beyond reproach, or that Shakespeare's Hamlet, who likewise wins our sympathy, is beyond reproach? Certainly God is portrayed in the divine speeches as censuring Job: mercilessly, at times sarcastically, he exposes the limitations of Job's knowledge and wisdom. Yet, if we take at face value Job's responses to what God says, he is not only humbled but enlightened and reconciled with God. This suggests *prima facie* that these speeches have a more positive purpose than to portray God as being lost for a response other than 'bluster' to the issue Job has raised.

The attempt to understand these speeches is all too often made without reference to the wider conceptual background that they have in the Old Testament. The book of Job is not the only place where the jarring disjunction between one's experience of reality and what one expects from God in God's world finds expression. Such a disjunction is after all the subject of the many laments in the Psalter. Of particular importance for our present purpose, however, are those texts in the Psalter and elsewhere (Pss. lxxiv 12–17, lxxxix 10–13 [9–12]; Isa. li 9–11; Job xxxviii 8–11, xl 25–xli 26 [xli 1–34]) which reflect the ancient near eastern *Chaoskampf* and in which God's primaeval victory over chaos is referred to or invoked in contexts in which chaos seems to persist. Jon D. Levenson has recently focussed attention anew upon such texts in a book bearing the suggestive title

Creation and the Persistence of Evil (San Francisco, 1988).[8] There is not space here to provide more than the briefest indication of his conclusions in this interesting and stimulating book. He writes of a generally overlooked tension in the underlying theology of these texts. On the one hand they speak of God's primaeval victory over his chaos adversary to create the world and establish order. On the other hand, they also speak not of the elimination of the adversary – Leviathan, the Sea, Rahab, etc. – but only of its confinement. They thus 'raise obliquely the possibility that the enemy's defeat may yet be reversed. They revive all the anxiety that goes with this horrific thought' (pp. 17–18). These texts courageously acknowledge the jarring disjunction between present experience and belief in God's absolute sovereignty. The result is a dialectic of myth and history, hymn and lament that on the one hand 'avoids the cheery optimism of those who crow that "God's in his heaven –/ All's right with the world"', but, on the other, 'does not allow for an unqualified acceptance of the pessimism that attributes to innocent suffering the immovability of fate. The absence of the omnipotent and cosmocratic deity is not accepted as final, nor his primordial world-ordering deeds as confined to the vanished past. Present experience, which seems to confirm these propositions, is not seen as absolute' (p. 24):

> The failure of God is openly acknowledged: no smug faith here, no flight into an other-worldly ideal. But God is also *reproached* for his failure, told that it is neither inevitable nor excusable: no limited God here, no God stymied by invincible evil, no faithless resignation before the relentlessness of circumstances. It is between the Scylla of simplistic faith and the Charybdis of stoic resignation that the lament runs its perilous course. The cognitive pressure on faith and realism to fly apart from each other is, in every generation, so intense that the conjunction of the two in these texts continues to astound. The *cri de coeur* of the complainants is unsurpassable testimony not only to the pain of their external circumstances, but also the pain of their internal dissonance, which only the creator God of old can heal. (pp. 24–5)

What comes to expression in such texts is that the 'world is not inherently safe; it is inherently unsafe. Only the magisterial intervention of God and his eternal vigilance prevent the cataclysm. Creation endures because God has pledged in an eternal covenant [the Noachic covenant] that it shall endure and because he has, also in an eternal covenant, compelled the obeisance of his great adversary [Leviathan, the Sea, Rahab, etc.]' (p. 17).

Job exposed the yawning chasm between the harsh reality of life and what orthodox piety, as represented by his companions, declared to be the automatic harvest of the righteous. For this truthfulness he is commended by God as against his three friends who did not speak 'what is right' about God (xlii 7–8). But disjunction is pressed by Job at the expense of the conjunction of realism and faith. Present experience is allowed to eclipse

---

[8] See especially ch. 2, 'The Survival of Chaos After the Victory of God'. On the *Chaoskampf* theme see also J. Day, *God's Conflict with the Dragon and the Sea* (Cambridge, 1985).

faith, and lament and plea grounded in hope and trust are replaced by the bitter accusation that God is unjust and his creation a travesty. It is for this that Job is rebuked and censured, and it is against this that God rouses himself to speak from the whirlwind – not to assert himself like a bully against Job, coercing him into humiliating submission, but to declare his mastery in and over creation, and so to renew his ancient pledge and in this way reawaken faith. God is not absent or otiose, but has manifested himself and declared anew his commitment to his creation, has given his word of promise. In this word Job places his trust. 'I had heard of thee by the hearing of the ear, but now my eye sees thee' (xlii 5).

It is not, however, a simplistic fideism that Job now exercises, as though his relentless insistence, against the claims of his companions, upon the presence of evil in the world had now been quietly disclaimed and dropped. The suffering remains, just as surely as Job himself at this stage of the narrative is still on the ash heap. Nor do the divine speeches anywhere seek to refute what Job has claimed on this issue. But the declaration of these speeches, like other texts elsewhere in the Old Testament, that the power of chaos, though not eliminated, is confined, and that God has given his pledge to his creation, renders evil less absolute than it would otherwise be. Such a faith is not only honest and courageous; it is also a reasonable and not just a blind faith, a pious whistling in the dark, for it contains at least the seed of a theology of redemption in the sense that if evil is somehow inherent in the creative process, so too is the overcoming of evil.[9]

Of course all theodicies ultimately fail or at best have limited plausibility. In our century of Auschwitz who can believe otherwise? And the dialogue between Job and his friends is a reminder of how empty and unworthy pious explanations can sound in the ears of those who suffer the unspeakable brutalities inflicted upon them by fellow human beings or the tragedies that nature visits upon them. There must be no trivializing of these. Yet if we are not to sink into a deep and melancholic pessimism which will then feed upon itself, we are surely beckoned to acknowledge the good that is also at work among us seeking to overcome the evil, and to see in this the redemptive work of God who has given us the vision of his kingdom, and not only to see but to give ourselves to participation in this as children of, and co-workers with, God.

It is a great pleasure to contribute this essay to a volume in honour of John Emerton to whom I owe a lasting debt of gratitude for the help and encouragement he has given me over the years, and whose friendship I count among my blessings.

[9] For a perceptive discussion of this see Maurice Wiles, *God's Action in the World* (Oxford 1986), especially chapter 4.

6   Qoheleth

Otto Kaiser

1

Although it has only twelve chapters, the book of Qoheleth poses a number of problems for the reader who has deduced its lateness and pseudonymity from the nature of its language.[1] The connection with King Solomon, which is suggested by the superscription in i 1 (cf. *b*. Megilla, fol. 7*a*), is founded on a failure to recognize i 12–ii 11 (26) as a 'royal fiction', and the usual translation of the Hebrew *qōhelet* on a misunderstanding by the ancient versions, which overlooked the original meaning of the term, 'assembly leader'.[2] We should probably picture the writer as a scribe who also worked as teacher, recording the results of the discussions which he led in school. By using catch-phrases and favourite expressions,[3] and by exhausting the stylistic possibilities of Hebrew proverbial wisdom and of poetry,[4] he has lent his work the unmistakable flavour of fine writing.

The prominence which Qoheleth gives to the personal-account form, and the emphasis which he places on the individual path to knowledge, correspond to his break with the ideas which were presupposed in the wisdom tradition of his people:[5] he clearly lived at a time when old beliefs were being questioned, and when the individual, no longer able to depend

---

This chapter was translated by Dr Stuart Weeks.

[1] See, already, J. G. Eichhorn, *Einleitung in das Alte Testament*, 3 (Leipzig, 1783), pp. 716–17. On the attempt by D. C. Fredericks, *Qoheleth's Language* (Lewiston, 1988), to deny the late character of the language, see the critical reviews by A. Hurvitz, *HS* 31 (1990), pp. 144–54, I. Kottsieper, *ZAW* 102 (1990), pp. 148–9, and particularly A. Schoors, *The Preacher Sought to Find Pleasing Words. A Study of the Language of Qoheleth* (Leuven, 1992), pp. 221–4.

[2] C. F. Whitley, *Koheleth. His Language and Thought* (Berlin, 1979), pp. 4–6, suggests that the word is to be translated 'sceptic', with reference to the Syriac *qhl*. This has been accepted by D. Michel, *Qohelet* (Darmstadt, 1988), but has, rightly, so far won little wider acceptance.

[3] See O. Loretz, *Qoheleth und der alte Orient* (Freiburg, 1964), pp. 167–80.

[4] See O. Loretz, *Qoheleth*, pp. 180–5, 212–16, and J. A. Loader, *Polar Structures in the Book of Qohelet* (Berlin, 1979), pp. 18–27. On his use of citations, see, e.g., R. N. Whybray, 'The Identification and Use of Quotations in Ecclesiastes' (*SVT* 32, 1981), pp. 435–51, and D. Michel, 'Qohelet-Probleme. Überlegungen zu Qoh 8, 2–9 und 7, 11–14', *Theologia Viatorum* 15 (1979/80), pp. 81–103 (= *Untersuchungen zur Eigenart des Buches Qohelet* [Berlin, 1989], pp. 84–115).   [5] See especially Loader, *Polar Structures*, pp. 29–111.

upon them, was forced to find his own way. Qoheleth therefore presents himself as a teacher in a time of change, who feels compelled to contrast tradition with situation, the traditional words of the wise with his own observations, and to draw his own conclusions. Moreover, if it is not really marked, the influence of Greek-Hellenistic writing and thought is certainly demonstrable.[6] Along with his reserve towards Jewish apocalyptic,[7] and his lack of any engagement with apocalypticism, this allows us to infer that Qoheleth worked around the middle of the third century BC.[8] Geographical and climatic assumptions in the text suggest that he worked in Palestine, and we can probably think of him as resident in Jerusalem.[9]

Qoheleth's sophisticated observation of human life leads him to criticize traditional school-wisdom, and its belief that individuals bear complete responsibility for their good or bad fortune in life. Indeed, his critical reflections encourage even modern readers to remain conscious of the limits of human endeavour, and of the inadequacy of their insight into God's *'obere Haushaltung'*.[10] With its message, repeated over and over, that there is no lasting reward for man's arduous labour, that all which he gains is transitory, and that he is too ignorant of the present to think himself master of the future, the book of Qoheleth is indeed a ghost at the banquet among the other books of the Bible.[11]

2

It is difficult to detect any deliberate structure in the book as a whole,[12] and only in i 3–iii 15 do we find what is obviously a carefully planned composition.[13] Most of this section is taken up by the 'royal fiction', the fictional nature of which is clear: only i 12–ii 11 suggests that the speaker is royal, and the idea exerts no further influence on the text after iii 1. Indeed, the viewpoint in iv 13ff., vii 19, viii 2ff. and x 16ff. is clearly that of a subject, not a ruler. In i 12–ii 11 (26), then, Qoheleth is putting a king's mantle on his

---

[6] See R. Braun, *Kohelet und die frühhellenistische Popularphilosophie* (Berlin, 1973), and O. Kaiser, 'Judentum und Hellenismus. Ein Beitrag zur Frage nach dem hellenistischen Einfluß auf Kohelet und Jesus Sirach', *VuF* 27 (1982), pp. 68–88 (= *Der Mensch unter dem Schicksal* [Berlin, 1985], pp. 135–52), which is critical of Braun.

[7] The evidence normally cited, iii 21, can hardly bear this weight. See Michel, *Untersuchungen*, pp. 126–37, 166–83, and cf. A. Fischer, *Furcht Gottes oder Skepsis? Studien zur Komposition und Theologie des Buches Kohelet* (Dissertation, Marburg, forthcoming).

[8] See especially M. Hengel, *Judentum und Hellenismus* (3rd edn, Tübingen, 1988), pp. 210–37 (E. tr., *Judaism and Hellenism*, 1 [London, 1974], pp. 115–28).

[9] See H. W. Hertzberg, 'Palästinische Bezüge im Buche Kohelet', *ZDPV* 73 (1957), pp. 113–24.

[10] See J. G. von Herder, *Vom Geist der Ebräischen Poesie*, first published in 1782, and to be found in vol. 12 of the collected works edited by B. Suphan (Berlin, 1880), p. 23.

[11] See H.-P. Müller, 'Der unheimliche Gast. Zum Denken Qohelets', *ZThK* 84 (1987), pp. 441–64.   [12] See the comprehensive study in Michel, *Qohelet*, pp. 21–45.

[13] See Michel, *Untersuchungen*, pp. 1–84 (cf. 245–7), and A. Fischer, 'Beobachtungen zur Komposition von Kohelet 1,3 – 3,15', *ZAW* 103 (1991), pp. 72–86.

own shoulders, in order to underline the universal validity of what he is saying: lasting reward is denied even to him, the mightiest, wisest and richest of all men, who is able to do whatever he desires. Even he is mortal, and dependent on the day-to-day fortune granted him by God.

No continuous structure can be discerned in iii 16–xii 7, where there are only shorter compositions, of varying length. These presuppose Qoheleth's position as developed in i 3–iii 15, deal with other areas of life, pre-empt possible objections, and finally draw out the consequences.[14] Unity is given to the book, then, by its language and theme, not by some overall structure. It does, though, possess an outer prologue and epilogue in i 1–3 and xii 8–14, with a corresponding inner foreword and afterword in i 4–11 and xi 7–xii 7. This is the first indication that the book has probably achieved its present form only through secondary redaction. Since the epilogue in xii 8–14 is clearly divided into two parts, verses 8–11 and 12–14, there are obviously two epilogists responsible for it, and the only difficulty lies in determining the extent to which general compositions, such as i 3–iii 15, were already available to the first epilogist.

Apart from xii 8–11, the work of this first epilogist is probably to be found also in the superscription of i 1aα, which originally had the short form 'Words of Qoheleth', and in verse 2, the book's characteristic motto, which has been attached to verse 3, part of the composition i 3–iii 15, and now constitutes, along with verse 1, the outer prologue. He clearly considers '"Utter vanity", says Qoheleth, "all is vanity"' to be a summary of Qoheleth's teaching, and places it at both the beginning and end of the book (i 2, xii 8). The rhetorical question in i 3, 'What lasting reward is there for man, from all the toil at which he toils under the sun?', was originally intended to be the superscription for the composition about cycles in i 3–iii 15. With the negative answer implicit in it, though, it now serves as a sort of basis for verse 2: while everything is *hebel*, transitory and vain as a breath of air (cf. Ps. xxxix 6*b*, 12*b*),[15] there can be no lasting reward for man, whatever he does or does not do.

The second epilogist was unhappy with this summary and interpretation of a book which he identified in i 1aαβb as the work of Solomon, 'the son of David', and he felt that it would be more appropriately summarized by an admonition to fear God and to keep the Law, with a view to the coming final judgement, when God would expose every hidden thing (cf. xii 13–14).[16] He

---

[14] See Michel, *Untersuchungen*, pp. 245–73, and Fischer, 'Furcht Gottes'.

[15] G. S. Ogden, *Qoheleth* (Sheffield, 1987), p. 21, has rightly pointed out that *hebel* in Qoheleth cannot mean that life is futile and pointless, and so it is unwise to translate it as 'absurd', as do M. V. Fox, *Qoheleth and his Contradictions* (Sheffield, 1989), p. 37, and Michel, *Qohelet*, p. 86 (cf. *Untersuchungen*, p. 51).

[16] There has been considerable debate about whether the second epilogist in xii 14 envisages eschatological rather than perpetual judgement, but the issue is unresolved. See A. Lauha, *Kohelet* (Neukirchen-Vluyn, 1978), p. 223, and Fischer, 'Furcht Gottes'.

also made insertions in xi 7–xii 7, which share the viewpoint of this summary. There he points out to the young man that God will call him to account for his behaviour (xi 9*b*), reminding him that youth and ungreyed hair are fleeting (xi 10*b*), and that he would be well advised to remember his creator even in the days of his youth (xii 1*a*).

3

Read in the light of the preceding verse, which was placed there by the first epilogist, i 3 appears to be a concise summary of Qoheleth's message, though he did not necessarily write it himself. Human life, characterized by toil and labour, is ultimately as profitless as the playing of the wind and the cycle of the waters, as i 4–11, the first reflection within the composition i 3–iii 15, points out. If everything on earth happens in the same purposeless and circular way, then the desire for lasting reward, and with it any overall meaning and purpose in life, is *a priori* impossible. For Qoheleth, familiar observations about nature provide an analogy for everything which happens under the sun, including human activity. Just as the heavenly bodies, the winds, and the waters all go round and round without result, so too are human undertakings denied any lasting consequence. To imagine that one is exempt from this basic, structural law, while understandable, is simply a symptom of the congenital short-sightedness which keeps humans from seeing the past, as well as the future. The rule observed in nature, Qoheleth believes, permits no exceptions, even for humans.

This reflection was presumably placed at the beginning of his composition, which stretches to iii 15, by Qoheleth himself. In its basic character, it corresponds to the riddle poem about the appropriate time[17] in iii 1–8, and the rhetorical question in iii 9, which reveals its meaning. Central to this poem is an experience familiar to humans of every age: one cannot just do what one wants, when one wants, but must recognize each time the appropriate moment, and act accordingly. In Israelite wisdom, this idea is especially associated with the motif of speaking and being silent at the proper time (see, e.g., Prov. xv 23; Ecclus xx 6–8).[18]

The farmer must sow and reap at the right time, if his work is to show any profit (cf. Is. xxviii 23–9), and this is also true more generally in life. With its twelve contrasting pairs, the poem taken over by Qoheleth[19] in iii 2*b*–8*a*

---

[17] See K. Galling, 'Das Rätsel der Zeit im Urteil Kohelets (Koh. 3, 1–5)', *ZThK* 58 (1961), pp. 1–15.

[18] See also G. von Rad, *Weisheit in Israel* (Neukirchen-Vluyn, 1970), pp. 182–8 (E. tr., *Wisdom in Israel* [London, 1972], pp. 138–43), and W. Bühlmann, *Vom rechten Reden und Schweigen. Studien zu Prov 10–31* (Freiburg and Göttingen, 1976), pp. 259–67.

[19] Going further than R. N. Whybray, 'A Time to be Born and a Time to Die. Some Observations on Ecclesiastes 3: 2–8', *Bulletin of the Middle Eastern Culture Center in Japan* 5 (1991), p. 480, I would include not only verses 1–2*a* but also verse 8*b* in the framework of the quotation.

teaches the importance of awaiting the right time for any undertaking in a particular situation. The idea of observing the right time runs through these twelve pairs, and in them it means finding the right occasion for a given action. The meaning is transformed, however, by placing verses 2*a* and 8*b* at the beginning and end, and thus giving the times a fateful character: the community has as little control over the time of war or peace as has the individual over the time of his birth or, excluding suicide,[20] the time of his death (cf. viii 8). This interpretation is supported by viii 6–8 and again in ix 11–12. Time is qualified for humans, in a way they cannot know, and so the latter passage stresses that their abilities do not completely guarantee success: it is not always the best runners who win the race, the best fighters who win the battle, or the most prudent, intelligent and well informed who attain wealth and position. Despite their abilities, time and chance can play terrible tricks on all humans, who, unable to discern clearly whether a time is favourable or not, become entangled in a net of misfortune.

Such is the plight of man: not only has he no guarantee that his behaviour will bring about the desired result (iii 9), but he is completely at the mercy of time and chance. The depths to which he can fall through fate are illustrated in iv 1–3, by the example of the oppressed suffering at the hands of their oppressors. The idea here is not merely one of times which are qualitatively predetermined in a general way, like days which are blessed by God and beneficial for everybody (e.g. the Sabbath, cf. Gen. ii 3). Rather, the assumption is that its time has a positive or negative significance for each individual action. Although this corresponds to the basic premise of astrology, there is no sign that Qoheleth has been influenced by this art. Indeed, astrology's promise to shed light on the future is in complete opposition to his conviction that men are denied the ability to understand the character of the time: set by God, it is comprehensible to him alone.

So we come to iii 10–15, which is decisive for an understanding of the book, and which concludes the section i 3–iii 15.

> I observed the business which God has given to the sons of men for them
>   to be busy with.
> He makes everything fine[21] in its time,[22] and has put duration in it;[23]
> only divine action remains unfathomable for men, from start to finish.
> I know:
> There is nothing better for them (i.e. men), than to be happy and to
>   enjoy themselves for as long as they live.[24]

[20] See L. Wächter, *Der Tod im Alten Testament* (Stuttgart, 1967), pp. 89–97.

[21] 'Fine' here corresponds to late Hebrew/Rabbinic usage. See Marcus Jastrow, *A Dictionary of the Targumim, the Talmud Babli and Yerushalmi, and the Midrashic Literature* (London and New York, 1903), p. 585b.

[22] On the present tense, and the meaning of the verse, see B. Isaksson, *Studies in the Language of Qoheleth* (Uppsala, 1987), pp. 79–81.

[23] See F. Ellermeier, *Qohelet* I/1 (Herzberg, 1967), pp. 309–22.

[24] For a pronoun with a singular suffix referring back to a plural antecedent, cf. *GK* 145*m*.

> So for every man who can eat, and drink, and take pleasure in his work,
>   this too is a gift of God.
> I know: everything which God makes endures for eternity,
> No-one can add to it, and no-one can subtract from it. But God acts[25]
>   (thus) so that (men) are fearful before him.
> That which is,[26] was, long ago,
> and that which will be, has been, long since.
> For God seeks (out) what has drifted away.[27]

This, then, is the human condition: God has imposed unremitting planning and activity, but has withheld any understanding of times, the character of which is for ever changing (although in the end, by their very structure, they bring nothing new). Men are forced to plan and to act as though they can thereby guarantee the consequence of their action, but, with the character of the times determined by God, they are merely groping in the dark. Everything which humans do is a gamble, and in their plans they have to reckon with every possibility (xi 1–6). So it is that they need a reliable companion in case their plans or actions go wrong (iv 9), quite apart from the fact that man is a social creature (iv 9–12), whose activity is meaningless without some relationship to another human (iv 8).

Even were he a second Solomon, able to fulfil all his desires (ii 3–11), a man could achieve no lasting gain from anything he did. Even then, his wisdom would be no comfort, as it could go no further than recognizing the mysteriousness of his existence (viii 1–9), and the transitoriness, in this sense futility, of what he was doing (cf. 16–18 with vii 23–4 and viii 16–17). To be sure, wisdom would give him some advantage over the fool (ii 14a), but death makes them equal (ii 14b), and time finally erases the memory of both (ii 16–17).[28] Were he to leave a good inheritance, there would be no guarantee that his heir would be capable of managing or maintaining it, and then there is the pain he might feel in leaving his hard-earned cash to men who had not worked for it (ii 18–21). Yet, in reality, this man is no Solomon, and he cannot be sure that his hard-earned property will even survive long enough for him to bequeath it to his son (v 13–15), or that he will be able to enjoy the fruits of his labour himself, while still capable of pleasure (vi 1–10).

So there is no lasting reward for a man's work, and his wisdom ensures neither his success (cf. also ix 13–16) nor the immortality of his name. He may attain wealth, and procure any pleasure, but cannot be sure either of

---

[25] On the durative sense, cf. Isaksson, *Studies*, p. 126.

[26] On the tense, cf. Isaksson, *Studies*, pp. 82–3.

[27] On the problems in verse 15b, see R. N. Whybray, *Ecclesiastes* (Grand Rapids and London, 1989), pp. 75–6, following Franz Delitzsch, *Hoheslied und Koheleth* (Leipzig, 1875).

[28] But see, e.g., Prov. x 7; Ecclus xxxvii 26, xxxix 11 and xli 12–13.

enjoying it himself or of leaving it to a worthy heir. Moreover, everything which he plans and undertakes has a risky outcome, and he does not know whether he is acting in accordance with the character of the time, as determined by God. While that is so, man can never be absolutely certain that proper behaviour will ensure him the long and successful life promised by the sayings, instructions and songs of the wise:[29] it can happen that things work out for the righteous just as though they were sinners, and for sinners as though they were righteous (viii 10–15). Further, the righteous man has no lasting reward even if he is granted a long and happy life, for every human action is ultimately 'as fleeting as the wind, and as fruitless as trying to catch it in one's hands'. In this sense, the first epilogist has correctly summarized his master's teaching in i 2, and the answer to the thematic question in i 3 must, in accord with Qoheleth's reflection, be negative.[30]

4

We have not yet considered iii 12–15, which is the climax of the whole composition. In verses 12–14, Qoheleth draws out two conclusions: denied lasting gain, the human must be content to hold on to the transitory future which is granted him, as the only one available (verse 12); since he has no control over it, this is always a gift of God (verse 13), granted wholly at God's discretion (cf. ii 24–6, and especially 26*aba*).[31]

Although we would feel obliged to mention this central, *carpe diem* theme of Qoheleth, neither the first nor the second epilogist picks it up, and the latter instead gives prominence to the concept of the 'fear of God', which is to be found for the first time in iii 14. The significance of this idea for Qoheleth's thought should not be underestimated. The need to act as though success depended upon it, while one is lacking insight into the time, which could alone guarantee that success, is the basic contradiction in human existence, and implies that all success is a gift of God. This is interpreted in iii 14: God has arranged things thus, so that men will fear him. If men could determine their own success or failure, God would be no more the lord of all reality.

Of course, we need to ask whether the 'fear of God' in Qoheleth should

---

[29] See, e.g., Ps. xxxvii; Prov. iii 13–18; Job viii 8–22, xxxiv 10–12.

[30] See i 14*b*, 17*b*, ii 1*b*, 15*b*, 17*b*, 21*bβ*, 23*b*, 26*b*, iv 4*b*, 8*bβ*, 16*b*, v 9*b* (15*b*), vi 2*b*, 9*b*, vii 6*b*, 10*b*, 14*a*(*a*).*b*, xi 8*bβ*2, and contrast Ogden, *Qoheleth*, pp. 17–22, with Fox, *Qoheleth*, pp. 29–51, and A. Lange, *Weisheit und Torheit bei Kohelet und in seiner Umwelt* (Frankfurt a.M., 1991), pp. 102–15, who translate *hebel* as 'absurd', as does Michel, *Qoheleth*, pp. 84–7.

[31] If one does not wish to take verse 26*aba*, or indeed verses 24*b*–26*aba*, as an addition by the second epilogist (cf. Lauha, *Kohelet*, p. 58), then one must take *hôtē'* in its original meaning of a man thwarted in his purpose.

be understood in its original meaning, awe before the numinous power of the deity,[32] or as a modification of the sapiential concept, where the expectation of divine justice implies that it must lead to a religious and moral perfection of life.[33] The latter is what we should expect, in view of Qoheleth's own wisdom background, and that this is indeed the case is shown by viii 12–13 (the authenticity of which has, wrongly, been questioned by some scholars).[34] Qoheleth here cites the basic wisdom position, that those who fear God prosper, and those who do not, do badly, an opinion which he has not found wholly valid, as there are exceptions (viii 14; cf. also vii 15). So iii 14, v 6 and vii 18 go back to Qoheleth himself, and express his own view.

On the basis of iii 14, we can only define the 'fear of God' generally, as the respect owed to God when the way of the world and shaping of the times are obscure.[35] However, v 6 and vii 18 allow us to be more specific, as each gives a context for the idea, and associates it with appropriate behaviour. Qoheleth, in iv 17–v 6 (v 1–7),[36] puts attentive listening in the temple before sacrifice (cf. 1 Sam. xv 22; Prov. xv 8, xxi 3; Ecclus xxxiv 21–3), and in v 3 (4) he cites the commandment about vows from the Torah (Deut. xxiii 22 [21]), so he can hardly have broken altogether with the scriptural faith and legal piety of his people – an important insight into the writer.[37] Anyway, the reason which Qoheleth gives for his advice, in iv 17b (v 1b), is interesting: bad behaviour comes from poor knowledge of the Torah, which presents the norms of religion and morality. Moreover, in the reasons which he gives in iv 17b, v 2, 3b, 5b (v 1b, 3, 4b, 6b), for warning against inappropriate garrulousness in prayer (v 1–2 [2–3]) and thoughtless oath-taking (v 3–5 [4–5]), Qoheleth shows that he probably accepts the validity of the basic wisdom position cited in viii 12b–13: a man who displays contempt in his behaviour towards God must count on having provoked God. The concluding instruction, in v 6b (7b), clearly implies that inappropriate behaviour towards God will, as a rule, result in punishment. Qoheleth's concept of the 'fear of God' does indeed stand in the sapiential tradition, and embraces some idea of the proper way to behave.

The last piece of evidence to be examined, vii 15–22, accords with this. The reflection begins in verse 15 with the observation that a righteous man

---

[32] See J. Becker, *Gottesfurcht im AT* (Rome, 1965), p. 55, or E. Pfeiffer, 'Die Gottesfurcht im Buche Kohelet', in H. Graf Reventlow (ed.), *Gottes Wort und Gottes Land* (Göttingen, 1965), pp. 132–58, especially p. 157.   [33] See Becker, *Gottesfurcht*, pp. 184–7, 249.

[34] Most recently, so far as I know, by K. Galling, *Prediger Salomo* (2nd edn, Tübingen, 1969). W. Zimmerli, *Das Buch des Predigers Salomo* (Göttingen, 1962), p. 216, rightly observes that verse 14 does not claim that the opposite *must*, but that it *may*, happen; therein lies the divine unknowability to which the wise subordinate 'order'.

[35] For iii 14, cf. also the definition by H.-P. Müller, 'Wie sprach Qohälät von Gott?', *VT* 18 (1968), pp. 507–21, especially p. 516, and Michel, *Untersuchungen*, p. 72.

[36] On the primary unity of iv 17–v 6 (v 1–7), see Lauha, *Kohelet*, p. 97.

[37] Contrast, Michel, *Qohelet*, p. 143.

can sometimes destroy himself through his righteousness, while the ungodly man can live long thanks to his ungodliness. The prohibitions which follow, in verses 16–17, show that man can actually cause his own death, before the time fixed for it, through his behaviour. The advice in verses 17–18, to avoid excess but to fear God, is explained in terms of avoiding the fate of both the over-righteous man and the fool, who can each bring about their own untimely death through their behaviour. The fear of God here is the prerequisite for proper behaviour, the middle way between presumptuous over-righteousness and foolish thoughtlessness. Verses 19–22 draw out the proper understanding of all this: verses 19–20 show that Qoheleth believes there to be no wholly righteous man on earth, and verses 21–22 illustrate the sort of over-righteousness which leads to untimely death – *viz.* demanding of others what one does not do oneself. The guarantor of this premature death can only be God, who causes it, and who knows even what is hidden (cf. xii 14).

The second epilogist's summary of Qoheleth's thought, in xii 13–14, stresses the need to fear God and obey his commands, so as to avoid his eternal judgement.[38] Although this accords with iv 17 (v 1), it is clearly one-sided, with its single-minded concentration on legal piety excluding more complicated thought. That God *as a rule* grants life and success to the righteous, but misfortune and early death to the ungodly, is not only recognized by Qoheleth to be a valuable teaching (cf. viii 12*b*–13), but is even proposed by Qoheleth himself in vii 15–22.[39] It is affirmed in iv 17–v 6 (v 1–7) that the human who behaves inappropriately towards God will have to reckon with God's wrath, and one such offence is the thoughtless treatment of the law of vows. Over and above all this, vii 15–22 shows that, for Qoheleth, the 'fear of God' and self-knowledge belong together. Finally, iii 10–15 warns against illusory confidence in the outcome of human action. For Qoheleth, fortune is always a free gift of God, never the consequence of human behaviour or action. The 'fear of God' in Qoheleth, then, is understood more broadly than in the second epilogist's legalistic sense, and its consequence is not so certain. If the epilogist has eschatological judgement in mind in xii 14, then he has left Qoheleth's thinking far behind.

5

In their summaries, the epilogists have omitted, or only partially taken up, Qoheleth's two central insights – that man can neither predict the

---

[38] See above, n. 16.

[39] iii 17 and xi 9*b* go back to the second epilogist. See especially Michel, *Untersuchungen*, pp. 248–51, 268 n. 31, and, e.g., H. Gese, 'Die Krisis der Weisheit bei Kohelet', in *Les Sagesses du Proche-Orient ancien* (Paris, 1963), pp. 139–51, especially p. 145, and his *Vom Sinai zum Zion* (Munich, 1974), pp. 168–79, especially p. 173.

consequences of his actions, as he is unable to see clearly the conditions in which they are undertaken, nor gain any lasting reward, as he is fated to die. They pass over both the advice in xi 1–6 to take account of every eventuality, and the admonition, which we would consider central, not to neglect the fleeting fortune which God has granted to man as his 'portion' for his ceaseless striving. With his summaries in i 2 and xii 8, the first epilogist has basically contributed to an understanding of Qoheleth as the messenger of the futility of all human action. So what we need finally to determine, is whether Qoheleth's *carpe diem* advice really is the proper conclusion of his reflection.

Early on, in the 'royal fiction', Qoheleth adds to the story a statement (ii 10*a*) that his work enabled him to indulge in every pleasure, and explains in 10*b* that 'this was my portion for all my work'. Here he is already using the word 'portion' (*ḥēleq*) in his own characteristic way, to mean the positive portion, or reward for life, which is allotted to man by God.[40] Reflecting on the law court as a place of unrighteousness (iii 16) and on God's purpose behind this, which is to remind men that they are no different from mortal beasts, Qoheleth concludes in iii 22 that 'there is nothing good for man except taking pleasure in what he does, for that is his portion. For who can see adequately what is going to happen after him?' In v 17–19 (18–20) he suggests that, when it is granted to man, happiness is a portion given to him by God for his efforts:

But this is what I have perceived as good and right, that a man eat and drink and enjoy himself in all his toil, at which he toils under the sun, throughout the span[41] of the days of his life, which God has given him;[42] for that is his portion. But for every man to whom God has given wealth and pleasure in his work, and whom he has empowered to enjoy it, to accept his portion and to take pleasure in his work, this is a gift of God. For (then) he does not give much thought to the length[43] of his life, for God keeps him busy with the enjoyment of his heart.

In ix 4–6, Qoheleth helps us to understand why it is best for man to forget about the fortune granted by God, as he reflects on his observation that death is the lot fixed for every man, whether his life is wise, foolish, pious or ungodly:

Indeed, he who is still numbered among the living has hope,
For: A live dog is better than a dead lion.
For the living know that they must die,
but the dead know nothing.
There is no more reward for them,

---

[40] He uses the word unspecifically in ii 21 and xi 2 to mean 'share'. Cf. M. Tsevat '*ḥālaq* II' in *ThWAT* 2, cols. 1015–20 (E. tr., *TDOT* 4, 447–51), and Michel, *Untersuchungen*, pp. 120–5.
[41] Literally 'number'.   [42] On the translation as perfect tense, cf. Isaksson, *Studies*, pp. 83–4.
[43] Literally 'days of his life'.

as their memory is forgotten.
Their loving, and their hating,
and their striving are long gone.
They have, for eternity, no more portion in all
that happens under the sun.

On his entry into the underworld, all a man's claims become extinct, and he is forgotten in the allotment of fortune, just as he has himself forgotten what his life had meant on earth. Like many earlier and later writers, Qoheleth derives from this a *carpe diem* conclusion, in ix 7–10:

Go, eat your bread with joy, and drink your wine with a happy heart;
for God has long since approved what you do.
Let your clothes be always white,
Let oil not be lacking on your head.
Enjoy your life with the wife whom you love, all the days of your fleeting
life, which he has given you under the sun.
For this is your portion in life and in your work, at which you work under
the sun.
Everything which you can do, do it with all (your) might;
for there is no action or planning, and no knowledge or wisdom in the
underworld,
to which you are on the way.

Qoheleth believes that it is best for a man to forget that, beyond the fortune which God grants him, he is doomed to die. At the same time, he gives explicit advice to think about death, as an incentive for man to take advantage of what he has at present: given what awaits in the underworld, that is all he is going to get. There is no contradiction here, and the two ideas are related to each other as is knowledge of a fact to the means of recognizing its truth. The reader may note that the invitations to enjoy are not subsequently condemned as vanities. They are the real conclusion which Qoheleth draws from his cryptic reflections, and this is why the advice in xi 9–xii 7, to enjoy one's youth, provides such a fitting end to his teaching.[44]

[44] See already R. Gordis, *Koheleth – The Man and his World* (2nd edn, New York, 1955), p. 121; D. Michel, *Untersuchungen*, p. 87; N. Lohfink, 'Qoheleth 5:17–19 – Revelation by Joy', *CBQ* 52 (1990), pp. 625–35; and now particularly M. A. Klopfenstein, 'Kohelet und die Freude', *ThZ* 47 (1991), pp. 97–107; cf. I. von Loewenclau, 'Kohelet und Sokrates – Versuch eines Vergleiches', *ZAW* 98 (1986), p. 338.

A house divided: wisdom in Old Testament
      narrative traditions

Robert P. Gordon

Wisdom texts and wisdom criteria

The credit (or otherwise) for setting the hare of Old Testament 'wisdom narrative' running must go to Gerhard von Rad, though in his *Theologie des Alten Testaments* he notes that Johannes Hempel had already suggested a link between narrative and wisdom back in 1936.[1] Von Rad's short essay on the Joseph narrative in Gen. xxxvii–1, published in 1953,[2] sought to demonstrate that these chapters were heavily influenced from Egyptian sources and were to be recognized as a form of early Israelite wisdom writing. The story of how the branches of the Joseph 'wisdom narrative' ran over the wall to affect other areas of Old Testament narrative is sufficiently well known to require only the briefest recapitulation here.

In his 1944 essay on historical writing in early Israel von Rad had developed the view that the reign of Solomon marked the beginning of a new phase in Israelite historical consciousness, and he had highlighted the (so-called) 'Succession Narrative' – 'the oldest specimen of ancient Israelite historical writing' (p. 12 [E. tr., p. 176]) – as exemplifying this new outlook.[3] In short, the author of the 'Succession Narrative' commends a more secular view of history according to which God remains involved in human affairs, but in a less visibly interventionist kind of way than had previously been imagined. Von Rad's 1953 essay on the Joseph narrative located these chapters in the same general period of the early monarchy and also, as we

---

[1] *Theologie des Alten Testaments*, 1 (Munich, 1958), p. 64, n. 24 (E. tr., *Old Testament Theology*, 1 [Edinburgh and London, 1962], p. 56, n. 30). See J. Hempel, *Gott und Mensch im Alten Testament* (2nd edn, Stuttgart, 1936), p. 65.

[2] 'Josephsgeschichte und ältere Chokma' (*SVT* 1, 1953), pp. 120–7 (E. tr., 'The Joseph Narrative and Ancient Wisdom', in *The Problem of the Hexateuch and Other Essays* [Edinburgh and London, 1965], pp. 292–300).

[3] 'Der Anfang der Geschichtsschreibung im alten Israel', *Archiv für Kulturgeschichte* 32 (1944), pp. 1–42 (E. tr., 'The Beginnings of Historical Writing in Ancient Israel', in *The Problem of the Hexateuch*, pp. 166–204).

have already noted, sought to demonstrate links between the narrative and Israelite wisdom traditions. Ten years later, in 1963, S. Talmon was characterizing the book of Esther as an 'historicized wisdom tale',[4] a term which B. S. Childs was soon happy to apply also to the story of the birth of Moses in Exod. i–ii.[5] Even more directly in the line of succession from von Rad stands R. N. Whybray's monograph on the 'Succession Narrative', published in 1968, in which the dual hypotheses of Egyptian influence and wisdom affiliation are again in evidence.[6] Not surprisingly, the account of Solomon's reign in 1 Kings iii–xi, with its emphasis on Solomonic wisdom, has also been subjected to the pull of the wisdom-circle approach.[7] The early chapters of Genesis[8] and the prophetic narrative of the book of Jonah[9] have also at one time or another had the wisdom rule run over them.[10]

However, this expansion of the surface area has not necessarily been matched by a consolidation of the underlying thesis of a category of wisdom-influenced narrative (whatever that may mean) within the Old Testament. If we take the supposed wisdom affinity of the Joseph narrative, for example, we shall find that D. B. Redford[11] and J. L. Crenshaw[12] dismiss the wisdom connection as unsustainable, though G. W. Coats manages to salvage a wisdom-influenced core in Gen. xxxix–xli which he thinks may have originated in the Solomonic period, or even in Egyptian court circles prior to the reign of Solomon.[13] Crenshaw, in point of fact, fails to find any evidence of 'wisdom narrative' among the various candidates that have been proposed. He argues that some of the defining

[4] '"Wisdom" in the Book of Esther', *VT* 13 (1963), pp. 419–55.
[5] 'The Birth of Moses', *JBL* 84 (1965), pp. 109–22.
[6] *The Succession Narrative. A Study of II Sam. 9–20 and I Kings 1 and 2* (London, 1968).
[7] See, for example, G. E. Bryce, *A Legacy of Wisdom. The Egyptian Contribution to the Wisdom of Israel* (Lewisburg and London, 1979), pp. 172–88; D. F. Morgan, *Wisdom in the Old Testament Traditions* (Oxford, 1981), pp. 52–3.
[8] Cf. L. Alonso-Schökel, 'Motivos sapienciales y de alianza en Gn 2–3', *Biblica* 43 (1962), pp. 295–316 (E. tr., 'Sapiential and Covenant Themes in Genesis 2–3', in J. L. Crenshaw [ed.], *Studies in Ancient Israelite Wisdom* [New York, 1976], pp. 468–80); W. Brueggemann, *In Man We Trust* (Atlanta, 1972), pp. 54–60; G. E. Mendenhall, 'The Shady Side of Wisdom: The Date and Purpose of Genesis 3', in H. N. Bream, R. D. Heim, C. A. Moore (eds.), *A Light unto My Path. Old Testament Studies in Honor of Jacob M. Myers* (Philadelphia, 1974), pp. 319–34.
[9] Cf. E. Sellin – G. Fohrer, *Einleitung in das Alte Testament* (10th edn, Heidelberg, 1965), pp. 485–6 (E. tr., *Introduction to the Old Testament* [London, 1970], p. 442). For a negative assessment see G. M. Landes, 'Jonah: A *Māšāl*?', in J. G. Gammie *et al.* (eds.), *Israelite Wisdom: Theological and Literary Essays in Honor of Samuel Terrien* (Missoula, 1978), pp. 137–58 (149–50). See also J. Day, 'Problems in the Interpretation of the Book of Jonah', *OTS* 26 (1990), p. 39.
[10] See J. L. Crenshaw, 'Method in Determining Wisdom Influence upon "Historical" Literature', *JBL* 88 (1969), pp. 129–42 (=pp. 481–94 in Crenshaw, *Studies*).
[11] *A Study of the Biblical Story of Joseph (Genesis 37–50)* (*SVT* 20, 1970), pp. 100–5.
[12] *JBL* 88 (1969), pp. 135–7 (=pp. 487–9 in Crenshaw, *Studies*).
[13] 'The Joseph Story and Ancient Wisdom: A Reappraisal', *CBQ* 35 (1973), pp. 285–97.

characteristics such as observation based on experience of life or belief in providence are too much a feature of other strands of Old Testament thought to support a special classification of 'wisdom narrative'. The only possible basis of recognition is the presence of stylistic or ideological particulars found peculiarly or primarily in the 'wisdom corpus'.[14] Whybray, whose own study of the 'Succession Narrative' had come under Crenshaw's strictures for alleged methodological weaknesses, seeks in his 1974 volume to establish terminological criteria by which wisdom writing may be identified.[15] But it is clear from Whybray's discussion that the vocabulary test can be used only with extreme caution. Only occurrences of the basic root *ḥkm* ('[be] wise') offer much hope of discovering wisdom-influenced material outside the traditional 'wisdom corpus', and even *'ēṣâ* ('counsel') is set aside as being used too frequently in non-wisdom sources to be much help (pp. 132–3). And so Whybray composes his list of passages representative of the Old Testament wisdom tradition largely on the basis of the occurrence of the *ḥkm* root, with occasional assistance from other terms deemed to be particularly characteristic of wisdom writing.

The methodological stringency advocated by Crenshaw, and by Whybray in his 1974 volume, undoubtedly courts the risk of overlooking wisdom-influenced or wisdom-related writing in the Old Testament, yet it is doubtful whether there is any realistic alternative. Moreover, since Crenshaw's pointed criticisms of the main attempts to identify 'wisdom *narrative*' within the Old Testament seem to the present writer to be fully justified, in what follows wisdom will be discussed principally as a theme within certain Old Testament narratives and mainly to the extent that the terminology suggests the presence of the theme.

There are three main narrative sections in the Old Testament in which the theme of wisdom may be judged to play an important role, namely, the chapters dealing with the making of the tabernacle, the 'Succession Narrative' and the account of Solomon's reign in 1 Kings iii–xi. The Joseph narrative, whose entitlement to inclusion is rightly challenged by Crenshaw on ideological grounds,[16] does not even score well in the vocabulary test. 'Wise' occurs twice in connection with Joseph's promotion (Gen. xli 33, 39), but the only other occurrence of the *ḥkm* root is in reference to the wise men who could not help Pharaoh with the interpretation of his dreams (xli 8). On the other hand, while it may be true that the incidence of *ḥkm* references in Exod. xxv–xl owes something to the repetitive style of the

---

[14] *JBL* 88 (1969), pp. 132, 136 (=pp. 484, 488 in Crenshaw, *Studies*).
[15] *The Intellectual Tradition in the Old Testament* (Berlin and New York, 1974).
[16] *JBL* 88 (1969), pp. 136–7 (=pp. 488–9 in Crenshaw, *Studies*). Cf. S. Weeks, *Early Israelite Wisdom* (Oxford, 1994), pp. 92–109.

section,[17] the importance of divinely given wisdom in the tabernacle tradition is self-evident and will be noted again in the second main part of this article dealing with the topic of Solomonic wisdom. First, however, there is the question of wisdom and the 'Succession Narrative'.

Several of the characters in the 'Succession Narrative' are characterized as 'wise'. However, one of the problems confronting any theory of wisdom influence is that not all the manifestations of wisdom in the 'Succession Narrative' are commendatory of the virtue. This applies especially to the 'wise' Jonadab's feeding of Amnon with ideas on how to seduce Tamar (2 Sam. xiii 3–5) and, less conclusively, to the exercise of wisdom by the wise woman of Abel in order to have the rebel Sheba beheaded and the city of Abel saved from destruction for having harboured him (2 Sam. xx 14–22 [16, 22]).[18] The two references to Solomon's wisdom in 1 Kings ii 6, 9 will be discussed later, but because of their frequent association with the 'Succession Narrative' it will suffice here to note that the biblical text itself seems to pose a question in the following chapter about the exercise of wisdom in the vindictive way of 1 Kings ii. A more positive attitude to wisdom may be seen in the story of the wise woman of Tekoa (2 Sam. xiv 2) who, at the end of her skilful performance, effusively credits David with 'wisdom like that of an angel of God' (xiv 20). But, taken overall, this scarcely adds up to a terminological banquet. It is also striking that the two leading 'exponents' of wisdom in 2 Samuel are women living away from Jerusalem – one of them at a considerable distance from the capital (cf. 2 Sam. xx 14). This does not easily inspire thoughts of a wisdom circle active in the Jerusalem area and purveying narratives reflecting their own image to a greater or lesser degree.

The occurrences of the *y'ṣ* root in 2 Sam. xv–xvii also have a bearing on our inquiry about wisdom and the 'Succession Narrative'. The story of the clash between the sound counsel of Ahithophel and the ruinous, for Absalom, advice of Hushai is told amusingly and with great skill in xvi 15–xvii 14. Hushai won the debate, it is observed in xvii 14, because 'the Lord had determined to frustrate the good counsel of Ahithophel in order that the Lord might bring disaster on Absalom'. If 'counsel' is a wisdom term within a wisdom-influenced 'Succession Narrative' then 'deconstructionism' would scarcely provide a term strong enough to describe what the narrative is doing to itself in 2 Sam. xvii. It would not just be a case of a wisdom narrative recognizing the possibility of bad counsel being ineffective, but of a wisdom writer describing powerfully and at length how in a

---

[17] Cf. Whybray, *The Intellectual Tradition*, p. 109.
[18] The 'ruinous' effect of the contributions of wisdom representatives in the 'Succession Narrative' is noted by Crenshaw (*JBL* 88 [1969], pp. 139–40 [=pp. 491–2 in Crenshaw, *Studies*]).

particular instance the wisdom and good counsel of a foremost exponent of wisdom ran contrary to the divine purpose and were humbled by Hushai's patter. This goes far beyond the pithy truism of Prov. xxi 30.

In his monograph on the 'Succession Narrative' Whybray argues for a general wisdom influence upon the narrative, and he notes two features of 2 Sam. xvii which point to the same source of inspiration, namely the cluster of similes on the lips of the two counsellors Ahithophel and Hushai (verses 3–13) and the author's evident ability to argue both sides of a case, for which Whybray finds a basic text in Prov. xxvi 4–5.[19] Whybray is still committed to the wisdom classification of the 'Succession Narrative' in his 1974 volume: the eight occurrences of the *ḥkm* root 'can hardly be put down to coincidence' (p. 89). However, the key term in the three chapters 2 Sam. xv–xvii is not 'wisdom' but 'counsel' (xv 31, 34, xvi 20, 23, xvii 7, 14, 23), and Whybray's vocabulary study now leads him to the conclusion that 'counsel', especially in Samuel-Kings, Isaiah and Jeremiah, has a political rather than a general wisdom connotation.[20] If this were so, we should have to concede that the story of the downfall of Ahithophel and his counsel would not be subversive of the wisdom theme in the 'Succession Narrative' in the way that might otherwise apply. However, Whybray's previous characterization of the whole narrative as primarily a political document intended to support the Solomonic régime[21] makes it difficult to maintain the distinction between 'wisdom' and 'counsel' in this particular instance. The 'wisdom' seen in action in the 'Succession Narrative' has, in any case, a distinctly political flavour in at least three of its occurrences (cf. 2 Sam. xiv 20; 1 Kings ii 6, 9). Moreover, in the earlier round Whybray found ample evidence of political counsel in Proverbs, whether in specific references or in more generalized statements capable of being applied to political situations (p. 60). It is arguably legitimate, therefore, to treat 'wisdom' and 'counsel' in the 'Succession Narrative' on a roughly equal basis. They both illustrate the ambiguity – or worse – of wisdom as a principle by which to determine human behaviour. In respect of Old Testament narrative, therefore, wisdom's house (cf. Prov. ix l) is divided, as the remainder of this study will also seek to show.

Solomon and the temple

As far as the *ḥkm* root – the primary item of wisdom vocabulary – is concerned, the largest concentration of occurrences in Old Testament narrative comes in the account of Solomon's reign in 1 Kings ii(iii)–xi.

---

[19] Whybray, *The Succession Narrative*, pp. 81–3.
[20] Whybray, *The Intellectual Tradition*, pp. 132–3.
[21] Whybray, *The Succession Narrative*, p. 55.

While the various occurrences may be grouped according as they reflect particular aspects of wisdom, whether political astuteness (ii 6, 9), judicial insight (iii 16–28) or 'encyclopaedic' knowledge (v 9–14 [iv 29–34]), from the standpoint of the biblical writer(s) this is insignificant as compared with the headline contribution that they make to the theme of the wisdom, divinely-given, by which Solomon established his kingdom and won an international reputation for himself as an uncommonly wise and successful ruler (iii 12, v 9–14 [iv 29–34], x 1–13).

The account of what is, from the biblical perspective, Solomon's crowning achievement – the building of the temple – makes interesting reading in the light of this general emphasis on wisdom in the Solomon narrative. First, we must note that the only occurrence of the *ḥkm* root in 1 Kings vi–vii, which deals with the construction of the temple and related matters, is in vii 14, and that it concerns Hiram, whom the king of Tyre seconded to Solomon because of his rare skill in bronze work. At first it appears, therefore, that the wisdom and temple themes are not much connected in 1 Kings, and this is partly true, as we shall see. There is, nonetheless, some attempt on the part of the biblical writer to place the building of the temple in the context of Solomonic wisdom. This appears to be the case when the king of Tyre, on hearing of Solomon's plan to build the temple, blesses God for giving David 'a wise son' to rule over Israel (v 21 [7]). Some writers, of whom Gosse is the most recent, relate this description of Solomon to his negotiating skills in the commercial field, but Kalugila has rightly questioned whether this is what it means in context.[22] Again, the treaty regulating relations between Israel and Tyre, and so ensuring the provision of materials and personnel for Solomon's building projects, is linked with God's endowment of Solomon with wisdom (v 26 [12]). Since, then, Tyre features in the Solomonic narrative to the extent that it assists the realization of Solomon's building plans, these wisdom references in ch. v are rightly seen as providing a context for the account of the building and furnishing of the temple in chs. vi–vii.

A different angle on Solomon's temple-building is suggested, on the other hand, by a comparison with the account of the construction of the tabernacle in Exod. xxv–xl. As already noted, there are various occurrences of the *ḥkm* root in these chapters, all of them relating to the skills required for the making of the tabernacle and its effects. But these all have to do with Bezalel and Oholiab, and with the rest of the people who were involved in the construction work. As in 1 Kings vi–vii, the verbs describing the construction are very often in the third person singular (literally 'and he

---

[22] See B. Gosse, 'La Sagesse de Salomon en 1 Rois 5, 21', *BN* 65 (1992), pp. 15–18 (17); L. Kalugila, *The Wise King. Studies in Royal Wisdom as Divine Revelation in the Old Testament and Its Environment* (Lund, 1980), p. 119.

made'), but there is never any question of their having Moses for subject, despite his special role in relation to the erection and inauguration of the tabernacle. Specifically, in Exod. xxxvi 8 it is 'all the skilled men' who make the tabernacle curtains, while in xxxvii 1 Bezalel makes the ark of the covenant (cf. xxxviii 22, and contrast Deut. x 1–5). At the end, Moses inspects the work, blesses the people and sets up the tabernacle (xxxix 43, xl 1–33). The situation is different in 1 Kings vi–vii. Here the third person singular verbs, with the exception of those in the Hiram section (vii 13–45), have Solomon for subject, and the whole account of the construction work contributes in this way to the glorification of Solomon, who 'built the House' (vi 1; cf. vi 2, 14, vii 51) and who is specifically credited with covering the inside of the temple with gold (vi 21) and with making all the temple furnishings (vii 48).

This focussing upon Solomon as the wise master-builder in 1 Kings vi–vii permits a further contrast with the Exodus account of the tabernacle. In the latter the construction of the tabernacle is accomplished by means of wisdom specially granted to Bezalel, Oholiab and the rest for this specific undertaking (see Exod. xxviii 3, xxxi 3, 6, xxxv 31, 35, xxxvi 1, 2). The basic skill of spinning yarn is exercised in the ordinary way (xxxv 25–6), but other skills are subsumed in the main action of the making of the tabernacle in accordance with divine ability specifically given (xxxv 34–5). This is, moreover, an inner-Israelite affair: the generation of the wilderness are the ones who are equipped for the making of the tabernacle. Bezalel is from the tribe of Judah and Oholiab from Dan (xxxi 2, 6); everyone else involved is Israelite. The narrative of the Solomonic temple, by contrast, knows nothing of a self-sufficient Israelite community provided with the requisite skills for the construction of the divine abode. The Tyrian king is asked to provide lumberjacks for Solomon because 'we have no-one so skilled in felling trees as the Sidonians' (v 20 [6]). According to v 32 (18) craftsmen from Israel, Tyre and Byblos prepared the timber and stone for the building of the temple. Finally, Hiram is brought from Tyre to use his skill in bronze for the making of various temple artifacts. Hiram's father was Tyrian, but his mother is linked with the tribe of Naphtali (vii 14) – though it has been suggested that this latter datum represents an attempt to domesticate Hiram within Israelite tradition.[23] There is, at any rate, no talk of divine inspiration or equipping of those directly involved in the building of the temple. To that extent the account of Solomon's activities is 'secular' as compared with the 'sacral' emphasis of the priestly tabernacle account; but the appearance of secularity may be owing, in part, to the writer's desire to magnify Solomon as the conduit of the divine wisdom and practical skill

---

[23] See M. Noth, *Könige* (Neukirchen-Vluyn, 1968), p. 148.

required for the building of the temple. A similar kind of point is made by Gosse in a recent note, when he argues that Solomon's employment of international labour is presented as another illustration of his wisdom.[24]

It is evident, then, that, in comparison with the account of the tabernacle in Exodus, the report of the building of the temple in 1 Kings vi–vii gives only limited attention to the wisdom theme.

Solomonic wisdom and retribution

If wisdom's role is implied more than expressed in the building narratives of 1 Kings vi–vii, there is some evidence of a more radical questioning of an aspect of Solomonic wisdom in 1 Kings ii–iii, in relation to Solomon's conduct early in his reign. First, we shall have to look at ch. ii, where the subject of Solomonic wisdom first appears, in what has become known as 'David's Testament' (verses 1–12). Here David is depicted as encouraging Solomon to find opportunity to remove two men who had done much harm to David during his reign. The charge against Joab is that he killed Abner and Amasa in peacetime and thereby involved the royal house in bloodguilt (verses 5–6), while Shimei's sin had been to call down curses on the hapless David as he fled from Jerusalem during the Absalom rebellion (verses 8–9). Shimei, however, had been promised on oath that he would not suffer for his opportunistic abuse of David (2 Sam. xix 16–23), and David now counsels Solomon to find a way out of this undertaking. In both cases, moreover, Solomon is charged to act according to his wisdom in order to relieve himself of these two potentially destabilizing elements within the kingdom ('according to your wisdom', verse 6; 'you are a wise man', verse 9).

On the surface, it looks as if 1 Kings ii is offering a defence of questionable actions by Solomon early in his reign, and this is how the chapter is often read: the removal of such as Adonijah, Joab and Shimei was necessary for the establishing of the kingdom under Solomon's rule (verses 12, 46).[25] T. Ishida goes so far as to identify the author of the 'Succession Narrative', including 1 Kings ii, as a supporter of Solomon and possibly an associate of the prophet Nathan.[26] Quite the opposite view

---

[24] B. Gosse, 'La Sagesse et l'intelligence de Salomon en 1 Rois 5, 9', *BN* 65 (1992), pp. 12–14; V. Hurowitz, *I Have Built You an Exalted House. Temple Building in the Bible in Light of Mesopotamian and Northwest Semitic Writings* (Sheffield, 1992), pp. 207–10, notes references to foreign peoples bringing building materials for the construction of various near eastern temples, their involvement usually being cited to indicate the superiority of the monarch engaged in the building.

[25] Cf. P. K. McCarter, '"Plots, True or False." The Succession Narrative as Court Apologetic', *Interpretation* 35 (1981), pp. 359–61; R. D. Nelson, *First and Second Kings* (Louisville, 1987), p. 30.

[26] 'Solomon's Succession to the Throne of David – A Political Analysis', in T. Ishida (ed.), *Studies in the Period of David and Solomon and Other Essays* (Tokyo, 1982), p. 187.

of the authorial stance of 1 Kings ii has also been represented, however, notably by *Tendenz* critics such as L. Delekat, who interprets the account of the Solomonic purges in verses 13–46 as frankly anti-Solomonic.[27] J. P. Fokkelman, representing a different type of literary criticism, suggests that the existence of verse 12 ('So Solomon sat on the throne of David his father, and his rule was firmly established') is meant to indicate that the killings reported in the rest of the chapter were *not* necessary for the consolidation of Solomon's rule.[28] B. O. Long, however, treats verse 12*b* as an opening bracket which, with verse 46*b*, frames the account of Solomon's elimination of dangerous opponents in order to secure his rule in Jerusalem.[29]

It is indeed difficult, as most critics sense, to read 1 Kings ii as other than basically protective of Solomon's reputation. Even the incidental-sounding reference to 'three years later' in verse 39 chimes in very well with the statement in vi 1 that Solomon set about the construction of the temple in his fourth year – as if to say that the blood-letting had all been completed before the construction work was undertaken. In the near east temple building was commonly undertaken by a king in his first year.[30] And yet there are indications in the chapter that this is not an unquestioning apologetic on Solomon's behalf. The give-away consists in the fact that so much of Solomon's activity relates to Adonijah's failed coup. Thus Adonijah is executed and Abiathar rusticated (ii 25–7), even though neither action is called for in 'David's Testament' in verses 1–12.[31] The failed coup also explains the linking together of the names of Adonijah, Abiathar and Joab in verse 22. Again, whereas the stated grounds for Solomon's obligation to dispose of Joab had been the latter's treachery towards Abner and Amasa (verse 5), Joab's flight to the altar in search of sanctuary comes directly upon his hearing of Adonijah's death and Abiathar's banishment (verse 28). The biblical writer makes the connection explicit and seems almost to put in a good word for Joab when observing that he 'had sided with Adonijah, though not with Absalom' (verse 28). After all, he has just told us in verse 26 that Abiathar escaped execution because of his previous association with the ark of the covenant and in consideration of his having

---

[27] 'Tendenz und Theologie der David-Salomo-Erzählung', in F. Maass (ed.), *Das ferne und nahe Wort. Festschrift L. Rost* (Berlin, 1967), p. 27; cf. F. Langlamet, 'Pour ou contre Salomon? La rédaction prosalomonienne de I Rois, I–II', *RB* 83 (1976), pp. 330–7.

[28] *Narrative Art and Poetry in the Books of Samuel*, 1, *King David (II Sam. 9–20 and I Kings 1–2)* (Assen, 1981), pp. 390, 409.

[29] *I Kings with an Introduction to Historical Literature* (Grand Rapids, 1984), p. 47.

[30] Cf. Hurowitz, *I Have Built You an Exalted House*, pp. 226–7.

[31] Cf. J. Kegler, *Politisches Geschehen und theologisches Verstehen* (Stuttgart, 1977), p. 198. Even if ii 1–12 does not presuppose the Adonijah coup as regards its content, its contextualizing between the account of the coup (i 5–53) and Adonijah's request for Abishag and his consequent death (ii 13–25) is what makes the silence of 'David's Testament' significant.

shared David's privations, doubtless during Absalom's rebellion when Abiathar (like Joab) remained loyal to David. But Solomon was determined to have Joab's life and ordered that he be struck down beside the altar, seeing that he would not come away from it.[32] The original grounds for eliminating Joab are restated (verses 31–3), but the reader knows by now that there is more to the execution of Joab.

Pretext also figures in the treatment of Shimei, who promises on oath (verses 38, 42–3) that he will limit his movements to the environs of Jerusalem. Since David had given Shimei his oath that he would not be punished for his raucous disloyalty during Absalom's rebellion (2 Sam. xix 23), Solomon's tactic is obviously to supersede his father's oath with a commitment of comparable gravity from Shimei.[33] There is the impression given, therefore, that the killings of 1 Kings ii have an element of legal pretext about them. The fact that the same verb (*pgʿ*) is used for Benaiah's killings on Solomon's orders (verses 25, 29, 31, 34, 46) as for Joab's crimes (verse 32) may also hint in this direction. The relevance of all this to the role of wisdom in the Solomon narrative of 1 Kings ii–xi will now become apparent as we consider a feature of ch. iii.

When, in his dream at the high place of Gibeon, Solomon is invited by God to make one request for himself, he asks for the gift of discernment so as properly to rule the people of Israel (iii 9). To this God replies:

Since this is what you have requested, and not longevity or wealth for yourself, *and since you have not asked for the death of your enemies* ... I shall do what you have asked. (iii 11–12a)

In point of fact Solomon is given not only the discerning heart that he requested, but also riches and conditional longevity (verses 12–14). In other words, all the elements of verse 11 are represented in verses 12–14, with the exception of the death of Solomon's enemies. Since the death, or removal otherwise, of his enemies is precisely what Solomon has been achieving in ch. ii, in the cases of Adonijah, Abiathar, Joab and Shimei, it is easy to read this reference in iii 11 to the king's not seeking the death of his enemies as some kind of oblique commentary on his previous actions. As a reading strategy this is certainly unexceptionable, but it is also a fair question whether the narrative itself is implying criticism of the earlier killings. And if it were to be argued that the inclusion of the death of the king's enemies with riches and long life in verse 11 assumes that one request is as legitimate as another, it remains the case that only the other two items are picked up in

---

[32] Fokkelman, *Narrative Art and Poetry*, p. 400, notes the contrast between the treatment of Adonijah and Joab, both of whom sought sanctuary at the altar.

[33] J. S. Rogers, 'Narrative Stock and Deuteronomistic Elaboration in 1 Kings 2', *CBQ* 50 (1988), p. 410, suggests that David's oath may have been reckoned to last only as long as David himself.

verses 12–14, and that this reference to enemies comes after the killings reported in ch. ii.

At this point, however, questions about source delimitation begin to affect the issue of reading strategy, for according to a widely held view the 'Succession Narrative' ends somewhere in 1 Kings ii, and 1 Kings iii 1 marks the beginning of a major new narrative segment.[34] This largely accounts for the tendency to treat the wisdom references in ii 6, 9 separately from those in the following chapters, sometimes with the additional justification that the 'wisdom' in ii 6, 9 is of the calculating, political sort and different from other manifestations of Solomonic wisdom in succeeding chapters, or even that Solomon does not officially acquire his wisdom until ch. iii.[35] But the discussion about the narrative affiliation of 1 Kings i–ii is by no means unidirectional. Over twenty years ago J. W. Flanagan argued that what appears as a 'Succession Narrative' was originally a 'Court History' to which has been added the 'Solomonic' material in 2 Sam. xi 2–xii 25 and 1 Kings i–ii.[36] P. K. McCarter has described 1 Kings i–ii as 'an apologetic document composed *in reference to* materials in Second Samuel',[37] which would apparently leave open the possibility of a Janus-like function of the chapters in relation to what precedes and what follows. Furthermore, in her unpublished dissertation, G. Keys has advanced strong stylistic arguments against including 1 Kings i–ii in the 'Succession Narrative' which she is happy to recognize within 2 Samuel.[38] Finally, in this brief selection of alternative estimations of 1 Kings i–ii, we should note K. I. Parker's discussion of 1 Kings i–xi as a rhetorical unit which, by its use of 'repetition as a structuring device', allows the reader to focus more sharply upon the two sides of Solomon's character.[39] For Parker, chs. i–ii and xi 14–43 function as 'frame stories', both having to do with the question of royal succession (pp. 21, 24–5).

It must now be evident that the hermetic sealing off of ch. ii from ch. iii is justified neither by the texts themselves nor by the state of recent opinion. And even if the conventional kind of boundary is retained we might still, with B. Halpern, regard chs. i–ii as 'skillfully resculpted to fit with the rest of the reign'.[40] Part of the 'resculpting', we suggest, actually takes place in

---

[34] Cf. Fokkelman, *Narrative Art and Poetry*, p. 410; K. K. Sacon, 'A Study of the Literary Structure of "The Succession Narrative"', in Ishida, *Studies in the Period of David and Solomon*, p. 52.   [35] See S. J. DeVries, *1 Kings* (Waco, 1985), p. 36.

[36] 'Court History or Succession Document? A Study of 2 Samuel 9–20 and 1 Kings 1–2', *JBL* 91 (1972), pp. 172–81.

[37] *Interpretation* 35 (1981), pp. 361–2.

[38] *The So-Called Succession Narrative. A Reappraisal of Leonhard Rost's Interpretation of II Samuel 9–20 and I Kings 1–2* (Ph.D. dissertation, Queen's University, Belfast, 1988), pp. 66–90.

[39] 'Repetition as a Structuring Device in 1 Kings 1–11', *JSOT* 42 (1988), pp. 19–27.

[40] *The First Historians. The Hebrew Bible and History* (San Francisco, 1988), p. 146.

ch. iii in an implied criticism of the vindictive actions by which Solomon secured his position as king. For all that he is glorified in chs. iii–xi as the ruler who saw the fulfilment of the Israelite imperial dream (iv 20–v 14 [iv 20–34]), there is elsewhere a hint of embarrassment at his corvée policy (ix 22–3; cf. v 27–31 [13–17]), while a candid account of his failings and their consequences is given in ch. xi. Indeed, our last sight of Solomon, apart from the standard concluding formula (xi 41–3), is of him reverting to the activity of ch. ii as he seeks the life of his rival Jeroboam and forces him to flee to Egypt (xi 40). This is a 'neat inclusio' to the story of a king who established his rule by such means and who, in the estimation of the biblical writer, came to undo much of his own and his father's achievements. The result was that his house too, like wisdom's, became divided (1 Kings xi 29–39, xii 1–24).

8   Wisdom in Solomonic historiography

André Lemaire

In his *status quaestionis* of about fifteen years ago, J. A. Emerton,[1] to whom this study is dedicated, noted that the influence of the sages upon Deuteronomy had been well evaluated in M. Weinfeld's synthesis, *Deuteronomy and the Deuteronomic School*.[2] According to Weinfeld, 'the authors of Deuteronomy and the deuteronomic school must be sought for, then, among circles which held public office, among persons who had at their command a vast reservoir of literary material, who had developed and were capable of developing a literary technique of their own, those experienced in literary composition, and skilled with the pen and the book: these authors must consequently have been the *sōferim-ḥakamim*';[3] at the same time, these latter seem only to have appeared as a socio-professional group in the time of Hezekiah, so that 'Hezekiah may be considered the historically true patron of *wisdom* literature'.[4] Meanwhile, in his methodological article on the influence of wisdom on the historical literature, J. L. Crenshaw[5] listed only 'Gen 1–11, 37, 39–50, Exod 34,6f, Deut, II Sam 9–20, 1 Kings 1–2, Amos, Habakkuk, Isaiah and Jonah'.

Even though there are some exceptions,[6] these positions which have been

This chapter was translated by Professor H. G. M. Williamson.

[1] 'Wisdom', in G. W. Anderson (ed.), *Tradition and Interpretation* (Oxford, 1979), pp. 214–37, especially 222–3.
[2] (Oxford, 1972), pp. 158–78, 244–74; cf. also Weinfeld, *Deuteronomy 1–11* (New York, 1991), pp. 55–7, 62–5.
[3] Cf. Weinfeld, *Deuteronomy and the Deuteronomic School*, pp. 177–8.
[4] *Ibid.*, pp. 161–2; on pp. 254–7, however, he recognizes the existence of a pre-deuteronomic Solomonic wisdom.
[5] 'Method in Determining Wisdom Influence upon "Historical" Literature', *JBL* 88 (1969), pp. 129–42, especially 129 (= J. L. Crenshaw [ed.], *Studies in Ancient Israelite Wisdom* [New York, 1976], pp. 481–94).
[6] Cf., e.g., A. Alt, 'Die Weisheit Salomos', *ThLZ* 36 (1951), pp. 139–44 (= *Kleine Schriften zur Geschichte des Volkes Israels*, 2 [Munich, 1953], pp. 90–9; E. tr., 'Solomonic Wisdom', in Crenshaw [ed.], *Studies*, pp. 102–12); M. Noth, 'Die Bewährung von Salomos "Göttlicher Weisheit"', in *Wisdom in Israel and in the Ancient Near East* (*SVT* 3, 1955), pp. 225–37; R. N. Whybray, *The Intellectual Tradition in the Old Testament* (Berlin, 1974), pp. 91–3, 154; G. E. Bryce, *A Legacy of Wisdom. The Egyptian Contribution to the Wisdom of Israel* (London, 1979), especially pp. 163–88.

adopted in contemporary exegesis appear somewhat paradoxical: even if it seems legitimate to associate the deuteronomic school with the group of scribes/sages which is attested from the reign of Hezekiah onwards, nevertheless, as far as the biblical tradition is concerned, it is not Hezekiah, but Solomon, who was the patron of wisdom, and it is surprising, to say the least, that the Solomonic history of 1 Kings iii–xi does not usually feature among the list of historical texts in which exegetes have uncovered wisdom influence. In this context of contemporary exegesis, it seems worthwhile to seek to clarify the role of wisdom in Solomonic historiography.

A brief statistical survey at once reveals the importance of this theme in 1 Kings iii–xi. In fact, derivatives of the root *ḥkm* appear there no less than nineteen times (*ḥokmâ* iii 28, v 9 [iv 29], 10 [iv 30] [*ter*], 14 [iv 34] [*bis*], 26 [12], vii 14, x 4, 6, 7, 8, 23, 24, xi 41; *ḥākām* iii 12, vi 21 [7]; *ḥākam* v 11 [iv 31]). This frequency should be compared with the eight occurrences in the whole of Deuteronomy,[7] one only in the book of Judges,[8] eight in the Succession Narrative[9] and above all the complete absence of *ḥkm* from the remainder of the books of Kings as also from the book of Joshua. Thus, leaving aside the song of Deborah (Judg. v 29), *ḥkm* is completely absent from the Deuteronomic History except for the Succession Narrative and the account of Solomon's reign;[10] it appears only between 2 Sam. xiii 3 and 1 Kings xi 41.

Even if these statistics do not challenge the suggestion that the Deuteronomic History could have been edited by the sages of the royal court of Jerusalem, they do show clearly that this theme was not a favourite of the deuteronomic historians from the end of the eighth century to the sixth century BC. They raise, rather, the question whether the link between wisdom and royalty was not characteristic of the Hebrew historical writers of the tenth century BC,[11] especially those of the Solomonic era.

I shall not discuss here the extent of the Succession Narrative,[12] but will simply accept that 1 Kings i–ii belongs to this work with its account of Solomon's accession to the throne and the consolidation of power in his

---

[7] Deut. i 13, 15, iv 6 (*bis*), xvi 19, xxxii 6, 29, xxxiv 9.

[8] Song of Deborah (v 29).   [9] 2 Sam. xiii 3, xiv 2, 20 (bis), xx 16, 22; 1 Kings ii 6, 9.

[10] Cf. B. Gosse, 'La Sagesse de Salomon en 1 Rois 5, 21', *BN* 65 (1992), pp. 15–18, especially 15.

[11] 'No Israelite king other than David (2 Sam 14:20) and Solomon is specifically credited with wisdom in the Old Testament' (R. N. Whybray, 'The Sage in the Israelite Royal Court', in J. G. Gammie and L. G. Perdue [eds.], *The Sage in Israel and the Ancient Near East* [Winona Lake, 1990], pp. 133–9, especially 133; cf. L. Kalugila, *The Wise King* [Lund, 1980], pp. 106–22, especially 122).

[12] Cf. recently E. Ball in L. Rost, *The Succession to the Throne of David* (E. tr., Sheffield, 1982), pp. xv–l; T. Ishida, 'Solomon's Succession to the Throne of David – A Political Analysis', in T. Ishida (ed.), *Studies in the Period of David and Solomon and Other Essays* (Tokyo and Winona Lake, 1982), pp. 175–87; J. W. Wesselius, 'Joab's Death and the Central Theme of the Succession Narrative (2 Samuel ix – 1 Kings ii)', *VT* 40 (1990), pp. 336–51, especially 336.

hands (1 Kings ii 46).[13] It may merely be noted that '*îš ḥākām* at 1 Kings ii 9 may be linked with the same expression at 2 Sam. xiii 3 and '*iššâ ḥᵃkāmâ* at 2 Sam. xiv 2, xx 16. In the opinion of most commentators,[14] this original account of Solomon's accession to power finishes at 1 Kings ii 46 and many think it was probably edited during the reign of Solomon, perhaps quite early in his reign; it is probably the work of one or more members[15] of the royal court about which he (or they) appear(s) to be well informed. We may note in particular the important political role played by the royal 'counsellors': *yō'ēṣ* 2 Sam. xv 12; *'ēṣâ* 2 Sam. xv 31, 34, xvi 20, 23, xvii 7, 14, 23; 1 Kings i 12; *yā'aṣ* 2 Sam. xvi 23, xvii 7, 15, 21; 1 Kings i 12.[16]

The leading role of wisdom in the Solomonic history of 1 Kings iii–xi emerges not only from the statistics about the usage of derivatives of the root *ḥkm* which were set out above but also, and above all, from the way in which wisdom is presented in this historiography:

(1) Right from the start of the Solomonic history, wisdom appears as a special gift granted to Solomon by Yahweh at the time of his dream at Gibeon: 'Behold, I am giving you a wise and understanding heart (*ḥākām wᵉnābôn*)' (1 Kings iii 12*a*).[17] As a sort of *inclusio*, wisdom is mentioned again at the end as a characteristic of the whole of Solomon's reign; the reference to 'his wisdom' (*ḥokmātô*, 1 Kings xi 41) is all the more significant in that the other parallel formulae which concluded the accounts of reigns in the Deuteronomic History never include this term, but rather *gᵉbūrātô*, 'his might, courage'.[18]

(2) This wisdom is portrayed as superior to that of all the other kings (see above, 1 Kings iii 12); it surpasses the wisdom of the Egyptians and that of the 'children of the East' (1 Kings v 10 [iv 30]). It is even described as

---

[13] Cf. T. Ishida, 'The Succession Narrative and Esarhaddon's Apology: Comparison', in M. Cogan and I. Eph'al (eds.), *Ah, Assyria ... Studies in Assyrian History and Ancient Near Eastern Historiography Presented to H. Tadmor* (Jerusalem, 1991), pp. 166–73.

[14] Note, however, the different opinion of J. Van Seters, 'Histories and Historians of the Ancient Near East: The Israelites', *Orientalia* 50 (1981), pp. 137–85, especially 156–67.

[15] On the possibility of an Abiatharid history revised by a Zadokite or a Nathanid, cf. A. Lemaire, 'Vers l'histoire de la rédaction des livres des Rois', *ZAW* 98 (1986), pp. 221–36, especially 231–2; A. Caquot, 'Samuel', *SDB* 11 (Paris, 1991), cols. 1048–98, especially 1095–8.

[16] Isa. i 26 may contain an allusion to the importance of royal counsellors in Jerusalem at the time of David, and it may be noted that the book of Proverbs insists on the importance of a plurality of counsellors (Prov. xi 14, xv 22, xxiv 6).

[17] This phrase was very probably part of the pre-deuteronomic account; cf. D. M. Carr, *From D to Q. A Study of Early Jewish Interpretations of Solomon's Dream at Gibeon* (Atlanta, 1991), pp. 32, 39–40.

[18] 1 Kings xv 23, xvi 5, 27, xxii 46; 2 Kings x 34, xiii 8, 12, xiv 15, 28, xx 20 (Hezekiah!).

'divine wisdom' or 'the wisdom of God'[19] (*ḥokmat ʾᵉlōhîm*, 1 Kings iii 28[20]).

(3) This wisdom is principally associated with the exercise of justice, as is demonstrated by the first account in 1 Kings iii 16–28, the famous 'judgement of Solomon'.[21] This account, which portrays two women appealing to the king, may be compared with that of the woman of Tekoa (2 Sam. xiv 1–22) because the principal conclusion of both is the recognition of the 'wisdom' of the king (2 Sam. xiv 20; 1 Kings iii 28). Furthermore, the association of wisdom and justice is underlined in other biblical texts (Deut. i 13, 15, xvi 19), while the primary role of the king in guaranteeing 'judgement and justice' (*mišpāṭ ûṣᵉdāqâ*) is clearly recalled by the Queen of Sheba (1 Kings x 9).

(4) This wisdom is also political wisdom.[22] It reveals itself in the organization of the administration of the kingdom (1 Kings iv 1–v 8 [iv 1–28]) and in the establishment of good diplomatic and commercial relations with the kings of neighbouring countries, especially Hiram of Tyre (1 Kings v 15–21 [v 1–7], ix 10–14,[23] 26–8, x 11–12, 22[24]) and the Queen of Sheba.[25] In particular, this earns Solomon international recognition, something carefully noted by means of words put into the mouths of foreign kings: Hiram of Tyre: 'Blessed be Yahweh this day, who has given to David a wise (*ḥākām*) son over this great people' (1 Kings v 21 [7]); the Queen of Sheba: 'your wisdom and prosperity (*ḥokmâ wāṭôb*) exceed the fame which I heard ... Blessed be Yahweh

[19] To be compared with 'the wisdom of the messenger of God (*ḥokmat mal'ak hāʾᵉlōhîm*)', attributed to David (2 Sam. xiv 20).

[20] Cf. also 1 Kings iii 12 and x 24, where Solomon's wisdom appears as a gift of God.

[21] For a literary analysis of this account, cf. H. and M. Weippert, 'Zwei Frauen vor dem Königsgericht. Einzelfragen der Erzählung vom "Salomonischen Urteil"', in B. Becking, J. Dorp and A. van der Kooij (eds.), *Door het oog van de profeten. Festschrift C. van Leeuwen* (Utrecht, 1989), pp. 133–60; W. A. M. Beuken, 'No Wise King without a Wise Woman (1 Kings iii 16–28)', *OTS* 25 (1989), pp. 1–10; K. A. Deurloo, 'The King's Wisdom in Judgement', *ibid.*, pp. 11–21; S. Lasine, 'The Riddle of Solomon's Judgement and the Riddle of Human Nature in the Hebrew Bible', *JSOT* 45 (1989), pp. 61–86.

[22] Cf. E. W. Heaton, *Solomon's New Men* (New York, 1974), especially p. 16; Bryce, *Legacy*, pp. 163–88.

[23] For an attempt at historical interpretation, cf. A. Lemaire, 'Asher et le royaume de Tyr', in E. Lipiński (ed.), *Phoenicia and the Bible* (Leuven, 1991), pp. 135–52.

[24] A. Lemaire, 'Les Phéniciens et le commerce entre la Mer Rouge et la Mer Méditerranée', in E. Lipiński (ed.), *Phoenicians and the East Mediterranean in the First Millennium B.C.* (Leuven, 1987), pp. 49–60, especially 51. On the relations between Hiram and Solomon, cf. recently F. Briquel-Chatonnet, *Les Relations entre les cités de la côte phénicienne et les royaumes d'Israël et de Juda* (Leuven, 1992), pp. 40–58.

[25] On the South Arabian historical context in the second half of the tenth century, cf. G. Gnoli, *Inventario delle iscrizioni sudarabiche II, Shaqab al-Manaṣṣa* (Paris and Rome, 1993), p. 31; M. Liverani, 'Early Caravan Trade between South-Arabia and Mesopotamia', to appear in the Acts of the International Congress *Arabia Antiqua, Rome, 1991*.

your God, who has delighted in you to set you on the throne of Israel'
(1 Kings x 7, 9).

(5) This wisdom is also the technical wisdom of one who undertakes works
of construction on a grand scale and sees them through to completion –
in particular the temple (1 Kings v 22 [v 8]–vi 37) and the royal palace (1
Kings vii 1–12), both of which were decorated by the bronze-worker
Hiram, who was himself 'full of wisdom (*haḥokmâ*)' (1 Kings vii 14).
The Queen of Sheba herself acknowledged that this was the practical
wisdom of a great builder (1 Kings x 4).

(6) Finally, this wisdom is also comprised of intelligence, knowledge and
the art of speaking well. It consists of riddles (*ḥîdâ*, 1 Kings x 1),
proverbs (*māšāl*, 1 Kings v 12 [iv 32]) and poems or songs (*šîr*, 1 Kings v
12 [iv 32]). This literary and scientific[26] skill is said to have been superior
to that of 'Ethan the Ezrahite, Heman, Calcol and Darda, the sons of
Mahol', who are reckoned as Judaean clan chiefs in 1 Chron. ii 6, and
perhaps also as superior to that of the 'children of the East'[27] and of
Egypt (1 Kings v 10 [iv 31]).

This rapid survey of the various aspects of wisdom in 1 Kings iii–xi
confirms beyond the shadow of a doubt the central role which it plays in
the biblical historiography of the reign of Solomon. It does not, however,
seem to be an isolated phenomenon in the historiography of the ancient
near east. Without going into great detail here,[28] and by concentrating
above all[29] on the West Semitic royal inscriptions of the ninth to eighth
centuries BC,[30] I should like to highlight briefly various themes which are
shared by the historiography of the ancient near east at the start of the first
millennium:

The king is better than the other kings of the country. This theme is
particularly prominent in the Phoenician inscription of
Kilamuwa 2–5: 'Gabbar became king over Y'dy, but accom-

---

[26] The interpretation of 1 Kings v 13 [iv 33] remains difficult and disputed; even when we have
taken into consideration the comments of M. V. Fox, 'Egyptian Onomastica and Biblical
Wisdom', *VT* 36 (1986), pp. 302–10, it still seems to be a question of a reference to a type of
encyclopaedic botanical and zoological knowledge, as proposed by Alt, 'Die Weisheit
Salomos'.

[27] The expression 'children of the East' (*b^enê qedem*) may refer to the Arameans (cf. Gen. xxix
1; Num. xxiii 7), to the Arabs (cf. Gen. xxv 6), or to the inhabitants of Transjordan.

[28] Cf., e.g., R. Gelio, 'Storiografia e ideologia in 1 R 3–10', in *La storiografia della bibbia. Atti
della XXVIII settimana biblica* (Bologna, 1986), pp. 29–52.

[29] For the neo-Assyrian domain, cf., e.g., F. M. Fales (ed.), *Assyrian Royal Inscriptions: New
Horizons* (Rome, 1981); H. Tadmor and M. Weinfeld (eds.), *History, Historiography and
Interpretation. Studies in Biblical and Cuneiform Literatures* (Jerusalem, 1983).

[30] Cf., e.g., J. M. Miller, 'The Moabite Stone as a Memorial Stela', *PEQ* 106 (1974), pp. 9–18;
J. Drinkard, 'The Literary Genre of the Mesha' Inscription', in A. Dearman (ed.), *Studies in
the Mesha Inscription and Moab* (Atlanta, 1989), pp. 131–54.

plished nothing. There was Banah, but he accomplished nothing. Then there was my brother Š'l, but he accomplished nothing. But I, Kilamuwa, the son of Tm-, what I accomplished not (even) their predecessors accomplished.'[31]

The king is superior to other neighbouring kings. This theme is expressed by the words '*l kl mlk*, 'above every king', in Karatepe A III 4, 6–7; C III 18; IV 1; it also recurs in the Barrakib inscription 11–15: 'I have taken over my father's house, and have made it better than the house of any powerful king. My brother kings were envious because of all the good fortune of my house'[32] (see also Panamuwa 12).

The prosperity and wealth of the country under the rule of the king who is being commemorated occurs in particular in the inscriptions from Karatepe and from Zenjirli. The country does not suffer from famine: it 'eats and drinks' (Panamuwa 9, parallel with 1 Kings iv 20) and it is full of corn and wine (*šbˁ wtrš*: Karatepe A III 7, 9; C IV 7, 9), 'wheat and barley and corn and millet were plentiful in his days' (Panamuwa 9).[33] Furthermore, the population grew rich and even lived in a degree of luxury (gold, silver, costly attire), as Kilamuwa boasts: 'Him who had never seen the face of a sheep, I made owner of a flock; him who had never seen the face of an ox, I made owner of a herd, and owner of silver and owner of gold; and him who had never seen linen from his youth, in my days they covered with byssus',[34] and the king possessed 'silver' (*ksp*) and 'gold' (*zhb*) (Panamuwa 11).[35] It is probably in the light of this historiographical theme that the wealth of Solomon should be evaluated historically.[36]

The king is glorified by his grand building works. The theme of the

[31] Cf. J. C. L. Gibson, *Textbook of Syrian Semitic Inscriptions*, 3: *Phoenician Inscriptions* (Oxford, 1982), pp. 33–5; cf. T. Ishida, '"Solomon who is Greater than David": Solomon's Succession in 1 Kings i–ii in the Light of the Inscription of Kilamuwa, King of Y'DY-ŠAM'AL', in J. A. Emerton (ed.), *Congress Volume: Salamanca 1983* (*SVT* 36, 1985), pp. 145–53.

[32] Cf. J. C. L. Gibson, *Textbook of Syrian Semitic Inscriptions*, 2: *Aramaic Inscriptions* (Oxford, 1975), p. 90.   [33] *Ibid.*, p. 79.

[34] Cf. Gibson, *Textbook*, 3, p. 35.

[35] Cf. Gibson, *Textbook*, 2, pp. 80–1.

[36] Cf. A. R. Millard, 'King Solomon's Gold: Biblical Records in the Light of Antiquity', *The Society for Mesopotamian Studies Bulletin* 15 (1988), pp. 5–11; Millard, 'Does the Bible Exaggerate King Solomon's Golden Wealth?', *BAR* 15 (1989), pp. 20–9, 31, 34; Millard, 'Texts and Archaeology: Weighing the Evidence. The Case for King Solomon', *PEQ* 123 (1991), pp. 19–27; J. M. Miller, 'Solomon: International Potentate or Local King?', *ibid.*, pp. 28–31; A. R. Millard, 'Solomon: Text and Archaeology', *ibid.*, pp. 117–18.

builder-king is well known from Akkadian royal inscriptions.[37] It recurs in most of the West Semitic royal inscriptions which magnify the king on account of his construction of temples, palaces and towns. Thus the Mesha inscription 3, 9–10, and especially 21–30: 'I built Qeriho, the parkland walls as well as the walls of the acropolis. I built its gates and I built its towers. I built the king's palace ... I built Aroer ... I rebuilt Beth-bamoth ... I rebuilt Bezer ... I built the temple of Medeba, the temple of Diblathayim and the temple of Baal-meon ...', and Barrakib 16–20: 'my fathers, the kings of Samal, had no good palace. They had indeed the palace of Kilamuwa, but it was their winter palace and their summer palace. However I have built this palace'[38] (cf. also Zakkur B 4–13; Hadad 13–14, 19; Karatepe A II 17).

The king is glorified by ambassadors who come from distant lands. This theme is well known from neo-Assyrian inscriptions.[39] It is attested in the Bible itself by the embassy of Merodach-baladan to Hezekiah (2 Kings xx 12–19). It should be noted that the sentence 'Everything which is in my house they have seen; there is nothing which I have not shown them' (2 Kings xx 15, cf. 17) is close to what is said in 1 Kings x 4–5 concerning the visit of the Queen of Sheba.

The king boasts of having been chosen by the national deity who has established him on his throne (*passim*).[40] The deity may eventually reveal himself to the king in a dream. This motif appears primarily in Egypt[41] with Thutmose IV[42] and Merneptah, and in Mesopotamia[43] with Nabonidus.[44]

Evaluation of the king's knowledge is less common. Nevertheless,

---

[37] Cf., e.g., S. Lackenbacher, *Le Roi bâtisseur. Les récits de construction assyriens des origines à Téglatphalazar III* (Paris, 1982).

[38] Cf. Gibson, *Textbook*, 2, p. 90.

[39] Cf., e.g., *ARAB* 1, sections 392, 590, 591, 794; cf. also R. Gelio, 'La délégation envoyée par Gygès, roi de Lydie, un cas de propagande idéologique', in Fales (ed.), *Inscriptions*, pp. 203–24.

[40] Cf. recently S. Ponchia, *L'Assiria e gli stati transeufratici nella prima meta dell' VIII sec. a. C.* (Padova, 1991), pp. 67–70.

[41] Cf. S. Herrmann, 'Die Königsnovelle in Ägypten und Israel. Ein Beitrag zur Gattungsgeschichte in den Geschichtsbüchern des AT', in *Wissenschaftliche Zeitschrift der Karl-Marx-Universität, Leipzig* 3 (1953–4), pp. 51–62 (=*Gesammelte Studien zur Geschichte und Theologie des Alten Testaments* [Munich, 1986], pp. 120–44).

[42] Cf. *ANET*, p. 449.

[43] Cf. A. L. Oppenheim, *The Interpretation of Dreams in the Ancient Near East* (Philadelphia, 1956), pp. 186–96, 245–55.

[44] Cf. J. Liver, 'The Book of the Acts of Solomon', *Biblica* 48 (1967), pp. 75–101, especially 80.

reference may be made to the inscriptions of Shulgi[45] and Ashurbanipal,[46] as well as to that of Yariris[47] in hieroglyphic Luwian, in which he boasts of knowing four scripts and twelve languages.[48]

Finally, 'wisdom' itself appears alongside 'righteousness/legitimacy' as an essential quality for a king. It guarantees him wealth, as Panamuwa 11 shows (*bḥkmth wbṣdqh*),[49] and the respect of other kings, as indicated by Karatepe A I, 12–13: 'Every king considered me like a father because of my justice, my wisdom and the kindness of my heart (*bṣdqy wbḥkmty wbn'm lby*)'.[50] In the neo-Assyrian realm only one text need be cited, that of Adad-nirari II (911–891), a near-contemporary of Solomon: '(The great gods) made perfect my features and filled my lordly body with wisdom . . .'[51]

The citing of these themes which are common to both Solomonic and royal ancient near eastern historiography shows clearly the extent to which 1 Kings iii–xi is rooted in royal near eastern ideology and propaganda, including the high value placed on the king's 'wisdom'.[52] Nevertheless, unlike the various royal inscriptions which have just been cited, the text of 1 Kings iii–xi has not been passed down to us on stone but through the channel of a literary tradition which was reread, recopied, corrected, revised and amplified, and which poses formidable literary-critical problems. Is it possible now to isolate and to date the redaction of 1 Kings iii–xi which has associated 'wisdom' so strongly with Solomon?

Since 1 Kings iii–xi is part of the Deuteronomic History, it is natural to think first of a final deuteronomic editor. It is true that certain verses in

---

[45] Cf. S. N. Kramer, 'Solomon and Šulgi: A Comparative Portrait', in Cogan and Eph'al (eds.), *Ah, Assyria*, pp. 189–95, especially 192–5.

[46] *ARAB* 2, sections 767, 843, 934 and, above all, 987.

[47] On this personality from Carchemish around 800 BC, cf. J. D. Hawkins, 'Some Historical Problems of the Hieroglyphic Luwian Inscriptions', *Anatolian Studies* 29 (1981), pp. 153–67, especially 157–60.

[48] Carchemish A 15b, 4; cf. P. Meriggi, *Manuale di eteo geroglifico*, 2 (Rome, 1967), p. 34, frag. 18; J. C. Greenfield, 'Of Scribes, Scripts and Languages', in Cl. Baurain, C. Bonnet and V. Krings (eds.), *Phoinikeia Grammata* (Liège-Namur, 1991), pp. 173–85.

[49] Cf. Gibson, *Textbook*, 2, pp. 80–1.

[50] Cf. F. Bron, *Recherches sur les inscriptions phéniciennes de Karatepe* (Geneva and Paris, 1979), pp. 13, 23, 63.

[51] Cf. A. K. Grayson, *Assyrian Royal Inscriptions*, 2 (Wiesbaden, 1976), p. 85, section 414; cf. also section 596 (Ashurnasirpal II) and above all R. F. G. Sweet, 'The Sage in Akkadian Literature: Philological Study', in Gammie and Perdue (eds.), *The Sage*, pp. 45–65.

[52] Cf. K. L. Younger, 'The Figurative Aspects and the Contextual Method in the Evaluation of the Solomonic Empire (1 Kings 1–11)', in D. J. A. Clines, S. E. Fowl and S. E. Porter (eds.), *The Bible in Three Dimensions* (Sheffield, 1990), pp. 157–75.

these chapters should probably be ascribed to one or to several deuteronomic editors: thus in particular iii 2–3,[53] 14a,[54] vi 11–13 (14?), viii 9(?), 16–61,[55] ix 1–9, 20–2, xi 2, 3b, 4–6, 7(?), 8, 11a, 13, 32–4b, 36b, 38–9,[56] 41–3*. However, any theory which associates the central theme of the Solomonic history – namely, wisdom – with a deuteronomic redaction in the seventh or sixth century BC seems very improbable. We have seen that the 'wisdom' of the king is completely absent from the remainder of the books of Kings, where the deuteronomic editors highlight instead 'his might/courage' ($g^e b\bar{u}r\bar{a}t\hat{o}$)[57] and his attitude towards the schism of Jeroboam (in Israel) or towards sacred prostitution ($q\bar{a}d\bar{e}\check{s}$) and then towards the 'high places' ($b\bar{a}m\hat{o}t$) (in Judah).[58] Furthermore, the verses which seem to be associated with a deuteronomic redaction do not develop this central theme of 'wisdom' and they appear already to presuppose the existence of this central theme in a document which the redactor has used (xi 41).[59] Finally, these verses are frequently critical of various aspects of Solomon's wisdom, and this is confirmed by Deut. xvii 16–17 which, with its aversion to the multiplying of horses, silver, gold and wives, is a scarcely veiled critique of several aspects of Solomon's wisdom.[60]

Is it necessary, then, to push this historiographical-sapiential redaction down into the post-exilic period, when a redactor might have transformed the deuteronomic redaction by adding in the central theme of wisdom? At first sight, such a solution seems rather difficult because it would presuppose an extensive reworking of chapters iii–xi in which the link between Solomon's wisdom and his wealth (cf. Prov. iii 16, viii 18), his exercise of justice, his politics and his building works seems natural. Furthermore, it would be difficult to see, on this hypothesis, why a late author should have felt the need suddenly to focus the whole of the Solomonic history on his wisdom; the mere association of two groups of

[53] The original account of the dream at Gibeon is obviously pre-deuteronomic because it contravenes the rule of the central sanctuary; cf. H. Cazelles, 'Les débuts de la sagesse en Israël', in *Les Sagesses du Proche-Orient ancien* (Paris, 1963), pp. 27–40, especially 34.

[54] The delimitation of these verses represents a minimal position. For a more detailed study, including other verses, cf. Carr, *From D to Q*, pp. 13–30; A. G. Auld, 'Salomo und die Deuteronomisten – eine Zukunftsvision?', *ThZ* 48 (1992), pp. 343–55.

[55] Cf. recently J. G. McConville, '1 Kings viii 46–53 and the Deuteronomic Hope', *VT* 42 (1992), pp. 67–79; E. Talstra, *Solomon's Prayer* (Kampen, 1993).

[56] Cf. H. Weippert, 'Die Ätiologie des Nordreiches und seines Königshauses (1 Reg 11:29–40)', *ZAW* 95 (1983), pp. 344–75, who unravels, probably with justification, a 'northern' redaction, favourable to Jeroboam, in xi 29–31, 37, 38b*, 40a*, with ancient Judean corrections in 34a, 35a, 36a, 40b*.   [57] Above, n. 15.

[58] Cf. Lemaire, 'Vers l'histoire'.

[59] Cf. Whybray, *Intellectual Tradition*, p. 92; P. K. McCarter, 'The Sage in the Deuteronomistic History', in Gammie and Perdue (eds.), *The Sage*, pp. 289–93, especially 290.

[60] On the links between Deut. xvii 14–17 and 1 Kings ix 26–xi 12, cf. M. Brettler, 'The Structure of 1 Kings 1–11', *JSOT* 49 (1991), pp. 87–97, especially 90–5.

Proverbs with Solomon (Prov. x 1, xxv 1) seems rather a weak base for such an undertaking.

Nevertheless, following R. B. Y. Scott,[61] two types of indication of relatively late reworking may be noted:

> On the one hand, several expressions[62] appear to date from the Persian period: 'Transeuphrates' (*'ēber hannāhār*) (1 Kings v 4 [iv 24]), 'the governors (*paḥôt*) of the country' (x 15), the use of the present participle with the verb 'to be' (*hāyâ mōšēl*, v 1 [iv 21]), and the (priestly) dating of 1 Kings vi 1;
> on the other hand, it should be noted that chapters iii–xi include several incoherences[63] or repetitions[64] in the present order of the Massoretic Text. Uncertainties in the order of the Massoretic Text seem to be reinforced by the different order of the text in the Septuagint (cf. especially LXX ii 35*a–o*, 46*a–l*,[65] v 14*a–b*, vi 1*a–d*, ix 9*a*, x 22*a–c*; see also xii 24*a–z*[66]). These differences pose in an acute form the problem of the co-existence of several early recensions of the Hebrew text in the second half of the first millennium BC. One should recognize with J. C. Trebolle Barrera that 'los cuatro o cinco siglos que median entre la redacción final de la obra histórica deuteronomística et la fijación definitiva de su texto fueron un epoca de creatividad y no de pura transmisión del texto a manos de copista'.[67]

The fact that chapters iii–xi were the object of late reworking therefore seems to be beyond dispute. Nevertheless, if 1 Kings v 1, 4, 9–14 (iv 21, 24,

---

[61] 'Solomon and the Beginnings of Wisdom in Israel' (*SVT* 3, 1955), pp. 262–79 (= Crenshaw [ed.], *Studies*, pp. 84–101); cf. also J. Gray, *I and II Kings* (London, 1972), pp. 115–17.

[62] However, the late character of the expressions mentioned by Scott ('Solomon and the Beginnings of Wisdom in Israel', pp. 268–9) but not taken up here seems very uncertain to me and, with the probable exception of x 15, does not really affect ch. x.

[63] Thus iv 20, v 1, 4, 5 (iv 21, 24, 25) seem to interrupt Solomon's administrative organization (iv 2–19, v 2–3, 6–8 [iv 22–3, 26–8]); v 9–14 (iv 29–34) interrupts the description of the economy; ix 24 looks like a gloss on ix 15, and ix 25, with its reference to sacrifices, would be more suitable towards the end of viii; x 26–8 seems to be the continuation of relations with Hiram (ix 14) which continue in x 11–12, 22. The account of the visit of the Queen of Sheba is interrupted by x 11–12; x 27 cuts into the notice about chariots (x 26, 28, 29); on these last verses, cf. D. G. Schley, '1 Kings 10:26–29: A Reconstruction', *JBL* 106 (1987), pp. 595–601.

[64] The marriage of Solomon with the daughter of Pharaoh (iii 1, vii 8*b*, ix 16, 24, xi 1); the prosperity of Judah and Israel (iv 20, v 1 [iv 21]); the domination of Transeuphrates (v 1, 4 [iv 21, 24]); the blessing of the assembly (viii 14, 55); Solomon's chariots (v 6 [iv 26], x 26, 28–9); an adversary raised up by God (xi 14, 23).

[65] Cf. D. W. Gooding, *Relics of Ancient Exegesis. A Study of the Miscellanies in 3 Reigns 2* (Cambridge, 1970); E. Tov, 'The LXX Additions (Miscellanies) in 1 Kings 2 (3 Reigns 2)', *Textus* 11 (1984), pp. 89–118.

[66] Cf. T. M. Willis, 'The Text of 1 Kings 11:43–12:3', *CBQ* 53 (1991), pp. 37–44.

[67] J. C. Trebolle Barrera, *Salomon y Jeroboam. Historia de la recension y redacción de 1 Reyes 2–12; 14* (Valencia, 1980), p. 371.

29–34)[68] especially are set on one side and if the Septuagint variants are taken into account, these late reworkings do not seem particularly to have affected the central theme of Solomon's wisdom, so that the latter appears to predate them.

We are obliged, therefore, to move back to a pre-deuteronomic redaction, all the more so as it seems to be precisely to such a redaction that xi 41 refers: 'The rest of the acts of Solomon, and all that he did, and his wisdom (*w^{e}ḥokmātô*), are they not written in the book of the acts of Solomon (*sēper dibrê š^{e}lōmōh*)?'[69]

The extent and date of the redaction of this book of the acts of Solomon have been studied by J. Liver.[70] Following the lead of S. Mowinckel,[71] he thinks that it was edited shortly after the schism of Israel from Judah and that it presented a political explanation for this event: 'The author was one of the wise men of Solomon's time from those same *ZQNYM* whose counsel Rehoboam disdained', one of the 'old men that had stood before Solomon his father while he yet lived'[72] (1 Kings xii 6), and probably one of those included in the benediction of the Queen of Sheba: 'Happy are these your servants, who stand continually before you and hear your wisdom' (1 Kings x 8). Such a member of the court, a royal counsellor, having been excluded from public life by Rehoboam, would have had the leisure, the qualities, the information[73] and the motivation to compose a presentation of Solomon's reign which would have finished with the earliest account of the revolt (*pš^c*, xii 19) of Israel by blaming it on the fact that the new king did not listen to the wise and moderating counsel[74] of the elders (xii 8).

[68] v 1, 4 (iv 21, 24) is probably to be dated to the Persian period (reference to Transeuphrates); v 9–14 (iv 29–34) seems to be more difficult to interpret and date; these verses, which are probably pre-deuteronomic (cf. Noth, 'Bewährung', p. 226), require a special study. Provisionally, see the remarks of S. Mowinckel, 'Israelite Historiography', *ASTI* 2 (1963), pp. 4–26, especially 7; Weinfeld, *Deuteronomy and the Deuteronomic School*, pp. 254–7; A. Lemaire, *Les Ecoles et la formation de la Bible dans l'ancien Israël* (Freiburg, 1981), especially pp. 78–80 and n. 325; N. Shupak, 'The "Sitz im Leben" of Proverbs in the Light of a Comparison of Biblical and Egyptian Wisdom Literature', *RB* 94 (1987), pp. 98–119, especially 117–19; B. Gosse, 'La Sagesse et l'intelligence de Salomon en 1 Rois 5, 9', *BN* 65 (1992), pp. 12–14.

[69] The Septuagint presupposes *sēper dibrê hayyāmîm*, 'the book of the annals', but this could be a case of harmonization with the conclusion of other reigns, and it is difficult to choose between these two variants.   [70] 'The Book of the Acts of Solomon'.

[71] 'Israelite Historiography', p. 7, 12–13; the pre-deuteronomic redaction of this book had already been proposed by M. Noth, *Könige I* (Neukirchen-Vluyn, 1968), pp. 175, 263; cf. also Noth, *Überlieferungsgeschichtliche Studien* (Halle, 1943), pp. 66–7 (E. tr., *The Deuteronomic History* [Sheffield, 1981], p. 57).

[72] Liver, 'The Book of the Acts of Solomon', p. 101.

[73] First-hand knowledge of administrative procedures and of the names of the chief administrators is presupposed, especially in chs. iv–v.

[74] The derivatives of *y^{c}ṣ* are attested nine times in xii 6–13. On the political significance of this counsel, cf. M. Weinfeld, 'The Counsel of the "Elders" to Rehoboam and its Implications', *Maarav* 3/1 (1982), pp. 27–53.

On this hypothesis it is intelligible that our author should have wished to underline a contrast with Rehoboam and an implicit criticism of his policy by highlighting the wisdom of his father, that is to say especially his political wisdom. Such a portrayal of Solomon's reign would have been all the more necessary because of the need to explain to the younger generation why Israel had revolted against the Davidic dynasty (*bêt dāwid*)[75] 'unto this day' (1 Kings xii 19), this latter expression marking the end of the book of the acts of Solomon.[76] Thus, just as the original account of the Succession Narrative probably stopped at the start of Solomon's reign (1 Kings ii 46), thereby justifying the new political situation, so the original account of Solomon's reign apparently stopped at the start of Rehoboam's reign and explained the reasons for the political situation which followed on from the schism.

In sum, setting aside the critical comments of the deuteronomic redactors and various later displacements and embellishments, the portrayal of Solomon's reign and of his wisdom such as appears in 1 Kings iii–xi seems generally to conform with the royal near eastern ideology of the start of the first millennium BC. This is known to us in particular from the West Semitic royal inscriptions, which sometimes already refer to the ruler's wisdom. And if this 'wisdom' was particularly emphasized by the author of the original book of the acts of Solomon, this was probably because (1) on the one hand, in contrast with David, Solomon seems never to have ventured into war[77] (1 Kings v 17–18 [3–4]; see also, perhaps, 1 Kings iii 7[78]); and (2) on the other hand and most importantly, this highlighting of Solomon's political wisdom was intended as an implicit criticism of Rehoboam's pretentious attitude at the Shechem assembly which, by refusing to follow the advice of his father's counsellors, was the primary cause of the revolt of Israel against the house of David.

[75] This syntagm appears on the fragment of an Aramaic stele from Tel Dan and probably on the Mesha Stele; cf. A. Biran and J. Naveh, 'An Aramaic Stele Fragment from Tel Dan', *IEJ* 43 (1993), pp. 81–98; A. Lemaire, 'La Dynastie davidique (*byt dwd*) dans deux inscriptions ouest-sémitiques du IXe s. av. J.-C.', *SEL* 11 (1994), pp. 17–19, and 'Epigraphie palestinienne: nouveaux documents I. Fragment de stèle araméenne de Tell Dan (IXe s. av. J.-C.)', *Henoch* 16 (1994), pp. 87–93.

[76] Cf. the comments of I. Plein, 'Erwägungen zur Überlieferung von I Reg 11$_{26}$–14$_{20}$', *ZAW* 78 (1966), pp. 8–24, especially 8–13; E. Lipiński, 'Le Récit de 1 Rois xii 1–19 à la lumière de l'ancien usage de l'hébreu et de nouveaux textes de Mari', *VT* 24 (1974), pp. 430–7, especially 436–7.

[77] Not even the creation of the kingdom of Damascus (1 Kings xi 14–25; cf. A. Lemaire, 'Les Premiers Rois araméens dans la tradition biblique', to appear in J. B. Humbert [ed.], *Les Araméens et la Bible* [Paris, forthcoming]) seems to have provoked a military reaction by Solomon.

[78] Cf. A. van der Lingen, '*bw'–yṣ*' ("To go out and to come in") as a military term', *VT* 42 (1992), pp. 59–66, especially 65–6.

Even though the socio-professional group of scribes/sages experienced important changes in Hezekiah's reign, it is probable that it existed as early as the time of the united monarchy and that it is to one of Solomon's royal counsellors that we owe the original account of his reign with its focus on wisdom.

9   Amos and wisdom

J. A. Soggin

At the end of the 1940s Johannes Fichtner published an important, pioneering study on 'Isaiah among the Wise'.[1] He argued mainly that wisdom in Israel was not, as had often been suggested, a purely post-exilic phenomenon, but that there were considerable traces of its existence in the writings of the eighth-century prophet Isaiah. He dismissed the possibility, however, that traces of wisdom could also be found in the other prophets of that century: Hosea, Amos and Micah; wherever such traces are allegedly found, one is dealing with later additions. It is interesting that, according to Fichtner, Isaiah mostly took a strong stand against the sages.

In the present chapter, which I wish to dedicate to one who is not only a colleague but also a friend, I intend to check on the assertion that there is no wisdom to be found in Amos.

First of all, this statement has not met with general approval. Terrien[2] and Crenshaw[3] have each written an essay dedicated to the subject, and the matter is further referred to explicitly in the commentaries of Wolff,[4] Mays,[5] Rudolph,[6] van Leeuwen,[7] and Paul,[8] as well as in my own.[9] Wolff[10] considers any 'admonition speech' (*Mahnrede*) to be derived from wisdom, a thesis which Rudolph rightly criticizes (see also van Leeuwen); the same is

[1] J. Fichtner, 'Jesaja unter den Weisen', *ThLZ* 74 (1949), cols. 75–80 (E. tr., 'Isaiah among the Wise', in J. L. Crenshaw [ed.], *Studies in Ancient Israelite Wisdom* [New York, 1976], pp. 429–38).

[2] S. Terrien, 'Amos and Wisdom', in B. W. Anderson and W. Harrelson (eds.), *Israel's Prophetic Heritage. Essays in Honor of James Muilenburg* (New York, 1962), pp. 108–15 (Crenshaw [ed.], *Studies*, pp. 448–55).

[3] J. L. Crenshaw, 'The Influence of the Wise upon Amos', *ZAW* 79 (1967), pp. 42–52; see also his *Old Testament Wisdom – An Introduction* (Louisville, 1981; London, 1982).

[4] H. W. Wolff, *Dodekapropheton 2: Joel und Amos* (Neukirchen-Vluyn, 1969) (E. tr., *Joel and Amos* [Philadelphia, 1977]).

[5] J. L. Mays, *Amos: A Commentary* (Philadelphia and London, 1969).

[6] W. Rudolph, *Joel, Amos, Obadja, Jona* (Gütersloh, 1971).

[7] C. van Leeuwen, *Amos* (Nijkerk, 1985).

[8] S. M. Paul, *Amos* (Minneapolis, 1991).

[9] J. A. Soggin, *The Prophet Amos* (Philadelphia and London, 1987).

[10] H. W. Wolff, *Amos' geistige Heimat* (Neukirchen-Vluyn, 1964), pp. 24–30 (E. tr., *Amos the Prophet: The Man and His Background* [Philadelphia, 1973], pp. 44–53).

true of the use of *hôy* in invectives, a proposal which is obviously untenable. In another article, Lindblom[11] accepts that there are analogies of style between the writings of the wise men and the prophets, even though none of the latter belonged to a wisdom school. Finally, Schmid[12] is right, in my opinion, to reject such formulae as 'ancient kin (or tribal) wisdom' (*Sippenweisheit*) and 'ancient covenant law' (*Bundesrecht*), which were frequently used in those years. He suggests instead that Amos and his contemporaries used the language which was common to the culture of the time. Indeed, McKane[13] maintains that, if anything, the prophets adopted a polemical stance over against the wise. It is therefore clear that scholarship is divided over the issue, a situation which justifies a fresh examination.

At the beginning of the present century a relatively simple argument was used to explain certain affinities with wisdom language in parts of the prophetical writings: wisdom was considered post-exilic, but it had been influenced by the language of the pre-exilic prophets.[14] Fichtner, however, protested against this assertion: while it is obvious, he maintained, that Israelite wisdom developed mostly in post-exilic times, there can hardly be any doubt that some elements of it must have existed already in pre-exilic times, as the book of Isaiah shows. And little wonder, I should like to add: ancient oriental wisdom is attested as early as Sumerian times and flourished in Mesopotamia, in Egypt[15] and in Syria (Ahiqar), and there is no reason why Israel and Judah should have been the only exceptions in the region.[16]

So far as I can see, one consideration has not been sufficiently borne in mind. A biblical author (or any author, for that matter) writes in his own style, and uses particular devices for expressing himself. In our case, these could incidentally have been borrowed from wisdom. But such a stylistic analogy does not turn a writing into a text dependent upon wisdom. Let me give a few examples, mostly taken from the essay by Terrien, whose translations I also quote.

An obvious case for some authors has been that of 'consecutive numerals ... used in pairs', as Terrien calls it (pp. 109–10), or of 'climactic parallelism', as it is often called elsewhere,[17] such as appears in the oracles

---

[11] J. Lindblom, 'Wisdom in the Old Testament Prophets', in *Wisdom in Israel and in the Ancient Near East (SVT 3, 1955)*, pp. 192–204.

[12] H. H. Schmid, 'Amos. Zur Frage nach der "Geistigen Heimat" des Propheten', *WuD* NF 10 (1969), pp. 85–103.

[13] W. McKane, *Prophets and Wise Men* (London, 1965), pp. 113ff.

[14] See, for instance, W. R. Harper, *A Critical and Exegetical Commentary on Amos and Hosea* (Edinburgh, 1910), p. cxxxvii.

[15] See the impressive display of parallels *apud* Paul, *Amos*.

[16] See Terrien, 'Amos and Wisdom', p. 109, nn. 3–4, for literature.

[17] See G. Sauer, *Die Sprüche Agurs* (Stuttgart, 1963), for the use of this device in wisdom.

against the nations (Amos i 3–ii 6). Wolff adopts a similar position.[18] As I
have noted in my commentary (pp. 15 and 31ff.), however, we are not here
dealing with an element borrowed from wisdom texts at all, but rather with
some kind of invective, maybe curses, which is expressed by means of a
rhetorical device which is used also, though not exclusively, in wisdom.
This applies to each of these texts, quite independently of the question of
the authenticity of any single one of them. 'The three transgressions of...,
yea, even four' are not individually listed in Amos, which is what normally
happens in wisdom texts. This is why I suggested in my commentary (p. 32)
that one ought to translate 'For the innumerable crimes of...' The
numerical formula is, incidentally, already well known from Ugarit; see,
for instance, *KTU* 1.17.II.26–46 (especially 32–46), a text which has
nothing to do with wisdom. Wisdom used the formula because of its
mnemotechnic and paedagogical value, as the wisdom texts cited by
Terrien show. In them the reader is confronted with real lists of items,
whereas in Amos he is not, as rightly noted by Mays. In Amos, it is just a
manner of speech.

Another example advanced by Terrien (pp. 110–11) is Amos ix 1–6, the
fifth vision (or, perhaps better, symbolic act[19]). According to him, only in
wisdom literature and in Ps. cxxxix 7–8 is it explicitly stated that Yahweh
has access to *šᵉʾôl*, a place normally considered out of his reach; the phrase
in Amos therefore represents something peculiar to wisdom.[20] (An
alternative approach is that of Whybray,[21] who says that other, non-wisdom,
texts imply the sovereignty of God over *šᵉʾôl*.) But does Ps. cxxxix say
exactly this, so justifying these assertions?[22] As far as I can see, it is again a
hyperbolic, rhetorical statement, typical of court language, like the phrases
which appear in the el-Amarna letter no. 264, lines 15ff., and the other
oriental texts listed by Mays, so that it should not be taken at face value. It
is therefore something of a negative parallel to Ps. cxxxix, as I suggested in
my commentary, p. 123.

Terrien, pp. 111–12, quotes a third text, iii 3–8, where 'the prophet uses
the didactic method of appealing to common sense'.[23] He readily concedes
that 'the use of the interrogative maxim is so widespread in the Old

[18] Wolff, *Amos geistige Heimat*, and *Joel und Amos*, pp. 167–8 (E. tr., p. 138).
[19] Cf. H. Graf Reventlow, *Das Amt des Propheten bei Amos* (Göttingen, 1962), pp. 49–50.
[20] See also Rudolph, *Joel, Amos, Obadja, Jona*, and Crenshaw, *Introduction*, p. 40.
[21] R. N. Whybray, 'Prophecy and Wisdom', in R. Coggins, A. Phillips and M. Knibb (eds.),
Israel's Prophetic Tradition. Essays in Honour of Peter Ackroyd (Cambridge, 1982),
pp. 181–99 (especially 188–90).
[22] For the problem, see W. Eichrodt, *Theologie des Alten Testament*, II–III (4th edn,
Göttingen, 1961), pp. 143–5 (E. tr., *Theology of the Old Testament*, 2 [London, 1967],
pp. 221–3).
[23] Similarly K. Koch *et al.*, *Amos – Untersucht mit den Methoden einer strukturalen
Formgeschichte* (3 vols., Kevelaer and Neukirchen-Vluyn, 1976).

Testament in general that it cannot be presented as an argument tending to show points of contact between the wise men and Amos', but he adds that the whole 'is strongly reminiscent of the teaching method of the wise'.[24] This is probably the closest Amos comes to wisdom and its disputation sayings. But again, it seems to be more a matter of style than of content: the questions are rhetorical because the answers are a foregone conclusion. As I suggested in my commentary, 'in this case the prophet has followed a tactic which we have already been able to note on other occasions. First of all he leads the people to agree to certain obvious truths by means of instinctive categories, for the most part inaccessible to logic; then finally he presents the final thesis of his speech' (p. 59). Similar tactics are used by Nathan (2 Sam. xii 1–12) and Isaiah (Isa. v 1–7). Since, incidentally, the prophets were also teachers, it seems unnecessary to postulate wisdom influence; one is dealing with a regular form of prophetic speech.

As the climax of this same poetic sequence on prophetic authority (Terrien, p. 112), Amos makes the statement of verse 7. The use of the word *sôd*, '(intimate) secret', belongs to wisdom literature (but also, I should add, to apocalyptic and the writings of Qumran), and this was recognized by the ancient translators: LXX παιδείαν, Aquila ἀπόρρητον, Theodotion βουλήν, Vulgate *secretum*. There is therefore an element of truth in this, but later studies[25] have demonstrated the probability that the verse is a deuteronomic insert – and this is not the place to examine the relation between Deuteronomy and the deuteronomistic school on the one hand and wisdom on the other.

At iii 10 Israel is accused of 'not knowing to do what is right' (*n^ekôhâ*);[26] further, in vv. 9–12 several expressions occur which are typical of wisdom style, such as the fixed pairs *'ôṣār – m^ehûmâ* and *da'at – n^ekōhîm*. But the context is not so much that of wisdom teaching as that of a special form of prophetic invective which uses the imagery and terminology of a trial in court.

In the indictment of Edom (cf. Terrien, p. 113), Amos states, 'And his anger did tear as a prey continually' (i 11), and in some wisdom texts the same idiom, *'ap + ṭārap*, appears (cf. Job xvi 9 and xviii 4). The text is not certain, however, and the majority of commentators propose reading *wayyiṭṭōr*, with the Vulgate and Syriac. Nevertheless, the problem here still seems to me to be one of method: if a wisdom text and a non-wisdom text use the same idiom, does it automatically follow that the latter has been influenced by wisdom?

[24] Similar points are made by Wolff, *Dodekapropheton 2*, Mays, *Amos: A Commentary*, Rudolph, *Joel, Amos, Obadja, Jona*, Koch *et al.*, *Amos*, and by S. Amsler, *Amos* (2nd edn, Geneva, 1982).

[25] S. Lehming, 'Erwägungen zu Amos', *ZThK* 35 (1958), pp. 145–69; W. H. Schmidt, 'Die deuteronomistische Redaktion des Amosbuches', *ZAW* 77 (1965), pp. 168–93.

[26] Cf. Terrien, 'Amos and Wisdom', pp. 112–13, and Wolff, *Dodekapropheton 2*.

Amos v 13, generally recognized as a late gloss, uses the term *maśkíl*, which belongs to the language of wisdom and apocalyptic; its later dating excludes it from our examination, however.

The facts that Amos twice uses the appellation 'Isaac' for Israel (vii 9, 16) and that he mentions Beersheba (v 5, viii 14), a cult centre which was connected with this patriarch and which was also used by the Edomites (but when?), reminds Terrien of 'the reputation of Edom for wisdom' (pp. 113–14). But the conclusion which he draws here is far-fetched.

Another element is proposed by Crenshaw: the doxologies of Amos (iv 13, v 8–9, ix 5–6; cf. viii 8) remind him of the same literary genre in Job v 9–16, ix 5–10, and at the end of the book.[27] All these passages in Amos have special problems of their own, however, beginning with the transmission of the text, which is often corrupt and therefore unclear. The further question arises whether the texts can be associated with Amos as his own, whether both Amos and Job are quoting from separate sources,[28] or whether, as has often been maintained, they are later additions to the work of Amos.[29]

Following Fichtner's seminal article, the problem of alleged wisdom influence on the pre-exilic prophets thus needs to be examined afresh. (This could be an excellent subject for a doctoral thesis.) As far as I can see, there are the following possibilities (not always mutually exclusive):

The prophets have been influenced in their phraseology, speeches and style by an ancient phase of Israelite and/or Judaean wisdom of which, however, little or nothing is known.

The prophets use stylistic devices which also belonged to wisdom literature.

The prophets are influenced by, or even quote, wisdom texts.

The texts in question are later, redactional additions to the prophetic books.

In all these cases the greatest caution should be exercised so that far-reaching conclusions are not drawn from materials which are still highly uncertain.

[27] Crenshaw, 'Influence', and *Introduction*, p. 122.
[28] So R. E. Clements, *Prophecy and Tradition* (Oxford, 1975), p. 78.
[29] See Mays, *Amos: A Commentary*, pp. 83–4; Crenshaw, 'Influence'; and cf. W. Berg, *Die sogenannten Hymnenfragmente im Amosbuch* (Bern and Frankfurt a.M., 1974), for details.

10 Hosea and the wisdom tradition: dependence and independence

A. A. Macintosh

It has long been supposed that the epilogue or last verse of the book of Hosea (xiv 10 [9]), replete with the language of the wisdom literature, was added later to Hosea's collected prophecies ('Whosoever is wise, let him understand *these matters*') in order to suggest to the reader the lesson that should be drawn from them.[1] More recently, a number of scholars[2] have drawn attention to the judicious choice of words in the didactic propositions which answer the (implied) catechetical question at the beginning of the verse. The proposition that 'the ways of Yahweh are straight and just men walk in them, while transgressors stumble on them' contains both the vocabulary and the antithetic structure which typifies the wisdom tradition. Yet the writer seems to have picked up particular words from the text of Hosea's prophecies: thus, 'stumble' (iv 5, v 5, xiv 2) and 'transgress' (vii 13, viii 1); even wisdom and understanding, which characterize the opening formula ('Whosoever is wise, let him understand these matters, whoever discriminating, let him take note of them'), form part of Hosea's own lexical stock (e.g. xiii 13, iv 14). Accordingly, what is clearly contrived in xiv 10 (9) is nonetheless carefully and sensitively contrived; its thought is essentially continuous with the material which it seeks to elucidate.

Recognition of the clear continuity between the epilogue, indubitably cast in the mould of a wisdom saying, and elements in the actual prophecies of Hosea raises the questions to what extent the prophet knew of the traditions of (early) wisdom, and what use he may have made of them.

A number of somewhat dogmatic answers have been given to the first of these questions. Thus, H. W. Wolff[3] finds in the proverb of viii 7 ('sowing

---

[1] The English translations of Hosea's words are my own and are taken from my forthcoming commentary in the ICC series. Translations of other biblical texts are taken from the NEB.

[2] E.g. G. T. Sheppard, *Wisdom as a Hermeneutical Construct* (Berlin and New York, 1980), pp. 129–36; C. L. Seow, 'Hosea 14:10 and the Foolish People Motif', *CBQ* 44 (1982), pp. 212–24; R. P. Gordon, reviewing Sheppard, *VT 32* (1982), p. 376.

[3] *Dodekapropheton*, 1: *Hosea* (Neukirchen-Vluyn, 1961), pp. xv–xvi (E. tr., *Hosea* [Philadelphia, 1974], p. xxiv).

the wind and reaping the whirlwind'), in the prophet's perceptions of the working of nature in ii 23–4 (21–2), as well as in his numerous similes and metaphors, clear evidence of the influence of wisdom upon Hosea's language. Earlier W. R. Harper[4] had noted laconically that 'Hosea is full of wisdom-thought'. Most thoroughgoing, perhaps, is G. Fohrer's conclusion that, because the prophecy contains so many elements of wisdom, Hosea 'was educated at a wisdom school which served primarily for the training of royal officials'.[5] More plausible are the approaches of Fichtner, Lindblom and Crenshaw;[6] for them, while there remains disagreement concerning the mode of the influence of wisdom upon the pre-exilic prophets, there can be no doubting their acquaintance with the popular sayings of the wise.

If such views are more plausible, they accord well with R. N. Whybray's[7] timely warning to the effect that wisdom has become a 'slippery word', debased by the tendency of modern scholarship to include more and more biblical material within its parameters. Whybray rightly stresses S. R. Driver's[8] definition of wisdom as the work of writers who 'applied themselves ... to the observation of human character as such, seeking to analyse conduct, studying action in its consequences and establishing morality upon the basis of principles common to humanity at large'. Yet if Proverbs, Job and Ecclesiastes alone fit this description in a strict sense and are properly styled 'wisdom literature', that is not to deny that other pieces of literature in the Old Testament share these concerns or that, preoccupied with other main themes, nonetheless they share something of such concerns (so essentially Whybray).

It is the contention of this essay that the prophet Hosea was much concerned with the preoccupations listed by Driver. He was greatly interested in the connection between thought and action and, above all, was convinced that wrong perceptions of reality, of the way things were, would lead inevitably to the demise and ruin of his people and nation. Yet this interest is harnessed to the particular endeavour to which, as a prophet, he was called. That endeavour was directed *more prophetarum* to the interpretation of the brute facts of contemporary history, to contemplation of the lessons of the past, and to the formulation of prayers *de profundis* for the restoration of an Israel whose false perceptions had been purged by the recognition of the truth.

[4] *A Critical and Exegetical Commentary on Amos and Hosea* (Edinburgh, 1905), p. 378.
[5] E. Sellin and G. Fohrer, *Einleitung in das Alte Testament* (10th edn, Heidelberg, 1965), p. 460 (E. tr., *Introduction to the Old Testament* [London, 1970], p. 419).
[6] J. Fichtner, 'Jesaja unter den Weisen', *TLZ* 74 (1949), cols. 75–80; cf. J. Lindblom, 'Wisdom in the Old Testament Prophets', in *Wisdom in Israel and in the Ancient Near East* (*SVT* 3, 1955), pp. 192–204; J. L. Crenshaw, 'The influence of the Wise upon Amos', *ZAW* 79 (1967), pp. 42–51.   [7] 'Slippery Words IV. Wisdom', *ET* 89 (1977–8), p. 361.
[8] *An Introduction to the Literature of the Old Testament* (9th edn, Edinburgh, 1913), p. 393.

It was, of course, supremely in the sphere of religion that false perceptions were entertained by Ephraim. The contemporary cult, licentious and self-indulgent, was a clear indication of a people whose minds were given over to the promiscuous admiration of values inconsistent with the God who, in the Exodus, had brought them into being. Hosea's indictment of these false perceptions is effected by the quintessentially *prophetic* device of the parable;[9] thus, he likens Ephraim's attitude and perception to that of an unfaithful wife whose adulteries and even her pragmatic contemplation of reform can readily be rationalized in terms of enlightened self-interest (e.g. ii 9, 11 [7, 9]). Yet the prophet, in contemplating particular aspects of the Ephraimites' cultic promiscuity, also uses words and concepts which are palpably derived from the vocabulary of the (early) wisdom tradition. Thus, iv 15 contains the judgement that 'a people without discrimination shall stumble in confusion'. Discrimination, or the lack of it ($\sqrt{}$ *byn*), is a commonplace in Proverbs; the verb 'shall stumble in confusion' ($\sqrt{}$ *lbṭ*)[10] is found elsewhere only in the book of Proverbs (x 8, 10). It seems likely that Hosea's use of these words is free, unfettered by the need to conform to the tradition whence they came. Thus to predicate the saying of 'a people' (i.e. *his* people, the indefinite so poignantly definite[11]) rather than of the individual foolish talker (as in Proverbs) appears to reflect predominantly Hosea's prophetic endeavour.[12]

Similar freedom may be detected in the treatment of wisdom concepts in the saying of xiii 13. Here the context is Yahweh's proclamation of the imminent and terrible demise of Ephraim, whose guilt in respect of her wilful and capricious addiction to palace intrigues and bloodthirsty coups, indelibly recorded, was securely stored in the heart of her God (cf. ibn Ezra on verse 12). The verse, with its reference to Ephraim as an 'unwise son' (*bēn lōʾ ḥākām*), clearly reflects the language of wisdom (e.g. Prov. x 1, xiii 1, xv 20; and cf. 1 Kings v 21 [7]; 2 Chron. ii 11) where the positive expression indicates an astute, teachable young man adapted to a successful and harmonious life. In view of the explicit nature of the reference to the wisdom tradition, the verse is subjected to a full investigation. The text runs:

---

[9] Cf., e.g., Isa. v 1–7. *mšl* 'parable' (i.e. in the prophetic tradition, as opposed to the 'proverb' of the wisdom tradition) is styled by *BDB* as 'a prophetic, figurative discourse'. For its likely origins in 'mocking songs', see O. Eissfeldt, *Einleitung in das Alte Testament* (3rd edn, Tübingen, 1964), pp. 88–9, 123–6 (E. tr., *The Old Testament. An Introduction* [Oxford, 1965], pp. 66, 92–4).

[10] Ibn Janāḥ compares the Arabic cognate verb with meanings: I 'throw to the ground', and VIII 'tumble to the ground', expressions (so he says) which convey 'dire lameness'. For ibn Ezra, too, the Arabic cognate suggests the meaning 'like a man immobilized, who does not know what to do'. S. Morag's view (*lšʾlt yyḥwd lšwnw šl hwšʿ*, *Tarbiẓ* 53 [1984], pp. 504–5) that the verb means 'are inflamed with passion', though it fits the context of the verse in Hosea admirably, does so less well in the verses from Proverbs.   [11] *GK* 125c.

[12] Cf. and contrast Seow's detection of a 'foolish people' motif in the prophecies of Hosea (*CBQ* 44 [1982], pp. 212–24); he appears to suppose that the motif arises naturally from the stuff of the wisdom concepts themselves.

ḥbly ywldh yb'w lw hw' bn l' ḥkm ky 't l' y'md bmšbr bnym
Labour pains come upon him. He is not a wise son. When the time comes he will
have no success in giving birth.

The translation and interpretation here set forth owe much to the
treatment of it by A. B. Ehrlich.[13] The following considerations are
important: first, the verse is predicated of the masculine Ephraim and not of
a woman in labour; for she is the vehicle and not the tenor of the
comparison. Other instances where males are described as in a dire
situation, comparable to that of a woman in childbirth, are Isa. xxxvii 3 and
Jer. xxx 6; in both cases the image is clearly used because it is inherently
surprising to the ear of the hearer and consequently powerful in its effect.
Secondly, the term *mšbr bnym* denotes not the 'breach of the womb' (*contra*
Kimchi) but rather the final stage, following labour pains, of giving birth.
In this connection it is convenient to note that Rashi (cf. Targ. and ibn
Janāḥ) defines the term as the place of delivery (ibn Janāḥ), the *sella
parturiensis* (Rashi). Consequently the phrase in this particular context has
virtually a temporal sense (so, explicitly, ibn Janāḥ) and denotes the last
stages of giving birth.

A number of commentators have supposed that the verse reflects a
popular understanding of unsuccessful labour. Thus, the 'son who is not
wise/clever' refers to the foetus who does not present himself to the breach
of the womb at the proper time. As Ehrlich observes, however, there is the
consequent difficulty that in a single verse the vehicle of the comparison
changes from the woman in labour to the foetus. Counter-arguments to the
effect that *lw* denotes not that labour pains come *upon* Ephraim but rather
have come *in respect of him* (i.e. as the foetus of the simile) smack of special
pleading. Reference to Isa. xxxvii 3 makes plain that the metaphor is that of
the fruitless and terrible pains of unsuccessful labour and that it is here
applied to the nation, Ephraim.

The verb *y'md* (√ *'md*) is invested by commentators with a number of
meanings all of which depend, to some extent at least, upon the view taken
of the phrase as a whole (e.g., when interpreted of the foetus, 'he will not
present himself'). On the view adopted here it seems right to assume for it
the well-attested meanings 'abide, endure, persist'.[14] Thus Ephraim,
tormented as if by labour pains, will not endure or survive to the point
when giving birth would normally afford relief (cf., again, Isa. xxxvii 3).
Hence the point of the statement is that the persistent torment is a prelude
only to doom and failure (cf. Isa. xxvi 17–18).

This treatment of the verse, though dependent on Ehrlich's main

[13] *Mikrâ ki-Pheschutô*, 3 (Berlin, 1901; republished, New York, 1969), pp. 391–2; cf.
Randglossen zur hebräischen Bibel (Leipzig, 1912), p. 209, where, though he arrives at a
similar conclusion, his treatment of the text is more radical.
[14] *BDB*, p. 764, col. 1, sections 3 c, d, f, and 4.

contention, nevertheless differs from it. Ehrlich connects the final phrase more closely with that which precedes it and suggests that Ephraim is not a wise/clever son since otherwise he would not remain so long in a situation like that of a woman in the last phase of labour. The difficulty is that *ky* is not elsewhere attested with the sense 'since otherwise'.

Turning now to the general sense of the verse, it may be suggested that the terrible consequences of the indelible record of the nation's guilt are expressed by the powerful metaphor of a woman in labour, racked with excruciating pain, whose endeavours are doomed to failure. The sense conveyed is precisely contrary to that expressed in John xvi 21 (cf. Isa. lxvi 7–9) where, in successful birth, the pain is replaced by joy for that 'a man is born into the world'. Elsewhere, it should be noted, it is the prophets and not the authors of wisdom literature – and not even Job – who make use of this figure of speech (cf. Mic. iv 9–10; Isa. xxvi 17–18[15]). Here, explicitly, the utter depths of Ephraim's suffering will be manifested in its unproductive failure.

If the vehicle of the metaphor is the notion of labour pains doomed to failure, the tenor (viz. Ephraim) is further defined by a parenthetical sentence: 'he is not a wise son'. As has been said, the words are derived from the very core of the old wisdom tradition and, in the way of a formal contrast with it (negative for positive), suggest that Ephraim is unteachable (cf. Kimchi), insensitive to moral concerns and ill-equipped for success (cf., with Jerome, vii 11). Yet the words allow of a further interpretation. For, at the beginning, when Yahweh loved his young son, he sought to lead him forth (from Egypt) with 'bonds of friendship' (so, as I suppose, *ḥbly 'dm*, xi 4). Here, with a reference in word-play to that saying, the nation is to be oppressed with labour pains (*ḥbly ywldh*). Accordingly, the use of the word 'son' forms a connection between the nation perceived initially as the object of Yahweh's love (xi 1–4) and the nation, at its end, as the object of his fury. It is this son, on whom was set so much affection, who now, through his folly and immorality, is doomed, like a wretched woman, not to survive to the time of successful delivery, to the *mšbr bnym*, the birth of sons. Thus the theme and counter-theme, the tenor and the vehicle of the comparison, are woven together by Hosea with extraordinary skill. The tenor is defined in concepts drawn from the wisdom tradition; the vehicle is of a sort with the dire warnings of the prophetic tradition. The whole serves well to articulate an urgent prophetic judgement.

The use of the term *ḥkm* ('wise') to denote technical skill as well as sagacity in the field of ethics and morality is well attested; indeed the latter concept

[15] The argument of this paper is not affected by J. Day's contention ('A Case of Inner Scriptural Interpretation', *JTS* ns 31 [1980], pp. 309–19) that Isaiah is here dependent on Hosea.

has been thought to have had its origins in the former.[16] At all events, texts such as Jer. x 9, Isa. xl 20, Exod. xxxi 6 (craftsmanship in manufacturing), and Ezek. xxvii 8 (seamanship) unequivocally speak of wisdom ($\sqrt{}$ ḥkm). In the writings of Hosea the natural world and agriculture are used extensively as a rich quarry for similes and metaphors and there can be no doubt that the author was knowledgeable and even technically competent in these fields. For knowledge of fruit trees and vines, see ix 10, 13, 16, x 1, xiv 6; for the use of technical details of domestic animals, ploughing and agriculture, see iv 16, viii 7, x 4. One such verse (one of the most difficult in the book) is, I believe, indicative of Hosea's use of this technical wisdom, viz. x 10:

b'wty w'srm w'spw 'lyhm 'mym *b'srm lšty 'yntm*
It is my wish that I discipline them; and so nations will be gathered against them, *because they have bound themselves to two wicked policies.*

Here b'wty denotes (so Jerome and Rashi) 'in accordance with my good pleasure'. w'srm is understood (with the versions and rabbinic commentators) to be an imperfect form of the verb ysr.[17] The verb is well known to the book of Proverbs, where the notion of discipline (mwsr) finds an important place in its portrayal of a proper relationship between a father and his son.

It is the clause marked* *which reflects technical competence, and my understanding of it is derived from the tenth century rabbinic lexicographer ibn Janāḥ.[18] According to him the word 'wntm (sic the qᵉrê[19]) is related to the words m'nh (1 Sam. xiv 14) and m'nyt (Ps. cxxix 3) meaning 'furrow' and derived from the root 'nh II (see BDB, pp. 775–6). These nouns, he says, denote properly 'a furrow made by a ploughman around a place which he intends to plough and called lǧnt' (i.e. in Arabic). The verb 'sr is attested of the harnessing of cows to a waggon (1 Sam. vi 7) and this is its meaning here. The phrase as a whole means 'in their being harnessed to two ploughing beasts'. Although this is the apparent (Arabic ẓ'hr) meaning, the phrase in fact conveys the making of the lǧnt since that action is comprised in the more general reference to ploughing. In the context it is the nation's persistence in two wicked attitudes or policies (Arabic 'ṣr'rhm 'ly mdhbyn) that is set forth.[20]

The verse as a whole continues the argument of verse 9. That the classical

[16] E.g. G. von Rad, Theologie des Alten Testaments, 1 (Munich, 1957), pp. 415–16 (E. tr., Old Testament Theology, 1 [Edinburgh and London, 1962] p. 418).
[17] For the daghesh forte, see GK 60a, 71 and Morag, Tarbiz 53 (1984), p. 491.
[18] His Kitâb al-Usûl (ed. A. Neubauer, Oxford, 1875), written in Arabic, is a masterly forerunner of the modern lexicon. See pp. 537–8 for his views as here set out.
[19] It is possible to defend the kᵉthîb as having the same sense; the details are set out in my forthcoming commentary.
[20] Ibn Janāḥ goes on to interpret the two wicked policies/attitudes as those of Ephraim and Judah. This particular deduction is dependent upon the reference to Judah in the following verse which, in common with most modern commentators, I understand to be a later gloss.

outrage perpetrated by the Benjamites in Gibeah (Judg. xix–xxi) should evoke the response of a punitive gathering of Israel against them was a reflection of Yahweh's essential preoccupation with justice. The subsequent iniquity of Ephraim, conforming indeed to the classical outrage of Benjamin, evoked in him the same response. It was, then, his good pleasure that he should discipline them, and the contemporary gathering of hostile nations[21] matches the gathering against the Benjamites. The use of the verb *'sp* seems to reflect its use in the tradition formulated in Judg. xx 11 (cf. verse 14): 'all the Israelites to a man were massed against the town'. Thus the impending doom of Ephraim is the result of the people's persistence in the evil attitudes to which, from the time of Gibeah, they had so firmly tied themselves. In this respect they were like the ploughman with his team of oxen who, prior to ploughing a field, marked out his task with delimiting furrows. It is this which constitutes the twofold nature of the nation's perfidy. Where the vehicle of the metaphor is concerned, the agents of the ploughman's intention and of his effecting it are the twin ploughing-animals who make both the initial delimiting furrows and also the completed plough.

The connection between ploughing, intention and thought can be illuminated by the verb *ḥrš*, which means not only 'plough' but also 'devise (as one who works in, practises) usually evil but also good'[22] (cf. Prov. iii 29, vi 14, xii 20, xiv 22). This connection is brought out explicitly by another writer in the wisdom literature, viz. Job: 'This I know, that those who plough mischief and sow trouble reap as they have sown' (iv 8). Hosea, too, makes use of this same figure of speech and he does so in verses proximate to that at present under review. It should be noted that here, as in Proverbs, ploughing can define both good and evil intention:

Your sowing shall be in accordance with what is right; your reaping in accordance with goodness; give yourselves to ploughing the fallow. And then there is the season to seek Yahweh till he comes to rain down blessing for you. Wickedness is what you have ploughed; you have reaped what is wrong; you have consumed the produce of deceit. For you trusted in your policy and in the number of your warriors (x 12–13).[23]

In his sustained use of the imagery of ploughing, Hosea has undoubtedly used concepts quarried from the field of wisdom sayings and, in particular, of those sayings which reflect the unity perceived between the moral order and the successful practice of technical agricultural expertise. It has been argued that such sayings reflect the accommodation of Yahwism to the agricultural ideas of Canaanite belief; thus, Yahwism 'had not basically

---

[21] Notably, Assyria. If the plural 'nations' is significant, then cf. 2 Kings xvii 24 for various nationals serving in the Assyrian army.   [22] *BDB*, p. 360, col. 2, sections 2 and 3.
[23] The verb *ḥrš* also occurs in verse 11; but what is there conveyed (Ephraim's vocation), though connected with the content of the verses here reproduced, nonetheless differs from it.

any special relationship to the arable land, the productive soil (*'dmh* in contrast to the nomadic steppe, Jer. ii 2)'. 'The ancients ... felt awe at the chthonic mystery: to plough the earth was a hazardous exercise ... requiring revelation and instruction by the deity.'[24] Certainly Hosea was at pains, confronting the wrong perceptions of his contemporaries, to emphasize that the productivity of the land was exclusively under the control of Yahweh (ch. ii, especially verses 23–25). And another prophet, this time in Judah, makes use of technical agricultural expertise in order to convey his sense of wonder at the continuity of revelation here and in the sphere of ethics and morality (Isa. xxviii 23–9). Its source is explicitly 'the Lord of Hosts, whose purposes are wonderful and his power great' (xxviii 29).

If in x 10 Hosea makes use of material derived from the wisdom tradition, he does so in order to show that evil actions are derived from evil attitudes. But he does not restrict himself *more sapientium* to a heuristic maxim of the sort found in Prov. xii 20, 'Those who plot ($\sqrt{hr\check{s}}$) evil delude themselves, but there is joy for those who seek ($\sqrt{y^\prime\varsigma}$) the common good.' His particular prophetic concern is to apply the principle to the realities of the contemporary situation which, in turn and simultaneously, are illuminated by reference to events in Israel's past. There, too, evil actions had followed evil attitudes: 'Israel, you have sinned from the time of Gibeah. It is there that they adopted their attitude' (x 9).

The moral consistency of Israel's God would seem to dictate that his punishment was inevitable now exactly as then. Yet Hosea is always alive to the possibility of repentance, and x 12, quoted above, gives expression to his prayer that Ephraim would dare to plough a new furrow of good intention.

In all this Hosea is his own man. If he knows the motifs of the wisdom tradition, he makes use of them, as he does of elements from other traditions, to forge a new theme, his own theme. His prophetic endeavour reflects the unity of thought which cannot but be attributed to an author of wide knowledge and consummate artistry. That, for example, forms of speech whose *Sitz im Leben* is the law court also occur in his prophecies is highly probable. On the other hand, the wholesale commitment of a large number of Hosea's sayings to varied and complex forensic categories (typical of Wolff's commentary) suggests over-interpretation. There is no need to suppose that Hosea was unable to communicate other than in clichés, and the supposition that he should have done so is, in view of the rich texture of his craft, most unlikely.

Hosea's use of words and themes from the wisdom tradition is

---

[24] G. von Rad, *Theologie*, p. 34 (E. tr., p. 25).

characterized by similar independence of thought. They are but one element woven into the texture of his prophecy. They are not merely introduced and repeated as if from an authoritative source; they are modified and transformed to find their place within a particular revelation of the eighth century BC which had its own urgent and immediate authority. It was the 'word of the Lord which came to Hosea, the son of Beeri' (i 1). It came to him whose bones have, for so long, sent forth new life from the ground where they lie (cf. Ecclus xlix 10).

11   Isaiah and the wise

H. G. M. Williamson

In discussions of the connections between wisdom and the prophets it is usually Isaiah who has attracted most attention. Although chs. xl–lv have frequently been studied from this point of view,[1] the present chapter will focus on Isaiah of Jerusalem, for it is here, with Fichtner's work, that this whole movement in scholarship is generally held to have begun, and it is around this figure that many of the questions of method have been raised. I shall first survey some of the principal contributions to this discussion before moving on to offer some more general reflections.

1   Survey of research

Fichtner's brief but programmatic article[2] notes that Isaiah is sharply critical of 'the wise', whom he identifies with Judah's politicians (e.g. iii 1–3, v 21, xxx 1–5, xxxi 1–3), that a number of his sayings are reminiscent of what we find in the book of Proverbs (e.g. compare v 21 with Prov. xxvi 5, 12, 16, xxviii 11, and xxix 13 with Prov. xxvi 23), and that his portrayal of the future ideal ruler in ix 5–6 and xi 2 includes features which are extolled in the wisdom writings. From these observations he suggests that Isaiah originally belonged to the class of the wise but that he turned against his background at the time of his call because wisdom had become divorced from its divine origins (cf. vi 9–10), though he nevertheless retained the hope that eventually a ruler would be raised up who would restore the original ideal.[3]

---

[1] For a survey, cf. D. F. Morgan, *Wisdom in the Old Testament Traditions* (Oxford, 1981), pp. 114–19.

[2] J. Fichtner, 'Jesaja unter den Weisen', *ThLZ* 74 (1949), cols. 75–80, reprinted in *Gottes Weisheit. Gesammelte Studien zum Alten Testament* (Stuttgart, 1965), pp. 18–26 (E. tr., 'Isaiah among the Wise', in J. L. Crenshaw [ed.], *Studies in Ancient Israelite Wisdom* [New York, 1976], pp. 429–38).

[3] Cf. R. T. Anderson, 'Was Isaiah a Scribe?', *JBL* 79 (1960), pp. 57–8; R. Martin-Achard, 'Sagesse de Dieu et sagesse humaine chez Ésaïe', in *maqqél shâqéd: Hommage Wilhelm Vischer* (Montpellier, 1960), pp. 137–44; and J. Becker, *Isaias – der Prophet und sein Buch* (Stuttgart, 1968), pp. 17–18.

Taking Fichtner's article as his starting point, Whedbee[4] seeks to extend and refine his analysis. Despite some later criticisms of his work, Whedbee is well aware that the mere use of certain speech forms, such as parables or proverbs, is not sufficient to establish wisdom influence on Isaiah; indeed, he criticizes Fichtner on just this ground, and also rejects the suggestion that Isaiah had himself once been a professional wise man. Nevertheless, Whedbee argues that influence may be discerned when there is a coincidence of distinctively wisdom-like form and content, and this he finds in the parabolic material of i 2–3, v 1–7, and xxviii 23–8, in the proverbial sayings at x 15 and xxix 15–16, and in two of the 'summary-appraisals', as identified by Childs,[5] at xiv 26 and xxviii 29. Whedbee emphasizes as much the wisdom style of argumentation as the use of proverbial language itself. He then moves on to consider Isaiah's use of the 'woe oracles', whose background he tentatively finds in (old) wisdom, following Gerstenberger,[6] and where again the content frequently coincides with the concerns of the wisdom writers. Finally, he studies the particular term 'counsel' (*'ēṣâ*), which he thinks Isaiah appropriated from wisdom circles but filled with new content in order to oppose some of the very conclusions which they themselves drew from it.

A third study which requires mention in this context is Jensen's detailed analysis of *tôrâ* in Isaiah.[7] In general, he is sympathetic to Fichtner's and Whedbee's approach, though he raises a number of telling criticisms on matters of detail. In particular, he finds Whedbee's discussion of *'ēṣâ* unconvincing because, amongst other things, it involves ascribing to the wise the opinion that Yahweh himself was not necessarily wise (cf. Whedbee, p. 134; Jensen, p. 49). His positive proposal concerns the use of the word *tôrâ* in what he takes to be the authentically Isaianic passages i 10, ii 3, v 24, viii 16 (and 20?), and xxx 9. In each case he maintains that the meaning is 'wise instruction' and that the idea of a priestly, legal or prophetic *tôrâ* is less suitable, if not impossible. Isaiah made use of this word 'because it was a term of the wisdom tradition that he wished to appropriate for his continuing debate with wisdom circles' (p. 120), and it relates both to foreign policy and to internal social concerns.

Finally, the links between Isaiah and the wise are also positively evaluated by Wildberger in the concluding discussion of his great

[4] J. W. Whedbee, *Isaiah and Wisdom* (Nashville and New York, 1971).

[5] B. S. Childs, *Isaiah and the Assyrian Crisis* (London, 1967), pp. 128–36.

[6] Cf. E. Gerstenberger, 'The Woe-Oracles of the Prophets', *JBL* 81 (1962), pp. 249–63. It may be noted in passing that this theory has not gained wide acceptance, not least because *hôy* never once occurs in the wisdom literature; see the survey, with literature, by H.-J. Zobel, *ThWAT* 2, cols. 382–8 (E. tr., *TDOT* 3, pp. 359–64).

[7] J. Jensen, *The Use of* tôrâ *by Isaiah. His Debate with the Wisdom Tradition* (Washington, 1973).

commentary on Isaiah i–xxxix.[8] He too accepts that various words and literary forms as used in Isaiah reflect the influence of the wisdom tradition, and this conclusion is bolstered by a (negative) comparison with the other eighth-century prophets. He enters the important *caveat*, moreover, that Isaiah's polemical statements on the subject, such as xxix 14, do not imply a rejection of 'wisdom' *per se*, as Fichtner implied,[9] but arise directly out of the differing evaluations of the specific situations which are under consideration.

All the studies summarized so far have in common a confidence that we know what is meant by 'wisdom' and that it is therefore possible to draw comparisons between it and the critically reconstructed words of Isaiah. This confidence was based upon a scholarly consensus which prevailed during the middle decades of this century. It accepted, among other things, that substantial parts of the book of Proverbs were pre-exilic (this in contrast with an earlier view that they were largely post-exilic), that they were associated in large measure with the professional scribes or 'sages' of the Judean court who could to some extent be compared with their counterparts in other countries, especially Egypt, and that the influence of their work could also be seen in some of the other literature of the period, such as the Joseph story (Gen. xxxvii–1) and the Succession Narrative (2 Sam. ix–xx; 1 Kings i–ii).

This consensus, however, is no longer so widely accepted.[10] The important changes as they affect Isaiah have been well summarized by Whybray.[11] In particular, attention has become increasingly focussed on native Israelite wisdom (often referred to as 'clan wisdom' or *Sippenweisheit*) which was by no means exclusively associated with the court. This tradition was far more broadly based in social terms than 'royal wisdom'[12] and also found expression in a wider variety of literary forms. Whybray finds that the logical conclusion of this trend in research is expressed by Murphy, who concluded that wisdom was 'an approach to reality which was shared by all Israelites in varying degrees', and who continues: 'Such an understanding

[8] H. Wildberger, *Jesaja. 3. Teilband: Jesaja 28–39. Das Buch, der Prophet und seine Botschaft* (Neukirchen-Vluyn, 1982), pp. 1614–32.

[9] This approach was taken to an extreme by W. McKane, *Prophets and Wise Men* (London, 1965), but his argument that 'old wisdom' was completely secular and anthropocentric, and therefore inherently inimical to the prophetic 'word', has been widely rejected; cf. S. Weeks, *Early Israelite Wisdom* (Oxford, 1994), pp. 57–73.

[10] Cf. especially Weeks, *Early Israelite Wisdom*.

[11] R. N. Whybray, 'Prophecy and Wisdom', in R. Coggins, A. Phillips and M. Knibb (eds.), *Israel's Prophetic Heritage. Essays in Honour of Peter R. Ackroyd* (Cambridge, 1982), pp. 181–99.

[12] Cf. R. N. Whybray, 'The Social World of the Wisdom Writers', in R. E. Clements (ed.), *The World of Ancient Israel. Sociological, Anthropological and Political Perspectives* (Cambridge, 1989), pp. 227–50.

was not a mode of thinking cultivated exclusively by one class; it was shared at all levels of society that interpreted daily experience.'[13]

In the light of these considerations, Whybray maintains that studies of Isaiah and the wise tend to move 'in the realm of shadows'. While appreciative, for instance, of Whedbee's attempt to introduce method-ological rigour into the discussion, he does not find the results convincing, principally because (in the case of proverbs and parables) he does not 'really dispose of the problem of a common heritage of speech and ideas, which might account for many of these similarities but which, if designated by the term "popular wisdom", would tend to empty the word "wisdom" of any specific content' (p. 191). Several other scholars have expressed the same point of view,[14] and in this they reflect the much greater caution which now prevails as regards finding wisdom influence on parts of the Old Testament outside the wisdom literature proper.[15] Whybray also repeats his doubts as to whether there ever was a distinct professional class of 'sages' in the pre-exilic period,[16] a proposition which enables him to dispense quickly with both Fichtner's and Jensen's work and with further parts of Whedbee's. This particular point, however, has not attracted such widespread support.

Finally, brief mention should be made of the fact that in current studies of Isaiah there is a tendency on the part of some scholars to deny ever larger amounts of material to the eighth-century prophet, and this includes a number of the passages which have featured prominently in the research summarized above. Werner, for instance, has argued that Isaiah never wrote about God's 'plan', and finds that all references in his work to '$\bar{e}\bar{s}\hat{a}$ are post-exilic at the earliest.[17] Similarly, it is not uncommon to find the opinion that some of the parabolic and proverbial material, such as xxviii 23–9, is post-Isaianic. If such views could be substantiated, they would, of course, have a significant effect on 'biographical' considerations, such as the view that Isaiah himself once belonged to the class of the sages, though they would not necessarily have such a far-reaching impact on other exegetical considerations.[18] Needless to say, the matter remains highly

[13] R. E. Murphy, 'Wisdom – Theses and Hypotheses', in J. G. Gammie *et al.* (eds.), *Israelite Wisdom: Theological and Literary Essays in Honor of Samuel Terrien* (New York, 1978), pp. 35–42.

[14] E.g. R. E. Clements, *Prophecy and Tradition* (Oxford, 1975), pp. 79–82; E. W. Davies, *Prophecy and Ethics. Isaiah and the Ethical Traditions of Israel* (Sheffield, 1981), pp. 29–36.

[15] See especially the influential essay of J. L. Crenshaw, 'Method in Determining Wisdom Influence upon "Historical" Literature', *JBL* 88 (1969), pp. 129–42 (=Crenshaw [ed.], *Studies*, pp. 481–94).

[16] Cf. R. N. Whybray, *The Intellectual Tradition in the Old Testament* (Berlin, 1974).

[17] W. Werner, *Studien zur alttestamentlichen Vorstellung vom Plan Jahwes* (Berlin, 1988).

[18] For a rigorously diachronic study in this regard, cf. J. Vermeylen, 'Le Proto-Isaïe et la sagesse d'Israël', in M. Gilbert (ed.), *La Sagesse de l'Ancien Testament* (Leuven, 1979), pp. 39–58.

contentious, and it would be unwise to build a detailed case on such considerations alone.

2   The way forward

It might appear from our survey thus far that the study of Isaiah and the wise has run its course. In the first phase of research the underlying presupposition was that of two static and isolated traditions, wisdom and prophecy; they could therefore be compared and mutual influence detected. If, as more recent work has suggested, these boundaries are not so rigid, then it emerges that the process of comparison was invalid from the outset, so that there is little left to be said. Within the rules of the game as it has generally been played, this negative conclusion would seem to be justified, but the question remains, have we been playing the right game? After all, Old Testament literature is not by any means all of the same sort. There are differences, not only of form, but also of theological outlook and emphasis, among the many blocks of material, individual books and, indeed, parts of books, that remain to be accounted for, and, furthermore, these seem to criss-cross through the literature in ways that are not adequately accounted for either by the conventional distinctions between, say, wisdom and prophecy, or by the suggestion that all such distinctions are more apparent than real. There are elements of truth in both these approaches, and the need is to retain that truth without falling into the past errors of either under- or over-emphasis on classification.

An approach to our material which takes account of these considerations has been suggested by Morgan,[19] and he also emphasizes the need to remember that wisdom itself developed over the course of time. Though we do not have enough material to chart this development in the pre-exilic period, he maintains that it is probable that some influence of the prophets is also likely to be attested in the narrowly defined wisdom literature in its finished form. Though Morgan's own interests and presentation differ from those of the present chapter, his more flexible approach suggests two areas in the study of Isaiah which seem worth exploring a little further.[20]

First, there is the area of epistemology. Two points need to be distinguished here. On the one hand, there is the question how Isaiah himself 'knew' what God's will for Israel was; there are no doubt many elements which might be considered in answer to this question, but they are

[19] D. F. Morgan, 'Wisdom and the Prophets', in E. A. Livingstone (ed.), *Studia Biblica 1978.* 1. *Papers on Old Testament and Related Themes* (Sheffield, 1979), pp. 209–44; *Wisdom in the Old Testament Traditions,* especially pp. 76–83.
[20] Considerations of space preclude discussion either of the possibility of some late 'wisdom' glosses in Isa. i–xxxix (e.g. ii 22) or of the possible light which might be shed from Isaiah on the wider history of education in ancient Israel; cf. A. Lemaire, *Les Ecoles et la formation de la Bible dans l'ancien Israël* (Fribourg and Göttingen, 1981), especially pp. 37–8 and 61–5.

not our concern here. On the other hand, there is the question how Isaiah expected Israel to know God's will, a question central to determining the basis and nature of the prophet's general invective.[21] Isaiah certainly uses a variety of formulae to indicate that his announcement of the judgement which he sees coming as a consequence of Israel's sin is in some sense a word of God, so that it answers to the first point just raised (see, for instance, i 2*a*, 10*a*, 20*b*, 24*a*, etc.). At the same time, however, he clearly expects his audience to concur with the justice of his condemnations on the basis of what they themselves know (or should know) of God's will, and here, as is well known, he does not appeal, as some of the other prophets do, to their infringement of the law of Moses, nor to the fact that their behaviour was incompatible with a relationship with the God who had saved them in the past and had made them his own. Rather, their behaviour was quite simply wrong when judged by any natural standard. It does not require special revelation to know that, for instance, children owe respect to their parents (i 2*b*–3), that the perversion of justice in the courts is unacceptable (i 21–3), that oppression of the weakest in society is offensive (iii 13–15), or that drunkenness is antisocial (v 11–12). It is true that some (though not all) of these concerns also find expression in Pentateuchal law, but they are by no means distinctive, and Isaiah does not refer to them specifically as infringements of law; rather, they are shared by other ancient near eastern societies and in particular, of course, by the wisdom literature, as scholars such as Fichtner and Whedbee have made clear.

This latter fact does not, however, make them exclusively the concerns of wisdom either. Rather, the point is that at this particular level both Isaiah and the wisdom writers share a common epistemological basis whose conclusions, in a Yahwistic society, are not unreasonably interpreted as an expression of God's standards of behaviour.[22] (It is in this way, I suggest, that the value of Jensen's study of *tôrâ* in Isaiah may be appreciated; both Isaiah and Proverbs attest an alternative means of God's instruction to the commoner Mosaic *tôrâ*. That does not make *tôrâ* exclusively a wisdom term, however.) Equally intelligible is the fact that both bolster their position by appeals to nature (e.g. i 3, xxviii 23–9) and to the natural standards of decent human behaviour (e.g. v 1–7). And consequently, the value of a comparison of Isaiah and the wise at this point is that it gives us valuable background information about the commonly accepted, if frequently flouted, assumptions in the society of Isaiah's day from which we can appreciate better the rhetorical effectiveness of his indictments.

---

[21] This is a distinction which S. Deck tends to overlook in her otherwise valuable discussion, *Die Gerichtsbotschaft Jesajas: Charakter und Begründung* (Würzburg, 1991).

[22] Cf. J. Barton, 'Natural Law and Poetic Justice in the Old Testament', *JTS* ns 30 (1979), pp. 1–14, and 'Ethics in Isaiah of Jerusalem', *JTS* ns 32 (1981), pp. 1–18.

The second area that clearly requires comment concerns Isaiah's relationship with the king's political advisers, especially in the events leading up to Sennacherib's invasion of Judah in 701 BC. These advisers have often been labelled 'the wise' (particularly because of Jer. viii 8–9 and xviii 18), and at one time it was widely believed that the early parts of the wisdom literature should be ascribed primarily to them. This was part of the consensus which, as we have already noted, has been broken down. Even if we cannot, therefore, be so confident about the precise background of this group or, indeed, be certain whether they can even properly be called a 'class', it remains the case that there obviously were such advisers,[23] that Isaiah clashed with them over the correct course of action to be followed, and that in at least one passage (xxix 14) he explicitly refers to 'the wisdom of their (i.e. the people's) wise men'.

From the two passages which fall principally for consideration (xxx 1–5 and xxxi 1–3[24]), it is widely agreed that in the period prior to Sennacherib's invasion Hezekiah had involved Judah in a wider revolt against Assyrian hegemony and that an appeal for help had been made to Egypt. It is this latter fact alone which Isaiah repudiates, and it may be significant that in doing so he does not refer directly to the king. Because there are many uncertainties in establishing the details of Isaiah's attitude to the events of this time, it is not clear whether he also repudiated the very notion of revolt against Assyria or whether he supported the revolt but disagreed with the manner in which it was pursued.[25]

In these passages, Isaiah's condemnation goes much further than a difference of opinion about which course of action it would be pragmatically best to follow. To court Egypt is an act of rebellion and sin, because the plan is not God's and has been undertaken without consulting him (xxx 1–2, xxxi 1). More than that, by putting faith in the Egyptian military (xxx 2b, xxxi 1), it allows mere men to usurp the place which rightfully belongs to God alone (xxxi 3a). The plan is therefore doomed to failure by its very nature (xxx 3–5, xxxi 3b).[26]

Such a radical position seems to go beyond what it would be reasonable to expect that 'the wise' could work out for themselves. It would be possible for them to argue, for instance, that their policy was compatible with faith,

---

[23] Cf. R. C. Van Leeuwen, 'The Sage in the Prophetic Literature', in J. G. Gammie and L. G. Perdue (eds.), *The Sage in Israel and the Ancient Near East* (Winona Lake, 1990), pp. 295–306.

[24] Opinions are sharply divided about the authenticity of verse 2. While caution demands that it should not be used for reconstructing Isaiah's own words, it seems nevertheless to be fully in accord with his point of view.

[25] See the full survey of opinions in F. J. Gonçalves, *L'Expédition de Sennachérib en Palestine dans la littérature hébraïque ancienne* (Paris, 1986), pp. 137–269.

[26] Cf. H.-J. Hermisson, 'Weisheit und Geschichte', in H. W. Wolff (ed.), *Probleme biblischer Theologie. Gerhard von Rad zum 70. Geburtstag* (Munich, 1971), pp. 136–54 (149–52).

while on the other hand it is not clear that Isaiah's words automatically exclude all human activity. Isa. vii 3–4 can certainly be interpreted as an encouragement to Ahaz to withstand Syria and Ephraim in battle (cf. Deut. xx 3) within a context that presses the need for faith (verse 9), and xxxi 1*b* (and xxx 1, according to Wildberger, p. 1152) may imply a similar outlook. Equally, there are some sayings in the book of Proverbs which suggest a position which at least moves in the direction of Isaiah's condemnation (e.g. xvi 9, xix 21, xxi 30–1), though they are admittedly less radical than his blanket condemnation, and the problems of dating individual proverbs leave uncertainty as to whether they may not themselves have been influenced by the prophetic outlook.[27] It would be a mistake, therefore, either to suggest that Isaiah condemned the wise because they adopted a wholly secular approach to policy or to argue that he was in some way trying to recall the wise to what their own tradition should have taught them (cf. Whedbee, pp. 125–6). Rather, as with his pronouncement of judgement against social sin and injustice, there was what may loosely be called a prophetic element which was combined with other data in wider currency amongst his contemporaries.

Does this conclusion imply inconsistency on Isaiah's part? Does he waver between theological deduction and prophetic insight? This is certainly the impression which some studies of his teaching imply, even if the matter is rarely spelt out so crudely. But in recent years there have been voices raised in favour of an underlying consistency in Isaiah's thinking. Thus Barton, who argues for 'natural law' as the basis of much of Isaiah's social condemnations, goes on to suggest that 'this understanding of the basis of ethics in Isaiah allows one to see a coherence between his condemnation of social injustice and his political oracles; for in these, too, he stresses the perversity or blindness to an obvious order of priorities manifested by those who encourage the Egyptian alliance ... The trouble with human alliances is that they exalt human strength above its natural place' ('Natural Law', pp. 6–7, developed in 'Ethics'). Similarly, Gonçalves recognizes a lower order of coherence in that preparation for war entailed social oppression (cf. xxii 8–11), but then goes on to make very much the same point as Barton: 'La confiance dans les moyens militaires et l'injustice se rejoignent dans le fait qu'elles expriment chacune à sa façon le refus de la seigneurie de Yahvé et constituent, aux yeux du prophète, les deux principales manifestations de l'orgueil judéen' (*L'Expédition*, pp. 267–9).

Behind all this, it is difficult not to see the reflection of the vision of the Lord, 'high and lifted up', in chapter vi (note especially the repeated use of this description in chapter ii as indicative of all pride which must, therefore,

[27] The expression of a similar point of view in the Egyptian wisdom text of Amenemope certainly leaves open the possibility that it was shared by the wisdom writers from the start.

be brought low). It was the reality of God's exaltation which gave everything else in society and nature its subordinate but ordered place. It was this towards which the wisdom writers (however defined) in Isaiah's day were struggling, giving him a strong point of contact with them in many respects, but ultimately his prophetic vision outstripped theirs and so also brought him into conflict with them. Though it was apparently rejected at the time, there are indications that his understanding was nevertheless eventually absorbed – probably in the synthesizing saying 'The fear of the Lord is the beginning of wisdom' (Prov. i 7), certainly in the climax of the book of Job, and perhaps even, paradoxically, by wisdom's most radical critic, Qoheleth (Eccles. xii 1–8).

12   Jeremiah and the wise

W. McKane

The wise against whom the pre-exilic Judahite prophets conducted a polemic were statesmen in the service of the kings of Judah on whose expertise and sagacity (*'ēṣâ*) the kings relied for advice and policy.[1] The book of Jeremiah contains chapters which set out Jeremiah's conflict with both kings and statesmen, especially on a matter of foreign policy, namely the kind of response which should be made to the imperial ambitions of Nebuchadrezzar.

The 'princes' or 'counsellors' as statesmen are certainly one class of the 'wise' or 'scribes', but they do not exhaust the class, and one (viii 8–9) or perhaps two (ii 8)[2] passages in the book of Jeremiah refer to 'wise' or 'scribes' who are Torah-scholars and specialize in the interpretation of the law. The 'wise' were an educated class equipped for different professions, and so their pursuits might be religious or literary (Proverbs) rather than political. Whybray[3] expressed doubt about the attempt to turn 'wise' into a class title, but the antithesis which the pre-exilic prophets construct between 'word' and 'counsel', between the revealed word and the concerting of policy by specialists, makes it clear that they are directing their criticism against a claim to know-how and sagacity and are opposing it with a prophetic claim. It is the prophet informed by Yahweh who is the authentic source of the policy which Judah should follow. This conclusion does not depend on a narrow or exclusive interpretation of 'wise' but on the observation that the 'wise' or 'scribes' with whom the pre-exilic Judaean prophets collide are certainly 'statesmen' and 'counsellors' and that their stock-in-trade is *'ēṣâ* ('counsel'), wisdom which derives from knowledge, calculation, experience and conference, and which has a source different from the *dābār* ('word') of a prophet.

---

[1] W. McKane, *Prophets and Wise Men* (London, 1965), pp. 65–91.

[2] McKane, *Prophets and Wise Men*, pp. 102–12. The main issue is whether 'those who handle the law' (ii 8) are simply to be equated with the priests (Kimchi, Cornill, Streane, Rudolph, Weiser) or whether they are a separate body of scholars, perhaps a special branch of the priesthood (Duhm, Volz, Carroll). Volz identifies them with the scribes and wise of viii 8–9, and describes them as forerunners of the post-exilic wisdom teachers.

[3] R. N. Whybray, *The Intellectual Tradition in the Old Testament* (Berlin, 1974). See my review in *JSS* 29 (1975), pp. 243–8.

There is one passage in Jeremiah (xviii 18) which deals with different kinds of specialists and indicates their specialities: priest/Torah; wise/counsel; prophet/word. The circumstance that it implies that Jeremiah does not utter a true 'word' (*dābār*) does not affect this classification.[4] The principal matter is that it associates the wise particularly with *'ēṣâ*. It was the claim of the wise to possess this quality of intellectual discernment and judgement, and that the wellbeing of Judah was dependent on its exercise, which was contested by the pre-exilic Judahite prophets.

The investigation of this in respect of Jeremiah depends on the assumption that reliable information about relations between the statesmen and Jeremiah can be had from those chapters which a long line of commentators (Duhm, Cornill, H. Schmidt, Volz, Rudolph, Weiser, Bright)[5] have attributed to Baruch and which they considered to have historical value and a biographical character. Nicholson,[6] on the other hand, has contended that the intention of ch. xxvi is theological rather than biographical, and that its unity can be demonstrated if this is properly appreciated. It is 'preaching to the exiles' and is shaped throughout by Deuteronomists. Its theme is that Judah rejected the word of a prophet and incurred exile as a punishment. Its origins are later than the end of the pre-exilic period and its concern is not historical but theological or homiletical. Its interest is disengaged from Jeremiah's life and times and from the conflicts which arose from his message. It belongs to the homiletical concerns of the exiles, but it preserves historical information, though this is divorced from its main purpose.

But, even if ch. xxvi is an 'edifying story' created by the Deuteronomists, this does not dissolve the literary incohesiveness of verses 17–19 or verses 20–3. The same should be said of Rietzschel's supposition[7] that the barrier to relating verses 20–3 to the preceding part of the chapter is erected by the wrong assumption that these verses are set in the context of biography – a Passion Narrative of the prophet Jeremiah. Similarly, there is the

[4] Duhm and Cornill delete 'and the word from [the] prophet' and argue that the sense of the verse is that the resources of law and counsel will enable Jeremiah's enemies to concert plans which will bring about his downfall (also H. Schmidt, without the deletion of 'and word from [the] prophet'; cf. Volz, Rudolph). Carroll supposes that the verse rests not on the conflict of Jeremiah with classes of the establishment, but reflects opposing ideologies of a later period.

[5] B. Duhm, *Das Buch Jeremia* (Tübingen and Leipzig, 1901); C. H. Cornill, *Das Buch Jeremia* (Leipzig, 1905); H. Schmidt, *Die grossen Propheten* (Göttingen, 1915); P. Volz, *Der Prophet Jeremia* (Leipzig, 1928); W. Rudolph, *Jeremia* (Tübingen, 1947, 3rd edn, 1968); A. Weiser, *Das Buch des Propheten Jeremia* (6th edn, Göttingen, 1969); J. Bright, *Jeremiah: Introduction, Translation and Notes* (Garden City, 1965).

[6] E. W. Nicholson, *Preaching to the Exiles: a Study of the Prose Tradition of the Book of Jeremiah* (Oxford, 1970), especially pp. 66, 106; Nicholson, *The Book of the Prophet Jeremiah 26–52* (Cambridge, 1975).

[7] C. Rietzschel, *Das Problem der Urrolle. Ein Beitrag zur Redaktionsgeschichte des Jeremiabuches* (Gütersloh, 1966), p. 99.

claim by Carroll[8] that, if the assumption that ch. xxvi is biography is surrendered, inconcinnities previously insurmountable cease to be troublesome. But even a later edifying narrative disengaged from the historical Jeremiah may not be broken or inconsequential. A good story, whatever its nature, is expected to hang together, and the thought that fiction is relieved of this requirement of literary consistency which is demanded of historiography has no foundation. Without our becoming too involved in the critical analysis of ch. xxvi it will be enough to say that when verse 16 is reached the chapter has run its course and a satisfactory conclusion has been arrived at. The recall of Micah's acquittal by 'the elders of the land' (who have not previously appeared in the chapter) at verses 17–19 is explicable as an appendix which cites a historical precedent to support the verdict of the statesmen, but the notice of Uriah's condemnation by Jehoiakim is less relevant.

Hossfeld/Meyer[9] divide ch. xxvi into a core narrative empty of historical value (verses 2a, 4a, 6, 7, 8b, 9–12, 14–16) and a deuteronomistic redaction (verses 1, 2b, 3, 4b, 5, 8a, 13, 17–24). The deuteronomistic redaction is more considerable than that of Thiel[10] (verses 3–5, 6*, 12–15*), and the core narrative, unlike the Baruch report of Thiel, has no biographical content. Reventlow's view[11] of ch. xxvi is similar to that of Hossfeld/Meyer. It sets out from the assumption that the key to the structure of ch. vii is the recognition that it is an Entry Torah, and that in ch. xxvi elements of the *Gattung* have been modified and relocated in the interests of a more dramatic form of narrative. The distance of ch. xxvi from historical interest and content is shown by the obscuring of the sacral character of the legal procedure rehearsed in the chapter, by the addition of *hāʿîr* ('city', verses 6, 9) in order to enlarge the area of conflict, and by the introduction of the statesmen. The form in which the charge is laid against Jeremiah – a threat against the city (verse 11) – is a deliberate stratagem on the part of the author to establish that Jeremiah's offence is treasonable, but it is evidence of the temporal and cultural distance from the sacral legal procedure which was originally envisaged (similarly Carroll). But, even if Jeremiah predicted only the destruction of the temple, such a prediction implies the destruction of Jerusalem and is enough to explain the concern and intervention of the statesmen. The attempt to enforce a distinction between 'sacral' and 'political' and to argue that an explicit reference to the city was necessary to

---

[8] R. P. Carroll, *Jeremiah, A Commentary* (London, 1986).

[9] F. L. Hossfeld and I. Meyer, 'Der Prophet vor dem Tribunal. Neuer Auslegungsversuch von Jer 26', *ZAW* 86 (1974), pp. 45–6, 48–9.

[10] W. Thiel, *Die deuteronomistische Redaktion von Jeremia 26–45 mit einer Gesamtbeurteilung der deuteronomistischen Redaktion des Buches Jeremia* (Neukirchen-Vluyn, 1981), pp. 3–4.

[11] H. Graf Reventlow, 'Gattung und Überlieferung in der "Tempelrede" Jeremias, Jer 7 und 26', *ZAW* 81 (1969), pp. 341–52.

change 'blasphemy' into 'treason' and to account for the intervention of the statesmen is highly artificial.

If the incompatible attitudes towards Jeremiah attributed to the 'people' (verses 8, 16, 24) are left aside as a subsidiary problem, verses 1–16 indicate that the priests and prophets of the Jerusalem temple were so incensed by Jeremiah's utterance that they represented to the statesmen that it deserved the death penalty. The statesmen, however, reached the verdict that, even for so extreme and politically untimely a prediction by a prophet, the death penalty was inappropriate. It may not be concluded that they thought Jeremiah's prediction wise, or that they were expressing sympathy or agreement with it (despite verse 16, 'for he has spoken to us in the name of the Lord our God'), but only that in their judgement the oracle of a prophet, however wild and politically disconcerting, should not be punished by the state.

The mention of Ahikam at verse 24 recalls the view which appears widely in the exegesis of ch. xxxvi (Duhm, Streane, H. Schmidt, Rudolph, Weiser, Bright) that Jeremiah had the sympathy and even the agreement of the family of Shaphan and could rely for his protection on the exercise of their influence. Shaphan the scribe had been Josiah's chief official and had acted for the king in the events which preceded the implementation of his reform (2 Kings xxii), and his sons had followed their father as statesmen. Gemariah, a son of Shaphan, had tried to dissuade Jehoiakim from burning Jeremiah's scroll, and it is supposed that a religious concern can be traced running through Shaphan and his family, and that the latter shared Jeremiah's convictions. But Shaphan's association with Josiah's reform was a political duty and does not increase the probability that his sons, as ministers of the king and members of the establishment, would embrace Jeremiah's predictions that Judah would be defeated and dissolved,[12] though this thesis, largely accepted, needs further consideration in connection with ch. xxvi.

So far as xxvi 24 goes, it is difficult to reconcile with what precedes it in ch. xxvi, both because of the hostility of the people to Jeremiah, which it assumes is not wholly consistent with the attitudes earlier attributed to them, and especially because the body of the statesmen had found in favour of Jeremiah (verse 16). Nor does he seem to depend for his safety on the influential intervention of Ahikam (cf. Carroll). Certainly the people are associated with the priest and prophets of the Jerusalem temple in seizing Jeremiah and threatening him with death (verse 8), and verse 9 may indicate that they thronged him in a menacing way, and that they caused an affray which triggered the intervention of the statesmen (verse 10).

[12] *Pace* H. Schmidt; E. W. Nicholson, *Preaching to the Exiles*, especially p. 44, n. 2.

However, 'all the people' (verse 16) are associated with the statesmen in the verdict that Jeremiah does not deserve to be put to death.

The principal matter is that the statesmen as a body reached this conclusion, and Ahikam's special role as Jeremiah's protector has been explained (Duhm, Volz, Rudolph, Weiser) on the uneconomical assumption that it illustrates the inconstancy of the *dēmos*, their fickleness, and the oscillation of their moods between support and menace. The representation of verse 24 that there was popular hostility to Jeremiah and his predictions (which may be true), and that his safety depended on the sympathy of Ahikam and his clandestine agreement with Jeremiah that non-resistance to Babylon was the policy which Judah should follow, is puzzling in the context of ch. xxvi (cf. Streane; the connection of verse 24 with the rest of the chapter is not clear).

The issues at ch. xxxvi are simplified to the extent that there is an impressive exegetical consensus which survives differing critical estimates of the chapter. Whether it is a Baruch report (Thiel[13] detects deuteronomic encroachment only at verses 3, 7, 31) or a deuteronomic narrative, set in the exilic period, whose interests are theological or homiletical,[14] the representation is thought to be that the statesmen are expressing agreement with the contents of Jeremiah's scroll (verses 16, 25) and their solidarity with his convictions.[15]

Nicholson[16] has challenged the interpretation of the attitude of the statesmen to Jeremiah offered in *Prophets and Wise Men* (pp. 118–20); he has impressive support, and so far as the Masoretic Text is concerned he may be correct. I had argued that *pāḥᵃdû*, used at verse 16 to describe the reaction of the statesmen to the reading of the scroll, signals alarm at the possibility of the bad political consequences of Baruch's proclamation, and that it is not the shudder of shocked piety coupled with the acceptance of the truth of the prophetic word. If it were the latter (Duhm, H. Schmidt, Rudolph, Weiser, Bright), their report to the king should be connected with an attempt on their part to persuade him that Jeremiah must be heeded. If it were the former, their report to Jehoiakim should have been that Jeremiah's action might have dangerous political consequences, might damage public morale and weaken the resolve to resist the Babylonians, and that measures to obviate this threat ought to be taken.

Nicholson lays weight on *pāḥᵃdû* (verse 16) and *wᵉlōʾ pāḥᵃdû* (verse 24), urges that this is a calculated antithesis and that *wᵉlōʾ pāḥᵃdû* contrasts the

---

[13] W. Thiel, *Die deuteronomistiche Redaktion von Jeremia 26–45*, pp. 49–51.

[14] E. W. Nicholson, *Preaching to the Exiles*, p. 39.

[15] Carroll concludes that ch. xxxvi is unhistorical, but he makes the historical judgement that the counsel of the statesmen was not in agreement with that of Jeremiah.

[16] E. W. Nicholson, *Preaching to the Exiles*, pp. 43–4, n. 2.

contemptuous rejection of Jeremiah's scroll with the fearful but believing response of the statesmen to Jeremiah's words. At verse 24 the coupling of *wᵉlōʾ qārᵉᶜû ʾet bigᵉdêhem* lends some support to this exegesis, since the latter indicates that Jeremiah's words made no impression of penitence and that they were not received as a prophetic communication which should be heeded and acted on. The contrast would then be between the concerned, agitated and believing response of the statesmen to the words of a prophet and Jehoiakim's high-handed, objectionably theatrical dismissal of it which *kol ᶜᵃbādāyw* applauded.

It should be noticed, however, that the LXX at verse 16 reads συνεβουλεύσαντο for *pāḥᵃdû*, and that this describes a different reaction from the MT. The statesmen no longer shudder at the thought that a prophetic prediction must be true (if this is the meaning of the MT), but, having heard Jeremiah's words, they go into conference in order to consider all their implications and decide that they must be reported to the king. There is nothing in the LXX to suggest that their intention was to persuade Jehoiakim that Jeremiah's words were true, or that Judah's policy towards Babylon should be revised to take account of them and that they should act on them. The sense is, rather, that the outcome of their conference is the conclusion that the public reading of the scroll is a politically dangerous action and that Jehoiakim must be informed of it. Hence the antithesis between *pāḥᵃdû* (verse 16) and *wᵉlōʾ pāḥᵃdû* (καὶ οὐκ ἐξέστησαν, verse 24), which has been thought exegetically decisive, has disappeared. The question then has to be asked whether the LXX at verse 16 does not preserve a more original text than the MT. At any rate it is plain that the *Vorlage* of συνεβουλεύσαντο is not *pāḥᵃdû* but perhaps *wayyiwwāᶜᵃṣû*.[17] In that case the antithesis between the believing response of the statesmen to Jeremiah's scroll and its insolent dismissal by Jehoiakim and all his officials would be a secondary creation of the MT, and *pāḥᵃdû* may have originated as a mirror form of *wᵉlōʾ pāḥᵃdû*.

Another matter is the ascertaining of the identity of 'all his officials' (verse 24). It is certain that the expression cannot be equated with 'all the statesmen' (verse 12) for at least two reasons. Three statesmen (Elnathan, Delaiah, Gemariah [MT, the last-mentioned a minus in LXX^BS*]) who expressed dissent with Jehoiakim's cutting up and burning of Jeremiah's scroll are ruled out, and 'all his officials' is not the same as 'all the statesmen'. Moreover, the attitude of the three statesmen to the scroll (xxxvi 25) cannot be differentiated from that of all the statesmen (verse 12) who were present in the room of Elishama the scribe, who *ex hypothesi* reported Baruch's reading of the scroll to Jehoiakim with the intention of

[17] E. Hatch and H. A. Redpath, *A Concordance to the Septuagint*, 2 (Oxford, 1897), p. 1303.

persuading him that its contents were true, and who demanded a positive response. Hence, however 'all his officials' are to be identified, they are a separate group from 'all the statesmen' (Rudolph). It may be that they were an inner circle of boon companions of the king, a court coterie (NEB, REB, 'courtiers'; H. Schmidt, a palace entourage; Rudolph, *Höflingen*). It is unlikely that *ʿᵃbādîm* has so lowly a reference as that of 'domestic servants', though the LXX has so rendered it (οἱ παῖδες αὐτοῦ), with *kol* ('all') a minus. The LXX translates *ben* (verse 26) as υἱῷ, but it is improbable that the *Vorlage* of οἱ παῖδες αὐτοῦ is *bānāyw* and that it is the king and his sons who express dismissive contempt for Jeremiah's intervention.

If συνεβουλεύσαντο is preferred at verse 6 and if the attitude of Elnathan, Delaiah and Gemariah to Jeremiah's scroll is the same as that of all the statesmen (verse 12), it should not be supposed that their protest (MT, verse 25) implies that they believed Jeremiah's words, but only that they objected to Jehoiakim's exhibition of contemptuous disregard for them. The circumstance that Gemariah is a son of Shaphan (verse 12) should not be thought to have special significance, and *lᵉbiltî* or *biltî* (original *liśrōp*) is a minus in LXX$^{BS^*}$, whose two statesmen are Elnathan and Gedaliah. It may be that *lᵉbiltî or biltî* is a secondary insertion in the MT and μή is not represented in LXX$^{BS^*}$ (πρὸς τὸ κατακαῦσαι τὸ χαρτίον), though it is retained in Ziegler's text.[18] *lᵉbiltî* or *biltî* could be a modification which matches *pāḥᵃdû* at verse 16 and *wᵉlōʾ šāmaᶜ ʿᵃlêhem*, which is also a minus in LXX, is the other part of it. According to LXX$^{BS^*}$ (verse 25) Elnathan and Gedaliah counselled Jehoiakim to burn the scroll, and we should assume that they were representing the 'counsel' which emerged out of the conference (συνεβουλεύσαντο) of the statesmen (verse 16). Hence there is nothing in LXX$^{BS^*}$ to support the conclusion that a shudder ran through the ranks of the statesmen when they heard the scroll read because they believed Jeremiah's words, so that they tried to persuade Jehoiakim to act on them. Nor is there longer reason to suppose that Elnathan, Delaiah or Gedaliah (or Gemariah) were particularly strong in their support of Jeremiah, so that they stand apart from the remaining statesmen in this regard, not being able to contain a protest against Jehoiakim's manner of expressing his rejection of Jeremiah's scroll.

The absoluteness of the distinction between the counsel of the statesmen and the word of the prophet is exegetically correct, but there is a lingering doubt whether it may not be an incomplete account of the matter and one that is too tidy and schematic to describe adequately the union of divine and human involved in the reduction of the prophetic encounter with Yahweh to the words of an oracle. The neat dissection of the 'counsel' and

---

[18] J. Ziegler, *Ieremias, Baruch, Threni, Epistula Ieremiae* (Göttingen, 1957), p. 397.

'word' in *Prophets and Wise Men* has thus caused me increasing dissatisfaction as the years have passed. 'Word of God' is not literal and Yahweh does not speak Hebrew. The language of the prophetic word is human, but the prophet is utterly convinced that it comes from God and that its authority is unquestioned. Nevertheless, the process by which the unspeakable encounter with God is converted into human language is a deeply mysterious transmutation and it cannot happen without a filtering of the transcendence of the experience through the total humanity of the prophet, the complicated whole of anguish, discernment and convictions.

Hence it is not the case that wisdom or counsel has no part in the production of 'word of God'. The foundation of the prophet's words is certainly that of divine authority, but its composition is an articulation of this into the pain of his commitment and into an analysis of the great issues which confront Judah, one which differs sharply from the 'counsel' which king and statesmen are implementing. We may not conclude that there are no elements of wisdom and counsel in a prophetic utterance, no deep discernment or appreciation of the perilous course which the ship of state must steer, no concern similar to that of the king and his statesmen, no exercise of political judgement.

There are decisive differences. The prophet founds his words on divine authority and does not make the claims for 'counsel' which are characteristic of the policy of the statesmen. Reliance on a self-sufficient counsel which leaves the will of God out of the reckoning and depends entirely on a cerebral power deriving from intellectual discrimination and expertise developed by experience is mistaken and is a kind of apostasy. The circumstance that the advice offered by Jeremiah and the statesmen respectively is nearly always contrary, especially with regard to the biggest issue – how to respond to the imperial advance of Nebuchadrezzar – has the effect of obscuring Jeremiah's words as a 'counter-counsel' to the counsel of the statesmen, both of which focussed on matters which appeared most urgent and of greatest consequence to Judah in the early sixth century BC. This is well illustrated in the report of the response made by Jeremiah to Zedekiah's request for prophetic guidance: 'If I divulge (*'aggîd*) God's will to you, you will put me to death and if I offer you counsel (*'î'āṣ^ekā*), you will not listen to me' (xxxviii 15).[19]

The contribution to the understanding of the nature of prophetic wisdom made by Wildberger[20] should be noticed. Wildberger offers the

---

[19] Duhm remarks that ch. xxxviii is from Baruch and is historically reliable. Thiel (*Die deuteronomistische Redaktion von Jeremia 26–45*, p. 54) finds traces of a deuteronomistic redaction only at verses 2, 22. Nicholson (Carroll; cf. Bright) supposes that chs. xxxvii and xxxviii are variant accounts of the same events.

[20] H. Wildberger, *Jahwewort und prophetische Rede bei Jeremia* (Zürich, 1942), especially pp. 120–5.

kind of dissection of divine and human within prophetic speech whose rejection is implied by what is said above. The gist of his contention is that the prophetic message is given to the prophet by Yahweh, so that this element is 'word of God', but that the other constituents of prophetic speech, furnishing explanation, giving reasons and so on, are supplied by the prophet himself as his own reinforcement of the message and the supplying of a context for it. The attempt to solve the union of the divine and the human in a prophetic word and to account for human discernment in it ought not to proceed by its division into separate compartments and the assumption that a part is 'word of God' or *Offenbarung*. The subsequent affirmations that both are essentially one and that 'word of God' is not 'verbal inspiration' do not undo the damage.

There is one chapter of the book of Jeremiah, in particular, which illustrates the point that the sharp conflict which normally obtains between Jeremiah and the statesmen has the effect of masking the fact that they are mostly offering contrary advice on the same issues. At ch. xxix there is the first reproduction of a letter in the Hebrew Bible (Streane[21]); circumstances demand it, and there seem no good reasons for doubting that a part of it is authentic.[22] Jeremiah is concerned to communicate with those who were deported to Babylon in 597. He is in Jerusalem, and so physically separated from them, and he can tender his advice and press his case only by sending them a letter. The historical moment is one when his view of how relations with Babylon should be managed appears to have coincided with the policies of Zedekiah and the statesmen, or at any rate, with those of the statesmen who, for a time, had gained the ascendancy (cf. H. Schmidt).

What prompted Zedekiah to send envoys to Nebuchadrezzar is unclear, but the view that it was a routine matter of handing over tribute (Cornill, Rudolph[?]) is less probable than the suggestion that, in view of the unrest among neighbouring small states in relation to Babylon and the unlikelihood that Zedekiah had been entirely uncompromised and free of rebellious tendencies (xxvii 3), the purpose of the embassy was to reassure Nebuchadrezzar of Zedekiah's and Judah's submissive loyalty to the Babylonian king (Rudolph[?], Weiser, Bright, Nicholson[?]). That Eleasah was a son of Shaphan and Gemariah of Hilkiah (verse 3) – if it is the Hilkiah of 2 Kings xxii – should not be thought significant. It ought not to be assumed that Jeremiah was availing himself of a special relationship which

[21] A.W. Streane, *The Book of the Prophet Jeremiah together with The Lamentations* (Cambridge, 1913), p. 173.

[22] Duhm remarks that Baruch's book is the foundation of the chapter, but that many details betray the influence of the books of Kings (also Streane; cf. Thiel, *Die deuteronomistische Redaktion von Jeremiah 26–45*, pp. 9–19; Nicholson, *Preaching to the Exiles*, pp. 97–100). Carroll denies any historical value to the chapter; it is either exilic or post-exilic and the Jeremiah who appears in it is not a historical figure.

he had with these two statesmen, or with Eleasah in particular (cf. Duhm, Rudolph, Weiser, Bright, on ch. xxxvi; Streane on xxix 1), and that his letter to the exiles was smuggled into the diplomatic bag (cf. Cornill, 'entrusted to Eleasah'). Jeremiah's letter is a prophetic oracle and is prefaced with 'These are the words of the Lord of hosts, the God of Israel' (verse 4), but the counsel which he offers the Judaean exiles in Babylon to settle down and accept their subject state, to look to a long future of its continuance, to abandon a feverish urge to rebel, and to fashion a regimen which would contribute positively to the common life of a foreign community, must have temporarily coincided with the policy of Zedekiah and his statesmen to damp down warlike postures towards Babylon both in Jerusalem and among the exiles at this juncture. Hence it was a reinforcement of Zedekiah's embassy to Nebuchadrezzar, and the message which it conveyed, to have an accompanying letter from Jeremiah whose purpose was to promote quietness and to encourage positive attitudes to Babylonian suzerainty among the exiles in Babylon.

Barton's conclusion[23] is connected by analogy with Jeremiah's attitude to international diplomacy. The concept of 'international customary law' to which Barton relates Amos i 3–ii 5 is regarded by the prophet as one which ought to have been generally acknowledged but which was not necessarily followed in fact. It was not a universally accepted ethos arising out of a common humanity, but it should have been. That was Amos' point of view. In our terms this suggests that counsel is not necessarily inimical to morality or to the prophetic word. Counsel and the prophetic word need not be incompatible, but they often are. Their sources are so different that a confluence is improbable, but they may coincide.

It is a privilege to pay homage to Professor Emerton's scholarship and to celebrate a long and happy association with him.

---

[23] J. Barton, *Amos's Oracles against the Nations: A Study of Amos 1.3–2.5* (Cambridge, 1980), pp. 5, 39–44.

13 The wisdom psalms

R. N. Whybray

All the other chapters in this part of the volume deal with specific texts. To write about 'the wisdom psalms' is a different proposition, somewhat akin to making bricks without straw, for there is no scholarly agreement at all about the number or the identity of such psalms, or even about the existence of such a category.[1] One of the main reasons for this lack of consensus is the ambiguity of the terminology – not only of 'wisdom' and 'psalm', but also of other terms which have had a place in the discussion such as 'cult' and 'school'. The object of the present contribution is not to add one more to the many attempts to identify the wisdom psalms in the Psalter, but to reconsider the question 'What is a wisdom psalm?' and to discuss the function of those psalms which have been, rightly or wrongly, so designated.

The existence in the Psalter of a number of psalms having an especial affinity with the concept of 'wisdom' supposedly to be found in the books of Proverbs, Job and Ecclesiastes was postulated by Hermann Gunkel.[2] Gunkel recognized, however, that they do not constitute a *Gattung* like the other types of psalm which he identified: that is, that they have no distinctive *form* of their own, but can only be distinguished by other criteria.[3] Their purpose was didactic, and they had from the first no connection with public worship in the temple as did the other kinds of psalm.

H. L. Jansen[4] and Sigmund Mowinckel[5] attempted greater precision with regard to the background and authorship of such psalms. Mowinckel spoke of them as examples of a 'private learned psalmography' and saw them as the work of scribal teachers in 'wisdom schools' connected with the Second Temple, in contrast with the temple singers who were the authors of the other psalms in the Psalter.

---

[1] For details see R. N. Whybray, 'The Social World of the Wisdom Writers', in R. E. Clements (ed.), *The World of Ancient Israel* (Cambridge, 1989), pp. 244–5.

[2] H. Gunkel and J. Begrich, *Einleitung in die Psalmen* (Göttingen, 1933), ch. 10.

[3] Gunkel also recognized another group, the 'royal psalms', which likewise has no distinctive form.

[4] *Die spätjüdische Psalmdichtung* (Oslo, 1937).

[5] 'Psalms and Wisdom', in *Wisdom in Israel and in the Ancient Near East* (*SVT* 3, 1955), pp. 205–24; *The Psalms in Israel's Worship*, 2 (Oxford, 1962), ch. 16 (E. tr. of *Offersang og Sangoffer* [Oslo, 1951]).

Since Mowinckel, and until very recently, most discussion of this subject was devoted to attempts to establish criteria for the identification of 'wisdom psalms'. But little progress was made along these lines. The same arguments, linguistic, formal, intentional, thematic were continually advanced, but without establishing a consensus. With regard to literary form, E. Lipiński remarked in 1979 that 'l'étude de la forme littéraire des psaumes sapientiaux est pratiquement au point mort'.[6] On the question of life-setting, R. E. Murphy (1963) concluded: 'all things considered ... it must be admitted that the precise life-setting of these poems eludes us'.[7] With regard to contents, G. von Rad in his major study of Israelite wisdom (1970) expressed the thoughts of many of his contemporaries when he offered a description of the wisdom psalms which was, for him, uncharacteristically imprecise: 'It is a general impression ... of a certain erudition and didactic quality, a preponderance of theological thoughts, etc., which entitles us to separate these psalms from the great body of cultically orientated psalms.'[8] The vagueness of these criteria (note the 'etc.') leaves the matter open to extremely subjective judgements.

R. E. Murphy, although he wrote in general terms of a 'shared approach to reality', devoted one half of his article 'A Consideration of the Classification "Wisdom Psalms"' to counting up the *number* of relevant features present in particular psalms, having considered the question how many of these were necessary for a psalm to 'qualify'. He concluded that Ps. i is (*sic*) 'the most successful example', the others being Pss. xxxii, xxxiv, xxxvii, xlix, cxii and cxxviii. His method did not permit the inclusion of Ps. lxxiii, a psalm very widely accepted by other scholars.[9]

Recent scholarship has tended to discuss the question of 'wisdom psalms' in a broader context. This new approach is closely connected with what B. S. Childs has called a 'hermeneutical shift' in the understanding of the Psalter as a whole.[10]

Since the work of Mowinckel it had been generally accepted that the psalms are mainly liturgical compositions intended for use in the 'cult' – that is, in the public worship of Israel. It was also widely assumed that the 'wise men' thought to be the authors of the wisdom books had no use for, or at least were indifferent to, this 'cult'. It was partly on this basis that psalms, several of which do not have the form of prayers – that is, are not addressed to God – were classified as wisdom psalms. It has recently been more and

[6] *SDB* 9, col. 121.
[7] 'A Consideration of the Classification "Wisdom Psalms"' (*SVT* 9, 1963), p. 161.
[8] *Wisdom in Israel* (London, 1972), p. 48 (E. tr. of *Weisheit in Israel* [Neukirchen, 1970], p. 70).
[9] L. G. Perdue, *Wisdom and Cult* (Missoula, 1977), pp. 261–343, applying the criteria of form, language and themes, distinguishes between 'proverb poems', ''Ashrê poems' and 'riddle poems'.
[10] *Introduction to the Old Testament as Scripture* (London, 1979), p. 513.

more recognized, however, that to deny that such compositions can be used for purposes of worship is to take a very narrow view of worship – a fact illustrated by the subsequent use of the entire Psalter both liturgically and in private devotion throughout almost the whole of Christian history up to the present time.

That there was a close connection in ancient Israel between religious observance and instruction is attested in such texts as Exod. xii 25–7. It can also be argued that all liturgical texts have a didactic function in that the confessions of faith which they make are also a kind of self-instruction in which worshippers remind themselves of the articles of that faith, as well as serving as lessons for the instruction of children. To make an *absolute* distinction in this connection between 'wisdom psalms' and the other psalms in the Psalter is, then, mistaken. Even Mowinckel's 'wisdom schools' among the ranks of whose teaching staff the authors of these psalms were, he supposed, to be found, were attached to the temple in Jerusalem. If this was the case, it is reasonable to suppose that the recitation of these psalms was in some way connected with worship: wisdom and worship, if they were ever separate, came together here. This would account for the fact, often felt to be difficult to account for, that these psalms came to be incorporated into a Psalter consisting mainly of psalms of a liturgical character.

But it has become clear that another, private kind of worship underwent significant development at some relatively late stage in the formation of the Psalter. Private prayer, especially petitionary prayer asking for God's help in times of adversity, was of course practised throughout Israelite history; it is frequently attested in the Old Testament, especially in the historical and prophetical books. Later there developed a custom of *regular* daily private worship. Daniel is said to have prayed to God and praised him regularly three times a day (Dan. vi 10–11); the author of Ps. cxix claims to do so seven times a day (verse 164), so unconsciously inaugurating the later custom of the recitation of the Breviary. The author of Ps. i declares blessed the individual who *meditates* (*yehgeh*) on Yahweh's teaching (*tôrâ*) day and night.

Whatever may be meant by 'meditate' in Ps. i – the word may refer primarily to the practice common among the ancients generally of reading to oneself aloud or half aloud – it was evidently a private, personal activity, and there can be no doubt that it was a prayerful one.[11] Such private

---

[11] See especially J. Reindl, 'Weisheitliche Bearbeitung von Psalmen' (*SVT* 32, 1981), pp. 333–56; C. Westermann, *Ausgewählte Psalmen* (Göttingen, 1984), pp. 203–6 (E. tr., *The Living Psalms* [Edinburgh, 1989], pp. 292–6); J. L. Mays, 'The Place of the Torah-Psalms in the Psalter', *JBL* 106 (1987), pp. 3–12; A. R. Ceresko, 'The Sage in the Psalms', in J. G. Gammie and L. G. Perdue (eds.), *The Sage in Israel and the Ancient Near East* (Winona Lake, 1990), pp. 217–30.

devotions may be supposed also to have inspired the composition of *new* psalms. Of these, Ps. cxix is a clear example; but other psalms, perhaps especially those which reflect some kind of spiritual struggle (xlix, lxxiii), may have originated in the same way.

The Psalter as 'book'[12]

In recent years there has been a renewed interest in the Psalter as a carefully organized, single 'text'. Whereas it had often been assumed that it was a more or less haphazard collection of liturgical poems and of small groups of poems, many scholars have now discerned in it a deliberate arrangement in which psalms originally intended for a variety of roles in the public liturgy of the temple were given a quite new function as parts of a *book*, intended to be read *consecutively* by private individuals.

It is now widely recognized that Ps. i had a major role to play in this process, having been especially composed, or at least selected, to act as a preface or introduction to the whole Psalter, instructing the reader in what spirit it was to be read and studied. This psalm is not a prayer in form. It is not addressed to God. It sets out, in the manner of a teacher of wisdom, the respective fates of the righteous and the wicked, characterizing the righteous as the person who delights in, and meditates upon, the law, or 'teaching' (*tôrâ*) of Yahweh, a term which for this writer has a wider connotation than the Law of Moses. He may have been thinking of Yahweh's deeds in the past which served as a 'text' for the instruction of later generations (compare Ps. lxxviii), but also of the Psalter itself as a 'sacred text' or book of instruction. Such a use of the Psalter did not, of course, exclude the liturgical use of many of the psalms in the worship of the temple while the temple lasted.

If this is a correct reading of Ps. i, we should expect to find traces of editorial work within the Psalter itself, intended to make it more evidently the kind of book which the author of Ps. i had in mind. Such editorial work might take several forms: a particular arrangement of the existing psalms, additions made to some psalms to adapt them more closely to their new role, and, possibly, the addition of some entirely new psalms to the collection. There is in fact evidence of all three kinds of activity.

It may be thought that the evidence for a comprehensive ordering of the whole Psalter is very slight: psalms notably conforming to the guidelines

---

[12] On what follows see especially G. H. Wilson, *The Editing of the Hebrew Psalter* (Chico, 1985); W. Brueggemann, 'Bounded by Obedience and Praise', *JSOT* 50 (1991), pp. 63–92; J. C. McCann, Jr, 'The Psalms as Instruction', *Interpretation* 46 (1992), pp. 117–28; G. H. Wilson, 'The Shape of the Book of Psalms', *Interpretation* 46 (1992), pp. 129–42, in addition to the works mentioned in note 11.

laid down by Ps. i are scattered, apparently at random, throughout the book. Moreover, the paean of worship in Pss. cxlvi–cl may hardly seem appropriate to the quiet individual meditation proposed by Ps. i. But, as Reindl pointed out, meditation is not an end in itself: it is intended to lead to acts of praise; and the final verse of Ps. cl – 'Let everything that has breath praise the Lord' – expresses the goal of the meditation prescribed in Ps. i. As for the apparent randomness of the arrangement, it must be remembered that the opportunities for reordering will have been very restricted, since much of the Psalter had already been formed into larger or smaller collections. But the fact that the new material is scattered throughout the Psalter may have had its own advantage in that a constant reminder to the reader of the way in which he was intended to read would have been more effective than if such reminders had been gathered into one place.

There is also evidence of the deliberate arrangement of some pairs and small groups of psalms which have been placed together so that the reader who is reading the Psalter consecutively as a book may have his thoughts guided in particular directions. For example, Pss. xc–xcii, which belong formally to different *Gattungen*, evince a development of thought when read consecutively. Ps. xc reflects on the infinitude of God and the ephemeral nature of man, and ends with an entreaty to God to take account of these things and to bless rather than punish. Ps. xci continues the theme, but expresses confidence that God will in fact protect his servants, and concludes with a divine oracle in which such protection is promised. Ps. xcii is a psalm of thanksgiving for these mercies. Again, Pss. cv and cvi both meditate on Yahweh's saving actions on behalf of Israel in the past; but whereas Ps. cv simply thanks God for what he has done, Ps. cvi directs the reader's thoughts into more sombre channels with a catalogue of Israel's rebellious actions which provoked God's anger, concluding with a prayer for continued forbearance. It is unlikely that these and other groupings of psalms were purely fortuitous. They served to bring about the interpretation of one psalm by another and so to provoke meditation.

It is also clear that some psalms have been expanded by additional verses with a similar purpose in mind. An obvious example is Ps. cvii, a psalm of corporate thanksgiving, to which a final verse has been added which is a general recommendation to ponder what has just been read about Yahweh's redeeming love – a verse strongly reminiscent of the final verse of Hosea (xiv 10 [9]) which is similarly concerned to present that book as a text whose teaching ought to be read and pondered.[13] Another example is Ps. xxxii, where an individual thanksgiving is interrupted in verses 8–9 by a

---

[13] See W. Beyerlin, *Werden und Wesen des 107. Psalms* (Berlin, 1978).

passage addressed not to God but to the reader by someone claiming to be an instructor. Other examples of this editorial process could be cited.

A late psalmography

If it is the case that already existing psalms were arranged, and others adapted, in order to provide instructional and devotional reading matter for the individual, it is only a small further step to suppose that whole new psalms may have been composed – apart from Ps. i, which has already been considered – to further this purpose, and that such psalms may have been added to the already existing collections. Ps. cxix, which is exclusively concerned with meditation on Yahweh's teaching, and which is believed by some scholars to have a crucial position within the organization of the Psalter as a whole,[14] is an obvious example of such a psalm.

Such late psalms need to be set in a wider context. The one hundred and fifty psalms in the biblical Psalter are part of a much larger genre. There are, for example, psalms embedded in a number of narrative books of the Old Testament. More important for our present concern are the post-biblical psalms. Psalm composition did not come to an end with the close of the biblical period; on the contrary, it appears to have flourished more than before if we may judge by the number of extant examples. Apart from the Psalms of Solomon and the Prayer of Manasseh there are psalms in Ecclesiasticus, the Greek additions to Daniel, Judith and Tobit, and also in the literature from Qumran and in the New Testament. The relevance of this later stage of psalm composition for the study of the biblical psalms was already recognized by Mowinckel; but no comprehensive study of the history and development of Jewish psalmody has yet appeared.

The existence of such late psalmody raises the question what is meant by the term 'psalm': how does it differ from other religious poetry? Most of the late psalms may seem superficially to be no different from the biblical psalms because they are imitative: they use the forms and characteristic expressions of the biblical psalms and often show clear signs of familiarity with those psalms; but those forms have been adapted to new situations. Mowinckel pointed out that the composition of psalms became in itself a pious practice. Ben Sira (Ecclus xxxix 5–6) regarded it as a sign of divine inspiration. For the exiled Tobit (Tob. xiii 1), who is represented as composing *and writing* a psalm of praise and thanksgiving, it was, perhaps, a kind of substitute for a *sacrifice* of thanksgiving which he was unable to offer. Some of these psalms may have been intended for liturgical worship; but others, especially those embedded in prose works, are more likely to

---

[14] Westermann considers that it once stood at the conclusion of the Psalter before its final redaction: *Ausgewählte Psalmen*, p. 205 (E. tr., *The Living Psalms*, p. 294).

have been intended from the first simply to be devotional poetry to be read by individuals.

The stage in the development of Jewish psalmody to which the instructional or devotional psalms in the biblical Psalter belong is not easy to determine. Some of them possess fewer formal psalmic features than some of the post-biblical psalms. But it would be mistaken to put them all in the same category and to label them simply 'wisdom psalms'. To use the term 'wisdom' to cover all types of religious thought in ancient Israel would be to deprive it of all specific meaning. It would be justifiable to call a psalm a 'wisdom psalm' only if its resemblance to some part of the Old Testament wisdom books – Proverbs, Job or Ecclesiastes – were so close as to be undeniable. The term is in any case hardly a precise one, given the great variety of attitudes to reality exemplified in those books, and the vagueness of ideas about the *Sitz im Leben* of wisdom that still prevails in Old Testament studies.

The psalms which most closely correspond in their entirety to the wisdom literature certainly include Pss. xxxiv, xxxvii and lxxviii. The intention of Ps. xxxiv, whose form is basically that of a thanksgiving psalm but which also uses a variety of other features, is clearly stated in verse 11, an address from a 'father' to his 'sons' closely corresponding to similar formulae in Prov. i 8, iv 1, v 1, 7, vi 20, vii 1:

> Come, O sons, listen to me;
> I will teach you the fear of the Lord.

Ps. lxxviii begins with a similar formula, being addressed to 'my people'; it is also a teaching psalm inviting the reader to reflect on Israel's past history. Ps. xxxvii has no corresponding formula, but consists of instruction addressed to an individual mainly in the form of admonitions and statements strongly reminiscent of Proverbs. It also contains two 'example stories' (verses 25, 35–6) in which a teacher seeks to impress his teaching on his pupils by recounting his own – true or fictitious – past experiences, a form otherwise peculiar to Proverbs (iv 3–9, vii 6–23, xxiv 30–4). The categorical insistence that

> I have been young, and now am old;
> yet I have not seen the righteous forsaken
> or his children begging their bread

strongly resembles an attitude expressed in Proverbs and Job, although this by itself would be insufficient for the psalm to 'qualify' as a wisdom psalm.

A number of psalms, indeed, have been designated 'wisdom psalms' because they express a radical or sceptical view similar to that of the book of Job. (It should be noted, however, that not all scholars regard Job as a wisdom book.[15])

Ps. xlix specifically claims the status of wisdom literature: in the introductory verses the author, who addresses 'all peoples' and 'all inhabitants of the world', states his intention to 'speak wisdom (*ḥokmôt*)'. Ps. lxxiii makes no such assertion; but it is couched in the form of a personal confession which should probably be seen as an 'example story'. Its account of an individual's wrestling with the problem of retribution has affinities with Job.

Apart from Pss. xxxvii and xlix, the word 'wisdom' (*ḥokmâ*) occurs in several other psalms: li 8 (6), xc 12, civ 24, cxi 10. But since in these cases the verses in which the word occurs appear to have been added to give the psalm in question a 'wisdom' character, these psalms cannot be regarded as original 'wisdom' compositions. (A possible exception is Ps. xc, which von Rad believed to be a wisdom psalm in the same vein as Ecclesiastes.[16]) In Ps. xciv, although the word does not occur, a section containing wisdom language and ideas has been inserted into a psalm of lamentation (verses 8–14).

Some psalms have been classified as wisdom psalms on the basis of criteria which are inadequate in that the features singled out are not in fact exclusive to the wisdom literature. Thus many psalms are concerned either positively or negatively with the dogma of retribution, and others stress the ephemeral character of human nature. But these are matters which are frequently treated elsewhere in the Old Testament. On the level of form and language, equally faulty criteria have been applied.[17] Thus it has frequently been claimed that the exclamation 'Happy is/are . . . !' (*'ašrê*), which occurs twenty-six times in the Psalter, is characteristic of the wisdom literature. However, this expression occurs only eight times in Proverbs, once in Job, and once in Ecclesiastes, while more than half the total number of occurrences in the Old Testament is accounted for by the Psalter itself. There is good reason to believe that its origins are to be located in the liturgy of the temple.[18]

[15] E.g. C. Westermann, *Der Aufbau des Buches Hiob* (3rd edn, Stuttgart, 1978) (E. tr., *The Structure of the Book of Job* [Philadelphia, 1977]); see also the reservations of K. J. Dell, *The Book of Job as Sceptical Literature* (Berlin, 1991).

[16] G. von Rad, *Theologie des Alten Testaments*, 1 (Munich, 1957), p. 452 (E. tr., *Old Testament Theology*, 1 [Edinburgh and London, 1962], pp. 453–4.

[17] For a recent discussion of linguistic criteria see A. Hurvitz, 'Wisdom Vocabulary in the Hebrew Psalter: A Contribution to the Study of "Wisdom Psalms"', *VT* 38 (1988), pp. 41–51. On 'wisdom vocabulary' in general see R. N. Whybray, *The Intellectual Tradition in the Old Testament* (Berlin, 1974).

[18] See, for example, H. Cazelles, *'ašrê*, *ThWAT* 1 (1973), col. 482 (E. tr., *TDOT* 1 [rev. edn, Grand Rapids, 1977], p. 446).

It may be concluded that the use of 'wisdom psalms' as a blanket term for all those psalms in the Psalter which express serious thoughts on religious matters as distinct from spontaneous expressions of faith, confession, praise, distress, etc. (von Rad's 'preponderance of theological thoughts') is a mistaken one. This terminology may be useful if it extends the corpus of wisdom literature by identifying those few psalms and parts of psalms which have marked affinities with the acknowledged wisdom books; but a too indiscriminate use of it tends to weaken the distinctiveness of the notion of 'wisdom' in Old Testament studies, and also draws attention away from the question of the character of the Psalter considered as a whole.

It is both a pleasure and an honour to participate in this tribute to a distinguished Old Testament scholar who has always been concerned in his work to stress the importance of the meanings of words and their proper use.

14   Wisdom and Daniel

B. A. Mastin

According to J. M. Schmidt, L. Noack, writing in 1857, was the first scholar to describe apocalyptic as the product of wisdom.[1] Some while before this, however, J. G. Eichhorn had claimed that what Daniel learnt in Babylon in the sixth century BC had contributed in a significant way to his book.[2] More recently, discussion of such topics has usually taken as its starting-point G. von Rad's assertion that the roots of apocalyptic are to be found in wisdom, and not, as is frequently supposed, in prophecy.[3] But, because this theory has rightly not won wide acceptance, and also because E. W. Nicholson[4] and M. A. Knibb[5] have provided valuable summaries and critiques both of von Rad's position and of the responses of other scholars to it, there is no need to cover this ground again here. Instead, attention will be concentrated on a modified form of von Rad's hypothesis which has a number of adherents.

Von Rad himself includes the interpretation of dreams among the activities of the wise,[6] and in the fourth edition of his *Theologie des Alten Testaments* he gives this increased prominence as a factor which lies behind the emergence of apocalyptic.[7] H.-P. Müller sees here the key to a correct understanding of the link between wisdom and apocalyptic. He believes

---

[1] *Die jüdische Apokalyptik* (Neukirchen-Vluyn, 1969), pp. 13–14. Schmidt refers to Noack's *Der Ursprung des Christenthums* (Leipzig, 1857). I have not had access to this, or to the second edition of Schmidt's work.

[2] *Einleitung in das Alte Testament*, 3 (3rd edn, Leipzig, 1803), pp. 384–7.

[3] *Theologie des Alten Testaments*, 2 (Munich, 1961), pp. 314–28 (E. tr., *Old Testament Theology*, 2 [Edinburgh and London, 1965], pp. 301–15); *Theologie des Alten Testaments*, 2 (4th edn, Munich, 1965) contains a revised and much fuller treatment of the subject which has not been translated into English, but, since I have not been able to obtain this, I have used the seventh edition (Munich, 1980), pp. 316–38; *Weisheit in Israel* (Neukirchen-Vluyn, 1970), pp. 337–63 (E. tr., *Wisdom in Israel* [London, 1972], pp. 263–83).

[4] 'Apocalyptic', in G. W. Anderson (ed.), *Tradition and Interpretation* (Oxford, 1979), pp. 207–11.

[5] 'Prophecy and the Emergence of the Jewish Apocalypses', in R. Coggins, A. Phillips and M. Knibb (eds.), *Israel's Prophetic Tradition. Essays in honour of Peter R. Ackroyd* (Cambridge, 1982), pp. 165–9.

[6] *Theologie*, 1st edn, p. 320 (E. tr., p. 307); cf. *Weisheit*, pp. 358–60 (E. tr., pp. 280–1).

[7] P. 331; cf. pp. 323–5 (in the seventh edition).

that apocalyptic is related, not to the wisdom movement in general, as von Rad holds, but more specifically to mantic wisdom, though he recognizes that other sources, such as the prophetic movement, have also made important contributions to it.[8]

Mantic wisdom is learning which is connected in some way to the work of the diviner, and our detailed knowledge of it comes mainly from texts which have been discovered in Mesopotamia. A large number of these deal with the meaning of omens, and the nature of this literature can be illustrated from the translations of explanations of dreams by A. L. Oppenheim[9] and of the series *Šumma izbu*, which is concerned with abnormal human or animal births, by E. Leichty.[10] The characteristic form of the entries is, 'If *x* happens, then *y* will take place'; for example, 'If [in his dream] he cuts down a poplar: peace of mind. If he cuts down a tamarisk: no peace of mind.'[11] One other type of material which is related to mantic wisdom will be mentioned on p. 168 below.

Daniel and his three companions were taught 'the literature and language of the Chaldeans', but their outstanding ability was bestowed on them by their God, who enabled Daniel to become expert at determining the meaning of dreams (Dan. i 4, 17). The only aspects of the diviners' work to which the author(s) of Daniel refer are the interpretation of omens and the giving of advice to the king, both of which could properly have been undertaken by a pious Jew, so in the stories Daniel functions at court and is even put in charge of all the wise men of Babylon (Dan. ii 48; cf. iv 6 [iv 9], v 11) without compromising his religious beliefs. This would not, of course, have been possible in real life. Yet Daniel's wisdom is superior to that of the other diviners because God endows him with it, not because he is cleverer or more learned than they are (Dan. ii 19, 27–8, 47; cf. iv 3–6, 15 [iv 6–9, 18], v 8, 11–12). Indeed, one of his achievements is of a different order from theirs. The wise men protest that telling Nebuchadnezzar what he has dreamed is outside the competence of any human being, and they add that no ruler has previously asked such a thing (Dan. ii 10–11),[12] but Daniel is able to fulfil this highly unreasonable demand because God reveals to him what he needs to know (Dan. ii 19). Thus, on the one hand, it would not be surprising if mantic wisdom had made a significant contribution to the

---

[8] 'Mantische Weisheit und Apokalyptik', in *Congress Volume: Uppsala 1971 (SVT* 22, 1972), pp. 271, 292.

[9] 'The Interpretation of Dreams in the Ancient Near East, with a Translation of an Assyrian Dream-Book', *Transactions of the American Philosophical Society* ns 46 (1956), pp. 257–9, 263–94.

[10] *The Omen Series Šumma Izbu* (Locust Valley, 1970).

[11] Oppenheim, 'Interpretation of Dreams', p. 285.

[12] This assertion is, however, incorrect, though the author of Dan. ii presumably thought it was true; see p. 167 and n. 33 below.

stories of chapters i, ii, iv and v, which are about the education and work of diviners, though on the other hand, since Daniel does not operate on the same level as the Babylonian sages, contrasts between mantic wisdom and what is related here may be expected too.

The influence of mantic wisdom has also been found in Dan. vii–xii. Thus, for example, J. J. Collins comments that here, as in the stories, 'a wise interpreter' decodes 'revelation [which] is given in a veiled symbolic form',[13] while P. A. Porter argues that 'the peculiar physical characteristics ascribed to the various beasts [in Dan. vii and viii] are ultimately traceable to Mesopotamian mantic wisdom traditions'.[14]

The purpose of this essay is to estimate the role of mantic wisdom in the production of the book of Daniel by discussing, in the limited space available, a representative selection of the topics which bear on this issue.

1

S. B. Reid claims that the appeal to mantic wisdom cannot shed light on the origin of apocalyptic. He thinks that 'when [Müller] tries to define mantic wisdom as a hybrid of both prophecy and wisdom, the term "mantic" becomes meaningless, for it is defined by terms which themselves are never defined'.[15] But, first, Müller does not 'define mantic wisdom as a hybrid of both prophecy and wisdom'. His point is rather that, though mantic wisdom was the ground from which apocalyptic developed, there were other contributory factors, of which prophecy was one. Secondly, it is possible to provide a precise definition of mantic wisdom. In Mesopotamia, texts which were drawn up by diviners have survived, and mantic wisdom is what is contained in this material, together with an understanding of the principles lying behind the practice of divination which are implicit in it. Far less is known about mantic wisdom in Israel or Judah, but it is reasonable to assume that the interpreters of omens in Mesopotamia and Palestine shared a basically similar outlook, even though it is perhaps unlikely that mantic lore was identical in all respects in both areas. Such learning persisted into the Hellenistic Age, and for present purposes it is sufficient to refer in this connection to J. C. VanderKam's demonstration that 1 Enoch was greatly influenced by it.[16]

Reid rightly observes that 'mantic activity ... is not related to wisdom literature alone, nor should it be confined to a classification under

---

[13] 'The Court-Tales in Daniel and the Development of Apocalyptic', *JBL* 94 (1975), p. 230.
[14] *Metaphors and Monsters* (Lund, 1983), p. 15.
[15] *Enoch and Daniel* (Berkeley, 1989), p. 14, citing Müller, 'Mantische Weisheit', p. 292.
[16] *Enoch and the Growth of an Apocalyptic Tradition* (Washington, 1984).

prophetic activity and literature nor under priestly activity and literature'.[17] But he incorrectly concludes from this that mantic wisdom is one of the 'outmoded categories' whose use he believes invalidates the debate about the origin of apocalyptic.[18] Since the various branches of mantic activity can be distinguished, it may properly be asked how far data which are relevant to the work of the interpreter of omens have moulded the book of Daniel.

2

Although Daniel and his three companions function as wise men at a heathen court, the tales of Dan. ii, iv and v owe much to native Israelite tradition.

As far as I am aware, F. Bleek was the first scholar to claim that Dan. ii is modelled on Gen. xli.[19] It is now generally agreed that Dan. ii, iv and v and Gen. xli have the same basic structure, apart from the omission of a reward for the hero in Dan. iv. A foreign king gives his wise men tasks which are too difficult for them (Dan. ii 2–11, iv 3–4 [iv 6–7], v 7–8; Gen. xli 8), but, because they are helped by their God (Dan. ii 19, 23, 30, 47, iv 5, 6, 15 [iv 8, 9, 18], v 11, 14; Gen. xli 16, 38–9), Daniel and Joseph are successful where the wise men fail (Dan. ii 25–45, iv 16–23 [iv 19–26], v 25–8; Gen. xli 25–32), and they are rewarded by being raised to high positions at court (Dan. ii 48–9, v 29; Gen. xli 40–6).

Two recent theories about the affinities of Dan. ii must, however, be considered briefly. First, S. Niditch and R. Doran hold that Gen. xli and Dan. ii, together with Dan. iv and v, which they do not discuss in detail, belong to the same literary type, which also occurs both in the Syriac version of Ahiqar 5–7 and in folktales from other parts of the world.[20] Yet, as P. J. Milne emphasizes, Niditch and Doran 'were not able to identify a type or form that fully describes' either Gen. xli or Dan. ii,[21] and so all the resemblances between these chapters cannot be accounted for by appealing to the background in folklore to which these scholars refer. Secondly, R. R. Wilson thinks that six so-called Egyptian prophecies 'all follow a pattern which is roughly similar to the one found in Daniel 2, 4, and 5', and he believes that this Egyptian material may well have influenced these stories. Wilson says that the prophecies 'picture a wise speaker standing in the presence of the king and delivering messages dealing with present and

---

[17] *Enoch and Daniel*, p. 22.   [18] *Ibid.*, p. 24.
[19] 'Ueber Verfasser und Zweck des Buches Daniel; Revision der in neuerer Zeit darüber geführten Untersuchungen', *ThZ* 3 (1822), p. 280.
[20] 'The Success Story of the Wise Courtier: A Formal Approach', *JBL* 96 (1977), pp. 179–93.
[21] *Vladimir Propp and the Study of Structure in Hebrew Biblical Narrative* (Sheffield, 1988), p. 197.

future social and political conditions',[22] but, despite these points of contact with Dan. ii, iv and v, there are much closer parallels between these chapters of Daniel and Gen. xli. Neither of these hypotheses can replace the view that Gen. xli was a source for Dan. ii, iv and v.

The traditional critical position that the Joseph stories were composed some while before the exile, which continues to be widely held, is likely to be correct, though even if they were drawn up during the exile, as some scholars suppose, Gen. xli would have been available to the author(s) of Dan. ii, iv and v. Because of the striking resemblances between Gen. xli and these sections of the book of Daniel, it is probable that it was used as a model for them. In that case, though these narratives are set in Babylonia, themes taken from a tale about mantic activity which was almost certainly written in Palestine play an important part in them.

If, as is widely, though not universally, agreed, the Daniel of Ezek. xiv 14, 20, xxviii 3 lies behind the figure of Daniel himself, there may be a point of contact with traditions about another diviner which were transmitted in Palestine. The words addressed to the ruler of Tyre in Ezek. xxviii 3, which the RSV translates, 'you are indeed wiser than Daniel; no secret is hidden from you',[23] may well indicate that this Daniel is endowed with mantic wisdom. The fact that the ruler of Tyre is compared with him suggests that he may have come from Syrophoenicia, and his inclusion with two non-Israelites, Noah and Job, in Ezek. xiv 14, 20 is consistent with this. Ezekiel is probably referring to the Dn'il who appears in the Aqhat epic, though this is not to say that he knew that text. While Dn'il is not a diviner, he employs magic arts, which can in principle be distinguished from mantic activity but which are often associated with it, and so a development which led to the attribution of mantic skills to Daniel would be readily intelligible.[24] Thus a notable diviner, who was perhaps Syrophoenician but

---

[22] 'From Prophecy to Apocalyptic: Reflections on the Shape of Israelite Religion', *Semeia* 21 (1981), p. 91. For translations of the Egyptian prophecies, see A. Erman, *Die Literatur der Aegypter* (Leipzig, 1923), pp. 65–73, 132–48, 152–7 (E. tr., *The Literature of the Ancient Egyptians* [London, 1927], pp. 36–44, 94–108, 111–15); H. Gressmann (ed.), *Altorientalische Texte zum Alten Testament* (2nd edn, Berlin and Leipzig, 1926), pp. 48–50; and W. Spiegelberg, *Die sogenannte demotische Chronik* (Leipzig, 1914), pp. 13–22. One of these texts, however, the Prophecy of the Lamb, diverges from the pattern outlined by Wilson in that the prophecy is read to the Pharaoh after the lamb's death, while another, the Demotic Chronicle, is the written exegesis of a number of oracles.

[23] *Pace* K. W. Carley, *The Book of the Prophet Ezekiel* (Cambridge, 1974), p. 189, the NEB's rendering, 'Is no secret too dark for you?', need not mean that 'the ruler has attempted to probe forbidden wisdom' (cf. G. R. Driver, 'Linguistic and Textual Problems: Ezekiel', *Biblica* 19 [1938], p. 177).

[24] See H.-P. Müller, 'Magisch-mantische Weisheit und die Gestalt Daniels', *UF* 1 (1969), pp. 79–94, and J. Day, 'The Daniel of Ugarit and Ezekiel and the Hero of the Book of Daniel', *VT* 30 (1980), pp. 174–84, for discussions of the issues examined in this paragraph, and, for different estimates of the material, H.-M. Wahl, 'Noah, Daniel und Hiob in Ezechiel xiv 12–20 (21–3): Anmerkungen zum traditionsgeschichtlichen Hintergrund', *VT* 42 (1992), pp. 542–53, and the articles he cites on p. 546, nn. 23, 24.

about whom Ezekiel presumably learnt in Judah, may well have given his name to the hero of stories which in all likelihood originated in the eastern Diaspora.[25]

As far as I am aware, no direct links have been discovered between the interpretations which Daniel provides in Dan. ii, iv and v and ancient near eastern omen literature. Yet, in showing how Daniel, like Joseph, was more successful than the other sages at a heathen court, and in describing how God revealed the future to Nebuchadnezzar and Belshazzar, the author(s) of these chapters shared many of the presuppositions of mantic wisdom. They affirmed that God may choose to communicate with men through dreams, and implicitly they emphasized the immutability of the divine decrees.[26] Although the diviner's skills were rejected out of hand in deuteronomic circles (Deut. xviii 10–14), there were, as J. C. VanderKam has demonstrated, many basic similarities between prophecy and divination.[27] Mantic lore has been employed in these stories to express in a new way themes which were already familiar as part of the Jewish heritage.

Some features of Dan. i, ii, iv and v may well reflect acquaintance with the activities of diviners. For example, when Nebuchadnezzar establishes whether his wise men are able to interpret his dream by insisting that they first relate it to him, and tells them that failure to do this proves that they have conspired to lie to him (Dan. ii 5–9), the author may have in mind the distrust of the diviners' professional honesty which is attested in both cuneiform and Greek literature. Thus, Sennacherib is said to have divided the haruspices into groups so that they could not collude when they gave him an answer about an important matter,[28] while Xenophon recounts both how the father of the elder Cyrus had his son taught how to divine, so that he would not be at the mercy of soothsayers, who might wish to deceive him,[29] and how he himself knew enough about divination to be able to check the main findings of Silanus, a soothsayer who was plotting against him during the expedition of 401–399 BC.[30] A much closer parallel to Dan. ii is afforded by this material than by either Nabonidus' dispute with

[25] W. L. Humphreys, 'A Life-Style for Diaspora: A Study of the Tales of Esther and Daniel', *JBL* 92 (1973), pp. 221–3.

[26] Müller, 'Mantische Weisheit', pp. 280–90 (who omits eschatology from the corresponding list in *ThWAT* 2 (1977), col. 935 (E. tr., *TDOT* 4 [Grand Rapids, 1980], pp. 377–8), claims that it is easier to explain five features which are characteristic of apocalyptic literature if mantic wisdom lies behind it. I had hoped to examine one of these, determinism, in this essay, but, because of lack of space, this subject must be left for treatment elsewhere.

[27] 'The Prophetic-Sapiential Origins of Apocalyptic Thought', in J. D. Martin and P. R. Davies (eds.), *A Word in Season. Essays in honour of William McKane* (Sheffield, 1986), pp. 168–73, 176.

[28] H. Tadmor, 'The "Sin of Sargon"', *Eretz-Israel* 5 (1958), pp. 154–9 (in Hebrew). I am grateful to the Rev. A. A. Macintosh for his kindness in providing me with a translation of this article.   [29] *Cyropaedia*, I. vi. 2.   [30] *Anabasis*, V. vi. 29.

the priests of Babylon[31] or Darius I's alleged massacre of the Magi,[32] which are frequently believed to lie behind it, while D. Flusser's comparison of the demand which Nebuchadnezzar makes with the testing of seven oracles by Croesus[33] suffers from the disadvantage that he has to assume that an earlier form of the narrative in Daniel has been misunderstood.

In sum, Dan. i, ii, iv and v are heavily indebted to native Israelite tradition: three of the stories are modelled on Gen. xli, all the stories propagate themes which were part of the Jewish heritage, and Daniel may have been named after a Canaanite diviner who had become domesticated in Israel. But at the same time, the detail of the stories is on occasion influenced by an awareness of non-Israelite mantic practice, the author(s) accept the legitimacy of divination, and some of its characteristics colour their thought.

3

Three issues raised by the vision reports of chapters vii–xii must now be considered.

First, Porter finds the source of the animal imagery in Dan. vii–viii in mantic wisdom,[34] and claims that 'nearly all of the peculiar features characterizing [these] animals ... are anticipated in the *Šumma izbu* series' (p. 18). But, as he himself concedes (p. 19), there are no parallels in the extant portions of *Šumma izbu* to some of these features. Moreover, he goes beyond the evidence when (p. 17) he compares 'it had three ribs in its mouth' (Dan. vii 5) with 'if an anomaly holds its lung(s) in its mouth' (*Šumma izbu* XVII 16'), since the Akkadian word used is *ḫašû*, which means '(1) human lungs, (2) belly, entrails, (3) animal lungs',[35] but not ribs. In addition, as Professor W. G. Lambert, who has kindly allowed me to consult him on this point, observes, what is described in Dan. vii 5 is surely a wild animal with some other creature's ribs in its mouth, while in *Šumma izbu* XVII 16' there is the very different picture of an anomaly whose own lungs are in its mouth.[36] Porter associates 'the ten-horned beast [which] is neither named nor likened to any specific species' with 'numerous birth-omen texts beginning "If an *izbu* [= anomaly]..."' (p. 28), but it is unsatisfactory to look here for the origin of the terrible fourth beast, since, as Leichty notes, 'usually ... [the term *izbu*] refers to sheep'[37] – a position which Porter accepts (p. 21). Porter has not succeeded in showing that the author of Dan. vii knew the series

---

[31] *ANET*, pp. 312–5.   [32] Herodotus, *Histories*, III.78–9.

[33] 'The Four Empires in the Fourth Sibyl and in the Book of Daniel', *IOS* 2 (1972), p. 156, citing Herodotus, *Histories*, I.46–9.   [34] *Metaphors and Monsters*, pp. 15–29.

[35] *CAD*, VI, pp. 143–4.   [36] Private communication dated 18 January 1993.

[37] *Šumma Izbu*, p. 3, n. 4.

Šumma izbu. Although there are much better parallels to the animals of Dan. viii in *Šumma izbu*, this is not sufficient by itself to demonstrate that they were borrowed from it, and, if the animals of Dan. vii were not taken from *Šumma izbu*, it is less likely that the animals of Dan. viii were.

There is no space to discuss either F. C. Burkitt's suggestion that Dan. viii 3–5, 20–1 has an astrological background,[38] or the hypotheses of R. Eisler[39] and A. Caquot[40] that this is true of Dan. vii 2–14 and Dan. vii 4–6 respectively, but attention may be drawn to Caquot's criticism of Eisler's views[41] and to J. Day's examination of those of Burkitt and Caquot.[42] The theories of these three scholars are unconvincing.

Secondly, there are striking similarities between Dan. viii 23–5, xi 3–45 and three so-called Akkadian prophecies, and W. G. Lambert concludes that 'it is certainly possible, perhaps even probable, that the author of Daniel adapted the style of a traditional Babylonian genre for his own purposes'.[43] A. K. Grayson says that the phraseology used in the *vaticinia ex eventu* of these texts 'is borrowed from omen literature', but he thinks that 'the relation of the prophecies ... to divination is purely stylistic' and that 'there is no meaningful connection with omen literature'.[44] But in that case, though the scribes who composed the prophecies were familiar with mantic wisdom, the Jewish author(s) of Dan. viii 23–5, xi 3–45 may have known it only at second hand, through the texts which were their model.

G. F. Hasel supposes that the scheme of four world empires which appears in Dan. ii and vii is also found in the Dynastic Prophecy, which is one of the Akkadian prophecies mentioned above, though he himself admits that the differences between this text and Daniel are so pronounced that 'even [an] indirect relationship seems to be out of the question'.[45] Moreover, Collins correctly objects that in the Dynastic Prophecy the 'sequence [of empires] is not numbered ... and there is no indication that the number four is given any definitive status'.[46] There is no link here between Daniel and mantic lore.

Thirdly, Collins maintains that 'the understanding of revelation is the same in both halves of the book. Revelation is given in a veiled symbolic form, which must then be decoded by a wise interpreter.'[47] There are many basic similarities between the visions of Dan. vii and viii and the stories of

[38] In F. Cumont, 'La Plus Ancienne Géographie astrologique', *Klio* 9 (1909), p. 273.
[39] *ΙΗΣΟΥΣ ΒΑΣΙΛΕΥΣ ΟΥ ΒΑΣΙΛΕΥΣΑΣ*, 2 (Heidelberg, 1930), pp. 660–70.
[40] 'Sur les quatre bêtes de *Daniel* VII', *Semitica* 5 (1955), pp. 5–13.   [41] *Ibid.*, p. 10, n. 2.
[42] *God's Conflict with the Dragon and the Sea* (Cambridge, 1985), pp. 154–5.
[43] *The Background of Jewish Apocalyptic* (London, 1978), p. 16. See further pp. 9–16, 18–20.
[44] *Babylonian Historical-Literary Texts* (Toronto and Buffalo, 1975), pp. 13, 16, 22.
[45] 'The Four World Empires of Daniel 2 against its Near Eastern Environment', *JSOT* 12 (1979), pp. 21–4, 28–30. The quotation is from p. 24.
[46] *Daniel with an Introduction to Apocalyptic Literature* (Grand Rapids, 1984), p. 50.
[47] 'Court-Tales in Daniel', p. 230.

Dan. ii, iv and v, but, as Collins concedes,[48] interpretation of scripture (cf. Dan. ix 2, 24–7) is less assuredly a part of mantic wisdom, and, as was noted above, Dan. xi 3–45 is in all likelihood modelled on Akkadian prophecies, which are at one remove from omen literature. This also tells against Collins's opinion that 'the most plausible background' for Dan. xi 2–xii 4 is the accounts from the ancient near east of messages spoken in dreams.[49] There is a general affinity between the world of the diviner and Dan. vii–xii, but other sources have made major contributions to these chapters as well.

4

VanderKam holds that 'divination supplied a thought-world and suggested certain media for revelations about the future' to 'the scholars who produced the earliest Jewish apocalypses', but he rightly adds that 'it would be simplistic to claim that "apocalyptic" derives either from "wisdom" (of whatever kind) or "prophecy". The Jewish writers of apocalyptic works drew on both and much more.'[50] The choice of Jewish diviners at a foreign court as the heroes of the stories of Dan. i–vi, and the subsequent composition of vision reports which provide Daniel with a different but related role in the disclosure of the future, demonstrate the authors' interest in mantic lore. They shared many of the presuppositions of mantic wisdom, and some of its characteristics coloured their thought. But the beliefs of the learned scribes who produced the book of Daniel were not compromised by the fact that the religious synthesis which prevailed in the circles to which they belonged was more favourable to divination than either the Deuteronomists or Second Isaiah had been. Their extensive knowledge of documents that were later to be included in the Old Testament, of ancient Canaanite myths which had become domesticated in Israel, and of material from their pagan environment, lay behind what was in large measure a new presentation of themes which already had a central place in the Jewish religious tradition. Mantic wisdom has made an important contribution to the book of Daniel, but care must be taken not to over-emphasize the part it plays.

It is a great pleasure to dedicate this essay to my former teacher Professor J. A. Emerton, to whom I am heavily indebted for many kindnesses and whose encouragement has meant much to me.

[48] *Ibid.*, p. 232.　　[49] *Daniel*, p. 105.　　[50] *Enoch*, p. 190.

15   Ecclesiasticus: a tract for the times

John G. Snaith

Often Ben Sira's own words have been used to describe his book: he spoke of himself as 'a gleaner following the grape-gatherers' (xxxiii 16).[1] Rightly regarded as one of the last of the traditional wisdom writers, he gathered up the loose ends of his predecessors in that genre. Such a description, however, does not do him enough credit, as it ignores the differences that exist between his own book and the work of the authors of Proverbs and Ecclesiastes. Certainly he gleaned a great deal from the Old Testament[2] and used widely the literary genres of both wisdom literature and psalmody[3] as well as adding others. But the real, lasting significance of his book can best be seen against the historical background of its authorship – only when we look at the political and social circumstances of Sirach's own time can we appreciate that he is not just summing up the past, but using the wisdom tradition positively for his own time. The phrase 'a tract for the times', often used of the book of Daniel and its relevance to Maccabean times, is no less true of Ecclesiasticus just before the Hellenistic reform. However, Sirach writes in his own name (l 27) without attributing his words to some ancient worthy as do Proverbs and Ecclesiastes, which both claim Solomonic patronage (though in different ways); even the author of Daniel hid behind an exilic personage. The Greek translation by Sirach's grandson even betrays a strong family interest, almost like a family firm of publishers! To see the reasons and circumstances of both authorship and translation we should examine the historical situation when Sirach wrote.

1

Although Sirach, like other wisdom writers, largely disregards specific historical events, we can deduce an approximate date for the authorship of his book in the original Hebrew from the Preface which his grandson wrote to his Greek translation. He says that he 'came to Egypt in the thirty-eighth

---

[1] Biblical quotations are cited from the REB.
[2] See J. G. Snaith, 'Biblical Quotations in the Hebrew of Ecclesiasticus', *JTS* ns 18 (1967), pp. 1–12.
[3] See A. A. Di Lella, *The Wisdom of Ben Sira* (Garden City, 1987), pp. 21–30.

year of king Euergetes'. Two of the Ptolemies of Egypt were called Euergetes. The first reigned for only 25 years, and the second began to rule in 170 BC, at first jointly with his brother, and died 53 years later in 117 BC. There was a short break, but the thirty-eighth year from his accession brings the grandson's arrival in Egypt to 132 BC, a date commonly accepted. Given that the grandson was about 30 years old when he emigrated to Egypt and allowing 25 years for a generation, then Sirach himself was active in Jerusalem in the late 180s just before the Hellenistic reform which led to the Maccabean revolt. This fits well the long panegyric in 1 1–21 on 'the high priest Simon, son of Onias', commonly linked with Simon II, who died in 196 BC after 23 years in the post – a length of office worthy of such a panegyric, particularly as the high priest was the principal native Jewish leader in Ptolemaic and Seleucid times.

It is important to note that Sirach wrote in the period before the Hellenistic reform and the Maccabean revolt – a period from which there is little other extant literature. Alexander the Great had conquered Palestine in his whirlwind passage through the middle east in 332, thus ending two centuries of Persian domination. At the division of Alexander's empire on his death in 323 his generals started a long struggle, contending who should obtain which parts of it. Palestine thus became a bone of contention between Asian and African powers, the Seleucids in Syria and the Ptolemies in Egypt. In 301 Ptolemy I gained control, Palestine remaining within the Egyptian sphere of influence until the Seleucid Antiochus III started extending Syrian influence in the near east. After an initial defeat by Egypt at Raphia in 217, Antiochus took advantage of the accession in Egypt of a young, inexperienced king, soundly defeating the Egyptian army at Panium near the source of the Jordan in 198, so Palestine became Syrian again. Following Alexander's conquests, Greek mercenary soldiers had married local girls and settled down, so that Greek-type cities had sprung up throughout the near east. It had become a Hellenistic world dominated by Greek ideas, Greek customs, Greek values. Pious Jews opposed to free-thinking Greek ways must have huddled together inside Jerusalem to defend the faith. It is noteworthy that little new Hebrew literature survives from Jerusalem at this time: additions were made to larger prophetic collections, with authors' personalities sunk in the prophets of old. Ecclesiastes appeared with its questioning spirit, using Solomon as a kind of sponsor. Such literary activity probably arose through a lack of self-confidence then prevalent in Palestine. Yet Sirach breaks with this, signing his book in his own name (1 27): here is no leaning on Solomonic tradition as in Ecclesiastes and the Wisdom of Solomon, but straightforward authorship in the Greek fashion.

With Greek culture surrounding Sirach, it would be no surprise to discover in his work 'a Jewish declaration of war against Hellenism', as R.

Smend stated.[4] It is probably true that 'the deadly spirit of accommodation and compromise was rampant'.[5] Doubtless Sirach disliked this intensely, but this does not justify Smend's contentious remark. He implies that Sirach was wholly conservative, clinging to the past. Sirach certainly introduces Jewish piety into the wisdom movement, but it would be quite wrong to imply that he rejected all Hellenism. This article hopes to demonstrate how Sirach shows a positive attitude to Hellenistic culture: surrounded by Greek influence he sought to show pious Jews how to live with Greek culture positively, not rejecting it altogether. It was in this arena of competing Hebrew and Greek cultures that Sirach 'was moved to compile a book of his own on the themes of learning and wisdom, in order that, with this further help, scholars might make greater progress in their studies by living as the law directs', as the grandson wrote in his preface. As 'a gleaner following the grape-gatherers' (xxxiii 16) he gathers much wisdom thought from books like Proverbs, but also applies himself to celebrating the history of his people in the long hymn on famous men (xliv–l) as well as borrowing material from Egyptian proverbial literature and Hellenistic aretalogies. But Hellenistic society may be seen clearly in some of his advice on social life and manners.

2

Signs can certainly be seen in Sirach's book of people adopting Greek ideas and practices, as for example in medicine (xxxviii 1–19). Later there was considerable feeling in rabbinic Judaism against the medical profession: in the Mishnah (*Kiddushin* iv 14) it is said that 'the best among physicians is destined for Gehenna'. Earlier in 2 Chron. xvi 12, Asa, king of Judah, is strongly criticized for consulting a doctor rather than seeking God's guidance for his foot disease. Supporting his more progressive view Sirach refers to the incident at Marah (xxxviii 5; cf. Exod. xv 23–5), where the Lord instructs Moses to throw a log into the water to sweeten it, presumably due to the chemical qualities in the water. Sirach thus implies that drugs can be used beneficially, as God initiated something similar on that occasion, approving Greek ideas as against negative pious attitudes. Not that religious practice is neglected altogether: when you fall ill, you are advised to 'pray to the Lord' (xxxviii 9), 'amend your ways' (verse 10) and 'bring a fragrant offering' (verse 11); but then 'the doctor should be called' (verse 12), because 'a time may come when your recovery is in his hands' (verse

[4] Quoted by M. Hengel, *Judentum und Hellenismus* (Tübingen, 1969), p. 252 (E. tr., *Judaism and Hellenism*, 1 [London, 1974], p. 138).

[5] A. A. Di Lella, 'Conservative and Progressive Theology: Sirach and Wisdom', *CBQ* 28 (1966), p. 139.

13). Thus Sirach commends new Greek medical ideas while keeping his options open on religious observance.

Further openness to the world of Greek customs may be seen in xxxi 12–xxxii 13, where he discusses dining customs and table manners. Good table manners require one to be sensitive to others (xxxi 14–15) and not to reach out greedily for food (verses 14, 18); he also recommends temperate drinking (verses 25–30). He gives guidance for hosting banquets (xxxii 1, 2) even to the rather obvious points of not interrupting musical entertainment (verse 3) and of leaving promptly at the right time (verse 11). The whole passage could well be used as advice on attending formal dinners today! Before leaving the passage we should note the concluding advice:

> And one thing more: give praise to your Maker,
> who has filled your cup with his benefits.   (verse 13)

This concluding couplet of suitable religious advice resembles that which concluded the earlier passage on medical matters:

> He who sins before his Maker
> shows himself arrogant before the doctor.   (xxxviii 19)

Further, A. A. Di Lella is surely right to detect cautions against 'the futility of Greek speculation into the nature of reality':[6]

> Do not pry into things too hard for you or investigate what is beyond your reach.
> Meditate on what the Lord has commanded: what he has kept hidden need not concern you.
> Do not busy yourself with matters that are beyond you: even what he has shown you is beyond the grasp of mortals.
> Many have been led astray by their theorizing, and evil imaginings have impaired their judgements.   (iii 31–4)

Before Jason's Hellenistic reform many people in Judah must have envied, even aped, fashionable Greek ways: 'no smoke without fire'. The move towards Greek ways must have commanded some popular support: Greek customs spread in Alexander's wake rapidly with the foundation of so many Greek cities in Palestine. Greeks gloried in intellectual curiosity, which frequently led on to advances in philosophy and science; but their opinions were often uncertain – shifting sand to base one's life on – and Sirach sought firm foundations amid the conflicting currents of Greek speculation. Sirach's view of such Greek intellectualism is aptly summed up in xix 24:

> Better to lack brains and be God-fearing
> than to have great intelligence and transgress the law

[6] A. A. Di Lella, 'Conservative and Progressive Theology', p. 142.

(where he means, of course, the Mosaic law, not administrative law).

Greek influence was traced in Ecclesiasticus itself by T. Middendorp[7] in many instances where he claims that Sirach quotes Greek writers. It is puzzling how Middendorp can detect so many quotations by Sirach of Greek works in the largely non-extant Hebrew. Detecting quotations of Greek in the original Hebrew in a work much of which is extant only in Greek translation seems an oddly unreliable method. J. T. Sanders[8] has examined Middendorp's work in detail and concludes that we must think of Sirach's 'unconscious use of Hellenic material that has entered into the mainstream of Hellenistic thinking and speech'. R. Pautrel[9] claimed to find Stoic influence in the book, summed up particularly in the verse: 'The end of the matter is this: God is all' (xliii 27); the unity of creation and all humanity under one God was hardly limited to Stoics alone – the Old Testament shows belief in it! It may well be that Sirach here is borrowing a Stoic phrase to describe God's almighty power: it may indicate that he knew Stoicism (hardly surprising), but he need not have believed the philosophy.

Sanders's thesis[10] that Sirach had read Theognis' Greek work seems likely; Theognis' primarily practical advice in a gnomic setting is just what Sirach was promoting, and that would appeal to him. Middendorp claims certain passages were 'lifted' from Theognis, thus overstating the case. Would we say that Sirach was 'lifting' from the Bible when he uses biblical phrases, as he does so often in xliv–li? Surely he was using Greek literature in a similar way to bring the two worlds of Hebrew and Greek literature together because he saw this happening in the growing Greek culture of Palestine in the early second century. Jason's Hellenistic reform and the subsequent Maccabean revolt showed just how right he was.

M. Hengel[11] claimed that in the hymn of wisdom's self-praise (chapter xxiv) there are in verses 3–7 'unmistakable parallels' to statements in Hellenistic Isis aretalogies. Under Ptolemaic rule this Egyptian goddess is known to have been worshipped at Acco in Phoenicia, and Hengel suspects she may have been known in Jerusalem. Whether Sirach was aware of close similarities to such pagan literature in his great hymn to wisdom is questionable: he may well have used contemporary literature as widely as possible to show how 'God (i.e. Yahweh) is all' (xliii 27).

Sirach's historical position near the 'dividing line' between Egyptian and Greek periods in Palestine is illustrated also by close parallels with

[7] T. Middendorp, *Die Stellung Jesu Ben Siras zwischen Judentum und Hellenismus* (Leiden, 1973).
[8] J. T. Sanders, *Ben Sira and Demotic Wisdom* (Chico, 1985), pp. 27–45, especially p. 45.
[9] R. Pautrel, 'Ben Sira et la Stoïcisme', *RSR* 51 (1963), pp. 535–49.
[10] J. T. Sanders, *Ben Sira*, pp. 29–38.
[11] M. Hengel, *Judentum und Hellenismus*, pp. 284–8 (E. tr., I, pp. 158–9).

Egyptian literature. In a detailed review of Sirach's relations with Egyptian traditions, Sanders gives considerable space to the Papyrus Insinger,[12] composed by someone prior to Sirach's time, probably in the pre-Ptolemaic era. Several topics discussed in the two works are identical, and are often treated in the same order, an almost certain sign of borrowing. It certainly seems clear that Sirach had read this Egyptian work in addition to the Greek work of Theognis. Sanders even claims that the Egyptian author[13] 'is more like Ben Sira, in both style and content, than is any other collection of proverbs, Theognis included, save only the book of Proverbs itself'.[14] In addition to the Papyrus Insinger and an Egyptian-inspired aretalogy Sirach seems to have used 'The Instruction of Duauf', otherwise known as 'The Satire on Trades', which was probably the source of many ideas and expressions found in xxxviii 24–xxxix 11. This passage should probably be seen as two separate poems, xxxviii 24–34 and xxxix 1–11, treating the skilled craftsman and scribe separately, although they are joined by a kind of inclusio as the scholar/scribe is mentioned in both xxxviii 24 and xxxix 1. The Egyptian author ridicules sculptor, carpenter, gem-maker, barber, merchant, builder, gardener and others. Not only are many details similar but both works conclude triumphantly with praise of the scribe.

In thus quoting Egyptian wisdom literature Sirach continues the precedent set in the book of Proverbs, which in xxii 17–xxiii 11 quotes from the Egyptian Instruction of Amenemope, composed probably in the thirteenth century, but much copied thereafter.

Another trait of the international wisdom tradition is Sirach's use of numerical proverbs, where a specified number of things is quoted, the last going one better, as it were, as in xxvi 5–6:

> Three things there are that alarm me,
> and a fourth I am afraid to face:
> scandalmongering in the city,
>   a mob controlling the assembly,
> and false accusation – all harder to bear
>   than death;
> but a wife's jealousy of a rival brings heartache
>   and grief,
> and everyone feels the lash of her tongue.

This is a passage which illustrates Sirach's negative view of women, a view coming from contemporary life. Even the description of the good wife in

[12] J. T. Sanders, *Ben Sira*, pp. 69–75.
[13] J. T. Sanders claims the author of Papyrus Insinger is one Phibis, but J. Ray in his review of Sanders's book notes that 'he misleads by calling the text Phibis which is probably the name of the copyist, and is usually read Phebhor' (*VT* 35 [1985], p. 383).
[14] J. T. Sanders, *Ben Sira*, p. 105.

Prov. xxxi 10–31 starts with the words: 'Who can find a good wife?' Such numerical proverbs of varying length appear also in xxiii 16, xxv 1–2 and xxvi 28.

The book of Job had discussed innocent suffering: indeed we should probably call this the main theme of the book, a theme frequently present in international wisdom literature. Suffering is not a theme that springs immediately to mind when reading Ecclesiasticus, but it is there. In ii 1 Sirach advises:

> My son, if you aspire to be a servant of the Lord,
> prepare yourself for testing.

The verse introduces a short section on the endurance of hardships.

Such links with Greek and Egyptian texts show a wide familiarity with ancient literatures. Sirach himself said:

> He who is well travelled knows much... (xxxiv 9)

> Travel increases a person's resources. (xxxiv 10)

Also, to show that this was really his own experience and that he was not just copying others, he writes:

> In the course of my journeyings I have seen much
> and understand more than I can put into words. (xxxiv 11)

This is a personal statement of great importance because it illustrates one major characteristic of the book: no other wisdom writer allows his own personality to show at all, let alone sign off with his own name as Sirach does in l 27.

Not only did Sirach speak of foreign travel as a way he had acquired wisdom; he also had considerable experience of participation in important meetings. He advises:

> Make yourself popular in the assembly
> and show deference to the great. (iv 7)

This is to be achieved by cooperation with Lady Wisdom:

> She will advance him above his neighbours
> and find words for him when he speaks in the assembly. (xv 5)
> The assembly welcomes a word from a wise man
> and ponders what he says. (xxi 17)

Such a man will enjoy wide fame:

> The nations will tell of his wisdom
> and the assembled people will sing his praise. (xxxix 10)

All this is seen as very different from the craftsmen who 'rely on their hands' (xxxviii 31): they are skilful at their own craft and essential to public life, yet are 'not in demand at public discussions' (xxxviii 33). Thus wisdom as a practical craft yields precedence to wisdom as 'the law of the Most High' as interpreted by the ideal scribe described in xxxix 1–11 who, interestingly in the light of Sirach's own wide experience, also 'travels in foreign countries' (verse 4).

But, experienced as Sirach may have been in foreign travel, adept as he was in borrowing and adapting foreign wisdom literature (some not extant today), we should not conclude that he only used foreign texts and customs. No-one can deny he was a loyal Jew: many features of his work show this, as the next section will indicate.

3

Sirach's position as a loyal Jew is clearly shown in his identification of wisdom with the Jewish Torah and in the passage in which he praises Israel's ancestors. But it is seen in other, shorter passages too. In l 25–6 he shows considerable animosity towards traditional enemies of Judah in a neat numerical proverb:

> Two nations I detest,
> and a third is no nation at all:
> the inhabitants of Mount Seir, the Philistines,
> and the senseless folk that live at Shechem.

The Philistines, proverbial enemies of Israel, had been subdued by David, but the word may occur here for those 'who had accepted paganism and Hellenization'. 'The inhabitants of Mount Seir', the Edomites, had helped the Babylonians in devastating the land after the exile, occupying southern Judah after 586; when the Jews returned from Exile, they became bitter enemies. But, as the climax of the numerical proverb comes 'the senseless folk that live at Shechem', the Samaritans, bitter enemies of the Jews in the post-exilic period. (Sirach does not even deign to name them.) Such intense hostility to the Samaritans forms a useful prelude to the tensions evident later.

For Sirach wisdom is no longer general instruction, nor is true wisdom found in the various foreign works he cites: 'All wisdom is from the Lord: she dwells with him for ever' (i 1). Wisdom is found by obedience to the law:

> If you long for wisdom, keep the commandments,
> and the Lord will give it you without stint.   (i 26)

Wisdom is now the law of Moses, not just wise men's instructions; nor is it possessed by other nations, but, in spite of its 'dwelling-place in high heaven' (xxiv 4), it 'came to be established in Zion' (xxiv 10). In chapter xxiv fusion between Wisdom and Torah is achieved in Wisdom's own hymn in verses 1–22. The verse following the hymn rams the point home:

> All this is the book of the covenant of God Most High,
> the law laid on us by Moses.   (xxiv 23)

As verses 10–12 show, wisdom (= the law) is at home only in Jerusalem. The law is now all-important:

> All wisdom is the fear of the Lord
> and includes the fulfilling of the law.   (xix 20)

The law becomes a priority in faith:

> Better to lack brains and be God-fearing
> than to have great intelligence and transgress the law.   (xix 24)

The exclusive importance placed on the law by later Sadducees and Pharisees is clearly well on its way. Meditating on what man has been given by God is far preferable to (Hellenistic?) speculations:

> Do not pry into things too hard for you
> or investigate what is beyond your reach.   (iii 21)

Similarly, speculation founded on interpretation of dreams is condemned. Divination and undue attention to dreams had been expressly forbidden in the Torah (Lev. xix 31; Deut. xviii 10–14), yet Sirach sees need to refute them yet again in xxxiv 5. For 'paying heed to dreams is like clutching a shadow or chasing the wind' (xxxiv 2), 'unless they are sent by intervention from the Most High' (xxxiv 6). Clearly Sirach was well aware of the importance attached to dreams in the Bible as, for example, with Joseph and Daniel. Here we find him critical of dreams from a psychological viewpoint, yet taking care not to condemn the use of dreams for divine revelation. So he is criticizing the present while honouring the past.

Before moving to the impressive recital of the past heroes of the faith (chapters xliv 1–xlix 16), we should note how that survey is flanked by references to Enoch (xliv 16, xlix 14). Noah also is mentioned in the first passage (xliv 17–18) and Adam, Joseph, Shem and Seth in the second (xlix 15–16), but Enoch is given priority on birth. Margaret Barker[15] has studied alternative strands of Judaism as seen in the book of Enoch, showing that there were several 'heretical' groups honouring Enoch at that time. Here we see Sirach mentioning him as a prominent figure in his hearers' minds.

In this section, 'the praise of the fathers', we see where Sirach's priorities

---

[15] M. Barker, *The Older Testament* (London, 1987), pp. 8–80.

lay. After a general introduction, including those who are 'unremembered' and are 'as though they had never lived' (xliv 9), he begins his list, not with Adam, who appears only at the end (xlix 16), and then only briefly, but with Noah, who saved the human race after the flood (xliv 17–18). Abraham (xliv 18–21) is then noted for obedience to God, for initiation into the Jewish rite of circumcision and for the promise of a large inheritance for the twelve tribes. Isaac (xliv 22–3) fares as we might expect of an undistinguished son carrying on his father's tradition, but he is credited with fixing tribal boundaries. Strangely, only one verse is given to Jacob (xliv 23), and Joseph is omitted altogether.

Moses (xlv 1–5) is credited with miracles, commandments and hearing God's voice from a cloud. Nothing is said about delivering his people from Egypt. Perhaps in Ptolemaic Palestine Sirach wished to avoid all mention of Egyptian oppression. Certainly liturgical matters come before political and social, as appears from the long, detailed account of Aaron in his fine robes as priest (xlv 6–22). Similar interest in obscure liturgical vestments and ceremonial is prominent also with Phinehas (xlv 23–6), whose description is almost as long as that of Moses, though short compared with Simon, the high priest, later. Sirach may here be fighting a political battle to emphasize that Phinehas was the legitimate successor to the high priesthood as, according to 4 Macc. xviii 12, there were currently disputes about the authentic succession of high priests. This may perhaps suggest why Sirach does not explain in detail the 'zeal' mentioned in verse 23, where Phinehas ends a plague by transfixing both an Israelite man and a Moabite woman with one thrust of his spear, thus pinning them together – such priestly 'zeal' is better ignored!

Joshua (xlvi 1–8) is introduced with a pun on his name: 'great saviour of the Lord's people' recalls the derivation of the Hebrew $y^e h \hat{o} \check{s} \bar{u} a^c$ from $y^e h \hat{o}$ (Yahweh) and the verb $h \hat{o} \check{s} \bar{i} a^c$ ('he saved'). He thus 'well deserved his name'. Sirach recalls several incidents in the biblical account, including Joshua brandishing his sword against Ai (verse 2) and the sun's eclipse (verse 4). The judges are not treated individually (verses 11–12); Samuel receives verses 13–20, where we should note the predominance of the miraculous element in the rout of the Philistines (verse 18) and the predictions of Samuel's ghost after his death (verse 20). Saul is ignored (apart from Samuel establishing the monarchy in verse 13), and there appears a prophetic rather than a royal succession:

> After him (Samuel) there arose Nathan
> to prophesy in the reign of David. (xlvii 11)

Using prophetic succession like this denigrates even further the unmentionable Saul. A brief account is given of David's reign (xlvii 1–11). Little account is taken of David's political and military achievements: the stress is laid on ordering festivals and temple music (even though the temple was not yet built).

After Aaron and Phinehas it is no surprise that Sirach devotes eleven verses to Solomon (xlvii 12–22), stressing temple worship like the Chronicler. The account includes literary skill in 'proverbs and riddles'; yet Sirach, well-balanced here, admits Solomon's adultery (verse 19) and blames him roundly for the breakaway of Ephraim to form the northern kingdom. Indeed, it is only because 'the Lord never ceases to be merciful' that 'he let a scion of David survive' (verse 22): the imputation is clearly that David's royal line was allowed to survive because of Solomon's piety. Jeroboam's revolt is correctly interpreted as due to Solomon's policies (verse 23). The prophetic succession continues with Elijah (xlviii 1–11) and Elisha (verses 12–14), after whom the northern tribes are exiled and

> Only a very small nation was left
> under a ruler from the house of David.   (verse 15)

Interestingly, Hezekiah's water-engineering comes to the fore (verse 17), probably because it was in Jerusalem; it precedes even the Assyrian invasion which brought Isaiah into prominence (verses 18–21). Isaiah is also credited with comforting 'the mourners in Zion' (verse 24), which reminds us that Deutero-Isaiah in Babylon is a modern discovery! Josiah receives three verses (xlix 1–3), and destruction comes upon Jerusalem from an unnamed 'foreign nation', leaving Jeremiah maltreated, even though he was called to 'build and to plant' (verse 7). Ezekiel appears complete with chariot and cherubim (verse 8), but still there is no mention of Babylon. Important with regard to the growth of the canon is the reference in verse 10 to 'the bones of the twelve', as this shows that the book of the twelve minor prophets had already been put together in Sirach's time. In verses 11–13 we find Zerubbabel, the Lord's 'signet ring', and Jeshua the priest erecting the temple, and the list concludes with Nehemiah, restoring walls, gates and houses of Jerusalem. Only Enoch, Joseph, Shem, Seth and Adam remain – a sop to the apocalyptists? – before he dwells at considerable length on the high priest, Simon II (l 1–21).

Simon, the high priest, seems to rise from among the heroes of the past: this is natural, as he was the nearest to a political leader in the years before the Maccabean revolt, and Sirach needed to be polite. But it was Simon's son, Jason, who in the early second century initiated a sweeping Hellenistic reform, including the construction of a Greek-style gymnasium within Jerusalem (2 Macc. iv 7–16). Sirach wrote before this, but not very long beforehand. So we may assume that Greek customs were spreading rapidly through Judah in the years before that reform. What Sirach may have been doing, then, was reminding loyal Jews of their historical and cultural background, showing them how they could integrate Greek ways with their Jewish faith without disloyalty to God. Whether inhabitants of Jerusalem were influenced by Sirach's work we do not know, but his grandson certainly got the idea. On emigrating to Egypt he found Jews there forgetting inherited loyalties and way of life, so he translated his grandfather's work into Greek for their benefit.

Sirach stressed the value of the past in xliv–1, but such appreciation of history appears elsewhere too. For example,

> Consider past generations and see:
> was anyone who trusted the Lord ever disappointed?   (ii 10)

However politically motivated the work may or may not have been, Sirach was certainly a pious man at heart, and it seems right to close, as he did so often, by illustrating that piety. The Jewish practice of almsgiving is commended in:

> As water quenches a blazing fire,
> so almsgiving atones for sin.   (iii 30)

and

> When one begs for alms, do not look the other way,
> so giving him cause to curse you.   (iv 5)

The section on banquets concludes with:

> And one thing more: give thanks to your Maker
> who has filled your cup with his benefits.   (xxxii 13)

Condemnation of the adulterous woman concludes with:

> All who survive her will learn
> that nothing is better than the fear of the Lord,
> nothing sweeter than obeying his commandments.   (xxiii 27)

Similar pious sentiments conclude sections in iv 28 and xix 17.

It is fitting that the longest passage of religious piety comes in the praise of the fathers of old, which is concluded with a special psalm (chapter li) that also closes the whole work.

With Hellenistic reform seemingly just around the corner in Jerusalem, Sirach wrote his book, ignoring the Jews still in Babylon, to provide a Zionist-like declaration of the values of traditional Judaism, a book treasured at Qumran and Masada, and found in the Cairo Geniza, and indeed well known to Jews and Christians throughout the world thanks to the Greek translation of a loyal grandson.

16 The Christian use and the Jewish origins of the Wisdom of Solomon

William Horbury

Not much is known of Wisdom as a Jewish book.[1] Its earliest attestations are Christian, not Jewish; yet its content strongly suggests that it is a non-Christian Jewish work.[2] Here clues to the Jewish origins and rôle of Wisdom are sought in the Christian witness to the book, and, less directly, in Jewish opinion as reflected in the Jewish inscriptions of Egypt.

Internal evidence suggests that Wisdom is a Greek compilation by a single writer, or by writers from the same school, who used more than one source; the work is consistent in its vocabulary and in its indebtedness to Greek thought, but exhibits contrasting changes of subject and style.[3] Profound familiarity with an interpreted Bible is used in order to develop

---

[1] For literature see J. A. Emerton, 'Commentaries on the Wisdom of Solomon', *Theology* 68 (1965), pp. 376–80; C. Larcher, *Etudes sur le livre de la Sagesse* (Paris, 1967); *Le Livre de la Sagesse* (3 vols., Paris, 1983, 1984, 1985) (bibliography by M. Gilbert); E. G. Clarke, *The Wisdom of Solomon* (Cambridge, 1973); D. Winston, *The Wisdom of Solomon* (Garden City, 1979) and 'Solomon, Wisdom of', in D. N. Freedman (ed.), *Anchor Bible Dictionary*, 6 (New York, 1992), pp. 120–7 (bibliography); D. Georgi, *Weisheit Salomos* (Gütersloh, 1980); M. Gilbert, 'Wisdom Literature', in M. E. Stone (ed.), *Jewish Writings of the Second Temple Period* (Assen and Philadelphia, 1984), pp. 283–324 (301–13), and G. Scarpat, *Libro della Sapienza*, 1 (Brescia, 1989) (bibliography); on Jewish use especially, L. Zunz, *Die gottesdienstlichen Vorträge der Juden* (2nd edn, Frankfurt a.M., 1892), pp. 111–12, and E. Schürer, revised by G. Vermes, F. Millar, M. Goodman, M. Black and P. Vermes, *A History of the Jewish People in the Age of Jesus Christ*, 3.1 (Edinburgh, 1986), pp. 568–79 (bibliography).

[2] The absence of specifically Christian conceptions is underlined by J. A. F. Gregg, *The Wisdom of Solomon* (Cambridge, 1909), p. xxi; note especially the lack of Christian messianic allusion in the passages on the righteous sufferer, the exodus and the patriarchs. For a critique of the theory of Christian authorship, as put forward by C. H. Weisse and others, see C. L. W. Grimm, *Das Buch der Weisheit* (Leipzig, 1860), pp. 25–6, and 244 (where he also rebuts H. Graetz's view that xiv 7, on the wood of Noah's ark, is a Christian gloss); in England S. P. Tregelles regarded Christian authorship as possible (n. 29, below).

[3] Georgi, *Weisheit Salomos*, p. 393; W. L. Knox, *St Paul and the Church of the Gentiles* (Cambridge, 1939), p. 81, surmised that the end of the source used in ch. x might have been deliberately suppressed.

the specifically biblical literary tradition.[4] The most likely place of origin is Egypt (section 3, below). Jerome claimed that (unlike Ecclesiasticus, which he knew in Hebrew) it existed 'nowhere among the Hebrews'; 'indeed', he added, 'the very style smells of Greek eloquence'.[5] Originally Jews will have known Wisdom in Greek, and later probably in Latin too. Sources or versions now lost may have circulated in Hebrew or Aramaic; that a Hebrew text representing at least some part of Wisdom existed for a time seems likely on the general ground that the book had high standing among Jews at the time of Christian origins (see below). The Peshiṭta of Wisdom was probably known to some Jews in antiquity, as it was in the thirteenth century.[6] (Compare the influence of the Peshiṭta on the Targum of another Solomonic book, Proverbs.[7])

1   Date

Much recent comment has set the book in Roman rather than Ptolemaic Egypt, under Augustus (C. Larcher; M. Gilbert, allowing also for a slightly later date) or Caligula (D. Winston, G. Scarpat). Yet, if early Christian material is left aside, the other evidence adduced permits dating either in the Greek or the Roman period. Thus, the Greek vocabulary includes many words not otherwise attested before the first century AD, but the body of first-century BC Greek literature is not large.[8] H. St J. Thackeray, on the other hand, suggested that the fluctuation between the forms οὐθείς and οὐδείς in Wisdom in BℵA would be most natural if the Greek text was originally produced about the end of the second century BC, when the two commonly appeared side by side; but further examples (down to AD 186)

---

[4] Larcher, *Etudes*, pp. 86–103; Clarke, *The Wisdom of Solomon*, p. 66 (Wisdom and the Targums); D. Dimant, 'Pseudonymity in the Wisdom of Solomon', in N. Fernández Marcos (ed.), *La Septuaginta en la investigación contemporánea* (Madrid, 1985), pp. 243–55, and 'Use and Interpretation of Mikra in the Apocrypha and Pseudepigrapha', in M. J. Mulder and H. Sysling (eds.), *Mikra* (Assen and Philadelphia, 1988), pp. 379–419 (410–15); A. N. Chester, 'Citing the Old Testament', in D. A. Carson and H. G. M. Williamson (eds.), *It is Written: Scripture Citing Scripture. Essays in Honour of Barnabas Lindars, SSF* (Cambridge, 1988), pp. 141–69 (162–4); L. Ruppert, 'Der leidende Gerechte', in J. W. van Henten, with B. A. G. M. Dehandschutter and H. J. W. van der Klaauw (eds.), *Die Entstehung der jüdischen Martyrologie* (Leiden, 1989), pp. 76–87.

[5] '... apud Hebraeos nusquam est, quin et ipse stilus Graecam eloquentiam redolet' (Jerome's Prologue to the books of Solomon translated from the Hebrew, in R. Weber *et al.*, *Biblia Sacra iuxta Vulgatam Versionem* [2nd edn, 2 vols., Stuttgart, 1975], 2, p. 957).

[6] On Aramaic quotations of Wisdom by Nachmanides, corresponding to the Peshiṭta Syriac, see Zunz, *Die gottesdienstlichen Vorträge*, p. 112, and A. Marx, 'An Aramaic Fragment of the Wisdom of Solomon', *JBL* 40 (1921), pp. 57–69.

[7] P. B. Dirksen, 'The Old Testament Peshitta', in Mulder and Sysling, *Mikra*, pp. 293–5.

[8] Winston's commentary, *The Wisdom of Solomon*, pp. 22–3; Schürer, *A History of the Jewish People* (revised), 3.1, p. 573 (comparative material is sparse, but such evidence as there is suggests Roman rather than earlier times).

of both spellings in the same document have now been collected.[9] Kinship with Philo is such as to suggest the priority of Wisdom, but assessment is not straightforward.[10] Finally, the historical circumstances presupposed seem to suit Greek or Roman government equally well. Wisdom's polemic against foreign rulers and idols might indeed suit Caligula's reign in particular, as noted by Luther, who took up the old Philonic ascription mentioned by Jerome.[11] Yet (to respond briefly to arguments advanced by Winston[12]) the attack on the wicked in v 16–23 fails to brand them clearly as idolaters, as would be natural on this view, and the chapters specifically on idolatry and ruler-cult (xiii–xv) lack the urgency to be expected when images were set up or threatened; contrast a gospel passage which is more plausibly associated with Caligula, Mark xiii 14–16, parallel with Matt. xxiv 15–18. The gradual development of veneration for dead children and far-off kings envisaged in Wisd. xiv 16–20 belongs to a broadly applicable euhemeristic account of the origins of the cult of the gods, and need not refer to the gradual growth of the specifically Roman ruler-cult or to the remoteness of the Roman emperor in particular. Similarly, the 'peace' of xiv 22 need not be Augustan, nor the κράτησις of vi 3 the Roman domination of Egypt (as Scarpat suggests), for the words may be used more generally here.

The high standing of Wisdom in the second-century church in both east and west is hard to understand, however, if the book was first known under Caligula. Wisdom is quoted by Irenaeus, Tertullian, Clement of Alexandria and the Teachings of Silvanus, Melito's Paschal Homily alludes to it, and the Old Latin version is probably second century. This early and widespread Christian use must presuppose considerable prior Jewish circulation and esteem.[13] The case for a pre-Roman date is strengthened if, as is probable, Clement of Rome quotes Wisdom at the end of the first

[9] H. St J. Thackeray, *A Grammar of the Old Testament in Greek*, 1 (Cambridge, 1909), p. 62; later examples in F. T. Gignac, *A Grammar of the Greek Papyri of the Roman and Byzantine Periods*, 1 (Milan, 1976), p. 97.

[10] See Larcher, *Etudes*, pp. 151–78 (Wisdom did not draw on Philo, but Philo could well have known Wisdom, although his dependence is not decisively clear); J. Laporte, 'Philo in the Tradition of Biblical Wisdom Literature', in R. L. Wilken (ed.), *Aspects of Wisdom in Judaism and Early Christianity* (Notre Dame and London, 1975), pp. 103–41 (105–6) (Philo used Wisdom).

[11] Jerome (footnote 5, above); Luther's Preface to his German version of Wisdom, translated in Larcher, *Études*, pp. 24–5; Larcher's commentary, *Le Livre de la Sagesse*, 1, pp. 134–5.

[12] Winston's commentary, *The Wisdom of Solomon*, pp. 22–3, 21–2, respectively.

[13] After some claimed allusions have been discarded, widespread early use is still allowed by R. T. Beckwith, *The Old Testament Canon of the New Testament Church* (London, 1985), pp. 388–9; Wisdom is the deutero-canonical book most frequently cited in the first three Christian centuries, according to F. Stuhlhofer, *Der Gebrauch der Bibel von Jesus bis Euseb* (Wuppertal, 1988), p. 147. The Old Latin is edited, with a wealth of information on Wisdom in the Church fathers, by W. Thiele, *Sapientia Salomonis* (Vetus Latina 11/1, Freiburg i. B., 1977–85).

century AD (Wisd. ii 24; xii 12, at 1 Clement iii 4; xxvii 5, respectively),[14] and if, as seems on the whole likely, knowledge of Wisdom is reflected, about forty years earlier, in Rom. i 18–32, ix 19–23. Probably, then, the book was already well established in Jewish currency at the time of Christian origins, and had taken its present Greek form by the early first century BC.

2   Status, authorship and authority

What status is it likely to have attained among Jews? Second-century *Christian* use already suggests that it was highly respected among them. As soon as evidence for Christian canonical judgements becomes plentiful, in the third and fourth centuries, Wisdom is found in a leading place among the non-canonical but acceptable adjuncts of the scriptures – the 'outside' or 'ecclesiastical' books, τὰ ἔξω or *ecclesiastici*;[15] books in this class were sometimes also called by the familiar term 'apocrypha', which covers prohibited books as well, but they were then singled out from the others as suitable for reading.[16]

Jews also spoke of 'outside books', both according to rabbinic texts and in the Jewish tradition on the canon reported by Origen;[17] moreover, Josephus' list of sacred books and the number twenty-two or twenty-four found in Josephus, the Greek Jubilees and 2 Esdras appear to be antecedents of the patristic lists of twenty-two Old Testament books, 'outside' which any other books widely revered and judged acceptable must

[14] So J. B. Lightfoot, *The Apostolic Fathers*, Part 1, *S. Clement of Rome* (2nd edn, 2 vols., London, 1890), 2, on the two passages; Beckwith, *The Old Testament Canon*, pp. 388–9; and Larcher's commentary, *Le Livre de la Sagesse*, 1, p. 146 (with caution). Gilbert, 'Wisdom Literature', p. 313, n. 101, finds similarity rather than relationship here; but the likelihood that Wisdom was known is strengthened by the knowledge of Judith shown in 1 Clem. lv.

[15] H. B. Swete, *An Introduction to the Old Testament in Greek* (2nd edn, Cambridge, 1914), p. 223, nn. 3–4; W. Horbury, 'Jews and Christians on the Bible: Demarcation and Convergence [325–451]', in J. van Oort and U. Wickert (eds.), *Christliche Exegese zwischen Nicaea und Chalcedon* (Kampen, 1992), pp. 72–103 (83–4).

[16] Jerome, Preface to the books of Kings (Weber, *Biblica Sacra*, 1, p. 365), and the Dialogue of Timothy and Aquila in Swete, *Introduction*, p. 206 (both mentioning Wisdom).

[17] M. Sanh. x 1, in the name of Akiba (those who read 'the outside books' [*hass^eparîm haḥîṣônîm*] have no share in the world to come); these books are explained in the Jerusalem Talmud, Sanh. x 1–2, 28a as books like Ben Sira, but in the Babylonian Talmud, Sanh. 100a as 'books of the *minim*'; the former explanation is followed here, with A. Geiger, *Urschrift und Übersetzungen der Bibel* (2nd edn, Frankfurt a.M., 1928), pp. 200–1, and L. Ginzberg, 'Some Observations on the Attitude of the Synagogue towards the Apocalyptic-Eschatological Writings', *JBL* 41 (1922), pp. 115–36 (126), reprinted in S. Z. Leiman (ed.), *The Canon and Masorah of the Hebrew Bible* (New York, 1974), pp. 142–63; for other views see J. Maier, *Jüdische Auseinandersetzung mit dem Christentum in der Antike* (Darmstadt, 1982), pp. 101–11. On Origen (preserved through a quotation in Eusebius, *HE* vi 25, 2) see N. R. M. de Lange, *Origen and the Jews* (Cambridge, 1976), pp. 52–3.

stand.[18] A book mainly current in Greek could be taken seriously by Jews, for Greek copies of sacred books were familiar, and used among Greek-speakers for public reading.[19] Wisdom's place in the church, a leading position in the class of non-canonical but acceptable books, could then be derived from Jewish usage of the end of the Second Temple period.

This is the view taken here, but some hold that the classification concerned was first brought in by learned Christians well after the rise of Christianity. Many western fourth-century church book-lists incorporate the 'ecclesiastical' books, without distinction, as canonical; may these lists reflect an older and longer canon, or even a pre-canonical liberty? As noted above, Wisdom was widely quoted in the church of the second and third centuries, and at the same time Christians complained that Jews had put various prophecies out of the accepted text or canon[20] – a rolling complaint in which Wisdom later on came to be specified (Isidore of Seville, *Eccl. Off.* i 12, 9).[21] Moreover, Greek and Latin MSS of the entire Old Testament include the 'ecclesiastical' books among the others, not separately, and the longer and shorter lists are closely linked, representing two versions of one ancient Judaean collection;[22] thus Wisdom normally appears among the Solomonic books, which in the shorter version number three (Proverbs, Ecclesiastes and the Song of Songs), but in the longer version five (these three, together with Wisdom and Ecclesiasticus). In recent interpretation, accordingly, against the background of debate on the origins of the canon, patristic recognition of a class of 'outside books' has been seen either as a late gesture towards conformity to a pre-Christian Jewish canon which had commonly been neglected in the church, or, if final Jewish acceptance of a shorter canon is put later than the rise of

---

[18] Lists are printed and discussed by T. Zahn, *Geschichte des neutestamentlichen Kanons*, 2.1 (Erlangen and Leipzig, 1890); Swete, *Introduction*, pp. 197–230; E. Junod and O. Wermelinger in J.-D. Kaestli and O. Wermelinger (eds.), *Le Canon de l'Ancien Testament* (Geneva, 1984), pp. 105–51, 153–210; on Jub. ii 23 see R. H. Charles, *The Book of Jubilees* (London, 1902), pp. xxxix–xl, 17–18, Beckwith, pp. 235–40, and Horbury, 'Jews and Christians', n. 20.

[19] M. Meg. ii 1, Tos. Meg. iv 13, discussed by J. A. Emerton, 'A Further Consideration of the Purpose of the Second Column of the Hexapla', *JTS* ns 22 (1971), pp. 15–28 (16–22).

[20] Justin, *Dial.* lxxi–iv; Tertullian, *Cult. Fem.* i 3; Origen, *ad Africanum* 13–15; *Ser. in Matt.* 28.

[21] Is Isidore's authority for this view (mentioned but unnamed) the Augustinian *Speculum*, 21 (quoted by Thiele, *Sapientia*, p. 242), on Wisdom as a pre-Christian Jewish book now not received by the Jews?

[22] Similarities are tabulated in D. Barthélemy, 'L'Etat de la Bible juive depuis le début de notre ère jusqu'à la deuxième révolte contre Rome (131–135)', in Kaestli and Wermelinger, *Le Canon de l'Ancien Testament*, pp. 9–45 (42–3); the likely age and Judaean origin of the LXX order are shown by P. Katz (W. P. M. Walters), 'The Old Testament Canon in Palestine and Alexandria', *ZNW* 47 (1956), pp. 191–217, reprinted in Leiman, *The Canon and Masorah*, pp. 72–98.

Christianity, as an approximation to current Jewish opinion.[23] This second view can be based on the presumption that both shorter and longer Christian canons were already represented among the Jews of the Second Temple period (D. Barthélemy and others), but it also fits the more libertarian thesis that movement towards a canon is essentially a Christian phenomenon of the patristic age (A. Jepsen and others).[24]

Here, however, in contrast with identifications of the canon as Christian, it is held that the patristic canonical lists, sometimes professedly of Jewish origin, reflect a genuine Jewish concern with the canon which, as has been argued elsewhere, was shared by Christians as part and parcel of their regular recourse to Jewish biblical knowledge.[25] Moreover, although the differing Christian treatments of the 'ecclesiastical' books probably reflect more and less welcoming Jewish attitudes towards the 'outside' books, it seems less likely that 'outside' books were counted *within* Jewish enumerations of the sacred writings in the Second Temple period. Thus in 2 Esdras xiv 44–7 the writer asserts the inspiration of apocryphal books not by simple enlargement of the number twenty-four, but by claiming yet greater authority for seventy hidden books *additional* to the public twenty-four. Qumran and New Testament evidence for use of books outside the list given by Josephus, rabbinic quotation of Ecclesiasticus, and the inclusion of 'outside books' in patristic quotations and biblical MSS, need not therefore imply that the circles concerned would have given a larger total if asked the number of the books, or that they had no thought of a canon. Rather, some at least of the books quoted and copied with the scriptures were probably classified as 'outside books'. The longer Christian Old Testament canon, therefore, which includes Wisdom and the other 'ecclesiastical' books to reach a total of forty-four books in Augustine, will represent a new Christian canon formed by an adaptation of earlier Jewish practice, rather than the survival of an earlier Jewish canon.

Recognition of Wisdom as an acceptable 'outside' book is already implied in the ante-Nicene period by the treatment of Wisdom in Melito

---

[23] These views are represented, respectively, by Beckwith, *The Old Testament Canon*, pp. 386–95, 436, and A. Tuilier, 'Les Livres Sapientiaux et le canon de l'Ancien Testament dans l'église ancienne', in *Letture cristiane dei Libri Sapienzali* (Studia Ephemeridis 'Augustinianum', 37; Rome, 1992), pp. 19–34.

[24] Barthélemy, 'L'Etat', pp. 9–45; A. Jepsen, 'Kanon und Text des Alten Testaments', *TLZ* 74 (1949), cols. 65–74, followed by A. C. Sundberg, *The Old Testament of the Early Church* (Cambridge, Mass., 1964), pp. 129–69; Sundberg, 'The Old Testament: a Christian Canon', *CBQ* 30 (1968), pp. 143–55, reprinted in Leiman, *The Canon and Masorah*, pp. 99–111; J. Barton, *Oracles of God* (London, 1986), pp. 35–81; G. M. Hahneman, *The Muratorian Fragment and the Development of the Canon* (Oxford, 1992), pp. 73–83.

[25] Horbury, 'Jews and Christians', pp. 80–6.

and Origen; both give canonical lists excluding Wisdom,[26] Origen's list being Jewish and Melito's probably Jewish, but both authors use Wisdom – in Origen's case, freely, but with clear statements that Wisdom is not canonical and is not universally accepted as authoritative.[27] In the Muratorian fragment, the naming of Wisdom after New Testament books and with debated Christian writings also probably indicates acceptable extra-canonical status,[28] rather than (as often held) inclusion in the *New Testament*.[29] Eusebius, similarly, reckons Wisdom among the Antilegomena or 'disputed books', recording its use by Irenaeus and Clement of Alexandria (*HE* v 8, 8; vi 13, 6), speaking circumspectly of 'the Wisdom known as Solomon's' or the author 'who published the All-virtuous Wisdom in his [Solomon's] character' (*HE* vi 13, 6; *PE* xi 7), but not denying the merit of the work; thus he supports the interpretation of 1 Kings v 12 (iv 32) as a reference to Solomon's physiological knowledge by appealing to the author of Wisdom, who will have taken the passage in this way (here he quotes Wisd. vii 17), as well as to the authentically Solomonic Eccles. i 9–10 (Eusebius, *PE* xi 7). Since twenty-two book reckonings on the lines followed by Melito were current among Jews by the time of Josephus, at the end of the first century AD, it seems likely that many Jews would by then have classed Wisdom as an approved 'outside' book.

Its Christian use was always accompanied, however, by questions on authorship. These are related to the broader Jewish and Christian debate on the Solomonic books, which may also throw light on Wisdom's origins

---

[26] Swete, *Introduction*, p. 203; Origen's 'outside' section has the Maccabees only, with a Hebrew title.

[27] *Princ.* iv 33; *Comm. in Joh.*, tom. xxviii 15 (13), discussed by J. Ruwet, 'Les "Antilegomena" dans les oeuvres d'Origène', *Biblica* 23 (1942), pp. 18–42; 24 (1943), pp. 18–58 (22–31).

[28] See B. F. Westcott, *A General Survey of the History of the Canon of the New Testament* (5th edn, London, 1881), p. 537, n. 8; Eusebius, as Westcott notes, treats the disputed books of both Testaments (Antilegomena) after the canonical books of both Testaments, when discussing Irenaeus and Clement of Alexandria (*HE* v 8, vi 13). The same method is followed by Athanasius and Epiphanius, and, as it seems, in the list underlying the Muratorian fragment – from which the preliminary Old Testament section is lost (Lightfoot, *Apostolic Fathers*, Part 1, *S. Clement of Rome*, 2, pp. 412–13). This interpretation is defended, with reference to the objections documented in the following footnote, by the present writer, 'The Wisdom of Solomon in the Muratorian Fragment', *JTS* ns 45 (1994), pp. 149–59.

[29] Wisdom is thought to be included in the New Testament here by H. von Campenhausen, *The Formation of the Christian Bible* (E. tr., London, 1972), p. 244; A. C. Sundberg, 'Canon Muratori: A Fourth Century List', *HTR* 66 (1973), pp. 1–41 (15–18) (urging that Wisdom is included in the New Testament not only by the Muratorian fragment, but also by Eusebius and Epiphanius); Larcher's commentary, *Le Livre de la Sagesse*, 1, p. 146; Beckwith, *The Old Testament Canon*, pp. 347, 390; Schürer (revised), *A History of the Jewish People*, 3.1, p. 574; Tuilier, *Les Livres Sapientiaux*, p. 20; and Hahneman, *The Muratorian Fragment*, pp. 200–5. Compare S. P. Tregelles, *Canon Muratorianus* (Oxford, 1867), pp. 53–5 (Wisdom, named among Christian books, was possibly itself Christian); Zahn, *Geschichte*, 2.1, pp. 103–5 (Philo was named as author in the original text of the fragment [see below], and Wisdom was accordingly put at the end of a still flexible list of apostolic writings, in view of Christian respect for Philo).

(section 3, below). The corpus was discussed with reference to 1 Kings v 12 (iv 32), on Solomon's manifold compositions (compare Eusebius, as just cited), and Prov. xxv 1, on their copying or selection by Hezekiah's company (the latter verse underlies Babylonian Talmud, Baba Bathra 15a: 'Hezekiah and his company wrote Isaiah, Proverbs, the Song of Songs and Qoheleth'). Ecclesiastes and the Song of Songs were central in early rabbinic debate, but Ecclesiasticus is mentioned in the same context, in Tos. Yadaim ii 13–14 (discussed below).

Christian views on the authorship of Wisdom can be set out as follows.

(1) *Solomon* was pervasively revered as author, doubts notwithstanding. An early comment on the Song of Songs – ascribed to Hippolytus by Anastasius of Sinai – names Proverbs, Wisdom, Ecclesiastes and the Canticle, in that order, as the Solomonic books selected by Hezekiah's company.[30] Towards the end of the patristic age both eastern and western opinion could view Wisdom as non-canonical, but genuinely Solomonic (so the pseudo-Athanasian biblical Synopsis, paras. 2, 45, and Isidore of Seville, *Eccl. Off.* i 12, 9). The same instinct affected Ecclesiasticus – often and early cited as Solomonic, concluded in Latin by Solomon's prayer (Ecclus lii), and numbered among 'the five books of Solomon'.[31]

(2) *The friends of Solomon*, an ascription known only from the Muratorian fragment, has been thought to arise from corruption or misunderstanding of the ascription to Philo (see below);[32] but this view should be treated with caution, for royal friends are prominent in the LXX,[33] Solomon's friend Hiram had a sapiential literary legend,[34] and it is possible, too, that Ecclesiasticus is in mind together with Wisdom (see below), Ben Sira being termed 'friend' as an imitator of Solomon.[35] The fragment as it stands then perhaps genuinely reflects an attempt to unite criticism with tradition.

(3) *Philo* was the author. This tradition must go back at least to the third

[30] N. Bonwetsch (ed.), *Hippolytus Werke*, 1.1 (Leipzig, 1897), p. 343; E. tr. by S. D. F. Salmond in *Hippolytus*, 1 (Edinburgh, 1868), p. 440.

[31] W. Thiele, 'Zum Titel des Sirachbuches in der lateinischen Überlieferung', in R. Gryson and P.-M. Bogaert (eds.), *Recherches sur l'histoire de la Bible latine* (Louvain-la-Neuve, 1987), pp. 43–9.

[32] 'Sapientia ab amicis Salomonis in honorem eius scripta', discussed by Tregelles, *Canon Muratorianus*, p. 53; cf. p. 55, n. *o*, where he allows that some might prefer his earlier view that the underlying Greek text hinted at LXX Prov. xxv 1 (φίλοι).

[33] LXX Prov. xxv 1 (Hezekiah); Dan. (Old Greek) iii 91, 94 (Nebuchadnezzar), v 23 (Belshazzar), vi 14 (Darius); Est. i 3 (Artaxerxes); compare Vulgate, Cant. v 1, 'amici' (LXX πλησίοι) (Solomon).

[34] Josephus, *Ap.* 109–20, summarized in Theophilus, *Aut.* iii 22, and quoted in Eusebius, *Chronicle*, i 17, 1–3; letters of other kings to Solomon are given in Eupolemus, quoted in Eusebius, *PE* ix 31–4.

[35] He is so called (ὀπαδὸς ... τοῦ Σολομῶντος) in the pseudo-Athanasian *Synopsis*, 46, translated in the first AV Prologue to Ecclesiasticus; that Ecclesiasticus *rather than* Wisdom is intended in the Fragment was suggested by W. O. E. Oesterley in R. H. Charles (ed.), *The Apocrypha and Pseudepigrapha of the Old Testament*, 1 (Oxford, 1913), p. 299.

century, and probably further, for it was known to Jerome from 'nonnulli scriptorum veterum' (footnotes 5 and 11). In Jerome's time it was therefore probably familiar among Greek-speakers as well as Latin Christians like Julian of Eclanum (see below).[36] The early readiness of Christians to identify Philo as the author of this highly revered book has been plausibly linked, in turn, with the traces of a quasi-hagiographic Christian legend of Philo found in Eusebius and elsewhere, perhaps deriving from the second-century Hegesippus.[37]

(4) *Ben Sira* wrote both Wisdom and Ecclesiasticus, according to Augustine, following what he took to be a standard view (*De Doc. Chr.* ii 8, 13: 'constantissime perhibetur').[38] He ultimately withdrew this attribution of Wisdom (*Retractations*, ii 30 [4], 2), perhaps so as not to infringe the book's authority by an opinion deemed doubtful; Julian of Eclanum in Italy thought that the ascriptions to Ben Sira and Philo were both uncertain (Augustine, *Op. imp. c. Iul.* iv 123). The attribution to Ben Sira is probably also reflected in those Greek and Latin texts of the Apostolic Canons which speak of 'the Wisdoms of the very learned Sirach'; compare the place of Wisdom just *after* Ecclesiasticus in one list in Epiphanius, the Gelasian Decree, Junilius and later Ebedjesu.[39] Jews in Galilee and the east highly esteemed Ecclesiasticus.[40] Was Augustine's attribution, perhaps learnt in Italy, shared by Jews in the west?

Thus authenticity was doubted in the church from early times, for the Philonic ascription was probably known in the second century. This doubt was not merely evoked by Wisdom's link with Ecclesiasticus; that would have readily suggested ascription to Ben Sira, but not to Philo. Jewish questions on authorship were probably already current when Christians first inherited Wisdom.

[36] Its influence seems likely to be a factor when Basil of Caesarea (*Letter* 190.3, to Amphilochius; PG 32.700–1) ascribes to Philo a tradition that the manna tasted however the eater pleased, but Wisd. xvi 20–21 rather than Philo appears to be in view, although the tradition is given in a developed form like that which it has in rabbinic midrash. (See rabbinic texts quoted by Winston, *The Wisdom of Solomon*, and cited by L. Ginzberg, *The Legends of the Jews*, vol. 6 [reprinted Philadelphia, 1968], p. 17, n. 99; for example, Exod. R. xxv 3, on Exod. xvi 4). Augustine also used this tradition (*Ad Inquisitiones Ianuari*, i 3 = *Letter* 54.3), but later noted that in the scriptures it could only be supported from Wisdom, which is not received as canonical by Jews (Augustine, *Retractations*, ii 46 (20), 2). With Wisdom here contrast Philo, *V.M.* i 208–9 (the manna tasted like honey-cakes, but the quails supplied the taste of flesh which would otherwise have been lacking).

[37] P. E. Bruns, 'Philo Christianus: The Debris of a Legend', *HTR* 66 (1973), pp. 141–5.

[38] For fuller study of the Augustinian passages cited here see A.-M. la Bonnardière, *Biblia Augustiniana, A.T. Le livre de la Sagesse* (Paris, 1970), pp. 46–57, 144–5, and 'Le Canon des divines écritures', in la Bonnardière *et al.*, *Saint Augustin et la Bible* (Paris, 1986), pp. 287–301.

[39] Swete, *Introduction*, pp. 204–9; Thiele, *Sapientia*, pp. 243, 245 (Apostolic Canons and Julian of Eclanum).

[40] Zunz, *Die gottesdienstlichen Vorträge*, pp. 106–11; Schürer (revised), *A History of the Jewish People*, 3.1, pp. 205–6.

The placing of Wisdom in biblical MSS sheds further light on views of status and authorship. In BℵA Wisdom is placed together with Ecclesiasticus *after* all the three Solomonic books transmitted in the Hebrew scriptures.[41] This placing, that most commonly found in both Greek and Latin biblical MSS, recurs in western book-lists such as Augustine's,[42] and in one of the three early Syriac MSS including Wisdom, the Paris MS (seventh or eighth century).[43] The varying opinions on status and authenticity just noted are thereby recalled; the two Wisdoms *can* be judged both canonical and Solomonic (the questions were separable, as Augustine shows), but they go down to a place after all the Solomonic books of the Hebrew canon.[44]

On the other hand, Solomonic ascription probably lies behind some traces of a closer link between Wisdom and Proverbs. Wisdom directly follows Proverbs in the comment ascribed to Hippolytus cited above, in the body of Pseudo-Chrysostom's biblical Synopsis, and in parts of the Latin and Syriac traditions,[45] including one of the three early Syriac copies, the Ambrosian MS B.21 Inferiore; in this MS, and sometimes elsewhere, Ecclesiasticus is divided from Wisdom and goes lower down.[46] In the light of this evidence some early quotations become notable, despite the uncertainty of inference from texts perhaps drawn from anthologies. Thus, in series of quoted texts, the order Wisdom-Proverbs and Wisdom-Song of Songs occurs in Tertullian, Wisdom-Proverbs-Ecclesiasticus-Ecclesiastes in Cyprian, and Wisdom-Ecclesiastes in Eusebius.[47] The application of the name (*All-virtuous*) *Sophia* to each of Proverbs, Wisdom and Ecclesiasticus

---

[41] In B the order is Proverbs, Ecclesiastes, Song of Songs, Job, Wisdom, Ecclesiasticus, in ℵA Proverbs, Ecclesiastes, Song of Songs, Wisdom, Ecclesiasticus.

[42] Thiele, *Sapientia*, pp. 231–2.

[43] For these MSS see J. A. Emerton, *The Peshitta of the Wisdom of Solomon* (Leiden, 1959), pp. xix–xx; on the Paris MS, Beckwith, *The Old Testament Canon*, pp. 195–7; on another of the three, the fragmentary British Library MS Add. 14,443, see W. Wright, *Catalogue of the Syriac Manuscripts in the British Museum acquired since the year 1838*, 1 (London, 1870), nos. XXVI, XXX, XXXI, XLII, showing that its contents appear to have followed the similar order Job, Proverbs, Ecclesiastes, Wisdom, Twelve Prophets.

[44] This placing implicitly questions the view that BℵA ignore the limits of the Hebrew canon (expressed for example by Swete *Introduction*, p. 225; Beckwith, *The Old Testament Canon*, p. 195).

[45] An association of Proverbs and Wisdom seems likely in the fourth-century Lucifer of Cagliari; Wisdom follows Proverbs in Cassiodorus' seventh-century Latin list, in the pseudo-Augustinian *Speculum*, in a group of Latin MSS, and in many Peshiṭta MSS (Thiele, *Sapientia*, p. 232).

[46] Wisdom is edited from this MS by Emerton, *Wisdom* (1959), and (in the Old Testament series issued by the Peshiṭta Institute, vol. 2.5) by Emerton and D. J. Lane, *Wisdom of Solomon* (Leiden, 1979); for the separate place of Ecclesiasticus here and in the Paris Syriac MS cited above see Beckwith, *The Old Testament Canon*, p. 196.

[47] Tertullian, *An.* xv 4 (Wisd. i 6; Prov. xxiv 12), and fragment in Praedestinatus i 60, in Thiele, *Sapientia*, p. 232 (Wisd. iii 1; Cant. viii 6); Cyprian, *Test.* iii 53 (Wisd. i 1; Prov. x 9; Ecclus iii 21; Eccles. vii 16); Eusebius, *P.E.* xi 7, cited above.

likewise suggests that these three books had been grouped together; compare rabbinic use of 'wisdom of Solomon' for both Proverbs and Ecclesiastes, and use of both 'wisdom' and 'proverbs' in forms of the Hebrew title of Ecclesiasticus.[48] Lastly, a comparable arrangement seems to have been current in Hebrew MSS, for Jerome (footnote 5) mentions a Hebrew copy of Ecclesiasticus, followed by Ecclesiastes and the Song of Songs. His report can perhaps be related to the debate on the question whether Ecclesiastes and the Song of Songs 'defile the hands' as sacred books (Mishnah, Yadaim iii 5; Tos. Yadaim ii 13–14), which suggests that the position of these two books when copied might not have been firm. In the church the order Ecclesiasticus-Ecclesiastes-Song of Songs occurs in Pseudo-Chrysostom's Synopsis (prefatory list; after Proverbs, without mention of Wisdom) and Cassiodorus (after Proverbs and Wisdom).[49] In the Tosefta the passage on Ecclesiastes and the Canticle follows a statement that 'the books of Ben Sira' and later books do not defile the hands; this sequence recalls, and just possibly reflects, the order of the books followed in the Hebrew copy mentioned by Jerome.

The grouping of Wisdom with Proverbs and Ecclesiasticus further confirms the prevalence of the Solomonic ascription in the church of the second and third centuries. On the other hand, an influential exegesis based on the Hebrew canon now bound Proverbs, Ecclesiastes and the Song of Songs closely together as Solomon's ethics, physics and contemplation (Origen, *Prol. Cant.*). The two Wisdoms were later usually listed and copied together after these three, as noted above – although occasionally Wisdom's strong Solomonic link parted it from Ecclesiasticus. Yet Jerome's report suggests that the placing of Ecclesiastes and the Song of Songs *after* Wisdom and Ecclesiasticus in some Christian usage long continued to have Jewish analogies.

Lastly, assessments of content throw further light on the authority of Wisdom. The long chapter on Wisdom which is common to the biblical Synopses in the names of Athanasius and Chrysostom begins by noting its 'teaching of righteousness' and 'prophecy concerning Christ'.[50] Wisdom was read and expounded in church,[51] and its 'teaching' was commended for catechumens (Origen, Athanasius, Jerome, Apostolic Canons), an assess-

[48] 1 Clement and Justin (Proverbs), Origen and Eusebius (Wisdom and Ecclesiasticus), are cited among examples in G. W. H. Lampe, *A Patristic Greek Lexicon* (Oxford, 1961), pp. 1001a, s. πανάρετος, 1246a, s. σοφία C.4; for Jewish usage see Zunz, *Die gottesdienstlichen Vorträge*, p. 111, n. *ee*, and Schürer (revised), *A History of the Jewish People*, 3.1, pp. 206–7.
[49] Swete, *Introduction*, pp. 205, 212.
[50] διδασκαλία δικαιοσύνης, προφητεία περὶ Χριστοῦ, in Ps.-Athanasius, *Synopsis*, 45 (PG 28.373) and Ps.-Chrysostom, *Synopsis*, on Wisdom (PG 56.368); the overlap between the two is set out by Zahn, *Kanons*, 2.1, p. 313, n. 1.
[51] Augustine, *De Praedestinatione Sanctorum* xiv 27, discussed by la Bonnardière, *Sagesse*, pp. 59–83; G. G. Willis, *St Augustine's Lectionary* (London, 1962), pp. 16 (Ambrose), 35, 39 (Augustine).

ment probably inherited from Jewish use, as Harnack held[52] (compare the educational value set by Ben Sira's grandson on his translation, in his Prologue). The book was also, however, read by Christians as a prophecy of the suffering and vindication of both Christ and the martyrs, at least from the end of the second century.[53] The anthologizing of important texts seen in this connection and in the quotation-series already noted would enhance Wisdom's prophetic status. Christians would accordingly incline to count Wisdom as inspired. Some Jews too had probably read Wisdom as prophecy, noting its consolation for martyrs[54] and Solomon's prayer for prophetic inspiration (vii 27), and perhaps already excerpting it in Greek florilegia. As Augustine shows, reception as prophecy could survive denial of Solomon's authorship. At the time of the rise of Christianity, then, Wisdom is likely to have been esteemed among many Jews not only as good teaching, but also as inspired prophecy.

This strong double reputation, preserved in Christian usage, distinguishes Wisdom from other Solomonic books which were viewed by some Jews and Christians as uninspired, or not fully inspired. Thus it was claimed that Ecclesiastes is merely Solomon's own wisdom, and it was asked whether this might be true of his other writings (Tos. Yadaim ii 14). Akiba appears in the Mishnah (Yadaim iii 5) as refusing, against the evidence of his brother-in-law, to accept Ben Azzai's unpalatable but plausible recollection that the inspiration of the Song of Songs as well as Ecclesiastes had been in question in earlier debate. For doubts of inspiration see also Aboth de-Rabbi Nathan, Recension A, i (Hezekiah's company said that Proverbs, Ecclesiastes and the Song of Songs drew upon proverbs, and were not among the scriptures); Jerome on Eccles. xii 13 (the Hebrews say that although Ecclesiastes seems to merit deletion, like other Solomonic writings which have become obsolete, it can be reckoned among the scriptures because of ch. 12); and views ascribed to Theodore of Mopsuestia (Proverbs and Ecclesiastes derive from prudence rather than prophecy, and the Song of Songs is just a wedding song).[55] Wisdom, less open to such objections, will have strengthened the Solomonic corpus. The same end

---

[52] A. Harnack, *Über den privaten Gebrauch der heiligen Schriften in der alten Kirche* (Leipzig, 1912), pp. 50–2, 85; Jerome (edification), Apostolic Canons (let the young men learn), cited nn. 5 and 39, above.

[53] Hippolytus, *Dem.* 9–10 (Wisd. ii; v, on the Jews' condemnation of Christ and future confusion); Cyprian, *Test.* ii 14; Augustine, *C.D.* xvii 20; on martyrdom, Tertullian alludes to Wisd. iii 8 (*Mart.* ii 4), Cyprian quotes Wisd. iii 4–8, v 1–9 (*Test.* iii 15–16, *ad Fortunatum de exhortatione martyrii* 12).

[54] In the midrash Jose ben Joezer (a possible model for Wisdom's sufferer, according to Ruppert, 'Gerechte', p. 86) has a legend with the Wisdom themes of intra-communal division and future judgement; see Ber. R. lxv 22.

[55] H. B. Swete, 'Theodorus of Mopsuestia', *DCB* 4, p. 940a; D. Z. Zaharopoulos, *Theodore of Mopsuestia on the Bible: a Study of His Old Testament Exegesis* (Mahwah, New Jersey, 1989), pp. 33–4; the resemblance to some rabbinic opinion is noted by Beckwith, *The Old Testament Canon*, p. 333, n. 138.

was reached by other ways when the books were linked with the wise king's progress to contemplation (Origen, cited above), or when, with a stress on inspiration recalling Wisdom, Jews read the Song of Songs as 'the song and praises which Solomon the prophet, king of Israel, spoke in the spirit of prophecy before the master of all the world, the Lord' (Targ. Cant. i 1).

On Jewish use about the time of Christian origins, probabilities noted so far can be recapitulated as follows. Wisdom will have been classified by the more precise as an acceptable 'outside book'. Many thought it Solomonic, although some doubted; when copied and stored it will have been associated with both Proverbs and Ecclesiasticus. It was widely viewed not only as sound teaching, but also as inspired prophecy, and Jews probably anticipated its Christian use in florilegia and catechesis. It will thus have supplied a prophetic element in the earthy Solomonic corpus, an end later achieved by other means.

3   Themes and origins

An Egyptian origin for Wisdom in its Greek form is commended by the known Greek literary productivity of Jews in Egypt, the translation into Greek of a similar book, Ecclesiasticus, especially for circulation in Ptolemaic Egypt, and the early and constant link between Wisdom and Ecclesiasticus in transmission. Syrian or Judaean origin would hardly account so naturally for a biblical pseudepigraph in Greek, which was also in debt to Greek thought.

Most surviving Jewish inscriptions from Egypt are in Greek, and of the period (second century BC to early second century AD) in which Wisdom was written. The metrical epitaphs in particular recall the Jewish taste for Greek verse seen in the Sibyllines and Ezekiel Tragicus, and they show up Wisdom's biblical stamp by contrast.[56] One who comes to Wisdom from the scriptures, like Jerome, finds 'Greek eloquence' in vocabulary, rhetorical devices and patches of rhythmical prose. The Greek scent is heightened by the Hellenic themes of untimely death and ethical example which Wisdom shares with the epitaphs. Yet Wisdom eschews Greek metre, fails to echo Greek poets,[57] and instead draws continually on the scriptures for readers who can understand. Not too much is conceded to the Greek literary tastes of Egyptian Jews.

The style therefore suits a Solomonic pseudepigraph. Motives for its

---

[56] W. Horbury and D. E. Noy, *Jewish Inscriptions of Graeco-Roman Egypt* (Cambridge, 1992), pp. xx–xxi.

[57] Larcher, *Études*, pp. 182–5, with the surmise that Greek was not the author's mother-tongue; some Jewish pride in the 'barbaric' biblical style is suggested by the present writer, 'Jewish Inscriptions and Jewish Literature in Egypt, with Special Reference to Ecclesiasticus', in J. W. van Henten and P. W. van der Horst (eds.), *Studies in Early Jewish Epigraphy* (Leiden, New York and Cologne, 1994), pp. 9–43 (18–20).

production seem most readily discernible in i–x, which conflict with views expressed elsewhere in the Solomonic corpus. Wisdom's attack on the powerful who deny after-life and divine revelation traverses opinion voiced in Ecclesiastes and (as is less often noted) in Ecclesiasticus, but recalls the Psalms of Solomon; the same disagreement seems to be partly mirrored in the inscriptions, and can be related to Pharisaic-Sadducaic struggle.

Ecclesiastes is countered not only on after-life and hedonism (Wisd. i–v against Eccles. ii 23–4, iii 20–2, v 18–20, ix 4–8), but also on a point which, as already noticed, continued to arouse debate – the nature of Solomon's paradigmatic wisdom; it was not human prudence acquired by ultimately pointless effort (Eccles. i 11–ii 17), but a priceless gift from above granted in answer to prayer (Wisd. vii–ix).[58] Similarly, Ecclesiasticus, even in Greek, has strong denials of after-life, coupled in one instance with hedonistic consolation (xiv 11–19; cf. x 11, xvii 27, xli 4; contrast Wisd. ii 1–9). Negative views on after-life also predominate in the verse epitaphs accepted by Jewish patrons in Egypt, and are implied too in the Greek inscription of the tomb of Jason in Jerusalem;[59] by contrast, the two clear references to after-life in the Egyptian epitaphs are in terms recalling Wisdom and the Psalms of Solomon.[60]

By the time of Wisdom the views of death and pleasure reflected in Ecclesiastes, Ecclesiasticus and many Jewish epitaphs would have been associated with Epicureanism.[61] In a Jewish context they could be attributed to Sadducees, regarded by Pharisees as persecutors, and holding tenets described by Josephus in terms recalling Epicureanism. The composition of a Greek Solomonic pseudepigraph against such views and in defence of a hope of immortality can be associated with traces of a similar defence in the biblical texts and versions, especially the LXX, including the longer Greek text of Ecclesiasticus (J. H. A. Hart's 'Pharisaic recension').[62] The shorter Greek text was also affected (xlviii 11), and many

[58] E. Meyer, *Ursprung und Anfänge des Christentums*, 2 (Stuttgart and Berlin, 1921), p. 364; M. Gilbert, 'La Figure de Salomon en Sg 7–9', in R. Kuntzmann and J. Schlosser (eds.), *Etudes sur le judaïsme hellénistique* (Paris, 1984), pp. 225–49 (239).

[59] Horbury, 'Ecclesiasticus', pp. 37–43; E. Puech, as cited there, and in his *La Croyance des Esséniens en la vie future: immortalité, résurrection, vie éternelle?* (2 vols., Paris, 1993), 1, pp. 184–5, urges that after-life is not excluded in the Greek inscription of the tomb of Jason, but this view seems less probable in the light of Ecclesiasticus and the Egyptian epitaphs.

[60] Horbury and Noy, *Jewish Inscriptions*, no. 33 = *CIJ* 1510, 1. 10 (ψυχὴ δ'εἰς ὁσίους ἔπετε), cf. Wisd. vii 27, Ps. Sol. xiv, and no. 36 = *CIJ* 1513 (εἰ δ' ὀλίγον ζῆσαι χρόννον κεκριμένον, ἀλλὰ ἐλέους ἐλπίδα ἀγαθὴν ἐγὼ προσδέχομαι), cf. LXX Job ii 9; Wisd. iii 4–5; xii 22; Ps. Sol. xiv 6.

[61] D. Seeley, 'Narrative, the Righteous Man and the Philosopher: An Analysis of the Story of the *Dikaios* in Wisdom 1–5', *JSP* 7 (1990), pp. 68–9, n. 6, rightly notes that polemical association of such views with Epicureans and Sadducees is likely, irrespective of the justice of the claims.

[62] See Geiger, *Urschrift*, pp. 175–6; R. Le Déaut, 'La Septante, un Targum?', in Kuntzmann and Schlosser, *Etudes*, pp. 147–95 (182–3); J. H. A. Hart, *Ecclesiasticus: The Greek Text of Codex 248* (Cambridge, 1909), pp. 310–4. On the development of eschatological themes in the LXX Psalms see J. L. W. Schaper, 'Eschatology in the Greek Psalter' (unpublished

ambiguous passages (e.g. ii 7–9) could be taken as expressing future hope –
a point which will have helped to confirm the popularity of the Hebrew text
as well. It therefore became possible for Ecclesiasticus and Wisdom to be
read together from the standpoint adopted in Wisdom. In the broader
context of the Solomonic corpus, the new book of Wisdom had redeemed
Solomon from the appearance of supporting the Sadducees, and had
enrolled him as a partisan of Pharisaic martyrs, an ardent prophet of
righteousness, immortality and judgement to come.

The Jewish origins and rôle of Wisdom can then tentatively be
reconstructed as follows. The Greek Wisdom was compiled on the basis of
sources now lost, probably in Egypt, but in touch with Judaean life and
thought. The first ten chapters reflect circumstances in which the
'Epicureanism' represented in Ecclesiastes, Ecclesiasticus and many Jewish
epitaphs seemed influential – perhaps near the beginning of the first century
BC, when Alexander Jannaeus reigned in Judaea and repressed the
Pharisees. The anti-gentile polemic of xi–xix, which is not without its
encouragement to non-Jewish sympathizers,[63] suits needs continually
present among the Jews of Egypt. Wisdom's inner-Jewish polemic
belonged to a powerful stream of opinion, accepted by Pharisees and
strengthened by martyrs. The book was therefore widely viewed as
Solomonic prophecy, and read as catechesis together with Ecclesiasticus,
which was soon interpreted agreeably with Wisdom; both had the standing
to gain recognition as 'outside books', and they might be linked more
closely with Proverbs than the debatable Ecclesiastes and the Song of
Songs. Yet Wisdom's authorship was questioned, it was current mainly in
Greek, and it lost esteem by contrast with Ben Sira. Its contribution of a
prophetic element to the Solomonic corpus as a whole was secured in
another way by the interpretation of the Song of Songs as inspired
prophecy. Meanwhile the Christians accepted Wisdom as teaching and
prophecy, developed its links with catechesis and martyrdom, and were
impressed by its points of contact with the Passion narrative; but they were
also aware of contested authorship and Jewish debate on the books of
Solomon. Now these speculations are offered to a student of Wisdom, with
admiration for his work and in gratitude for his teaching and his kindness
over many years. If 'Greek eloquence' may salute labours in the widest
range of Hebrew and Old Testament studies, Wisdom has words for the
spirit of his work: φιλάγαθον, παντεπίσκοπον.

dissertation, Cambridge, 1993), and in the Targums, Puech, *La Croyance*, 1, pp. 223–42.
Puech treats Wisdom on this subject without the stress laid here on contrary views in
Ecclesiasticus and elsewhere, but he notes that Wisd. i–v develops a passage which is itself
perhaps anti-Sadducaic, 1 Enoch cii 6–11 (*La Croyance*, 1, pp. 92–8, 202).

[63] J. P. M. Sweet, 'The Theory of Miracles in the Wisdom of Solomon', in C. F. D. Moule
(ed.), *Miracles* (London, 1965), pp. 115–26 (121–2).

Part 3

Themes

17   Were there schools in ancient Israel?

G. I. Davies

'The Old Testament evidence is slight.'[1] These words may stand as a warning not to expect too much from the pages that follow. Even some of those who have written at length on the question have acknowledged that their conclusions are to some extent provisional and hypothetical and so open to correction by future discoveries.[2] Some leading scholars in the field are no longer as sure as they once were that there were schools in ancient Israel.[3] Viewed as a whole, the tenor of scholarly discussion has moved from confident assertion[4] to doubt and even denial in recent years. This is undoubtedly a result of the nature of the evidence to which appeal has been made. Much of it either comes from other parts of the ancient near east, and so does not prove anything about ancient Israel, or represents what may (but also may not) be the products of Israelite schools, in the shape of writings which make no clear allusion to their authors or their place of composition or use. Explicit evidence from the Old Testament itself is indeed 'slight'. But it is not lacking altogether, and because of its importance it deserves to be noted before more indirect arguments are reviewed.

To begin with the one Old Testament reference to a school building (leaving Ecclus li 23 on one side), Elisha's disciples are said in 2 Kings vi 1 to have complained that 'the place where we sit before you is too small for us'. Although some have taken this as a reference to living quarters (so NRSV), the combination of *yšb* with *lpny* (for which cf. iv 38) is much more likely to refer to a place of instruction. This is evidence for a prophetic 'school', of course, but it shows that the idea of a school building or schoolroom was not unknown in Israel. J. L. Crenshaw has drawn attention to a possible

[1] J. A. Emerton, in G. W. Anderson (ed.), *Tradition and Interpretation* (Oxford, 1979), p. 226.
[2] E.g. A. Lemaire, *Les Ecoles et la formation de la Bible dans l'ancien Israël* (Fribourg and Göttingen, 1981), p. 84.
[3] Compare, e.g., R. N. Whybray's views in *Wisdom in Proverbs* (London, 1965), p. 18; *The Intellectual Tradition in the Old Testament* (Berlin and New York, 1974), pp. 31–43; and *Wisdom and Poverty in the Book of Proverbs* (Sheffield, 1990), p. 71.
[4] As exemplified in the works of H.-J. Hermisson, *Studien zur israelitischen Spruchweisheit* (Neukirchen, 1968), E. W. Heaton, *Solomon's New Men* (London, 1974), and Lemaire (n. 2).

reference to fees in Prov. iv 7, where *qnh* may well have its specific meaning 'buy' rather than the more general 'get' favoured by recent translations.[5] The verb *qnh* is in fact used with *ḥkmh* and its synonyms as object on numerous occasions in Proverbs and two of the other occurrences suggest even more strongly that the payment of fees to a teacher may be involved (xvii 16, xxiii 23).

As for teachers, Prov. v 13 offers clear evidence. The writer anticipates that negligent pupils will one day show remorse. Both the words used are participial in form, so that a 'non-professional' translation is theoretically possible ('those who taught me ... those who instructed me'), and the LXX and Vulgate take this line. But if, for example, parental instruction were meant, one would expect 'father' and 'mother' here. The reference is almost certainly to some kind of school, and the earlier verses of the chapter give some idea of the teaching that was being given there. Ps. cxix 99 is a further case.[6] Some occurrences of the word 'wise' (*ḥkm*) may involve teachers, as in Prov. xiii 14 and xv 7. 'Pupils' are mentioned twice in the book of Isaiah (viii 16, 14). The first of these passages has played a central part in attempts to establish that the classical prophets had their own 'schools' of disciples, but even if the language should be interpreted differently, it is still significant that the word *limmûd* is used, as it shows that the prophet's audience would be familiar with the idea of 'pupils' in a school of some kind. Similarly the passage from Deutero-Isaiah draws on knowledge of this situation, probably with specific reference to training in rhetoric and perhaps (cf. verses 5–6) to the corporal punishment which pupils had to undergo in school.[7] The later word for 'student', *talmîd*, occurs only once in the Old Testament, but in a passage which also mentions the teacher, here designated as *mēbîn* (1 Chron. xxv 8). The context makes it clear that this was a music school supposedly attached to the temple (cf. verses 6–7).

Much of this evidence, of course, comes from passages which are or may be late in origin, but 2 Kings vi 1 and Isa. viii 16 are likely to reflect pre-exilic conditions, and this is certainly to be reckoned with as a possibility for at least some of the verses cited from Proverbs.[8] In any case, to establish the

---

[5] 'Education in Ancient Israel', *JBL* 104 (1985), p. 602.

[6] In view of the late date of this psalm, however, the reference may be not to Israelite teachers but to pagan schools attended by Jews (cf. Dan. i 3–20).

[7] So Lemaire (n. 2), p. 39, noting further uses of the teaching image in xlviii 17 and liv 13. Isa. l 4–9 is one of the three biblical passages whose use by A. Klostermann in a pioneering study of schools in ancient Israel has been criticized by F. Golka, 'Die israelitische Weisheitsschule oder "des Kaisers neue Kleider"', *VT* 33 (1983), pp. 257–70. Golka argues that *limmûd* in l 4 means not 'pupil' but 'practised'. While this is possible for the first occurrence in the verse, it is much less likely for the second, so an educational background remains likely. Golka's objection to Klostermann's use of Isa. xxviii 9–13 is more soundly based: the passage is so unclear and imprecise that it proves nothing. On Klostermann's third passage (Prov. xxii 17–21) see below, n. 17.   [8] See further p. 203 below on Prov. xxii 29–xxiii 3.

Conclusion

existence of schools at any period of Old Testament history amounts to a positive answer to the question posed in our title, even if we may need to be discriminating as to the period(s) for which their existence can be proved or even inferred. If the evidence is indeed 'slight', this may be due to the fact that the Old Testament contains the religious traditions, and only some of them, from ancient Israel, rather than the educational literature of the schools, as G. Wanke has noted.[9]

1.

The indirect arguments have undoubtedly played a more prominent part in the discussion. The first is that, since it is well attested that schools existed in the rest of the ancient near east for the training of scribes and other officials,[10] then it is highly likely that in Israel, where many of the same religious and political institutions existed as elsewhere from the early monarchy onwards, a similar training would have been needed. It is sometimes objected to this argument that, whereas to write the cuneiform or hieroglyphic scripts required a long and intensive training which could only be provided in a scribal school, the alphabetic script that was used to write Hebrew (and Aramaic) could quickly be mastered and so competence in reading and writing might well have been passed on in the family (or work-place, where these differed). Against such an objection two points may be made at this stage. First, Egyptian and Babylonian schools were by no means only concerned with teaching scribes to read and write.[11] Even if Israelite boys learnt the alphabet at home, they still had much technical knowledge to acquire which was elsewhere transmitted in school. Secondly, there is a difference between being able to write and being able to write well.

[9] 'Der Lehrer im alten Israel', in J. G. Prinz von Hohenzollern and M. Liedtke (eds.), *Schreiber, Magister, Lehrer. Zur Geschichte und Funktion einer Berufstandes* (Bad Heilbrunn, 1989), pp. 51–9 (see p. 58). (I owe my knowledge of this volume to the computerized bibliography of Old Testament studies which is being prepared by Mrs. O. Lipschitz of Jerusalem.) Such a view gains support from the similar silence of most Egyptian and Babylonian literature about the schools that undoubtedly existed in other parts of the ancient near east, as E. W. Heaton noted (*Solomon's New Men*, p. 108, cited by Lemaire in J. G. Gammie and L. Perdue [eds.], *The Sage in Israel and the Ancient Near East* [Winona Lake, 1990], p. 171), but it also calls in question Lemaire's hypothesis (see below) that most of the biblical literature was composed for use in school. If that were so, one could reasonably expect to find more explicit references to its *Sitz im Leben*.

[10] See, for example, the essay by J. D. Ray in this volume, dealing with Egyptian wisdom literature. Schools also existed in Canaan, as shown by the fragments of lexical lists from Aphek (A. F. Rainey, 'Two Cuneiform Fragments from Tel Aphek', *Tel Aviv* 2 [1975], pp. 125–9; 3 [1976], pp. 137–40), the Shechem letter (*ANET*, p. 490, but some caution is required: see Crenshaw, 'Education in Ancient Israel', p. 606) and a table from Hazor (see H. Tadmor, 'A Lexicographical Text from Hazor', *IEJ* 27 [1977], pp. 98–102).

[11] This is evident, e.g., from the Egyptian school-texts which have recently been reviewed by R. J. Williams, such as the *kemyt* or 'compendium', which included epistolary formulae, a model letter and appropriate sentences for different kinds of correspondence (see Egyptian Literature [Wisdom], in *Anchor Bible Dictionary*, 2 [New York, 1992], pp. 398–9).

While it may well be true that some Hebrew inscriptions were written by laymen without any special training, the obvious difference between them and the writing on official ostraca, seals and monumental inscriptions points to the latter being the work of scribes who had been taught to form their letters carefully according to a standard practice.[12]

A different objection has been raised by F. W. Golka and E. Lipiński.[13] They note that elsewhere in the ancient near east scribal training was sometimes given not in schools but by a system of 'famulature' or apprenticeship to an expert in the profession. Golka stresses that this was the original procedure in Egypt (prior to c. 2100 BC) and argues that in Israel's newly adopted monarchic polity similar arrangements are likely to have been the norm. Against this it has been pointed out by Lemaire and Crenshaw that Israel had close contact with the developed Egyptian educational system of its own time, which was based on schools.[14]

Of course, even if this argument by analogy is accepted, it still remains open to discuss when Israel was first in a position to imitate the educational institutions of her neighbours. Many would argue that this took place in the time of David (or Solomon), when a bureaucracy with some Egyptian parallels had already been established according to 2 Sam. viii 16–18, xx 23–5 and 1 Kings iv 1–6. Others would date it later, perhaps in the eighth century, when large numbers of official documents begin to appear in excavated remains, believing that the tradition about Solomon's wisdom is largely legendary and in any case does not refer to a royal school or to writing.

The second kind of indirect argument has inferred the existence of schools in Israel from the character of certain biblical books (chiefly the so-called 'wisdom literature') which, it is held, points to their having originated in a school setting. Here too comparative evidence from Israel's neighbours plays an important part, for it can be shown that works comparable to Proverbs were used elsewhere as school texts, as in the case of the Egyptian 'Instructions'.[15] The early examples of this genre (before c. 1500 BC) commonly bore the name of royal figures either as authors or as recipients of the teaching given, but it is clear from the numerous copies which survive (many on ostraca) that they were widely used for the

[12] Cf. J. Naveh, *The Early History of the Alphabet* (Jerusalem, 1982), pp. 74–5.
[13] Golka, 'Die israelitische Weisheitsschule', pp. 257–70; Lipiński, 'Royal and State Scribes in Ancient Jerusalem', in *Congress Volume: Jerusalem 1986* (*SVT* 40, 1988), pp. 157–64.
[14] Lemaire, 'Sagesse et écoles', *VT* 34 (1984), pp. 275–7; Crenshaw, 'Education in Ancient Israel', pp. 609–10. Recent research has both added to and subtracted from the evidence in support of such connections: see M. V. Fox, 'Egyptian Onomastica and Biblical Wisdom', *VT* 36 (1986), pp. 302–10, and N. Shupak, 'The "Sitz im Leben" of the Book of Proverbs in the Light of a Comparison of Biblical and Egyptian Wisdom Literature', *RB* 94 (1987), pp. 98–119.   [15] Whybray, *Wisdom in Proverbs* (see n. 3), pp. 33–71.

education of officials over a long period. It is from one such composition, the *Teaching of Amenemope*, that an extract has apparently been made, with adaptations, in Prov. xxii 17–xxiv 22. Its conclusion is particularly interesting in that it holds out the prospect for the attentive student of a future career as a teacher as well as a courtier:

> Be filled with them, put them in your heart,
> And become a man who expounds them,
> One who expounds as a teacher.
> The scribe who is skilled in his office,
> He is found worthy to be a courtier.[16]

The second part of this passage has a close parallel in Prov. xxii 29:

> Do you see those who are skilful in their work?
> they will serve kings;
> they will not serve common people.

This verse itself is followed by three more (xxiii 1–3) which make specific reference to behaviour in the presence of a 'ruler' (*môšēl*). This implies that they are addressed to those who could expect to associate with the political leadership, even if the term need not imply the king himself. Thus it appears that the borrowing of this extract from an Egyptian Instruction was made with its original purpose still very much in mind, namely the instruction of would-be courtiers and officials.[17] Similar indications have been found in other parts of Proverbs, especially in chs. xvi–xxii and xxviii–xxix and in the statement in xxv 1 that the following collection was copied by 'the men of Hezekiah king of Judah'.

Golka, however, has drawn attention to signs of a popular origin, outside the royal court, for Proverbs. He noted U. Skladny's observation that Prov. xxv–xxvii seemed to be designed for artisans rather than courtiers and reasonably enough rejected Skladny's view that in these chapters court wisdom had been adapted for the lower classes.[18] It is much more natural to suppose that the movement was in the opposite direction. Three years after his original article Golka published a second study which draws on African parallels to show that even references to the king and the court need not necessarily indicate a court origin for Proverbs: ordinary citizens had good reasons to formulate and hand on both positive and

---

[16] Tr. M. Lichtheim, *Ancient Egyptian Literature*, 2 (Berkeley, 1976), p. 162.

[17] Klostermann already deduced an educational background for this section of Proverbs from xxii 17–21. Golka's objection to this on the basis of the subsequent discovery of the parallel in the *Teaching of Amenemope* is beside the point, as others have already observed (e.g. Lemaire, 'Sagesse et écoles', pp. 273–4; Crenshaw, 'Education in Ancient Israel', p. 603).

[18] *Die ältesten Spruchsammlungen in Israel* (Göttingen, 1962), pp. 56–7, 77; Golka, 'Die israelitische Weisheitsschule', pp. 268–9.

negative assessments of the national leaders.[19] A popular origin, of course, need not exclude a subsequent use of the material in schools for the training of officials, as Lemaire has affirmed and as Golka has been ready to admit.[20] Moreover Whybray, who like Golka believes that the sentence-literature has a non-courtly origin because of its attitudes to wealth and poverty, has equally firmly insisted that the 'instructions' in chs. i–ix and xxii 17–xxiv 34 breathe a quite different air of upper-class ethics.[21] They could perfectly well (though Whybray hesitates to draw the conclusion) have originated in official schools, like their Egyptian counterparts. It should also be noted that to establish an origin for many proverbs in 'popular tradition' is not necessarily to rule out a school setting for this.[22]

Thus, both from the analogy with other ancient near eastern peoples and from the character of some biblical writings, persuasive indirect arguments can be built up for the existence of schools in ancient Israel, and these arguments also imply that such schools would have been, at least in part, associated with the training of government officials.

Recent discussion of the problem has centred on two books which have both claimed to bring new evidence to bear on it. The distinctive feature of A. Lemaire's *Les Ecoles et la formation de la Bible dans l'ancien Israël* (1981) is his appeal to the evidence of Hebrew and other inscriptions (see especially pp. 7–33). Lemaire's expertise in this field and some important recent discoveries have made it possible for him to list eleven categories of epigraphic (or associated) evidence which, he maintains, should remove any remaining doubt about the existence of schools in ancient Israel (p. 32). These categories are: (1) abecedaries (Lachish, Kadesh-barnea, Kuntillet 'Ajrud, perhaps Aroer – also 'Izbet Ṣarṭah); (2) letters which are isolated or arranged in no recognizable sequence (perhaps Arad – also 'Izbet Ṣarṭah); (3) groups of similar letters (perhaps Lachish); (4) words written several times (Arad, Kadesh-barnea and perhaps Kuntillet 'Ajrud); (5) texts containing nothing but a single personal name (perhaps Lachish and Aroer); (6) formulae for the beginning of a letter (Kuntillet 'Ajrud); (7) lists of months (Gezer); (8) numbers, sometimes repeated (Kadesh-barnea, perhaps also Lachish and Arad); (9) sequences of numbers (units, tens,

---

[19] 'Die Königs- und Hofsprüche und der Ursprung der israelitischen Weisheit', *VT* 36 (1986), pp. 13–36.   [20] Lemaire, 'Sagesse et écoles', pp. 271–2; Golka, 'Die Königs–', p. 13.

[21] *Wealth and Poverty in the Book of Proverbs*, pp. 114, 116.

[22] B. Lang associates the book of Proverbs with a school setting, which he reconstructs in some detail on the basis of Prov. i 20–1 and parallel situations in other cultures (*Wisdom in the Book of Proverbs* [New York, 1986], pp. 7–12, 22–31; cf. Lang, *Frau Weisheit* [Düsseldorf, 1975], pp. 11–18, 24–32). He also argues – this is one of the new features of the English edition – that Prov. viii 12–31 presupposes that Wisdom was honoured in early Israel as a goddess who was the patron of ancient Israelite schools (*Wisdom in the Book of Proverbs*, pp. 5, 7, 57; contrast *Frau Weisheit*, p. 170: 'Frau Weisheit ist keinesfalls als "Göttin" zu bezeichnen.').

hundreds, etc.) with a unit of measurement (Kadesh-barnea); (10) drawings (Kuntillet 'Ajrud and probably Lachish); (11) possibly exercises for learning a foreign language (Phoenician at Kuntillet 'Ajrud). Each of these categories is based on careful analysis of particular inscriptions, noting cases of inexperienced writing and parallels to known types of Egyptian school exercises. They serve, in Lemaire's view, not only to establish the existence of schools but to contribute a host of new insights into Israelite education and its influence on the whole Bible.

For Lemaire the school is the *Sitz im Leben* of most if not all of the biblical writings as we have them (though not of all the oral compositions which lie behind them). Israelite education probably grew out of the Canaanite tradition, as the transitional evidence from 'Izbet Ṣarṭah (near the Canaanite scribal school of Aphek) and Gezer shows. The chronological distribution of the epigraphic evidence points to a multiplication and expansion of schools in the early eighth century BC and implies that by the end of the monarchy period literacy was extending even to the villages and the common people. The fact that letters from Arad and Lachish use different introductory formulae can be attributed to the existence of separate 'regional schools' for the intermediate level of education. Most of the epigraphic evidence is assigned by Lemaire to the 'elementary' stage of the curriculum, where the cheap but durable ostracon was the natural writing material, but there are indications of what must have been taught in the 'middle' stage in the letters and other administrative documents that have been found. At this and the final stage papyrus or leather was probably used, and these materials do not normally survive the centuries in Palestine. Evidence for these later stages of education must be sought primarily within the Bible. From this Lemaire deduces that at the higher levels separate royal, priestly and prophetic schools are likely in pre-exilic times, with only the priestly school(s) continuing after the Exile. Comparisons with Egypt and Babylonia suggest to him that texts which were to become 'classical' as opposed to 'occasional' were preserved by being copied in schools, so that the literary history of the Bible should be seen in terms of educational developments in Israel. For example, the fact that the final redaction of the Pentateuch is from a priestly hand is attributed by him to the fact that the royal schools where the deuteronomic/ deuteronomistic literature had taken shape were abolished at the Exile and their products were taken over and adapted by the priestly school(s) which continued to exist. These educational institutions and developments were also responsible for the growth and eventual closure of the canon, just as in Egypt and Mesopotamia at a much earlier period certain texts came to form the regular curriculum of all schools and were listed in catalogues, some of which have survived (references on p. 117, n. 289).

Lemaire's account of Israelite education is not based exclusively on epigraphic evidence: like his predecessors he fills out the picture by drawing on biblical and other ancient evidence at many points. He is also more cautious in relation to his description of schools in Israel than he is about their existence (p. 84):

De futures découvertes épigraphiques et de nouveaux essais de synthèse permettront sans doute de corriger telle ou telle hypothèse de détail faite en passant.

Subsequent writers on the subject have in fact gone well beyond correcting 'telle ou telle hypothèse de détail'. Already in 1983 Golka compared the whole edifice of the school hypothesis to 'the Emperor's new clothes'. Several scholars have doubted whether the epigraphic material assembled by Lemaire proves as much as he supposes.[23] They have argued that while it indicates a certain degree of literacy – though the extent of this is disputed[24] – it does not of itself show *how* people learnt, in a school or in some other way. The most penetrating, and not entirely negative, critique of Lemaire's argument so far as been provided by E. Puech.[25] Of the eleven categories of epigraphic evidence which Lemaire distinguished Puech accepts only four as convincing: (1) the abecedaries, though only those written on ostraca (to these he adds Arad Ostracon 90, with a new reading); (2) the isolated letters; (8) the repeated numbers; (9) the lists of numbers in order. Several of the other categories are much more reasonably to be viewed not as school exercises but as having had a function in the everyday life of the places where they were found: this applies, for example, to the blessings at Kuntillet 'Ajrud, which Lemaire took to be epistolary formulae, and the Phoenician texts from the same site, which are more likely to have been inscribed by Phoenician travellers. On the other hand Puech has himself noted further epigraphic arguments which support the existence of schools, such as the consistency of spelling and the order of the letters of the alphabet, allowing for a few dialectal variations, and the use of scarce equipment such as a stylus and ink (pp. 197, 201).

One question which has been raised a number of times, and also

[23] Golka, 'Die israelitische Weisheitsschule', p. 263, n. 19; Crenshaw, 'Education in Ancient Israel', pp. 605–6; M. Haran, 'On the Diffusion of Literacy and Schools in Ancient Israel', *Congress Volume: Jerusalem 1986 (SVT* 40, 1988), pp. 87–91; Shupak, 'The "Sitz im Leben"', p. 104, n. 7; Wanke in *Schreiber, Magister, Lehrer* (n. 9), p. 54; G. Barkay, in A. Ben-Tor (ed.), *The Archaeology of Ancient Israel* (New Haven and London, 1992), p. 350.

[24] Against Lemaire's view that by the eighth century literacy was widespread (*Les Ecoles*, p. 48; cf. A. R. Millard, 'An Assessment of the Evidence for Writing in Ancient Israel', in *Biblical Archaeology Today* [Jerusalem, 1985], pp. 301–12) must be set the doubts expressed by Haran, 'On the Diffusion of Literacy', pp. 82–5, and E. Puech (see below, n. 25), pp. 197, 200, both of them to some extent dependent on the sociological insights offered by S. Warner, 'The Alphabet – An Innovation and its Diffusion'. *VT* 30 (1980), pp. 81–90.

[25] 'Les Ecoles dans l'Israël préexilique: données épigraphiques', *Congress Volume: Jerusalem 1986 (SVT* 40, 1988), pp. 189–203.

answered, is why there is not more epigraphic evidence of schools in Israel if they really existed. There is very little in the Hebrew epigraphic material to correspond to the quantities of school exercises and other educational texts which have been found in Egypt and Mesopotamia. In a reply to Golka, however, Lemaire has pointed out that this is a common problem in archaeology, where only a fraction of the original data has survived and still less has been discovered, and in this case the problem is accentuated by the perishable materials (papyrus, leather) which were commonly used for writing in Palestine. That papyrus was indeed widely used for general purposes is proved by the impressions of papyrus on the back of numerous clay stamped bullae that have been found in excavations or appeared on the antiquities market.[26] In the same article Lemaire also drew attention to a further feature of the epigraphic evidence which is most likely to be due to the existence and expansion of school education: the sudden appearance of much more inscribed material from the eighth century onwards.[27] It may be added that from Jerusalem itself, where if anywhere a school must have existed, comparatively few complete inscriptions of any kind have survived, so that the absence of school exercises is put into perspective. Whether the reason is the use of perishable materials, the effectiveness of the Babylonian destruction, the later demolition and quarrying of the south-eastern hill, or simply that archaeologists have not so far excavated in the 'right' places, the fact remains that no archive of any kind has yet been found in Jerusalem which is comparable even to those which happen to be known from Samaria, Lachish and Arad. And by near eastern standards these 'archives' are very small indeed.

The second book published in the past few years to offer a new approach to the question about schools is the archaeological study of D. W. Jamieson-Drake.[28] His approach is not archaeological in the traditional sense of trying to identify specific material evidence, be it buildings or small objects, which could be connected with the existence of schools. Instead, following the lead of theorists such as the Cambridge archaeologist D. L. Clarke,[29] he sets up an explanatory model of Judaean society in the monarchy period on the basis of the excavations at a selection of sites, with a view to determining whether, and if so where and when, there was a sufficient degree of administrative control to make official schools a necessary or even likely feature of the system. The approach is explicitly sociological and anthropological, in line with much fruitful archaeological

[26] For several examples see N. Avigad, *Hebrew Bullae from the Time of Jeremiah: Remnants of a Burnt Archive* (Jerusalem, 1986), pp. 15, 17.
[27] Lemaire, 'Sagesse et écoles', pp. 278–81.
[28] D. W. Jamieson-Drake, *Scribes and Schools in Monarchic Judah: A Socio-Archaeological Approach* (Sheffield, 1991).
[29] See especially his *Analytical Archaeology* (2nd edn, London, 1978).

research today, and indeed Jamieson-Drake sees his work as an important first step in the application of such techniques to Palestinian archaeology in the biblical period. The chief parameters which he uses are the number and size of settlements, the occurrence of public works (fortifications and public buildings) and the presence of 'luxury items', i.e. items of limited availability which presuppose the existence of specialists who are not food-producers (see the lists and statistics on pp. 191–8). These include inscriptions.

Jamieson-Drake states the results of his investigation with some caution. He is aware of various ways in which his data are unsatisfactory, and expected correlations do not always occur. Nevertheless he believes that the evidence shows that Judah only became a strongly centralized state, with Jerusalem as the dominant centre, in the eighth and seventh centuries BC. It was only then, and only in Jerusalem, that the conditions were right for the existence of a school to train scribes who would exercise administrative control over the kingdom. This is confirmed, he holds, by the fact that those places in Judah outside Jerusalem where examples of writing are known were dependent on Jerusalem, either politically or economically. Jamieson-Drake considers briefly the widely held view that already in the time of Solomon Judah/Israel was a highly organized state, but he finds that the biblical evidence in favour of such a view is often suspect and in any case it does not fit in with the overall picture derived from his archaeological data.

This last claim may cause some surprise in view of the evidence that already in the tenth century BC Hazor, Megiddo and Gezer were strongly fortified cities, and in the light of the evidence (archaeological as well as biblical) for public works in Jerusalem at the same time. These examples expose two important limitations in Jamieson-Drake's account of Judaean society. First, it is based exclusively on archaeological data from southern Palestine, despite the fact (which he recognizes) that in the tenth century David and Solomon reigned over a kingdom which extended well to the north of these limits. Secondly, even for Judah he by no means gives a complete account of the archaeological evidence as it was known in 1991 when his book was published. This is partly because the data presented were apparently collected in the early 1980s. But it is also due to a failure on Jamieson-Drake's part to give a full account of what was already known (and published) even then. This is particularly true of inscriptions, for he pays little attention to the detailed epigraphical data presented by Lemaire and he seems to be unaware of the full range of the inscriptions from Arad that were published by Y. Aharoni in Hebrew in 1975 and in English in 1981. The latter omission leads him to underestimate the total number of inscriptions and to overlook those which Aharoni attributed to the ninth century and earlier.[30] Other kinds of evidence which would make an important difference to the picture are also overlooked. A striking example is the city wall at Lachish, which Jamieson-Drake attributes only to the eighth century, despite the fact that D. Ussishkin, the excavator, ascribes it and major related features of the city plan to Stratum IV of the ninth century.[31] Another example concerns the public buildings at Tel Beersheba. According to the lists and statistics on pp. 179–87 there were none in the monarchy period. But even a cursory glance at the excavation report published in 1973 would show the presence of storehouses/stables, a 'governor's house' and a water-system.[32]

No firm conclusions can be based on work which relies on inadequate data, however promising and complex its theoretical superstructure may be. The main fault in Jamieson-Drake's work lies, however, in the exaggeration of contrasts which are real enough and which a more comprehensive review of the evidence would probably still underline: between the massive bureaucracies of Egypt and Mesopotamia and the much smaller institutions of ancient Israel and Judah; between the simpler institutions of the tenth century and the more complex ones of the eighth century and later;[33] between Jerusalem and the rest of Judah, at least from 701 onwards. When these are seen as differences of degree rather than absolute differences, they are compatible with the existence of schools in Judah over a longer period and in more centres than Jamieson-Drake allows; but at the same time they should also warn against claiming too much, especially for the early monarchy period.

Were there schools in ancient Israel? The evidence, both direct and indirect, is sufficient to justify an affirmative answer, but one that must be qualified in several ways. The growing corpus of epigraphic evidence is beginning to place the matter beyond doubt, even though not all of Lemaire's 'categories' convince. Particular emphasis should be laid on the

---

[30] Prof. A. R. Millard first drew my attention to this defect in Jamieson-Drake's work. Ironically it may turn out that the neglect of these 'early' inscriptions is not so serious after all, as Ussishkin has proposed dates for the strata with which they are associated in the eighth century or later (cf. 'The Date of the Judaean Shrine at Arad', *IEJ* 38 [1988], pp. 142–57).

[31] D. Ussishkin, 'Excavations at Tel Lachish – 1973–1977; Preliminary Report', *Tel Aviv* 5 (1978), pp. 1–97 (p. 93).

[32] Y. Aharoni, *Beersheba, 1: Excavations at Tel Beer-Sheba, 1969–1971 Seasons* (Tel Aviv, 1973), pp. 13–18. Another omission is the tenth-century casemate wall at Gezer (see Y. Yadin, *Hazor* [Schweich Lectures: London, 1972], p. 148, n. 4, and W. G. Dever, *Recent Archaeological Discoveries and Biblical Research* [Seattle, 1990], pp. 97, 106). Further archaeological weaknesses in the book have been pointed out in the reviews of P. G. Dorrell, *PEQ* 114 (1992), pp. 155–6, and B. A. Mastin, *JTS* ns 43 (1992), pp. 145–7.

[33] There is an important study of the latter (not mentioned by Jamieson-Drake) by Y. Garfinkel, 'The Distribution of Identical Seal-Impressions', *Cathedra* 32 (1984), pp. 35–52 (Heb.).

remarkable but as yet little known inscriptions from Kadesh-barnea.[34] They are written in columns and use hieratic Egyptian signs for the numbers: one (no. 4) contains the same number (2382) nine times, another (no. 3) has two columns of mixed numbers and units of measurement and a third column with the numbers from 100 to 800 followed by the unit *grh*, and a third (no. 9) has the numbers from 100 to 500 preceded by the shekel sign. The most important of all (no. 6) contains nine columns, six on the recto and three on the verso, with sequences of the numbers from 1 to 10,000 which are in some cases accompanied by the signs for *ephah* (or *kor*) or 'shekel'. This is an especially valuable discovery, both because it gives the complete system of hieratic numerals used in Judah on a single inscription and because it can scarcely be anything but a practice exercise of a trainee scribe, like the others from Kadesh-barnea. It is admittedly strange to find such texts in an isolated fortress on the edge of the desert, but one must apparently conclude from them that training was given in the skills which we see being used by the writers of, for example, the Arad ostraca, where many of these signs (and others) reappear.[35] The *a fortiori* argument is a strong one: if we find evidence of such training in an outpost such as this, it must surely also have existed in the major centres of administration. It is hard to imagine a scribe becoming adept at the use of the extensive system of hieratic signs without much training and practice. Although reading the numerical signs on weights may have been within the competence of many a trader,[36] writing them accurately was a much greater skill.

But even after allowances have been made for the different interests of the biblical writers and the chances of archaeological discovery, there is at present insufficient evidence for envisaging such a widespread educational system as that sketched by Lemaire. Formal instruction may only have been given in the capital cities and the administrative centres that were dependent on them. Even this may only have been on a limited scale until the eighth century. There is evidence of Egyptian influence on Israelite education, both in parts of the book of Proverbs and in the use of hieratic numerals and other signs. But much of Proverbs will have been drawn from

[34] For the texts and references to the primary publications see my *Ancient Hebrew Inscriptions* (Cambridge, 1991), nos. 9.003–9.006 and 9.009. For a brief account of the finds see R. Cohen, 'Excavations at Kadesh-barnea 1976–1978: Addendum', *BA* 44 (1981), pp. 105–7.

[35] See the listings in my *Ancient Hebrew Inscriptions*, pp. 512–35, and the drawings on pp. xix–xxii; also the discussion in A. Lemaire, *Inscriptions hébraïques*, 1: *Les ostraca* (Paris, 1977), pp. 277–81. The majority of occurrences are in seventh- or early sixth-century texts, but there are several instances of the use of hieratic signs in eighth-century inscriptions. To these must now be added Pithos B from Kuntillet 'Ajrud, on which a large number of hieratic signs appear: this was pointed out to me by Dr. J. M. Hadley, following an earlier observation by Prof. V. Fritz.

[36] Cf. Puech, *Congress Volume: Jerusalem 1986* (*SVT* 40, 1988), p. 195.

traditional popular wisdom, which was disseminated in ways that remain unclear. There may have been 'schools' of a kind in the villages of Palestine, presided over by one or more of the village elders perhaps, but analogies for this have yet to be identified. As literacy became more widespread, it may have been disseminated informally, outside a formal school setting. But the more technical scribal skills were probably passed on, as elsewhere, through schools.

It is a pleasure for me to dedicate this essay, as a token of admiration, friendship and thanks, to a scholar who has always made the encouragement and teaching of the young a priority in his work.

18   The trees, the beasts and the birds: fables, parables and allegories in the Old Testament

Kevin J. Cathcart

In his introduction to the Old Testament, O. Eissfeldt divides narratives into two groups: poetic narratives and historical narratives.[1] The poetic narratives are subdivided further into several groups including myths, fairy-tales, fables, tales and sagas. Eissfeldt identifies examples of fairy-tale motifs in Num. xxii 22–35, where Balaam's ass is a talking animal, and 1 Kings xvii 1–6, where ravens bring food to Elijah. Like many scholars, he points out the excellent examples of fables in Judg. ix 8–15 (Jotham's fable) and 2 Kings xiv 9 (Jehoash's fable). In the allegories of Ezekiel, he notes the fable of the eagle, the cedar and the vine (xvii 3–10). Animals or vines appear together with humans in 2 Sam. xii 1–4, Nathan's parable of the poor man's ewe lamb, and Isa. v 1–7, the parable of the vineyard.

G. Fohrer, on the other hand, discusses fable, parable and allegory under the heading, 'The Literary Types of Wisdom and their Traditions'.[2] However, he includes most of the examples chosen by Eissfeldt and identifies them in the same manner, though we might note that he lists three allegories from Ezekiel: xvii 1–10, xix 1–9, xxxi 1–18. An 'extended' allegory is recognized in Eccles. xi 9–xii 8. Fohrer discusses the fairy-tale in his section on narrative literary types.[3]

C. Kuhl, discussing the literary character of the Old Testament, writes: 'In addition to this mythical material there is much in the Old Testament that smacks of the world of the *Märchen*, particularly in the writings of the prophets.'[4] Thus, he too cites Ezek. xxxi 1–18, the allegory of the great and wonderful tree, but he adds the example in Amos v 19 which speaks of the

---

[1] *Einleitung in das Alte Testament* (3rd edn, Tübingen, 1964), pp. 41–75 (E. tr., *The Old Testament: An Introduction* [Oxford, 1965], pp. 32–56).

[2] *Einleitung in das Alte Testament* (10th edn, Heidelberg, 1965), pp. 339–44 (E. tr., *Introduction to the Old Testament* [Nashville and New York, 1968], pp. 311–15).

[3] *Einleitung*, pp. 97–8 (E. tr., pp. 89–90).

[4] 'Neben diesen mythischen Stoffen findet sich im Alten Testament vieles, was aus der *Welt des Märchens* stammt. Besonders bei den Propheten wird oft auf solche Stoffe angespielt' (*Die Entstehung des Alten Testaments* [Bern, 1953], p. 47 [E. tr., *The Old Testament: Its Origins and Composition* (Edinburgh and London, 1961), p. 41]).

unfortunate man who escapes from the lion only to meet a bear, and is bitten by a serpent when he leans on the wall of his house. Yet Kuhl is at pains to stress that what we find in the Old Testament are not complete fairy-tales or folktales, but only allusions or single features.[5] He regards Isa. v 1–7 as a fable, and sees 'a glimmer of an original fable' in Ezek. xv, xvii and xix. However, the content of the fables of Jotham (Judg. ix) and Jehoash (2 Kings xiv) is thought to approach the parable and the allegory, 'forms of literary art whose object is to be vivid and impressive'.[6]

G. von Rad, in the introduction to his *Weisheit in Israel*, has a section entitled, 'The Forms in which Knowledge is Expressed' *(Erkenntnisbindende Formen)*, and there he discusses fable and allegory.[7] He acknowledges that very few fables have been preserved in the Old Testament and finds an explanation for this in 'the religious point of view which was determinative for the collection of Israel's literature'.[8] He takes as fables Judg. ix 8–15; 2 Sam. xii 1–4; 2 Kings xiv 9, but in his view the application of the fables to particular situations (e.g. political and historical situations) results in their acquiring allegorical features. Von Rad sees an advanced form of this development in Ezek. xvii and xix. Now it is surprising that he speaks of the 'two fables' in these chapters of Ezekiel, because immediately he wonders 'whether Ezekiel was using what was still genuine fable material'.[9] However, it is possible that von Rad, to judge by his view that the allegory of Eccles. xii 1–6 is a riddle, may have had some difficulty with the use of the term allegory or with allegorizing. It is precisely on this issue that J. L. Crenshaw is firmer in his assessment of the fable and the allegory in the Old Testament;[10] though, to be fair, it must be said that when Crenshaw asserts that in time 'it [the fable] disintegrated into pure allegory, particularly in prophetic hands',[11] he does so with direct support from von Rad.

---

[5] *Die Entstehung*, p. 47 (E. tr., p. 41). It is not necessary to review here the various criticisms and strictures against H. Gunkel, *Das Märchen im Alten Testament* (Tübingen, 1917) (E. tr., *The Folktale in the Old Testament* [Sheffield, 1987]). But see, for example, J. A. Wilcoxen, 'Narrative', in J. H. Hayes (ed.), *Old Testament Form Criticism* (San Antonio, 1974), p. 72: 'Strictly speaking, the *Märchen* is only indirectly relevant to OT form criticism. The extant narratives are not *Märchen*, even if they contain such motifs, and the prophetic allegories and eschatological visions are at least drastic alterations of hypothetical *Märchen*.' See also J. J. Scullion, '*Märchen, Sage, Legende:* Towards a Clarification of Some Literary Terms used by Old Testament Scholars', *VT* 34 (1984), pp. 321–36.

[6] 'literarischen Kunstformen, denen es auf Anschaulichkeit und Eindringlichkeit ankommt' (Kuhl, *Die Entstehung*, p. 48 [E. tr., p. 42]).

[7] *Weisheit in Israel* (Neukirchen-Vluyn, 1970), pp. 62–7 (E. tr., *Wisdom in Israel* [London, 1972], pp. 41–6).

[8] 'Das könnte an dem religiösen Gesichtspunkt liegen, der für die Sammlung der Literatur Israels massgebend war' (von Rad, *Weisheit in Israel*, pp. 62–3 [E. tr., p. 42]).

[9] 'Man kann fragen, ob Hesekiel noch echte Fabelstoffe' (von Rad, *Weisheit in Israel*, p. 65 [E. tr., p. 44]).

[10] 'Wisdom', in Hayes (ed.), *Old Testament Form Criticism*, pp. 245–7.

[11] 'Wisdom', p. 246.

M. H. Abrams defines the fable as 'a short story that exemplifies a moral thesis or a principle of human behaviour; usually in its conclusion either the narrator or one of the characters states the moral in the form of an Epigram'.[12] M. C. A. Korpel, after citing Abrams's definition, rightly adds that 'usually the acting figures are animals or (less frequently) plants'.[13] Now the distinction between a parable and an allegory is rather more difficult to describe. Abrams defines the parable as 'a short narrative presented so as to stress the tacit but detailed analogy between its component parts and a thesis or lesson that the narrator is trying to bring home to us'.[14] However, as we shall see below, there are Old Testament texts which can well be described as parables; but since there are further lessons or messages to be taken from them, they could just as well be interpreted as allegories. It may well be that strict definition serves a limited purpose and it seems futile to attempt to attach specific labels to every text of the parabolical and allegorical type. In the most recent article on parable, J. D. Crossan stresses that, in the Hebrew literary tradition, the *māšāl* (Gk παραβολή) had a 'wide range of application ... [and] is concentrated around the idea of comparison of one thing said and another intended'.[15] K. Nielsen, in a stimulating investigation of 'the tree as metaphor' in Isa. i–xxxix, has some sobering remarks on the limited interest which Old Testament scholars have shown in imagery and metaphor.[16] Though she might be critical of my emphasis on what she calls 'the special "Gattungen" of imagery: fable, parable, allegory', I am entirely sympathetic to her search for what is common to all forms of imagery.[17]

As Crenshaw reminds us, fables are absent from the wisdom literature of the Old Testament, and there are few allegories in that corpus.[18] This is surprising, for we are told in 1 Kings v 13 (iv 33) that Solomon 'discoursed about trees, from the cedar of Lebanon to the marjoram that grows out of the wall; and he discoursed about beasts and birds, and reptiles and fish'. After all, Solomon is the figure of the past upon whom all wisdom is focussed.[19] As it happens, many of the fables, parables and allegories of the

---

[12] *A Glossary of Literary Terms* (4th edn, New York, 1981), p. 6.

[13] 'The Literary Genre of the Song of the Vineyard (Isa. 5:1–7)', in W. van der Meer and J. C. de Moor (eds.), *The Structural Analysis of Biblical and Canaanite Poetry* (Sheffield, 1988), p. 121.   [14] *Glossary*, p. 6.

[15] 'Parable', in D. N. Freedman (ed.), *Anchor Bible Dictionary*, 5 (New York, 1992), pp. 146–7.

[16] *There is Hope for a Tree: The Tree as Metaphor in Isaiah* (Sheffield, 1989), pp. 25–35, especially 33–5. Note the useful review of the contributions of her Scandinavian colleague, A. J. Bjørndalen, 'Metodiske bermerkninger til spørsmålet etter allegorier; Det gamle Testamente', *Tidsskrift for Teologi og Kirke* 27 (1966), pp. 145–66; and *Untersuchungen zur allegorischen Rede der Propheten Amos und Jesaja* (Berlin, 1986).

[17] Nielsen, *There is Hope for a Tree*, p. 60.   [18] 'Wisdom', p. 245.

[19] J. A. Montgomery and H. S. Gehman, *A Critical and Exegetical Commentary on the Book of Kings* (Edinburgh, 1951), p. 129.

Old Testament do have acting figures which are trees, animals and birds. These particular examples are the subjects of the short survey that follows.

The tale of Balaam's ass (Num. xxii 22–35)

It is generally agreed that this tale of Balaam's ass stands uneasily after what precedes it. We are told in verse 19 that Balaam asked Balak's Moabite messengers to stay the night, so that he might learn the will of the Lord. God comes to him in the night, and tells him to go with the messengers, an order which Balaam promptly obeys (verse 21). However, in the next verse (verse 22), it is related that 'God was angry because Balaam was going' *(kî hôlēk hû̓)*. Are we to assume, with M. Noth, that there was an older version of the story of Balaam, in which there was no mention of the events recounted in verses 7–20?[20] In the older version Balaam must have set out of his own accord, and without consulting God about Balak's demand. Yet the tale of Balaam's ass looks very much like an independent piece – a folktale or fable which was adapted for insertion in the Balaam narrative (Num. xxii–xxiv).[21] According to Noth, 'with its clarity, with its artistic presentation of suspense and of dramatic heightening, the episode of the ass is a masterpiece of ancient Israelite narrative art'.[22]

Jotham's fable (Judg. ix 8–15)

This is one of only very few fables which have been preserved in the Old Testament. Von Rad describes it as a 'masterpiece of the most concise reasoning and linguistic style'.[23] It is written in rhythmic prose and should not be regarded as a poem, *pace* C. F. Burney,[24] von Rad,[25] R. G. Boling,[26] and some modern translators (NJB, NRSV). The structure of the fable can be compared to that of Aesop's fables, and the theme of rivalry between the trees is well known from antiquity. T. H. Gaster compares the Mesopotamian story of the quarrel between the tamarisk and the palm-tree; the fables of Aesop in which the fir-tree and the bramble boast to each other, and the pomegranate and the apple-tree dispute with each other, with the bramble calling out from a hedge for an end to the quarrel; and the Aramaic sayings

---

[20] *Das vierte Buch Mose: Numeri* (Göttingen, 1966), p. 157 (E. tr., *Numbers* [London, 1968], p. 178).   [21] J. Sturdy, *Numbers* (Cambridge, 1976), pp. 157, 165.

[22] 'Die Eselinepisode ist mit ihrer Anschaulichkeit, ihrer Kunst der Darstellung von Spannung und dramatischer Steigerung ein Meisterwerk altisraelitischen Erzählens' (*Das vierte Buch Mose*, p. 157 [E. tr., p. 178]).

[23] 'Dieses Meisterwerk straffster Gedankenführung und Sprachgestaltung' (*Weisheit in Israel*, p. 63 [E. tr., p. 42]).

[24] *The Book of Judges* (2nd edn, London, 1920), pp. 272–5.

[25] *Weisheit in Israel*, p. 63 (E. tr., p. 42).   [26] *Judges* (Garden City, 1975), pp. 166, 172–3.

of Ahiqar (*ANET*, pp. 429–30) which relate a fable of the bramble taunting the pomegranate.[27]

Jotham's fable is found in an address that he delivers to the Shechemites from Mount Gerizim. First, he tells the fable (verses 8–15), and then applies it to the current situation regarding his political opponent Abimelech, whom he wishes to discredit. Verses 16–21 are effectively the moral of the fable, and, when they are read together with verses 8–15, the whole unit takes on the appearance of a parable. The best recent study of the fable is B. Lindars's form-critical analysis.[28] With him and earlier critics, the fable in verses 8–14/15 must be taken as an originally independent piece. Lindars isolates a proverb in verse 15, *tēṣē' 'ēš min hāʾāṭād wᵉtōʾkal 'et 'arᵉzê hallᵉbānôn*, which 'only became a curse in the context of the conditional sentences'.[29] By adapting the proverb, the two conditional sentences in verse 15 were composed to match the application of the fable in verses 19–20, so that verse 15 replaced the original ending of the fable. (The ending, suggests Lindars, may originally have read, 'And the bramble said to the trees, I will be king over you.')

It has been proposed by Gaster that, when the bramble says to the trees, 'Come and take shelter in my shade' *(bᵉṣillî)*, there may be a play on the Mesopotamian 'in your/his shadow', meaning under the special protection of the king.[30] Perhaps even more apposite is the following passage from the Akkadian 'Love Lyrics of Nabû and Tašmētu':

The shade *(ṣil)* of the cedar, the shade of the cedar, the shade of the cedar, the king's shelter! The shade of the cypress is for his magnates! The shade of a sprig of juniper is shelter for my Nabû and my games![31]

The parable of the poor man's ewe lamb (2 Sam. xii 1–4)

This piece is without doubt one of the best illustrations of Old Testament parables, and possibly the most famous.[32] Nathan's parable follows the story of David's adultery with Bathsheba and his subsequent order to Joab to place Uriah at the battlefront. Now U. Simon has convincingly argued that the literary form of 2 Sam. xii 1–4 is a 'juridical parable', which he defines as follows:

The juridical parable constitutes a realistic story about a violation of the law,

[27] *Myth, Legend, and Custom in the Old Testament* (New York and Evanston, 1969), pp. 423–5.
[28] 'Jotham's Fable – a New Form-Critical Analysis', *JTS* ns 24 (1973), pp. 355–66.
[29] 'Jotham's Fable', p. 359.
[30] *Myth, Legend, and Custom*, p. 427, and reference there to A. L. Oppenheim, 'Assyriological Gleanings IV', *BASOR* 107 (1947), pp. 7–11.
[31] See the new edition of the text with translation in A. Livingstone, *Court Poetry and Literary Miscellanea* (Helsinki, 1989), p. 35.   [32] Crossan, 'Parable', p. 147.

related to someone who had committed a similar offence with the purpose of leading the unsuspecting hearer to pass judgement on himself. The offender will only be caught in the trap set for him if he truly believes that the story told him actually happened, and only if he does not detect prematurely the similarity between the offence in the story and the one he himself has committed.[33]

Like Jotham's fable, the fable of the poor man's ewe lamb probably had an independent existence, because, as von Rad points out, it only 'very approximately fits the offence which David had committed against Uriah'.[34] Be that as it may, the parable in verses 1–4 has been placed in its overall setting with considerable skill.

The ravens feed Elijah (1 Kings xvii 1–6)

The chapter begins with Elijah's sudden appearance and his announcement to Ahab of a drought. Then three incidents are described which have miraculous elements: the feeding of Elijah by ravens at the brook of Cherith (verses 2–6), the widow of Zarephath and the miracle of the flour and oil (verses 7–16), and the miracle of the resuscitation of the child (verses 17–24). This last incident has no apparent connection with the drought, though the child raised to life is often thought to be the widow of Zarephath's son. These stories have 'the characteristics of prophetic wonder legends'.[35] Indeed, the first two incidents are suggestive of the world of the *Märchen*. Therefore, there is no reason to emend MT '$\bar{o}r^e b\hat{\imath}m$, 'ravens' (verse 4) to '$^a r\bar{a}b\hat{\imath}m$, 'Arabs'. Feeding by animals and birds is found in similar fairy-tales in ancient and later times. In the words of Montgomery and Gehman, 'the divine provision of the prophet's food was simply miraculous'.[36] Though the Deuteronomist probably did not intend 1 Kings xvii 1–6 as 'fable', but as history, nevertheless there is a fairy-tale motif in the passage.

Jehoash's fable (2 Kings xiv 8–10)

A thistle in Lebanon sent to a cedar in Lebanon to say, 'Give your daughter in marriage to my son.' But a wild beast in Lebanon went by and trampled on the thistle. (verse 9)

---

[33] 'The Poor Man's Ewe-Lamb: An Example of a Juridical Parable', *Biblica* 48 (1967), pp. 220–1. Note also P. W. Coxon, 'A Note on "Bathsheba" in 2 Samuel 12, 1–6', *Biblica* 62 (1981), pp. 247–50.

[34] 'nur sehr ungefähr das Verbrechen, das David an Uria begangen hatte, trifft' (*Weisheit in Israel*, p. 64 [E. tr., p. 43]).

[35] G. H. Jones, *1 and 2 Kings*, 2 (London and Grand Rapids, 1984), p. 303.

[36] Montgomery and Gehman, *Kings*, p. 294.

This verse is part of a short passage (verses 8–10) which recounts Amaziah of Judah's challenge to Jehoash of Israel to meet him in battle. Amaziah's challenge ('Let us confront each other') has been described as 'couched in the knightly language of the duello'.[37] The fable is short, and so is its interpretation in verse 10. The passage as a whole recalls Jotham's fable (Judg. ix 7–21), already discussed above, for both fables involve talking plants and trees and operate in a political sphere. This fable, like others of the same genre that we have examined, does not completely fit the story which frames it. But it is incisive, and the whole piece, short as it is, is lively.

The parable of the vineyard (Isa. v 1–7)

Most commonly known as the Song of the Vineyard, the problem of its literary genre continues to provoke much discussion.[38] In a lengthy article on this passage, W. Schottroff, anticipating to some extent Simon's recognition of the 'juridical parable' in 2. Sam. xii 1–4, has argued that the Old Testament parable, in the form of a legal case, was meant to elicit from the hearer a verdict which was then unexpectedly applied to himself.[39] The Song of the Vineyard, he suggests, has these characteristics. More recently, G. A. Yee has proposed two literary forms 'conjoined', viz. a song and a juridical parable,[40] and A. Graffy offers the term 'self-condemnation parable'.[41] Schottroff rejects the view that a love song has been reworked and argues that it is more satisfactory to interpret the text in the light of the ancient near eastern disputation poem *(Streitdichtung)*, and understand it as a fable employed as a parable.

In her detailed study of the text, Korpel rejects the view that it is a fable, arguing that the vineyard is not an acting figure and verse 7 is not 'a moral thesis or a principle of human behaviour in a general sense'.[42] For the same reasons, she thinks it difficult to describe the passage as a parable, preferring to classify the genre of Isa. v 1–7 as an allegory. On the other hand, she does concede that elaborate imagery can be found in both parable and allegory. The sticking-point is basically around the question of whether the parable is to be distinguished from the allegory on the ground that the former has a single point of comparison. Nielsen, whose work on imagery in Isaiah has been referred to already, discusses the form of Isa. v

---

[37] *Ibid.*, p. 440.

[38] For a review of the many different views, see J. T. Willis, 'The Genre of Isaiah 5, 1–7', *JBL* 96 (1977), pp. 337–62.

[39] 'Das Weinberglied Jesajas (Jes 5 1–7): Ein Beitrag zur Geschichte der Parabel', *ZAW* 82 (1970), pp. 69–91.

[40] 'A Form-Critical Study of Isaiah 5: 1–7 as a Song and Juridical Parable', *CBQ* 43 (1981), pp. 30–40.   [41] 'The Literary Genre of Isaiah 5, 1–7', *Biblica* 60 (1979), pp. 400–9.

[42] 'The Song of the Vineyard', p. 154.

1–7 at length and prefers to describe this text as a 'metaphorical narrative'.[43] She recognizes a love song and a lawsuit but places rather more emphasis on the reinterpretation of the text in the eighth century and in the exilic period. Yet she does speak once of the vineyard parable.[44]

Korpel is convinced that the passage is an allegory, stressing that the 'multiple and ambiguous imagery would be unacceptable to the genre of the parable in its traditional meaning'.[45] Perhaps scholars are trying too hard to be precise about the genre of Isa. v 1–7. Even Korpel thinks it could be described as an 'allegorical parable'.

The allegory of the useless vine (Ezek. xv 1–8)

This passage divides into a parable of the vine (verses 1–5) and its interpretation (verses 6–8). The parable emphasizes the idea of the uselessness of the wood of the vine. L. Boadt observes: 'In contrast to the wonderful product of the grapes – wine – the product of the pruned wood is good for nothing but fuel for the fireplace.'[46] In Isa. v 1–7 Israel is compared to a vineyard and elsewhere (e.g. Ps. lxxx 9–16 [8–15]; Hos. x 1) she is a luxuriant vine. So the contrast here is striking, where Israel is compared to useless vine wood. W. Zimmerli, drawing attention to the question in verse 2 introduced by *mah* (cf. the similar beginning of the parable in Ezek. xix 2) and to further questions in verses 3–5, suggests that we have here an example of a parable 'stylized as a disputation saying'.[47] He also notes J. Lindblom's view that didactic wisdom literature has influenced the form of the passage.[48] Von Rad interprets the questions in verses 1–3 as 'school questions' *(Schulfragen)*, indicative of a type of educational activity.[49] He recalls as examples Amos iii 3–8; Job viii 11 and Prov. vi 27–8, though his preferred example of what he calls the 'catechetical-didactic style' is Isa. xxviii 23–9.

The interpretation of verses 6–8 is clear and explicit: Jerusalem (representing Israel) will be burned. However, there is no evidence to support the view that the two burned ends of the wood in verse 4 refer to Israel and Judah. Kuhl may be right in seeing a glimmer of an original fable in Ezek. xv, but it is nothing more than that.[50]

---

[43] *There is Hope for a Tree*, pp. 89–116.   [44] *There is Hope for a Tree*, p. 108.
[45] 'The Song of the Vineyard', p. 154.
[46] 'Ezekiel', in R. E. Brown, J. A. Fitzmyer, R. E. Murphy (eds.), *The New Jerome Biblical Commentary* (New Jersey, 1990), p. 316.
[47] 'als Disputationswort stilisiert' (*Ezechiel* [Neukirchen-Vluyn, 1969], p. 326 [E. tr., *Ezekiel 1* (Philadelphia, 1979), p. 318]).
[48] 'Wisdom in the Old Testament Prophets', in *Wisdom in Israel and in the Ancient Near East* (*SVT* 3, 1955), p. 201.   [49] *Weisheit in Israel*, p. 32 (E. tr., p. 18).
[50] *Die Entstehung*, p. 48 (E. tr., p. 42).

The parable of the eagles, the cedar and the vine (Ezek. xvii 1–10)

In form Ezek. xvii is not unlike Ezek. xv. However, materially it is more extensive with its animal plant fables, together with elements from the riddle. The cedar and the vine figured in Jotham's fable and Jehoash's fable. But here, as elsewhere, the form of the fable has, in von Rad's words, 'been greatly disintegrated by the prophet for his own purposes'.[51] The significance of *ḥîdâ*, 'riddle', in verse 2 has been much discussed. In truth, the 'riddle' is rare in the Old Testament and Judg. xiv 10–18 is the only pure example. Crenshaw sagely observes that the riddle is related to parable and allegory, but, after pointing out that A. Wünsche treated Ezek. xvii 1–10 as a symbolic riddle, he wonders what the real difference is between this passage and the allegory in Eccles. xii 1–7.[52] Yet we have already seen that von Rad thought the latter text to be a riddle. Possibly Ezek. xvii 1–10 should be treated as a parable. Indeed, one of the most succinct and relevant observations on the matter has been made recently by a New Testament scholar. J. Ashton points out that Ezekiel, having 'propounded his parable', is asked by God to 'explain it', so it is in this way that the parable is enigmatic or has a riddling quality.[53] T. Polk also stresses this aspect, noting that here *ḥîdâ* suggests 'riddling quality' and not a pure riddle.[54] Recently H. Simian-Yofre has added his weight in favour of interpreting Ezek. xvii 1–10 as a parable (he provisionally calls it a fable at the beginning of his article) and takes the subsequent verses 11–21 as a 'political interpretation' and verses 22–4 as a 'theological interpretation'.[55] However, he retains the description of it as a riddle as well as a parable ('enigma y parábola' = *ḥîdâ . . . māšāl* in verse 2). Perhaps, once again, it is necessary to caution against too rigid an adherence to these terms. Ezek. xvii 1–10 may well be a parable, but the chapter as a whole (verses 1–24) is best defined as an allegory. (JPSV, NRSV translate *māšāl* in verse 2 by 'allegory', REB by 'parable', NAB by 'proverb'.)

The allegory of the lioness and the vine (Ezek. xix 1–14)

This piece is a 'metaphorical account of the fall of the lamented'[56] and is, in effect, an allegory. It should be taken as a unity, even though there is an

---

[51] 'Die Gattung der Fabel ist hier vom Propheten für seine Zwecke schon stark desintegriert' (*Weisheit in Israel*, p. 65 [E. tr., p. 44]).   [52] 'Wisdom', p. 244.

[53] *Understanding the Fourth Gospel* (Oxford, 1992), p. 396. Note also his remarks on παραβολή and παροιμία: 'both words are employed in the LXX to translate the Hebrew *māšāl* and the evangelists themselves might not have been impressed by Jülicher's careful distinction between parable and allegory' (p. 398).

[54] 'Paradigms, Parables, and *Měšālîm*: On Reading the *Māšāl* in Scripture', *CBQ* 45 (1983), p. 578.   [55] 'Ez 17, 1–10 como enigma y parábola', *Biblica* 65 (1984), pp. 27–43.

[56] '(Bild-)Erzählung vom Fall der Beklagten' (Zimmerli, *Ezechiel*, p. 421 [E. tr., p. 392]).

apparent break between verses 1–9, where the image is that of a lioness with two cubs, and verses 10–14, where it is that of a vine. But it is only apparent, for the introductory '*imm^eka* of verse 10 is clearly connected with verse 2. However, Zimmerli may well be right in thinking that verses 10–14 were added to verses 1–9 at a later stage in the composition of the text. Certainly, the image and vocabulary of verses 10–14 are similar to those of chs. xvii and xxxi, as is the theme.

The first cub represents Jehoahaz but the identity of the second cub is disputed. It is thought by some to be Zedekiah because Jehoahaz and Zedekiah were sons of the same mother, Hamutal. But the second cub could just as well refer to Jehoiachin. Perhaps it is more important to note that the unidentified '*imm^eka*, *l^ebiyya'* and *gepen* stand for Judah and the Davidic house. The destructive fire in verse 14 has been compared by Boadt to the fire that went from the bramble to consume the cedars in Jotham's fable.[57]

The allegory of the great tree (Ezek. xxxi 1–18)

This oracle, addressed to the pharaoh of Egypt in all his pomp, probably originated among the Babylonian exiles. It can best be interpreted as an allegory, though of course Boadt is surely right when he sees in it 'characteristics of a fable, metaphor, allegory, judgment speech, and lament'.[58]

Verses 3–9 describe a great splendid tree; verses 10–14 give an account of its fall from great splendour and pride to wretchedness, and verses 15–18 contain a description of the journey of the mighty tree to Sheol. In particular, verse 13 illustrates the mood of the judgement oracles: 'On its fallen trunk the birds of the air all settled, and the wild beasts all sought shelter among its branches.' Yet the thrust of the whole passage is best found in verses 10–11: 'Because it grew so high, raising its crown through the foliage, and its pride mounted as it grew, I handed it over to a prince of the nations to deal with it.'

This survey is not meant to cover every example of fable, parable and allegory in the Old Testament. But the choice of those in which trees, plants, animals and birds figure is sufficiently extensive to illustrate usage and characteristics.

It is a pleasure to dedicate this contribution to Professor John Emerton, a friend for many years.

[57] 'Ezekiel', p. 318.   [58] 'Ezekiel', p. 323.

19   The personification of Wisdom

Roland E. Murphy

In the beginning was the word, i.e., the spoken word of the proverbial saying; in the end was a radiant wisdom (Wisd. vii 26), striding through creation (Ecclus xxiv 5), born of God and rejoicing in the created world (Prov. viii 22–31). There is no journey in the Bible comparable to this, just as there is no personification comparable to that of wisdom. Justice and peace may kiss (Ps. lxxxv 11 [10]), and alcohol may be a rowdy (Prov. xx 1), but only wisdom is given a voice that resembles the Lord's (Prov. viii 35, 'whoever finds me finds life'). In a summary of the state of research in wisdom literature, Professor Emerton once wrote, 'A controversial problem of Prov. 1–9 is that of the origin and meaning of the personified figure of Wisdom...'[1] Those words still hold true, not only for the book of Proverbs, but for all the biblical passages dealing with this mysterious figure.

Two aspects of the problem present themselves immediately. First, are we dealing with a personification, a hypostasis, or a person? This question cannot be answered effectively because there is no agreement on the meaning of these relatively abstract words as they are applied to wisdom. The theological baggage these words have acquired over the years is simply too heavy to bear. Readers will note the specificity of the title of this essay, but they are wary enough to take it in the sense of a directional sign. Second, although there is a similarity in all the pertinent texts, there is a bewildering variety of claims made for personified Wisdom. Are we talking about the same figure throughout the texts we shall examine? A summary analysis of the data will enable readers to form a judgement, perhaps one different from the writer. It is to be expected that wisdom should carry different meanings for different generations – even if the *written* expression of all these texts took place within a relatively short time, the post-exilic period.

In the first half of the century the studies of R. Bultmann, W. L.

'Wisdom', in G. W. Anderson (ed.), *Tradition and Interpretation* (Oxford, 1979), pp. 237–45, especially p. 241. The fascination of John Emerton with wisdom is manifested in his many studies of the text and translation of the book of Proverbs, and in his critical edition of *The Peshitta of the Wisdom of Solomon* (Leiden, 1959).

Knox, G. Boström, and H. Ringgren set the tone of future research.[2] They concentrated on the origins or the pedigree of Wisdom, the sources outside the Bible which influenced the development of the biblical figure. This research has been fruitful in many ways. Scholarly attention was continually called to this enigmatic figure. In addition, perhaps all the possibilities have been exhausted: an unnamed Assyrian or West Semitic goddess (in the Ahiqar text), the Canaanite goddess Ashtart or Asherah, the Egyptian Ma'at, the Hellenistic Isis, or a gnostic divinity before gnosticism itself.[3] However, even if the influence of one or another of these sources is not disputed, its measure is difficult to assess, and often the biblical meaning has been side-stepped. The studies have been both perceptive and exaggerated. No-one would discount the background role of *ma'at* in the fleshing out of Wisdom in the book of Proverbs, or the influence of Isis aretologies on Wisdom vii–ix. But in the end there is the feeling of Qoheleth's judgement in the bones of the biblical reader (Eccles. vii 23–4 – wisdom remains distant). Of course the theme of the impossibility of finding wisdom is frequent in the Bible (e.g. Job xxviii 10, 20). One reason is that wisdom carried different meanings for different generations of Israelites. It is not possible to hold wisdom at a specific historical level with a corresponding meaning. Thus, the identification by Sirach of Wisdom and Torah is only one meaning among others which the Bible serves up. This chapter intends to centre on the unfolding meaning(s) of personified wisdom in the contexts of the several books in which she appears.

Job xxviii

There is no dearth of literature and of interpretation for this enigmatic chapter. There are two principal questions. First, what is it doing here (in Job's mouth? or a later addition)? Second, what effect does the final verse (verse 28 with the traditional equation of wisdom and fear of the Lord) have on the wisdom poem? We must bypass here the critical problems of authorship and age. The message of the poem is clear to this extent: precious minerals can be taken from the earth by humans, but where is wisdom to be found (verses 12, 20)? The answer to this question seems to be

---

[2] R. Bultmann, 'Der religionsgeschichtliche Hintergrund des Prologs zum Johannesevangelium', in *Eucharisterion* (FS H. Gunkel; Göttingen, 1923), pp. 1–26; W. L. Knox, 'The Divine Wisdom', *JTS* 38 (1937), pp. 230–7; G. Boström, *Proverbiastudien. Die Weisheit und das fremde Weib in Spr. 1–9* (Lund, 1935); H. Ringgren, *Word and Wisdom. Studies in the Hypostatization of Divine Qualities and Functions in the Ancient Near East* (Lund, 1947).

[3] Cf. the summary treatments in B. Lang, *Frau Weisheit. Deutung einer biblischen Gestalt* (Düsseldorf, 1975), pp. 148–60, and also his *Wisdom and the Book of Proverbs* (New York, 1986), pp. 126–46.

unequivocal. It (wisdom does not seem to be personified here as a woman) is with God. But therein lies a problem: the final verse (xxviii 27) of the poem seems to indicate that God did something with wisdom. He surely knows the way to it, because 'he sees everything under the heavens' (verse 24). In verse 27 'he saw it and declared it; he established it and searched it out' (NRSV). What is the meaning of this activity? The answer of G. von Rad is helpful: wisdom is somewhere in the world, and yet separate from the works of creation. He denies that it is a personification (but then, what is it?) or a divine attribute.[4] His answer is that wisdom is 'the order given to the world by God', a mystery that humans cannot reach. Unfortunately, he does not correlate it with Ecclus i 1–10. Ben Sira provides a suitable if unexpected commentary, because some of the same verbs are used and the ideas are similar.

> It is he who created her;
> > he saw her and took her measure;
> > he poured her out upon all his works,
> upon all the living according to his gift;
> > he lavished her upon those who love him. (Ecclus i 9–10, NRSV)

Verse 9b reflects the phrasing of the MT of Job xxviii 27*a* (*eiden kai exērithmēsen*; *r'h* and *spr*). But the important insight is that God poured out (*execheen*) Wisdom (who was created before all other things, Ecclus i 4, NRSV) upon all his works. In other words, for Ben Sira wisdom is in this world, without quite being identical with it, since it is also a gift that he has lavished (*echorēgēsen*) upon 'those who love him', namely Israel. Compared to Ben Sira's interpretation, von Rad's view of the 'order given to the world by God' is rather jejune. But he opened up the possibility of recognizing that God put wisdom somewhere (in the world), even if humans have not found it, according to the poem of Job xxviii.

Proverbs

Wisdom is personified in an address she gives in i 22–33 and especially in ix 4–6 where she is contrasted with Dame Folly. But chapter viii contains the most important passage. As in ch. i, Wisdom's address is placed deliberately in a public arena that will ensure a wide audience. Her claims to value and virtue are clear and formidable: prudence, knowledge, counsel, advice, insight – all that rulers and leaders need. Then follows the astounding claim

---

[4] Cf. G. von Rad, *Weisheit in Israel* (Neukirchen-Vluyn, 1970), p. 194 (F. tr., *Wisdom in Israel* [Nashville, 1972], p. 148). It is significant that ch. 9 is entitled 'The Self-Revelation of Creation'.

in verses 22–31: she is born of God, and before any of the divine creative actions, in a timeless beginning. Verses 30–1 describe her position:

> I was beside him as an '*mwn*,
>   I was delight day after day
>   playing before him all the time,
> Playing on the surface of the earth,
>   and my delight (was) with humankind.

As yet no definitive argument has been made for the meaning of '*mwn* (crafts[wo]man, child, confidant, etc.).[5] It is not clear that Wisdom had a role *in* creation (but see Prov. iii 19 and the interpretation in Wisd. vii 22 and viii 6). There is more emphasis on joy and play than on any other activity of Wisdom. She is associated both with God (the pronominal suffix 'his' [delight] referring to God is found explicitly only in the LXX) and even more emphatically with human beings. This latter claim deserves more notice. The play of Wisdom and her pleasure to be with humankind can be understood to mean the concrete aphorisms and admonitions which the book of Proverbs offers. There is no other connection that one can work out between the figure of Wisdom in chapter viii and the rest of the book. However, if one turns to the Wisdom of Solomon, this 'delight' is made explicit in the very intimate relationship between Wisdom and humankind (chs. vii–ix). Wisdom never loses her association with God by reason of origin (reaffirmed in Ecclus xxiv 3 and Wisd. vii 25–6), but her destiny is to be among God's creatures (Wisd. ix 10–x 12).

In the book of Proverbs a new twist is given to the figure of personified Wisdom, because she is contrasted with another female, and her own relationship to human beings is described in erotic fashion. The other woman seems to be a composite of several 'women'. There is first of all the 'strange' woman (*'iššâ zārâ*; *nokriyyâ*), against whom the naive youth is frequently warned. Indeed, the attention given to this topic (the main subject in v–vii) is out of all proportion to the attention given to it in the rest of the book (cf. xxii 14, xxiii 27), and also in the Egyptian instructions (see Ptaḥḥotep and Ani). There seem to be two levels of meaning present. Just as Wisdom is personified as a woman, and is more than the teachings contained in Prov. i–ix, so the strange woman is more than sexual seduction, and has become personified as Dame Folly who also issues a (deadly!) invitation to youth (most explicitly in ix 13–18).

On the level of the book of Proverbs, what is the meaning of the

---

[5] Cf. the exhaustive study of '*mwn* by H. Rüger, "Amôn – Pflegekind: Zur Auslegungs-geschichte von Prv 8:30a', in *Übersetzung und Deutung, A. R. Hulst gewidmet* (Nijkerk, 1977), pp. 154–63.

personification of Wisdom? She clearly stands for the fullness of life promised by the sages to those who follow in her way (viii 35).[6] But the author has also framed her against the background of Israel's sad history by the sexual emphasis, and by the contrast between Lady Wisdom and Dame Folly. The issue is now life and death, fidelity to the Lord or infidelity. This is far more than a personification of 'world order', or the 'self-revelation of the world', as G. von Rad interpreted it. In the daily life of the post-exilic period Wisdom has been elevated to more than 'correct conduct'. She has assumed the burden of the covenant, fidelity to the Lord, in language reflecting the old struggle so mercilessly bared in the book of Hosea and elsewhere.

Ecclesiasticus xxiv

We have adverted above to Sirach's use of personified Wisdom at the beginning of his work, in i 1–10. In addition, one can point to iv 11–19, vi 18–31, xiv 20–xv 8, li 13–30. Of course, the most famous passage is ch. xxiv, if for no other reason than that here he identifies personified Wisdom – a task other sources avoided. Job xxviii underlined that Wisdom could not be found by humans, and Prov. viii emphasized her divine origins. Sirach uses similar language – the relationship between Prov. viii and Ecclus xxiv is undeniable – to increase the mystery of Wisdom, only to identify her in the end with Torah.

However, the lengthy description that Wisdom gives of herself does not demand such an identification. The twenty-two line speech (verses 3–22) delivered by Wisdom is in part a spin-off from Prov. viii. Attention is given to the setting (verses 1–2; but are her people the same as the assembly of the Most High?), and immediately Wisdom proclaims her divine origins: from the mouth of the Most High, like a spoken word, and also like a mist covering the earth (cf. Gen. i 2). She is in the entire world (notice the dimensions indicated in verses 4–5) and hence there can be no doubt about her ruling that world (verse 6). As God journeys through the vault of heaven (Job xxii 14), so does Lady Wisdom (verse 5). Although she rules over every people and nation, she seems unable to determine where to settle (verse 7a, *anapausin*, or *m^{e}nûḥâ*) until her creator commands her to pitch tent in Jacob/Israel; that is where her *klēronomia* (*naḥ^{a}lâ*) or inheritance is. Verse 9 seems interruptive, in that it returns to Wisdom's 'eternity', backwards and forwards. At one time this 'eternal' character of Wisdom may have been part of her international character. Now the specific

---

[6] It is significant that N. Habel found 'way' as the key symbol in Prov. i–ix; see 'The Symbolism of Wisdom in Proverbs 1–9', *Interpretation* 26 (1972), pp. 131–57. In any case, the way leads to *life*; cf. R. E. Murphy, *The Tree of Life* (New York, 1990), pp. 29, 104.

Israelite note grows stronger and stronger. From the temple in Jerusalem, she acts as priestess, directing liturgical service (*eleitourgēsa*). This trait is most unexpected. J. Marböck remarks that the intent is not to describe an hypostasis, but 'through the activity and attributes of Wisdom to show where and how the divine presence and activity can be explained. Only in this way can the accumulation of the most varied predicates from cosmic activity to cult, to beloved, to wife and mother (cf. 4:11–19; 14:20–15:10) be meaningfully understood.'[7] The significant term, *klēronomia*, in verse 12 is a kind of inclusio (see verse 7*b*) tying together this Jewish identity of Wisdom. The metaphor of taking root among the people is developed in the paradisal description of various types of tree, from Lebanon to En-gedi (verses 13–15). Hence Wisdom can issue an invitation to eat of her fruits – a mixed blessing since it increases hunger and thirst (verse 21)! Wisdom offers all the blessings of the 'land of milk and honey' (cf. Deut. viii 7–10), and she will make her followers themselves a veritable garden and forest (cf. Ecclus xxxix 13–14). The many-sided personality of Wisdom is never better illustrated than here. She was apparently the presence of God accompanying Israel down to the settlement in Jerusalem and dwelling in the 'tent'. Hence the forceful claim that Wisdom is the Torah (verse 23, and a verbatim use of Deut. xxxiii 4 [LXX]): 'the Law which Moses commanded us as a heritage for the congregations of Jacob'. This is more than a simple statement of the identity of Wisdom and Torah. As G. Sheppard has shown, Sirach has taken up into the sweep of this verse the acknowledgement of Israel's wisdom and understanding (Deut. iv 6–8) as well as the cancellation and remedy of Israel's folly in Deut. vi.[8]

To the paradisal growth of Wisdom's 'root' in verses 13–17 corresponds the comparison of the book of the Torah to paradisal rivers, the Pishon and Gihon (which serve as an inclusio), and others more realistic (Tigris and Euphrates). The effect of these images is to enhance Israel as the Promised Land where Wisdom dwells.

How are we to assess this identification of Wisdom with Torah? Since Ben Sira speaks of the 'book of the covenant of the Most High', it seems likely that he has in mind the whole Torah or Pentateuch. When we consider the centrality which the Torah came to assume in the post-exilic period, it is really not surprising that it should become the epitome of Wisdom. Wisdom dwelling among God's people is concretized in the Torah. It is not the other way around, as though the eternal pre-existent Torah is now identified with Wisdom. The Wisdom that took residence in Israel is now seen to be expressed in the entire Torah, not merely in law codes. We are dealing with a theology of presence.

---

[7] J. Marböck, *Weisheit im Wandel* (Bonn, 1971), p. 66.
[8] Cf. G. Sheppard, *Wisdom as a Hermeneutical Construct* (Berlin, 1980), pp. 63–6.

Baruch iii 9–iv 4

It is not difficult to single out this poem within the book of Baruch. It is a curious combination of the questions of Job xxviii 12, 20 (cf. Bar. iii 15) concerning the mysterious hiddenness of Wisdom, and of straightforward answers about the 'way of wisdom/understanding' (Bar. iii 20, 23, 27, 31, 36). The answer repeats that of Job, but with much less mystery. Wisdom is with God (Bar. iv 36), who has given her to Israel:

> She is the book of the commandments of God,
> the Torah that endures forever.   (iv 1)

Hence Baruch repeats the identification of Ben Sira (it is hardly possible to date the poem, but it gives the impression that the identification has already been made some time previously). Many scholars judge that the striking final verse of ch. iii is a later, even Christian, addition:

> Since then she has appeared on earth
> and moved among men.   (iii 38)

But there is no compelling reason for eliminating the verse; it is totally in line with Prov. viii 31 (cf. also Ecclus xxiv 7, 12, 18), and it loosens somewhat the rigidity of the identification with a book.

The reason for the poem is given at the outset; Israel is in exile because she has forsaken the fountain of wisdom (iii 10–12). This situation is all the more deplorable since the Lord has given the 'way to knowledge' or the Law to Israel (iii 36–iv 1). Hence there is no need to attempt impossible feats to find the way to wisdom (iii 29–30, inspired by Deut. xxx 12–13).

Wisdom vii–ix

These chapters are preceded by a short introduction in which pseudo-Solomon proclaims to his audience that he will tell them 'what wisdom is and how she came to be' (vi 22). But he says far more than this; in effect, he sings a love song to the beloved, Lady Wisdom. If one analyses his words, the following hard data emerge: the gift of the spirit of Wisdom is the answer to prayer (vii 7); she is simply incomparable to any other value, for she brings all good things to him because she is their mother (vii 12, *genetin*, 'creator', 'begetter'; cf. vii 22a, viii 4). He had been unaware of Wisdom's role in all this, but now he shares it that all may find the 'friendship with God' that she imparts. It is to God that Solomon must pray because even Wisdom must have God as a guide (*hodēgos*); he is behind everything, all the marvels of the universe (vii 16–20). More specifically, it is personified Wisdom, the *technitis*, or 'fashioner', of all things (viii 6), that taught Solomon. Wisdom not only had a role in creating (cf. viii 5–6 and Prov. viii

30, '*mwn*), but she is in effect the divine activity of God at work. This identity seems to be explained by the striking list of twenty-one predicates that follows (verse 22: 'in her is a spirit that is intelligent, holy', etc.). These characteristics of Wisdom exemplify her ever active and changing roles.

There is an explicit identification of Wisdom and Spirit. Wisdom is a spirit (i 6, vii 7) and she has a spirit (vii 22). C. Larcher[9] suggests that the author wishes to combine intelligence (wisdom) with power; *pneuma* in a particular way would connote divine activity at work. In vii 25 he will speak of Wisdom as 'the breath' (*atmis*) of the power, or omnipotence, of God. By her purity Wisdom pervades and penetrates all things (see also i 7, xii 1) – seemingly a reflection of the Stoic world-soul. Wisdom is transcendent and distinct from the world, yet immanent to it.

The relationship of Wisdom to pseudo-Solomon and to the world is the general burden of chs. vii–ix. Now in the delicate phraseology of vii 25–6 the relationship of Wisdom to God is described by metaphors that border on simple identity: *atmis* (breath), *aporroia*, an 'emanation' of the glory – so that she is without any impurity. Thus she can shine, reflecting the eternal light (Isa. lx 19), a mirror that replicates the divine activity, an image of the divine goodness itself (see the echo of these images in Heb. i 3; Col. i 15; 2 Cor. iv 4):

> For she is a breath of the power of God,
>   and a pure emanation of the glory of the Almighty;
>   therefore nothing defiled gains entrance into her.
> For she is a reflection of eternal light,
>   a spotless mirror of the working of God,
>   and an image of his goodness.   (vii 25–6; NRSV)

The thrust of this passage should be understood more in the sense of divine action through Wisdom; her divine origins have already been described. Here she is the pure light and activity of God at work in all the things she penetrates (vii 24). Hence Wisdom works in the human heart (cf. Prov. ii 10); she is at work in the world but especially within human beings (Wisd. i 4–6). She is 'the active cause of all things' (viii 5). We are dealing with a kind of soteriology, rather than an ontology; the emphasis remains on Wisdom's all-pervading influence. Her nature is such that she can penetrate everything (vii 22, 'penetrating through all spirits') and this is precisely to make souls holy, the friends of God (vii 27). It is no wonder that pseudo-Solomon determined to take her to live with him (viii 9). Wisdom is almost entirely given to winning over human beings; she is 'easily known by those who desire her' (vi 13), and in fact she never issues reproofs. This is striking in view of the generally high estimation of reprimand and

---

[9] Cf. C. Larcher, *Etudes sur le livre de la Sagesse* (Paris, 1969), p. 368.

correction in the role of acquiring wisdom (Prov. xii 1, xiii 1; Ecclus xviii 13–15, xx 1–3).

The love relationship between Wisdom and her suitor has already been mentioned (cf. viii 2), and there is a remarkable love affair between God and Wisdom. She lives with God (*symbiōsin*, viii 3; cf. *paredron* in ix 4) in a loving marriage relationship. This intimacy is itself a model for the intimacy that humans and Wisdom are to have with each other (viii 9, 16). Pseudo-Solomon prays that she may work at his side so that he may learn what pleases God. Theologically considered, there is nothing in the Old Testament that captures this picture: the relationship of God and Wisdom is the model for the relationship of humans and God. The prayer of Solomon at Gibeon (1 Kings iii 6–9) is a pale reflection of the intensity of the prayer in Wisd. ix 1–12. A 'listening heart' is replaced now by the gift of Wisdom who knows what God wants (ix 9), and she will guide and guard Solomon with her glory (ix 11) that is scarcely distinguishable from the divine light and power with which the angel of the Lord 'guarded' the people in the Exodus (Exod. xxiii 20).

This remarkable prayer of pseudo-Solomon ends on the all-important role of Wisdom in God's dealings with his creatures. C. Larcher entitles the section ix 13–18 in his commentary, 'Humanity has need of a revelation in order to know the will of God.'[10] Human beings simply cannot divine the will of God. All are aware of the human condition: our materiality weighs us down (the Platonic ring to ix 15 is clear, but does one have to read Plato to recognize this human weakness?). We cannot search out what is in the heavens (the frequent topoi of the inaccessibility of wisdom and transcendence of God). That is why the gift must come from God: 'unless you have given Wisdom and sent your holy spirit from on high' (ix 17). This verse recalls Solomon's request in ix 10–11 ('holy heavens'), but it reflects particularly the relatively rare occurrence of 'holy spirit' in the Old Testament (LXX: Ps. l 13; Isa. lxiii 10–11). The spirit and Wisdom are *sent* (cf. verse 10) and together they provide the knowledge of the divine plans, the ignorance of which on the part of human beings is lamented in verses 13–16. That particular emphasis on the soteriological character of Wisdom is sounded in the last verse, and will be continued explicitly in ch. x, and implicitly in the rest of the book dealing with the story of the plagues. Larcher rightly points out the universal import of pseudo-Solomon's prayer.[11] In effect, Wisdom overshadows the Torah. Wisdom's basic universalism and inclination towards interiority (cf. Prov. i–ix) is exploited, and the prayer envisions not just Israelites but human beings as such. In a similar way, the first fourteen verses of ch. x will relate how Wisdom saved a

[10] C. Larcher, *Le Livre de la Sagesse ou la Sagesse de Salomon*, 2 (Paris, 1985), p. 591.
[11] *Ibid.*, p. 604.

line extending from Adam to Joseph; it is anticipated by ix 18 which mentions that people 'were saved by Wisdom'.

Conclusion

A truly satisfying assessment of the theological meaning of personified Wisdom is hard to achieve, due mainly to the aura of mystery that surrounds her. One can detect various phases of emphasis in the emergence of this figure, from Job through to the Wisdom of Solomon. If they are respected, allowance can be made for specific meanings along the way. In Job Wisdom is associated with God, apart from whom it is not to be found – but *where* is Wisdom to be found? In the book of Proverbs she proclaims her birth from God, her (active?) presence before and during creation, and her delight to be with human beings. She appears to be the link between the practical, down-to-earth realities of daily living and life with God (Prov. viii 35). This gives a decidedly religious hue to the entire book, so different from the common verdicts of 'worldly' and 'profane' that past and recent scholarship has favoured.

In Sirach there can be no doubt about the identification of Wisdom with Torah; this is the specific meaning attached to her by Ben Sira. At the same time, this should not be understood in a restrictive manner. It is no doubt Ben Sira's view, but he has allowed the cosmic character of Wisdom to appear in i 9, and in her universal rule (xxiv 4–6). It can be said that the figure of Wisdom resists localization, or at least that the Torah does not confine her, despite Ben Sira's solution. Within his world-view, Wisdom answered to Torah in the final analysis. The same can be said of Baruch iii 9–iv 10. The identification with the Torah is as firm and clear as it is in Sirach. To a lesser extent, but clearly enough, the cosmic import is also to be found. The theme of Job xxviii is sounded. Only God *knows* Wisdom, but she is somehow also manifest in the creation, like the stars who said 'here we are' when he called them (Bar. iii 34). 'Afterward she appeared on earth and lived with humankind' (iii 37) – again a universal reference even if Wisdom is identified with the eternal Law. Finally there is the highly developed figure in the Wisdom of Solomon. She is spirit, all-pervasive, an artisan in creation, the divine consort, yet one to be taken by pseudo-Solomon as bride. She knows God's plans, and she is a divine gift who is also a saviour. The Bible has preserved an air of mystery about her even while dedicating so many lines to her.

Can anything of theological significance be made of such a chameleon-like figure? As indicated at the outset, little is to be gained by a classification of hypostasis or the like, or even of an analysis of the foreign influences that have contributed to her characterization (e.g. goddess figures). This historical approach to the wisdom texts is enlightening, but it is 'soft' on meaning. Personified Wisdom was understood by those who wrote about her and honoured her, not as a rival to the Lord, or even as a sympathetic (?) goddess. This direction of research fails to do justice to Wisdom herself, and to the place of wisdom in the Bible, as the following remarks intend to suggest.

First, from a literary-theological point of view, personified Wisdom is simply unequalled in the entire Old Testament. Yes, one can be rhapsodic about *rûaḥ* (spirit and various other meanings as well), *ḥesed*, *šēm*, *'emet*, and a host of other important biblical concepts. But personified Wisdom outshines them all in her claims – claims that affect God and humans. She is born of God, and that brings a sense of the divine presence and closeness to *all* of creation that is simply unequalled. She is not an intermediary. Such a role would make of the Lord a kind of absentee landlord. Far from this is the intimate association between Lord/Wisdom in the experience of human beings, as described by the sages. There is the curious and admirable mixture of what we today call transcendence and immanence. Wisdom is not to be found, because she is with God – but human beings are encouraged to fall in *love* with her, to pursue her and attain her as a gift from God. Immediately difficult questions arise from this scenario. She is to be pursued as a love partner, but is she also a gift? This seems to be intrinsic to her paradoxical nature, and it is not due to foreign influence on the Wisdom figure. It is genuinely Israelite.

Second, what is the effect of this exalted figure of Wisdom upon the wisdom literature, on the world-view and theology of the sages of the Old Testament? Nothing at all, if one is to judge from scholarly writings. In modern times scholars have failed to be comfortable in the study of the three (or five) books commonly termed wisdom literature. Although there has been a recent trend to recognize 'wisdom influence' on many other parts of the Bible – a tendency that was spurred on, if not inaugurated, by the study of the Joseph narrative by G. von Rad – there has not been a corresponding heightening of the importance of this literature. Attitudes have ranged from embarrassment (G. E. Wright[12] confessed that he did not know what to do with the wisdom literature in Old Testament theology) to condemnation (H. D. Preuss[13] found it dangerous to preach from these books). Evaluations were usually fixed by the so-called 'profane' character of the literature, such as the aphorisms and admonitions in Proverbs (and Sirach). More serious charges appeared when it became a commonplace to

---

[12] G. E. Wright, *God Who Acts: Biblical Theology as Recital* (London, 1952), pp. 103–4.

[13] H. D. Preuss, 'Erwägungen zum theologischen Ort alttestamentlicher Weisheitsliteratur', *EvT* 30 (1970), pp. 393–417, especially pp. 416–17; see also his *Einführung in die alttestamentliche Weisheitsliteratur* (Stuttgart, 1987), pp. 186–98.

speak of the 'crisis of wisdom' (a phrase too common even to document). One of the most frequent views is the placing of wisdom in the strait-jacket of 'order'. It was order in the universe that the sages were out to discover – moreover an order that was, or should be, manifest in the realm of reward/punishment or retribution. K. Koch[14] first delineated a persuasive view of the *Tat-Ergehen-Zusammenhang* (as opposed to *Vergeltung*, or divine judgement and intervention), according to which there is a mechanical connection between a good/evil deed and a good/evil consequence. This deed/consequence view can be illustrated by the well-known adage about the one who digs a pit for another but instead falls into it (e.g. Ps. vii 16 [15]). Such an evil deed was mechanically answered by a proper recompense. When this 'order' was seen to be a failure, the entire approach of the sages was faulted, and the 'crisis' appeared (very late, indeed) with the books of Job and Qoheleth. Was there no-one among the sages, or among anyone else in Israel, who could see through the chimera of deed/consequence? The alleged crisis had to wait for modern scholarship to discover it. There is no intent here to deny the error of the friends of Job in reasoning from suffering to sin in the case of Job himself, or to deny that Qoheleth was sceptical about the benefits of wisdom. What is unexplained in the modern views of wisdom is that the stout resistance these works offered to the doctrines of the sages did not kill the movement. On the contrary, Ben Sira and the unknown author of the Wisdom of Solomon carry on the tradition, and under the banner of personified Wisdom. The insights of the sages were purified by the opposition that Job and Ecclesiastes offered to a comfortable wisdom outlook.

One must leave to another time, and indeed to another person versed in history and philosophy and literature, a theological discussion which will be able to give Lady Wisdom her due. There is hardly a more powerful symbol for the human (as well as the divine) achievement among theologians of both East and West than that of *sophia*. One thinks of the ending of the famous story about King Darius' question to three bodyguards (1 Esdras iii–iv): great is truth and the strongest of all. The Latin form, really a proverb, is: 'magna est veritas et praevalet'. In fact, Zerubbabel, one of the bodyguards, prays thus: 'From you comes the victory; from you comes wisdom, and yours is the glory. I am your servant. Blessed are you, who have given me wisdom; I give you thanks, Lord of our ancestors' (NRSV, iv 59–60). Magna est sapientia et praevalet!

[14] K. Koch, 'Gibt es ein Vergeltungsdogma im Alten Testament?', *ZThK* 52 (1955), pp. 1–42 (E. tr., 'Is there a Doctrine of Retribution in the Old Testament?', in J. L. Crenshaw [ed.], *Theodicy in the Old Testament* [London and Philadelphia, 1983], pp. 57–87).

20   Wisdom and the goddess

Judith M. Hadley

It is fitting that this article should be included in a volume in honour of Professor J. A. Emerton, for it was he who first opened my eyes in wisdom to the study of Semitic goddesses.[1] The personification of Wisdom as a woman in the book of Proverbs as well as in the deutero-canonical books of Sirach, Baruch and the Wisdom of Solomon has been much discussed, and is the topic of another chapter in this volume. This chapter will consider Lady Wisdom (or Israelite *ḥokmâ*), and will examine whether or not this personification of Lady Wisdom refers to an actual person (divinity or hypostasis) or is merely a literary device.

Since W. F. Albright[2] advocated a Canaanite background to Proverbs, scholars have considered the possibility of a goddess being the inspiration for the figure of Lady Wisdom (or, in the case of G. Boström,[3] Lady Folly). In recent years, perhaps the most vocal advocate of the connection between Wisdom and a goddess has been Bernhard Lang.[4] The main texts which appear to give divine status to Lady Wisdom are Prov. i, viii and ix; Job

---

[1] I wish to thank Professor Emerton for his patience and guidance in my study of Semitic goddesses in general, and of Asherah in particular. It is with great pleasure and admiration that I offer him this small token of my esteem.

[2] 'The Goddess of Life and Wisdom', *AJSL* 36 (1919–20), pp. 258–94; also *From the Stone Age to Christianity* (Baltimore, 1946), pp. 367–71; but see R. N. Whybray, *Wisdom in Proverbs* (London, 1965), pp. 83–7, where he argues against this view, and J. A. Emerton, 'Wisdom', in G. W. Anderson (ed.), *Tradition and Interpretation* (Oxford, 1979), pp. 231–2.

[3] *Proverbiastudien: Die Weisheit und das fremde Weib in Spr. 1–9* (Lund, 1935).

[4] *Wisdom and the Book of Proverbs: An Israelite Goddess Redefined* (New York, 1986), and cf. O. S. Rankin, *Israel's Wisdom Literature* (Edinburgh, 1936), and G. Hölscher, *Das Buch Hiob* (Tübingen, 1937). Lang's *Wisdom and the Book of Proverbs* is a revision and translation of his doctoral dissertation, *Frau Weisheit* (Düsseldorf, 1975). Lang, in his foreword to *Wisdom and the Book of Proverbs*, asks that the English edition be considered his definitive statement on the topic, and so that is the work which has been consulted for this essay. I also wish to thank Professor Lang for sending me a copy of his as yet unpublished article on 'Wisdom' in K. van der Toorn, B. Becking *et al.* (eds.), *Dictionary of Deities and Demons in the Old Testament* (Leiden, forthcoming).

xxviii (although Wisdom is not explicitly personified here); Ecclus i 1–10 and xxiv 1–22; Baruch iii 9–iv 4; and Wisd. vii–ix, although other more isolated passages in Prov. i–ix, Ecclesiasticus and Wisdom also appear to give Lady Wisdom divine status. The consensus is that these texts in their present form are all relatively late,[5] although the dating of Prov. i–ix and Job xxviii is disputed (see below).

Many suggestions have been made for the origin of the portrait of Lady Wisdom. Some look to goddesses, e.g. Egyptian Ma'at or Isis, Canaanite Astarte, Mesopotamian Inanna, or even to a Persian provenance.[6] Others see her as a hypostasis of God's Wisdom.[7] Conzelmann sees her not only as a hypostasis, but also as a Person.[8] Still others prefer to explain the apparent divine imagery as a literary device.[9] In a much different vein, C. V. Camp, while admitting some echoes of goddesses, sees the image as an abstraction from women sages and counsellors (and biblical stories about them).[10] Another recent suggestion has been proposed by M. D. Coogan, that the divine attributes given to Lady Wisdom in Prov. i–ix and especially Job xxviii (as elsewhere in the deutero-canonical books) are a legitimization of the worship of more 'established' goddesses in Israel and Judah, such as

---

[5] Cf. Emerton, 'Wisdom', p. 229.

[6] Cf. H. Conzelmann, 'The Mother of Wisdom', in J. M. Robinson (ed.), *The Future of Our Religious Past: Essays in Honor of Rudolf Bultmann* (New York, 1971), pp. 230–1, and the references listed there, including H. Ringgren, *Word and Wisdom: Studies in the Hypostatization of Divine Qualities and Functions in the Ancient Near East* (Lund, 1947); cf. also those listed in nn. 3 and 4.

[7] See, e.g., R. Marcus, 'On Biblical Hypostases of Wisdom', *HUCA* 23 (1950–1), pp. 57–171, who follows the definition of hypostasis as given by Ringgren, *Word and Wisdom*, and R. N. Whybray, *The Book of Proverbs* (Cambridge, 1972), p. 50. It should be noted, however, that the term 'hypostasis' has no agreed definition; cf. H. Cazelles, 'La Sagesse de Proverbes 8, 22: Peut-elle être considérée comme une hypostase?', in A. M. Triacca and A. Pistoia (eds.), *Trinité et liturgie* (Rome, 1984), p. 53. The term is apparently taken over from Christology, where it is used in an attempt to provide some degree of individuality while still maintaining a monotheistic theology.

[8] 'The Mother of Wisdom', p. 232.

[9] R. E. Murphy, who believes that Wisdom cannot be a hypostasis or distinct person because of the strict monotheism of the post-exilic period, may be the most vocal advocate of this view; see, e.g., his 'Wisdom – Theses and Hypotheses', in J. G. Gammie et al., *Israelite Wisdom: Theological and Literary Essays in Honor of Samuel Terrien* (Missoula, 1978), pp. 35–42; 'Hebrew Wisdom', *JAOS* 101 (1981), pp. 21–34; 'Proverbs and Theological Exegesis', in D. G. Miller (ed.), *The Hermeneutical Quest* (Allison Park, 1986), pp. 87–95; *The Tree of Life: An Exploration of Biblical Wisdom Literature* (New York, 1990), pp. 133–49, etc.

[10] *Wisdom and the Feminine in the Book of Proverbs* (Sheffield, 1985); see also 'Woman Wisdom as Root Metaphor: A Theological Consideration', in K. G. Hoglund et al., *The Listening Heart: Essays in Wisdom and the Psalms in Honor of Roland E. Murphy* (Sheffield, 1987), pp. 45–76; and 'The Female Sage in Ancient Israel and in the Biblical Wisdom Literature', in J. G. Gammie and L. G. Perdue (eds.), *The Sage in Israel and the Ancient Near East* (Winona Lake, 1990), pp. 185–203; and S. Schroer, 'Weise Frauen und Ratgeberinnen in Israel', *BN* 51 (1990), p. 45.

Asherah.[11] It is my opinion that the apparent apotheosis of Lady Wisdom in the biblical literature is not a legitimization of the worship of 'established' goddesses, but rather is a literary compensation for the eradication of the worship of these goddesses.[12] This chapter will briefly consider only Prov. viii and Job xxviii, before returning to these suggestions and concluding with some possible solutions concerning the divine attributes of Lady Wisdom.

Proverbs viii

The passage in Proverbs that most suggests divine imagery for Lady Wisdom is Prov. viii 22–31, where Wisdom declares herself to be the first of all Yahweh's creations/acquisitions/children, and to have been present when Yahweh established the heavens and set the boundaries of the sea. McKane notes that LXX adds in verse 21, 'If I declare to you the things of daily occurrence, I shall remember to recount the things of old', and agrees with Toy and Gemser that this suggests an editorial bridge.[13] As McKane notes, 'this literary-critical observation reinforces a conclusion which follows from a consideration of the widely diverging characteristics of the wisdom tradition represented by the two passages. In the one it is Wisdom's role in a historical community, as the adviser of kings, as politician and instructress of men in the good life which is being described. In the other, attention is riveted on the place and precedence of Wisdom in a cosmological context.'[14] The reader recognizes that in verses 22–31 something new is being revealed; whereas in Prov. i–ix Wisdom appears like a great sage, in close contact with humans (sometimes with erotic

[11] 'The Goddess Wisdom – "Where Can She Be Found?"': Literary Reflexes of Popular Religion', communication given at the Society of Biblical Literature Meetings in Washington D.C., November 1993. I wish to thank Professor Coogan for furnishing me with a rough draft of this communication. For extensive bibliographies on Asherah as a goddess in Israel and Judah, see the following works by J. M. Hadley: 'The Khirbet el-Qom Inscription', *VT* 37 (1987), pp. 50–62; 'Some Drawings and Inscriptions on Two Pithoi from Kuntillet 'Ajrud', *VT* 37 (1987), pp. 180–213; 'Yahweh and "his asherah": Archaeological and Textual Evidence for the Cult of the Goddess', in W. Dietrich and M. A. Klopfenstein (eds.), *Ein Gott allein?* (Freiburg, 1994), pp. 235–68; and especially *Evidence for a Hebrew Goddess: The Cult of Asherah in Ancient Israel and Judah* (Cambridge, forthcoming).

[12] For a detailed examination of the gradual eradication of the worship of Asherah, see Hadley, 'Yahweh and "his asherah"'; and *Evidence for a Hebrew Goddess*.

[13] W. McKane, *Proverbs* (Philadelphia, 1970), p. 351; and see also C. H. Toy, *A Critical and Exegetical Commentary on the Book of Proverbs* (Edinburgh, 1899); and B. Gemser, 'The Instructions of Onchsheshonqy and Biblical Wisdom Literature' (*SVT* 7, 1960), pp. 102–28.

[14] *Proverbs*, p. 351. See also J. Ashton, 'The Transformation of Wisdom. A Study of the Prologue of John's Gospel', *NTS* 32 (1986), pp. 163–4; and cf. Lang, *Wisdom and the Book of Proverbs*, p. 60, who believes that Wisdom's assertion 'By me kings reign' in verse 15 is evidence of her divine status.

imagery[15]), here Wisdom is a much more exalted and remote figure, more comparable to Wisdom in Job xxviii (see below).

A key question in the discussion of Prov. viii 22–31 is the translation in verse 22 of *qānānî* as either acquired, established, conceived, formed or created by God.[16] Whybray believes that even if this term were to be translated 'begot', there would be no sexual connotation, as there might be in polytheistic religions. For Whybray, the act of Yahweh 'begetting' Wisdom would only be a metaphor for Yahweh's 'act of creation'.[17] Similarly, Whybray takes the verb 'born' in verses 24 and 25 as a metaphor for Yahweh's creation of Wisdom.[18] After a discussion of various ways of interpreting *qānānî*, McKane takes the verb to mean 'begotten'; 'Wisdom is begotten, not made, and is not a creature in the ordinary sense; her precedence is qualitative as well as temporal.'[19] McKane thus interprets Wisdom as a hypostasis as the child of Yahweh, begotten and not made.[20] Vawter argues eloquently for the position that here in Proverbs, as well as in Job xxviii, Wisdom was something which existed independently of Yahweh, and which Yahweh has acquired. He therefore translates *qānānî* as 'acquired'.[21] Whatever interpretation is to be accepted, Wisdom appears to be associated with God through some action of Yahweh's, either through creation, birth or acquisition. If acquired, however, Wisdom may be co-eternal, as Yahweh acquires that which already exists. However the association was formed, Wisdom was therefore present when Yahweh brought forth the various acts of creation. For Whybray, this shows Wisdom's priority in the order of creation.[22] R. B. Y. Scott, on the other hand, turns this 'possession' of Wisdom by Yahweh into one of Yahweh's attributes.[23]

Whether or not Wisdom herself assisted Yahweh in creation depends

---

[15] Cf. R. E. Murphy, 'Wisdom and Eros in Proverbs 1–9', *CBQ* 50 (1988), pp. 601–3.
[16] For bibliographies on the translation of *qānâ*, see Whybray, *Wisdom in Proverbs*, and M. Gilbert, 'Le Discours de la Sagesse en Proverbes, 8', in M. Gilbert (ed.), *La Sagesse de l'Ancien Testament* (Gembloux and Leuven, 1979), p. 209, and bibliography in n. 18; see also the various commentaries on Proverbs. For the strongest argument in favour of translating *qānānî* as 'acquired me', see B. Vawter, 'Prov. 8:22: Wisdom and Creation', *JBL* 99 (1980), pp. 205–16.
[17] *Proverbs*, p. 51, and cf. Gilbert, 'Le Discourse', p. 210. It must be noted that many discussions use 'post-exilic monotheism' as a dogmatic postulate, and not as a conclusion to be reconsidered with any new evidence; see, e.g., the various works by Murphy cited in n. 9, as well as P.-E. Bonnard, 'De la Sagesse personnifiée dans l'Ancien Testament à la Sagesse en personne dans le Nouveau', in M. Gilbert (ed.), *La Sagesse de l'Ancien Testament*, p. 133, 'Près de Yahweh, les sapientiaux, plus que jamais guidés par leur strict monothéisme, n'ont jamais imaginé aucune déesse'; among many others.
[18] *Proverbs*, p. 52.   [19] *Proverbs*, p. 353 (and cf. discussion starting on p. 352).
[20] *Proverbs*, p. 353, and cf. p. 357. The Christological origins of the term 'hypostasis' are intentionally alluded to here.
[21] 'Prov. 8:22', *passim*. Vawter further argues that in none of the biblical passages or their cognates is it necessary to translate *qānâ* as 'create'.
[22] *Wisdom in Proverbs*, p. 101.   [23] *Proverbs, Ecclesiastes* (Garden City, 1965), pp. 71–2.

upon the translation of '*āmôn* as 'master architect' or else 'little child'.[24] The picture of Wisdom as a little child may fit more appropriately the description of her frolicking amidst creation. C. Kayatz believes that these images of Wisdom as the divine child at play, existing before the creation of the world, and even as the one who legitimizes the king's rule (cf. Prov. viii 15–16), are a result of Egyptian influence and are ideas which are usually associated with Ma'at.[25] Whybray notes that the similarity is made all the more striking by the fact that often the deities described in such terms, both in Egypt and in Mesopotamia, are female ones. He believes that the author of this text in Proverbs may have been influenced by the extra-biblical literature, but he sees no evidence of divinity in Lady Wisdom here. 'She is no more than a poetical personification of the teaching of the wisdom teacher or, in verses 22–31, of an attribute of God.'[26]

The claim that Lady Wisdom is to be considered a divine figure may be strengthened if '*āmôn* were to be translated 'master architect', which might indicate that Wisdom was a 'co-creator' with Yahweh. McKane believes that the picture of Wisdom here as an architect is meant to emphasize her vast intelligence, and to magnify her authority by giving her a cosmological dimension.[27] D. Cox declines to choose between the two interpretations, believing that there is no textual reason to favour either reading. Therefore, 'it is possible that the author intended it to be a double concept: Wisdom as firstborn and favoured child of Yahweh, who, craftsmanlike, shares his creative activity'.[28] Nevertheless, the fact that Wisdom is said to be 'at his side' establishes Yahweh as the primary creator.[29]

Whichever interpretation is to be accepted, Prov. iii 19 indicates that Yahweh 'by wisdom founded the earth; by understanding he established the heavens'. Since Yahweh obviously needs Wisdom in order to create the heavens and the earth, then Yahweh must have been acquainted with Wisdom before the acts of creation could be performed. Although some scholars see this passage as poetic imagery,[30] others believe the passage

[24] See, e.g., Gilbert, 'Le Discours', p. 213, and the references there.
[25] *Studien zu Proverbien 1–9* (Neukirchen-Vluyn, 1966), pp. 86–7; see also n. 32 below; G. von Rad, *Weisheit in Israel* (Neukirchen-Vluyn, 1970), p. 199 (E. tr., *Wisdom in Israel* [London, 1972], p. 153).   [26] *Proverbs*, p. 50.
[27] *Proverbs*, p. 351; and see also G. von Rad, *Theologie des Alten Testaments*, 1 (Munich, 1957), pp. 446–7 (E. tr., *Old Testament Theology*, 1 [Edinburgh and London, 1962], pp. 448–9). This authority is especially so if it is connected with the Akkadian *ummânu*, which Bonnard, 'Sagesse', p. 121, asserts may be a kind of vizier (but cf. his references in n. 9 for the sense of 'noble', and cf. Cazelles, 'Sagesse', p. 54). For the Akkadian background see J. C. Greenfield, 'The Seven Pillars of Wisdom (Prov. 9:1) – A Mistranslation', *JQR* ns 76 (1985), pp. 17–18.
[28] *Proverbs: With an Introduction to Sapiential Books* (Wilmington, Del., 1982), p. 155.
[29] Bonnard, 'Sagesse', p. 120, asserts that neither 'maître d'oeuvre' nor 'nourrisson' fits the following image of a young girl dancing. He therefore applies the concept to Yahweh; and see Lang, *Wisdom and the Book of Proverbs*, p. 65.
[30] See, e.g., Whybray, *Proverbs*, p. 51, among others.

identifies Wisdom as a divine or at least personified figure (see above, and Ecclus i 1–9).

However, the question still remains: is this apparent apotheosis of Lady Wisdom a result of her actually being (or having been) a deity as such, or is it a literary device of some sort? To try to answer this question, we will also examine Job xxviii. First, however, a brief consideration of the various theories of the date of Prov. i–ix is in order.

Prov. i–ix seems to defy all attempts at a precise dating. Suggestions range from the early monarchic period to the early post-exilic era, with perhaps the majority of scholars placing it in the fifth to fourth centuries BCE.[31] Many scholars draw a comparison between Prov. i–ix and Egyptian wisdom instruction.[32] Whybray believes that the concept of Wisdom in chs. i–ix as a characteristic of God, who alone can dispense Wisdom, is the most fully developed in the whole book, and therefore belongs to the final editor, who placed this section at the beginning of the work to 'set the tone' of the book.[33] Lang believes that in Prov. i–ix late (i.e. post-exilic) vocabulary is notably absent.[34] Other arguments for an early dating of chs. i–ix come from two considerations: (1) that proverbs are an old form of literature, and hence the material could have been composed earlier. However, a possibility such as this is not proof; and (2) the association with Solomon. But, as Scott and others have shown, this association is a literary convention.[35] We will return to the implications of the dating of Prov. i–ix in the conclusion.

Job xxviii

The uniqueness of the book of Job and its lack of historical allusions have created difficulties for scholars in determining a date for this book also.

---

[31] Lang, 'Wisdom', dates the 'original' to the tenth/ninth century, with the edited version tentatively dated to the fifth century. Kayatz, *Studien*, also prefers a Solomonic date. Others who opt for an early date are L. G. Perdue, *Wisdom and Cult* (Missoula, 1977), p. 230, n. 29; G. Landes, 'Creation Tradition in Proverbs 8:22–31 and Genesis 1', in H. N. Bream *et al.*, *A Light Unto My Path: Old Testament Studies in Honor of Jacob M. Myers* (Philadelphia, 1974), pp. 279–93; and D. F. Morgan, *Wisdom in the Old Testament Traditions* (Atlanta, 1981), p. 113. For summaries of other views, see Cox, *Proverbs*, p. 89, as well as the other commentaries.

[32] Cf. Kayatz, *Studien*, pp. 15–75; McKane, *Proverbs*; Whybray, *Wisdom in Proverbs*; Murphy, *Tree of Life*, pp. 151–79; and D. Georgi, 'Frau Weisheit oder das Recht auf Freiheit als schöpferische Kraft', in L. Siegele-Wenschkewitz (ed.), *Verdrängte Vergangenheit, die uns bedrängt: Feministische Theologie in der Verantwortung für die Geschichte* (Munich, 1988), pp. 243–76.   [33] *Proverbs*, p. 14.

[34] *Wisdom and the Book of Proverbs*, p. 4.

[35] R. B. Y. Scott, 'Solomon and the Beginnings of Wisdom in Israel', in *Wisdom in Israel and in the Ancient Near East* (*SVT* 3, 1955), pp. 262–79, reprinted in J. L. Crenshaw (ed.), *Studies in Ancient Israelite Wisdom* (New York, 1976), pp. 84–101.

Nevertheless, most scholars date it to somewhere between 700 and 200 BCE, with perhaps the majority of scholars placing it in the early post-exilic period.[36] As far as ch. xxviii is concerned, some scholars believe that it is an independent poem, or 'Hymn to Wisdom', whereas others believe that the poem was still written by the author of Job.[37]

Verses 1–11 describe the activities of humanity in the search for precious metals and stones, but the question 'But where shall wisdom be found?' in verse 12 and the answer in verses 13–19 lead one to realize that the most precious acquisition of all is inaccessible to humans, and cannot be bought for any price. Even Abaddon (Sheol) and Death (who are personified here) have only heard rumours of it (verses 20–2). Only God knows the way to Wisdom, and noted Wisdom's presence in creation (verses 23–7). Gordis observes that, here in Job, Wisdom is called *haḥokmâ*, with the definite article, to distinguish it from *ḥokmâ*, 'its more mundane and practical counterpart'.[38] Furthermore, since only God understands Wisdom's path and knows where she is to be found, then 'what is available to man, therefore, is not transcendent Wisdom, the key to the universe and the meaning of life, but practical Wisdom (without the definite article), which expresses itself in piety and moral behavior'.[39]

Verses 23–7 are perhaps the most instructive. Especially, the verbs *yabbîṭ*, 'looks to', and *yir'eh*, 'sees', in verse 24 may indicate that God is seeking for Wisdom, which has her own independent existence and origin. Verse 23 may also suggest that Wisdom lies elsewhere, and that even God must 'find' Wisdom by following a path that leads to her own special abode. Habel admits that in this passage the author does not portray Wisdom as an attribute of God, but rather as a priceless figure whom even God wishes to

---

[36] For example, M. H. Pope, *Job* (Garden City, 1965), after an extended discussion on the previous suggestions for the date of the book of Job (pp. xxx–xxxvii), declines to give it a more precise dating apart from the seventh century BCE for the dialogue. R. Gordis, *The Book of God and Man: A Study of Job* (Chicago and London, 1965), pp. 216–18, places it between 500 and 300 BCE, with probabilities favouring the fifth rather than the fourth century (and see also the relevant notes on p. 361). J. C. L. Gibson, *Job* (Philadelphia, 1985), p. 3, dates the book to around 600 BCE, but he 'would not object if it were dated a little later'. J. G. Janzen, *Job* (Atlanta, 1985), p. 5, believes that it was 'written in the exile', and N. C. Habel, *The Book of Job* (Philadelphia, 1985), p. 42, tentatively suggests a date somewhere in the post-exilic era. See the commentaries and the discussions there for more opinions.

[37] So Gibson, *Job*, pp. 188–9, who also notes that F. I. Andersen, *Job* (London, 1976), and C. Westermann, *Der Aufbau des Buches Hiob* (2nd edn, Stuttgart, 1977) (E. tr., *The Structure of the Book of Job* [Philadelphia, 1981]), hold similar positions; Gordis, *God and Man*, p. 278, repeated in *The Book of Job: Commentary, New Translation and Special Studies* (New York, 1978), p. 298; Janzen, *Job*, p. 187, etc.; one notable exception is Pope, *Job*, p. xviii. For a good survey of the various positions see Habel, *Job*, pp. 391–2, who himself believes that this chapter is the poet's 'personal reflection on the debate thus far'.

[38] *God and Man*, p. 100.

[39] *God and Man*, p. 101; and cf. *Job*, pp. 298–9, where he says virtually the same thing.

seek out and acquire.[40] Nevertheless, most commentators are reluctant to attribute divine status to Wisdom. Gordis believes that 'for the biblical and post-biblical authors the personification and glorification of Wisdom is mythology, not religion; it is poetry, not truth ... In their most lavish paeans of praise to Wisdom, the Hebrew sages do not attribute to her any independent existence, let alone the status of a goddess or a divine being. She is indubitably the creation of God, His plaything, His companion, His delight, perhaps even the plan by which He fashioned the world, but nevertheless, completely God's handiwork, as is the entire cosmos.'[41] Janzen believes that 'looks to' and 'sees' in verse 24 should be interpreted as 'seeing to' or 'attending to' the matter in hand. He therefore translates 'When he attended to the ends of the earth/ and saw to everything under the heavens'.[42] This general reference to creation is then followed by more specific acts of creation in which Wisdom is mysteriously present; but it is only *in* these creative activities that God has seen, named, established, and searched out Wisdom. Janzen therefore concludes that Wisdom is found 'in' the creative act.[43] This is similar to Habel's conclusion, that 'in the process of ordering and establishing the limits of his cosmic design God discerned Wisdom. Thus Wisdom both precedes creation (Prov. 8:22ff.) and is revealed to God in the very creation process itself. Wisdom is apparently, therefore, the ordering principle of this creation process, the hidden design and designer behind all things.'[44] This is why Wisdom is unknowable for humanity, since humanity does not fully participate in God's creative process.

The poem ends with verse 28, which appears suspect for several reasons, perhaps primarily for the fact that here the divine name is used, and spelled with the consonants *'dny*, which usage is found nowhere else in the entire book. Pope believes that this new definition of Wisdom as 'the fear of the Lord', after an extended poem about the inaccessible nature of Wisdom, is rather abrupt, and is 'a standard affirmation and formulation of the conservative school (cf. Prov. i 7, iii 7, ix 10; Ps. cxi 10) which is appended as an antidote to the agnostic tenor of the preceding poem'.[45] Gibson, on the other hand, attributes the use of the term 'the Lord' here to a slip on the part of the author, owing to the familiarity of the phrase.[46] Habel goes one step further in considering that verse 28 is a pivotal verse, not only in this chapter but also for the first half of the book. He states that 'v. 28 provides a formal closure which on the one hand is orthodox and traditional, but on

---

[40] *Job*, p. 399. If *qānâ* in Prov. viii 22 is translated 'acquire', then the passage here could reflect that meaning.

[41] *God and Man*, pp. 34–5. Yet, as mentioned above, this may be begging the question, since we only know what has been transmitted, and not what may originally have been intended. The present context of this poem may not have been its original context.

[42] *Job*, p. 197.   [43] *Job*, pp. 197–8.   [44] *Job*, p. 400.   [45] *Job*, p. 183.   [46] *Job*, p. 198.

the other stands in direct counterpoint to the poem which it precedes and serves as a deliberate foil for the climactic protestation of the hero which immediately follows (chs. 29–31). The poet thereby emphasizes once again that the traditional orthodox answer, while it may need to be said as a formal statement, is not acceptable to Job.'[47]

There is another possible interpretation of this chapter. Job is often used as the mouthpiece of a criticism of the 'wisdom of the schools'; the substitution of tradition (e.g. Job xv 17–19) for experience (e.g. Job xii 1–8). Prov. viii suggests that pre-created Wisdom is accessible to humanity; that Wisdom is both 'transcendent' and 'practical'. In particular, that the (male[48]) sage has access to Wisdom of the ages, to the deep and mysterious things of creation, through his Muse – Wisdom. Job xxviii denies this. The deep and mysterious things are known only to God, and humans should be content with the moral and ethical Wisdom which is 'their' kind of Wisdom (verse 28).

Conclusion

From the preceding discussion it can be seen that in several places in Israelite wisdom literature, the figure of *ḥokmâ*, or Lady Wisdom, is described as a person, and even seems to have divine attributes. Nevertheless, scholars have been reluctant to give *ḥokmâ* full divinity. Perhaps the single strongest objection to considering Lady Wisdom as a divine figure in her own right is the fact that, to date, *ḥokmâ* is not listed in any onomastica or extra-biblical literature as a goddess. Lang believes that a version of the Ahiqar story from Elephantine 'refers to a goddess who bears exactly the same name as Israel's divine patroness of wisdom'.[49] In a footnote, he shows that he is using J. M. Lindenberger's translation of the passage.[50] However, in a review of Lang, Emerton notes that in the fragmentary text in question, it is never explicitly stated that wisdom is a goddess[51] (the word 'Wisdom' is restored in a lacuna).

---

[47] *Job*, p. 393, and cf. pp. 400–1.

[48] The predominantly male sage, despite the attempt of Camp and others to see a female rôle-model in this figure, even in both Lady Wisdom and Lady Folly. See, e.g., Camp, 'Wise and Strange: An Interpretation of the Female Imagery in Proverbs in the Light of Trickster Mythology', *Semeia* 42 (1988), pp. 14–36. Carol Newsom, 'Woman and the Discourse of Patriarchal Wisdom: A Study of Proverbs 1–9', in P. Day (ed.), *Gender and Difference in Ancient Israel* (Minneapolis, 1989), p. 157, says rather of Wisdom and Folly that 'together they define and secure the boundaries of the symbolic order of patriarchal wisdom'.

[49] *Wisdom and the Book of Proverbs*, p. 131.

[50] *The Aramaic Proverbs of Ahiqar* (Baltimore, 1983), p. 68.

[51] J. A. Emerton, review of B. Lang, *Wisdom and the Book of Proverbs*, *VT* 37 (1987), p. 127. See also Murphy, *Tree of Life*, pp. 158–9, who discusses the Ahiqar texts, and presents Ginsberg's translation in *ANET*, p. 428.

A pre-exilic date for Prov. i–ix (or at least a pre-exilic *Urtext*) is perhaps necessary for the view that Wisdom had been a deity that later lost her divine status, but this view does not explain very well the (re-emerging?) picture of the divine attributes of Wisdom in later, post-exilic works such as Ecclesiasticus, Baruch, Wisdom, or even Job.[52] Ecclus xxiv 1–22 especially has Wisdom established in heaven with God, 'in the assembly of the most High' (verse 2). It may be instructive that Lang, perhaps the most vocal advocate of a pre-exilic date for Prov. i–ix, is also the main modern advocate of *ḥokmâ* as a deity in her own right. Perhaps a better interpretation of the apparent apotheosis of *ḥokmâ* in Israelite wisdom literature is that the gradual eradication (or assimilation into Yahweh) of legitimate goddesses such as Asherah has prompted a counter-reaction where the feminine needs to be expressed.[53] Georgi follows a similar view, seeing a shift in Wisdom from an abstraction to a person to a heavenly character, taking her place at the side of Yahweh, which in pre-exilic times was filled by other female figures such as Asherah (at Kuntillet 'Ajrud) and Anat (at Elephantine). He further notes, however, that now Wisdom is not the wife of Yahweh, but rather the daughter.[54] Similar situations to this may be seen in the Hosean imagery of Israel as the bride of Yahweh and the 'demotion' of Asherah into a hypostasis of Yahweh. Now, here in the wisdom literature, can be seen a female figure of Lady Wisdom with seemingly divine attributes, but still very much 'under the thumb' of Yahweh, which may be an attempt at satisfying this apparent need for the feminine to be represented in the deity. This image of divine Wisdom extends into the New Testament and in Philo's male Logos as well. Unfortunately, an examination of this development is beyond the scope of this chapter.[55]

[52] Cf. R. H. Pfeiffer, 'Wisdom and Vision in the Old Testament', *ZAW* 52 (1934), pp. 93–101, reprinted in J. L. Crenshaw (ed.), *Studies in Ancient Israelite Wisdom* (New York, 1976), pp. 305–13. For a counter-argument see J. D. G. Dunn, 'Was Christianity a Monotheistic Faith From the Beginning?', *SJT* 35 (1982), pp. 318–21.

[53] See the works by Hadley cited in nn. 11 and 12 above.

[54] 'Frau Weisheit', p. 246.

[55] For this development, see, e.g., Georgi, 'Frau Weisheit'; Bonnard, 'Sagesse'; Whybray, *Proverbs*, p. 51; B. L. Mack, *Logos und Sophia* (Göttingen, 1973); H. C. Kee, 'Myth and Miracle: Isis, Wisdom, and the Logos of John', in A. M. Olson (ed.), *Myth, Symbol and Reality* (Notre Dame and London, 1980), pp. 145–64; and J. S. Kloppenborg, 'Isis and Sophia in the Book of Wisdom', *HTR* 75 (1982), pp. 57–84.

21 Wisdom at Qumran

A. S. van der Woude

Little has been written so far on wisdom at Qumran. A number of essays have been devoted to the 'Wiles of the Wicked Woman' (4Q184),[1] Lichtenberger[2] analysed 4Q185, and W. Lowndes Lipscomb and J. A. Sanders[3] contributed a short article on 'Wisdom at Qumran' to the *Festschrift* for S. Terrien. The latter authors have suggested that although many of the terms for 'wisdom' and 'insight' common in the biblical sapiential literature are found in the writings of the Qumran community, there is no undisputed evidence that its members ever composed wisdom texts.

In this essay, written in honour of my dear friend John Emerton, I do not propose to treat the complicated question how to draw the borderline between chokmatic and non-chokmatic compositions in the literature found at Qumran. On this problem, I adopt a pragmatic standpoint, the more so because the form-critical rules usually adopted in the case of Old Testament wisdom texts are to a large extent not applicable to similar early Jewish writings or parts of them. Consequently, I consider those Qumran texts as chokmatic whose contents include enough elements that remind us

---

[1] For the text see J. M. Allegro, *Qumrân Cave 4 I (4Q158–4Q186)* (Oxford, 1968), pp. 83–5, and the improvements made by J. Strugnell, 'Notes en marge du volume V des "Discoveries in the Judaean Desert of Jordan"', *RQ* 7 (1969–71), pp. 163–276, especially 263–8. Further studies on the text: H. Burgmann, '"The Wicked Woman": Der Makkabäer Simon?', *RQ* 8 (1972–6), pp. 323–59 (= id., *Zwei lösbare Qumrânprobleme* [Frankfurt a.M., 1986], pp. 33–69); M. Broshi, 'Beware the Wiles of the Wanton Woman. Dead Sea Scroll Fragment (4Q184) Reflects Essene Fear of, and Contempt for, Women', *BAR* 9/4 (1983), pp. 54–6; J. Carmignac, 'Poème allégorique sur la secte rivale', *RQ* 5 (1964–6), pp. 361–74; A. M. Gazov-Ginsberg, 'Double Meaning in a Qumran Work ("The Wiles of the Wicked Woman")', *RQ* 6 (1967–8), pp. 279–85; R. D. Moore, 'Personification of the Seduction of Evil: "The Wiles of the Wicked Woman"', *RQ* 10 (1979–81), pp. 505–19.

[2] H. Lichtenberger, 'Eine weisheitliche Mahnrede in den Qumranfunden (4Q185)', in M. Delcor (ed.), *Qumrân. Sa piété, sa théologie et son milieu* (Paris-Leuven, 1978), pp. 151–62.

[3] W. Lowndes Lipscomb and J. A. Sanders, 'Wisdom at Qumran', in J. G. Gammie, W. A. Brueggemann, W. Lee Humphreys and J. M. Ward (eds.), *Israelite Wisdom. Theological and Literary Essays in Honor of Samuel Terrien* (Missoula, 1978), pp. 277–85. The dissertation of J. E. Worrell, *Concepts of Wisdom in the Dead Sea Scrolls* (Claremont Graduate School, 1968), referred to in their paper, was not accessible to me.

of Old Testament sapiential writings. This may seem a somewhat unsatisfactory mode of delimitation, but its advantage may be that I do not consider a text as chokmatic which others want to assign to another literary category, e.g. a valedictory address or an admonition pertaining to the eschaton.

Not only in the canonical literature of the Old Testament, but also in the writings of early Judaism (including Qumran), wisdom is a term with multifarious meanings. Wisdom may refer to admonitions based on daily experience, more or less influenced by religious traditions, but also to a charisma imparted by God to a certain person. It can mean God's inscrutable knowledge, or the cosmological and ethical world order, and eventually even the Torah. The personification of Wisdom, already found in Proverbs, evoked her counterpart Dame Folly. Men may be invited to seek wisdom, but on the other hand it is said to have been given to all creatures and it can be described as a divine gift to the elect. All these different kinds and meanings of wisdom are attested in the Qumran documents. This signifies that the Qumran community shared in a common wisdom tradition. In order to illustrate this, it seems worthwhile to exemplify the different usages of wisdom in the Dead Sea scrolls by offering a rendering of (parts of) some of them. Then attention must be given to the question whether the Qumran writings show sapiential traits which are different from those of their religious *Umwelt*.

It should be emphasized that what follows is no more than a preliminary sketch which eventually should be elaborated on, and rectified by, a profound investigation into Qumran wisdom texts and terminology.

1   Some sapiential texts

In order to get an impression of the sapiential literature found among the Dead Sea scrolls I offer in this section a translation of, and a brief comment on, a number of sapiential documents (or portions of them) which attest to established wisdom traditions and the different aspects of wisdom inherited by the Qumran community.

A. The counterpart of Lady Wisdom

4Q184 (Wiles of the Wicked Woman)[4]

[1] [..........] brings forth vanity
and in a [..........].
Continuously she seeks misguiding

[4] For the text editions, see n. 1.

[and she ...... to] sharpen the wor[ds of her mouth (?)
.......] ² she mockingly fl[atte]rs,
deriding thoroughly with evil l[ips].
Her heart promotes indiscipline
and her innermost sn[ares.
Her eyes] ³ are defiled by iniquity
and her hands grasp the Pit.
Her feet go down to act wickedly,
walking in [evil] guilt.
[Her .....] ⁴ are the foundations of darkness
and many are the sins in her skirts.
Her [.....] are the depth of night
and her clothes [.........].
⁵ Her garments are complete darkness
and her adornments plagues of hell.
Her beds are couches of r[uin.
Her .....] ⁶ are depths of the Pit
and her lodgings couches of darkness.
In night times [she exerts] her dominion,
from the foundations of darkness ⁷ she pitches her dwelling.
She resides in the tents of the underworld,
in the midst of everlasting burnings;
she has no inheritance among all ⁸ who spread light.
She is the first of all the ways of evil.
She is a ruin to all who possess her
and a destruction to all ⁹ who take hold of her.
For her ways are the ways of death
and her paths the roads of sin.
Her tracks lead astray ¹⁰ to iniquity
and her path[s] to sinful guilt.
Her gates are the gates of Death,
at the entrance of her house Sheol treads.
¹¹ All who [enter unto her] shall not return
and all who possess her will go down to the Pit.
S[h]e lies in ambush in secret places
[and ....] ¹² all [.........].
In the city's squares she wraps herself up
and in the gates of the town she sets herself up:
nobody can interr[upt her] ¹³ from [her] pe[rpetual fornication].
Her eyes glance keenly hither and thither;
she wantonly raises her eyelids
to seek [out a ma]n ¹⁴ who is righteous to overtake him,
and a [per]fect man to make him stumble,
turning aside the upright from the way
and the righteous pious ¹⁵ from keeping the commandment;
making fools, by wantonness, of the steady[-minded]
and making those who walk uprightly change the statute;

causing to rebel [16] the humble ones from God
and turning their steps from the ways of righteousness;
bringing presumptu[ous]ness [into] their [hear]ts,
that they do not wa[lk] [17] in the tracks of uprightness;
leading men astray on the ways of the Pit
and seducing by flatteries the sons of men.

This text has been interpreted in various ways,[5] but the most convincing exegesis finds here the personified Folly as the counterpart of Dame Wisdom. We are, of course, reminded of the loose woman of the book of Proverbs who has forgotten the covenant of her God (Prov. ii 17) and tries to seduce men to join her (vii 10ff.) but whose house sinks down to Death (ii 18). Our poem elaborates upon motives already present in the book of Proverbs. Hell is the destiny of all who mix themselves up with this woman who inveigles men into committing iniquity.

Because Lady Wisdom elsewhere is never identified with the Qumran community, there is no compelling reason for interpreting her counterpart described in 4Q184 as the personification of a collective opposed to the Qumran sect. Line 17 rather suggests that Dame Folly is a danger to all men.

Since there are no indications in 4Q184 which unambiguously refer to the Qumran community, one may well doubt whether the writing originated in its ranks.

B. Wisdom as universal gift

4Q185[6]

I[9] For behold [10] as grass he sprouts and his beauty flowers forth like a blossom. As for his strength – when His [= God's] wind blows upon him, [11] his rootstock withers and the wind whisks away his blossom, so that on his spot nothing more exists [12] and nothing else is found than wind. One will seek him but not find him. There is no hope (left): [13] like a shadow are his days on ea[rth]. And now listen to me, my people, and pay attention [14] to me, simple ones; stand in fear of the [migh]ty deeds of our God and remember the wonders He did [15] in Egypt and his portents [in the land of Ham]. Let your heart tremble for fear of Him II[1] and do his w[ill ....] your soul according to his good mercies. Search out for you the way [2] (that leads) to life, the road [that ....] as a remnant for your children after you. Why would you give

---

[5] For studies on the text, see n. 1. Allegro interprets the woman as the Roman adversaries of the Qumran community (*PEQ* 96 [1964], pp. 53–5), Carmignac and Gazov-Ginsberg as a rival sect, and Burgmann as the Liar, i.e. Simon Maccabaeus. Broshi considers the text as an example of Essene fear of, and contempt for, women. Moore concludes that the woman is a personification of the seduction of evil, but Strugnell identifies her with Dame Folly, the counterpart of Lady Wisdom.

[6] Edition: Allegro, *Qumrân Cave 4*, pp. 85–7. See, however, the improvements of the transliteration by Strugnell, 'Notes en marge du volume V', pp. 269–73, and Lichtenberger, 'Eine weisheitliche Mahnrede'.

³ your [soul] to vanity [and your ..... to jud]gement? Listen to me, my sons, and do not disobey the words of the Lord. ⁴ Do not transgress [the way He commanded Ja]cob and the path He appointed to Isaac. Is not better one day ⁵ .... in wealth ...... in fear of Him without deviating because of the scare or the snare of the fowler? ⁶ .... and to ...... because of his angels, for there is no darkness ⁷ nor gloom (?) [with Him ......] he [....] his [good plea]sure and his knowledge. You then, ⁸ what can you understand [..........? Fr]om Him goes forth knowledge (?) unto every people. Happy is the man to whom She has been given, ⁹ the son of man .... Let not the wicked act like a madman by saying: She has not been given ¹⁰ to me and [I will] not [seek Her. For the Lord has given Her] to Israel and as a noble dowry He has endowed Her. All his people He has redeemed, ¹¹ but He has slain [.......... He has] rui[ned]. He who holds Her in honour says: Let one take Her as [a posses]sion ¹² and She will suffice him [and gi]ve what She yields. For with Her is [length of da]ys, fatness of bone, joy of heart, ri[ches and honou]r, ¹³ the mercies of her ... and the salvation of [her ......]. Happy is the man who wins Her and not ???, [nor in a spirit of] ¹⁴ deceit seeks Her, nor with flatteries holds fast to Her. As She is given to his fathers, so he himself will possess Her and [hold fast to H]er ¹⁵ with all the power of his strength and with all his [might], without e[n]d. He will give Her as a possession to his offspring ???

Lichtenberg opines that in this text 'nicht allein Israel angeredet wird, sondern sich deutliche Hinweise finden (leider hindert der beklagenswerte Erhaltungszustand an ganz sicheren Aussagen), daß auch die Völker in bezug auf die Weisheit/das Gesetz angesprochen sind'. The correctness of his thesis largely depends on the reconstruction of the text, especially in II, 8 and 10. In line 8 one has the choice between d^ch (knowledge) and r^ch (disaster), although it must be admitted that 'knowledge' is probably to be preferred for contextual reasons. It is difficult to reconstruct the text of line 10, but if Lichtenberger's proposal (followed above) is adopted, we can conclude that the wicked ($rš^cym$) must be identical with non-Israelites. Although our text speaks about the commandments given to Isaac and Jacob, the Law of Moses is not mentioned and Wisdom is not explicitly identified with it. Consequently, the drift of the text may well be that Wisdom is given to all peoples (cf. Prov. viii 1ff.; Ecclus xxiv 6). Apparently, Wisdom should not be equated unreservedly with the Law revealed to Israel. Wisdom embraces both *Schöpfungsweisheit* and *Toraweisheit*, although in the outcome these two were considered identical so that in the end Wisdom is equated with the Law of Moses. Our text testifies to this identification by the wicked's assertion that Wisdom is given to Israel only. The author of the text may indeed be protesting against this assumption.

Lichtenberger rightly emphasizes that the text is of pre-Qumranic origin, because of its defective mode of writing, its vocabulary and the free use of the divine names Yahweh and Elohim in the text of the document.

C. Wisdom as a practical course of life gained by experience

4Q424 (PAM[7] 43.502; 44.196; FE[8] 1452; 1785), edited for the first time by Eisenman and Wise[9] and labelled by them as 'The Sons of Righteousness', is another wisdom text, which reminds us of the admonitions of the book of Proverbs. Fragment 1 contains the following text (from lines 1–2 only a few letters are preserved):

4Q424, fragment 1

[3] ... outside and chooses to build it and covers its wall with plaster. He also .... [4] it will fall because of the thunder-shower. Do not take upon you a task with an underhanded person and with an unstable man do not [5] enter a furnace. For as lead he will melt and before fire he will not stand. [6] Do not put a sluggard in charge of a ??, for he will not carry out the work you commissioned to him. And do not send him any [7] instruction, for he will not clear one of your roads. Do not com[mission] a murmurer [8] to get provisions for your needs. Do not tr[ust] a man of cunning lips, [for he will ......] [9] your judgements. He will certainly speak deviously. After truth he will not delight ...... [10] with the fruit of his lips. Do not set over [your] property a man with a covetous eye ... . [He will not] [11] arrange what remains to you according to your wish ... ??...... [12] And at the time of harvest he will be found to be a renegade, quick to an[ger.....], [13] the simple ones, for he will surely swallow up ....

The text warns young people against crooked and incompetent men. Not every detail can be ascertained but the bearing of the text is clear. Lines 3 and 4 remind us of Jesus' words as recorded in Matt. vii 26–7. Enigmatic is the warning not to enter a furnace together with an unstable person.[10] Is 'furnace' used here metaphorically?

The assertion of Eisenman and Wise that the fragment refers to the Kittim, known to us, for instance, from the Habakkuk pesher, is unfounded. In the last line of the fragment they have mistaken the word *ptyym*, 'the simple ones', as *ktyym*.

Although one may designate the admonitions of 4Q424 as a sapiential text, its bearing is quite different from 4Q184 and 4Q185. Wisdom is here practical wisdom for life, acquired by experience, without typical Israelite, let alone Qumranic, traits.

---

[7] PAM = Palestine Archaeological Museum.

[8] FE = R. H. Eisenman and J. M. Robinson, *A Facsimile Edition of the Dead Sea Scrolls*, 1–2 (Washington, 1991).

[9] R. H. Eisenman and M. Wise, *The Dead Sea Scrolls Uncovered* (Shaftesbury, Rockport and Brisbane, 1992), pp. 166–7.

[10] The translation of *bkwr* by 'young man' (so Eisenman and Wise, *The Dead Sea Scrolls Uncovered*, p. 166) is not acceptable because the noun means 'first-born' (which makes no sense in the context).

D. Torah as Wisdom

4Q525 (PAM 43.650; 43.595; 43.596; FE 1547; 1542; 1543), called by Eisenman and Wise[11] 'The Demons of Death', is represented by a large number of fragments which as a rule are too small to allow us to reconstruct their original place in the manuscript. However, three larger fragments (fr. 3, col. II; fr. 5; fr. 14, col. II) have reached us, the first of which is particularly interesting because it contains a series of beatitudes, edited for the first time by Puech.[12]

4Q525, fragment 3, column II

[Blessed is he who speaks the truth] [1] with a pure heart,
  who does not slander with his tongue.
Blessed are they who hold fast to her statutes,
  who do not hold fast [2] to the ways of wickedness.
Ble[ssed] are they who rejoice in Her,
  who do not chatter in a foolish way.
Blessed are they who seek Her [3] with clean hands,
  who do not look for Her with a deceitful [heart].
Blessed is the man who reaches Wisdom
  and walks [4] in the Law of the Most High,
  who directs his heart to her ways,
  and contains himself by her disciplines,
  who always is pleased with her chastisement,
  [5] who does not forsake Her in the misery of [his] afflict[ions]
  and does not abandon Her in the time of distress,
  who does not forget Her [in the days of dr]ead
  [6] and does not des[pise] Her in the oppression of his soul.

If he always meditates on Her, and in his affliction is concer[ned with the Law of God, in his whole] [7]life [is attached] to Her [and places her constantly] before his eyes, lest he walk in the paths [of evil, he will... [8] ......] in unity and his heart will be perfect. Go[d,...... [9] ... and W[isdom will lift up] his [he]ad and among kings She will s[eat him...... [10] .... brothers .... [11] VACAT [12] [And] now, children, l[isten to me and do no]t turn aside [...

As evidenced by lines 3 and 4 as well as by line 6, Wisdom and the revealed Law of Moses are identified. We are reminded of Ecclus xxiv which testifies to the way in which wisdom became equated with the Law of Moses: the latter is full of wisdom, as full as the river Pishon and the Tigris at the time of first fruits, and overflows with understanding like the Euphrates and the Jordan at the time of harvest (Ecclus xxiv 25–6).

---

[11] Eisenman and Wise, *The Dead Sea Scrolls Uncovered*, pp. 168–79.
[12] E. Puech, 'Un hymne essénien en partie retrouvé et les Béatitudes. 1QH V 12 – V 18 (=col. XIII – XIV 7) et 4QBéat', *RQ* 13 (1988), pp. 59–88, and in particular E. Puech, '4Q525 et les péricopes des béatitudes en Ben Sira et Matthieu', *RB* 98 (1991), pp. 80–106.

According to the Beatitudes, the Law of the Lord must be obeyed in all circumstances, for it is the source of life and the instrument of blessing.

E. The purpose of the gift of wisdom

The Psalms scroll of Qumran cave 11 (11QPs^a)[13] includes a number of apocryphal compositions interspersed between the canonical psalms found in the manuscript. Three of these apocryphal hymns contain the original Hebrew text of Psalms I (= 11QPs^a 151), II (= 11QPs^a 154) and III (= 11QPs^a 155) of the five so-called Syriac non-canonical psalms which appear as 'filler' material in the Book of Discipline (k^{e}tâbâ d^e-durâšâ) by the tenth-century Nestorian bishop Elijah of al-Anbar.[14] The second and fourth strophes (verses 5–8 and 12–15) of Psalm II (11QPs^a, col. XVIII) describe the purpose of the gift of Wisdom.

11QPs^a 154 (Syriac II)[15]

1   With a loud voice glorify God;
    in the congregation of the many proclaim his majesty.
2   In the multitude of the upright glorify his name
    and with the faithful recount his greatness.
3   [Let] your souls [keep company] with the good ones
    and with the blameless to glorify the Most High.

[13] J. A. Sanders, *The Psalms Scroll of Qumrân Cave 11* (Oxford, 1965).

[14] The existence of these psalms was noted for the first time by S. E. and J. S. Assemani in their *Bibliothecae Apostolicae Vaticanae Codicum Manuscriptorum Catalogus*, Partis primae, Tomus tertius (Rome, 1759), pp. 385–6. In 1887 W. Wright published the text of the psalms on the basis of a manuscript in the University Library of Cambridge ('Some Apocryphal Psalms in Syriac', *PSBA* 9 [1887], pp. 257–66). E. Sachau discovered the same psalms in a manuscript of the Berlin royal library (*Verzeichnis der syrischen Handschriften der königlichen Bibliothek zu Berlin* [Berlin, 1899], p. 209). A. Mingana published the text of the psalms from two manuscripts kept in the Rendel Harris Library ('Christian Documents in Syriac, Arabic and Garshuni, edited and translated with a critical apparatus', *BJRL* 11 [1927], pp. 492–8 [= *Woodbrooke Studies,* 1 (1927), pp. 288–94]). In 1930 M. Noth presented a collated text of the five psalms, rendered them in German and translated three of them (II, III and IV) back into Hebrew ('Die fünf syrisch überlieferten apokryphen Psalmen', *ZAW* 48 [1930], pp. 1–23). A critical edition of the Syriac text of the psalms can now be found in W. Baars, 'Apocryphal Psalms', *Vetus Testamentum Syriace iuxta simplicem Syrorum Versionem*, Pars IV, fasc. VI (Leiden, 1972). For translations of the psalms, see M. Delcor, 'Cinq nouveaux psaumes esséniens?', *RQ* 1 (1958), pp. 85–102; M. Delcor, 'Cinq psaumes syriaques esséniens', *Les Hymnes de Qumrân (Hodayot)* (Paris, 1962), pp. 299–319; M. Philonenko, 'L'Origine essénienne des cinq psaumes syriaques de David', *Semitica* 9 (1959), pp. 35–47; A. S. van der Woude, 'Die fünf syrischen Psalmen (einschließlich Psalm 151)', in *Jüdische Schriften aus hellenistisch-römischer Zeit*, Band IV, Lief. 1 (Gütersloh, 1974), pp. 29–47; J. H. Charlesworth and J. A. Sanders, 'More Psalms of David', in J. H. Charlesworth (ed.), *The Old Testament Pseudepigrapha*, 2 (London, 1985), pp. 612–24.

[15] Lines 1–3a and 17b–20 are reconstructed from the Syriac.

⁴ Join together to make known his salvation
    and be not lax in making known his might
    and his majesty to all simple-hearted.
⁵ For to make known the glory of the Lord
    is Wisdom given,
⁶ and to recount his many deeds
    she is made known to man:
⁷ to make known to the simple-hearted his might
    and to afford the senseless insight into his greatness,
⁸ those who are far from her gates,
    who stray from her portals.
⁹ For the Most High is the Lord of Jacob,
    and his majesty is over all his works.
¹⁰ To a man who glorifies the Most High,
    He is favourable as to one who brings a meal offering,
¹¹ as to one who offers he-goats and bullocks,
    as to one who fattens the altar with many burnt offerings,
    as to the sweet-smelling fragrance from the hand of the righteous.
¹² From the gates of the righteous her voice is heard,
    from the assembly of the pious her song.
¹³ When they eat with satiety she is mentioned,
    and when they drink in community together.
¹⁴ Their meditation is on the Law of the Most High,
    their words on making known his might.
¹⁵ How far from the godless is her word,
    from all haughty men to know her.
¹⁶ Behold the eyes of the Lord
    are compassionate upon the good ones,
¹⁷ and upon those who glorify Him He increases his mercy;
    from an evil time He delivers [their] life.
¹⁸ [Bless] the Lord,
    who redeems the humble from the hand of the str[angers
    and deliv]ers [the blameless from the godless,
¹⁹ who establishes a horn out of Ja]cob
    and a judge [of the peoples out of Israel,
²⁰ who spreads his tent in Zion
    and abides for ever in Jerusalem].

Wisdom as the divine gift imparted to the righteous apparently refers here to the right knowledge of God which the simple folk and those devoid of insight do not have (verses 7–8), let alone the wicked and haughty men (verse 15). This wisdom manifests itself in meditation on the Law of the Lord (cf. verses 14–15), instruction of those who lack knowledge of God, and above all in the glorification of his mighty deeds, which according to the hymn is the purpose of the gift of wisdom and equals cultic sacrifices. The relationship of wisdom to liturgical praise is a conspicuous trait of the psalm which deserves special consideration.

Despite Delcor's and Philonenko's assertions,[16] neither the contents nor the vocabulary of this hymn and the other apocryphal psalms of 11QPs[a] unambiguously point to an Essene or Qumranic origin.[17]

F. Passionate devotion to Wisdom

11QPs[a] col. XXI, 11–17, contains the first part of another sapiential psalm which shows the earliest Hebrew text of Ecclus li 13ff. and li 30b.[18] It refers to Lady Wisdom as a nurse, a tutor and a mistress, passionately desired by the young man who putatively authored the psalm.

1 I was a young man; before I could err,
   I sought her.
2 She came to me in her beauty
   and I explored her in depth.
3 Even if the blossom falls off when the grapes ripen,
   they gladden the heart.
4 My foot trod in uprightness,
   for from my youth have I known her.
5 I inclined my ear but a little,
   but I found instruction in large measure.
6 She became a nurse for me,
   a tutor, to whom I dedicated the bloom of my life.
7 I purposed to give myself up to revelry,
   I was zealous for pleasure, without pause.
8 I burned in my desire for her
   and never took my eyes off her.
9 I bestirred my desire for her
   and on her heights I would not relax.
10 My hand opened [her gates]
   [and] her unseen parts I perceived.
11 I cleansed my hand within [her
   and found her in her purity].

In contradistinction to the Greek version of Ben Sira's grandson, this poem clearly shows erotic overtones: the wording of a number of verses is purposely ambiguous in their use of *mots à double entente* (cf., for example, the use of *yād* [verse 10] and *kap* [verse 11] in the sense of hand *and* phallus, of 'her unseen parts' [verse 10] as Wisdom's mysteries *and* genitals). 'Despite the intriguing fact that, in the preserved portion ... Wisdom is

[16] Cf. their studies mentioned in n. 14.
[17] Cf. van der Woude, 'Die fünf syrischen Psalmen', p. 35.
[18] Another Hebrew text of a much later date (11th cent. AD) forms part of one of the Cairo Genizah manuscripts. On the character and deficiencies of this manuscript and its relationship to the Greek version of Ecclesiasticus, see Sanders, *The Psalms Scroll*, pp. 79–80, and T. Muraoka, 'Sir. 51: 13–30: An Erotic Hymn to Wisdom?', *JSJ* 10 (1979), pp. 166ff.

never mentioned explicitly, there is no mistaking that the author's real concern was about a search after Wisdom and deep devotion to it, only he saw an extremely close analogy between this religious, ethical zeal and a man's intimate association and physical union with his female companion.'[19] The imagery is prepared by the book of Proverbs (cf. Prov. v 18–19, vii 4; see also Ecclus xv 2–3) and later on attested in the Wisdom of Solomon (viii 2). Those who love Wisdom attain the loftiest goal of human life. Since a version of the text appears already in Ben Sira, it did not originate in the Qumran community.

Of the wisdom writings translated above it cannot be said that they show unambiguous traits referring to the history, the religious customs or the beliefs of the Qumran community. The vocabulary used by their authors only occasionally reminds us of the sapiential terminology found in the writings ascribed to the Qumran community (e.g. 1QS, 1QH, 1QM). I therefore share the view of Lowndes Lipscomb and Sanders that the Qumran community itself did not compose wisdom documents, although its members certainly handed down writings of this kind and held them in esteem.

In contradistinction to this conclusion, Devorah Dimant[20] wants to attribute all sapiential texts discovered at Qumran to the Qumran community, with the exception of 4Q184, 4Q185, 4Q411 and 4Q412. As such she lists:

> Sapiential Work A (4Q416–18)[21]
> Sapiential Work B (4Q413; 4Q415)
> Wisdom Texts (4Q419; 4Q408)
> Book of Mysteries (4Q299–301; 1Q27)
> Various Sapiential Fragments (4Q410; 4Q423–6; 4Q474–81; 4Q487)
> Two Ways (4Q473)
> Parable of the Tree (4Q302a)
> Wisdom Text with Beatitudes (4Q525)
> Meditation on Creation (4Q303–305)
> Way of Righteousness (4Q420–1)
> Rule of the Farmer (4Q423; 1Q26)
> Rule ? (4Q524).

[19] Muraoka, 'An Erotic Hymn', p. 174.

[20] D. Dimant, 'The Qumran Manuscripts: Contents and Significance', in D. Dimant and L. H. Schiffman (eds.), *Time to Prepare a Way in the Wilderness. Papers on the Qumran Scrolls by Fellows of the Institute for Advanced Studies of the Hebrew University, Jerusalem, 1989–1990* (Leiden, 1993), pp. 23–49.

[21] D. J. Harrington and J. Strugnell, 'Qumran Cave 4 Texts: A New Publication', *JBL* 112 (1993), pp. 491–9, consider 4Q415, 4Q423 and 1Q26 as manuscripts of the same work (p. 492).

Dimant's identification of these manuscripts as wisdom compositions may eventually turn out to be a provisional one, not only because some other texts seem to belong to this category (cf., e.g., 4Q406–8), but also because it is doubtful whether all the documents labelled by her as wisdom texts should be regarded as such (cf., e.g., 1Q27; 4Q524).

More important is Dimant's attempt to assign the origin of these works to the Qumran community on the basis of the vocabulary used in the writings. In her paper, she is not very explicit on this score. The linguistic evidence which she adduces to support her thesis does not seem to be convincing.[22] The wisdom texts discovered among the Dead Sea scrolls are apparently compositions which were authored before the Qumran community came into existence.[23]

2   Charismatic wisdom given to the Teacher of Righteousness

The text portions dealt with above can be considered as more or less representative of the kinds of sapiential literature discovered among the Dead Sea scrolls. From their contents we can conclude that both wisdom in the sense of practical admonitions pertaining to conduct in life and wisdom as the secret of the cosmological and ethical world order (which eventually led to the identification of wisdom and Torah) played a role in the Qumran community in accordance with the attention given to wisdom and the appreciation of it in the sapiential literature of early Judaism in general. The only difference between Qumran and its spiritual *Umwelt* may be found in the particular knowledge imparted by God to the Teacher of Righteousness to which especially the *Hodayoth* (1QH) refer.

The authority that the Teacher of Righteousness claims for himself is based upon the divine illumination granted to him (1QH IV, 5; cf. IV, 6, 23, 27–8). According to 1QS II, 3 this illumination relates to life-giving wisdom (*śkl ḥyym*) and eternal knowledge (*d'̊t 'wlmym*). Because of the particular revelation imparted to him, the Teacher is 'a banner to the elect of righteousness' and 'an interpreter of knowledge pertaining to the wonderful

---

[22] Sometimes also the contents of the manuscripts which Dimant ascribes to the Qumran community plead against Qumran provenance; cf., e.g., 4Q416. In fr. 2, col. III of this document, the author admonishes his audience not to forsake the pursuit of knowledge because of poverty, and in case of marriage to cling to the prescribed rules. If this text stems from Qumranic ranks, it must make an appeal to outsiders (which is not likely), since poverty is incompatible with the community of property which obtained in the Qumran sect, and marriage is inconsistent with the celibacy of its members.

[23] H. Stegemann, *Die Essener, Qumran, Johannes der Täufer und Jesus* (Freiburg, Basel, Wien, 1993), draws a similar conclusion: 'Keiner der inhaltlichen Befunde verlangt ein Abfassungsdatum ... später als im 4. oder 3. Jh. v. Chr. Die Essener haben diese alten Weisheitsbücher hoch geschätzt, sie aber nicht erst selbst verfaßt, von ein oder zwei Ausnahmen vielleicht abgesehen' (p. 143).

mysteries' (II, 13). The wicked who seek smooth things (*dwršy ḥlqwt*) rage against him because God has put understanding (*bynh*) into his heart that 'he might open a fountain of knowledge (*mqwr dᶜt*) to all men of insight (*mbynym*)' (II, 17–18). 'Knowledge' apparently refers to the sound doctrine revealed to the Teacher. His opponents, however, 'withhold from the thirsty the drink of knowledge' (IV, 16) and reject the 'vision of knowledge' (*ḥzwn dᶜt*) granted to the Teacher of Righteousness (IV, 18).

The revelation imparted to the latter concerns the right understanding of God's will and knowledge about the final age (cf. CD I, 11–12; 1QpHab II, 7ff., VII, 4). The preaching of the Teacher conveys right insight. He is the true prophet whom God has instructed to proclaim his truth. Although the term *ḥkmh* apparently is not used in this connection, it should not be doubted that the revelation imparted to the Teacher was considered as charismatic wisdom.

We have subscribed to the view of Lowndes Lipscomb and Sanders that none of the wisdom texts discovered among the Dead Sea scrolls originated in Qumran. If this thesis is correct, the reason for the absence of sapiential texts authored at Qumran could be that after true wisdom was revealed to the Teacher of Righteousness, the members of his community were essentially interested in the knowledge imparted to him. Seemingly, they did not feel the necessity to elaborate on and to develop wisdom texts since eternal knowledge (*dᶜt ᶜwlmym*) was revealed to them by the Teacher of Righteousness.

Nevertheless, they did not do away with wisdom traditions. They copied sapiential literature handed down to them and to a large extent put their own convictions into words by means of inherited wisdom terminology. In this respect the members of the Qumran community shared the creed of early Jewish sapiential literature that correct conduct in life, fear of the Lord and clinging to his revealed will attest to insight and true knowledge, although they had their own ideas about the implementation of these requirements. Therefore, it does not come as a surprise that wisdom terminology also abounds in non-sapiential writings found among the Dead Sea scrolls.

22 The interpretation of wisdom in nineteenth-century scholarship

Rudolf Smend

1 Introduction

Several times during the course of this century, the Society for Old
Testament Study has provided general surveys of scholarly trends, but
initially wisdom played no noticeable role in them. In A. S. Peake (ed.), *The
People and the Book* (Oxford, 1925), wisdom was merely mentioned. H. W.
Robinson (ed.), *Record and Revelation* (Oxford, 1938), devoted only a few
pages to it, in O. Eissfeldt's discussion of 'modern criticism'. Not until 1951
was it treated in a chapter of its own, in H. H. Rowley (ed.), *The Old
Testament and Modern Study* (Oxford). The chapter was written by W.
Baumgartner, and this was continued – on an equal level – by J. A. Emerton
in G. W. Anderson (ed.), *Tradition and Interpretation* (Oxford, 1979). This
sequence clearly shows how wisdom gained – and retained – importance in
our field following the first quarter of this century.

The bibliographies which follow the surveys of Baumgartner and
Emerton make possible another peripheral observation. Nearly two-thirds
of the books contained in Baumgartner's bibliography (1951) arc in
German (48 out of 79), while in 1979, when Emerton compiled his, the
number had been reduced to less than a half (28 out of 60). Even if the
possible influence of the background of the two authors is taken into
account, these numbers are most likely symptomatic of the decreasing
weight of German-speaking scholarship in this field; corresponding
statistics for the period between 1979 and 1995 would show that even more
strikingly.

The first decades of the twentieth century form a contrast to this,
something even more strongly marked in the nineteenth century as summed
up in respect to Old Testament scholarship as a whole by J. Rogerson.[1]

This chapter was translated by Henrike Lähnemann.

[1] *Old Testament Criticism in the Nineteenth Century. England and Germany* (London, 1984).

Mainly on that account non-German literature is bound to play an even less important part in the following remarks than in those of Baumgartner and Emerton; a second reason lies unfortunately in the insufficient number of non-German books accessible to me.

Even for literature written in German, however, incompleteness is not too serious with respect to the interpretation of wisdom in the nineteenth century. Such a survey has not commonly been undertaken, and this contrasts with Pentateuchal criticism where great and far-reaching decisions were being taken. This too is impressively demonstrated by Rogerson's book, which in this respect takes the SOTS surveys further back: wisdom does not even appear in it. It vanishes completely under the shadow of greater themes, among which, of course, Pentateuchal criticism stands out as pre-eminent.[2] In this situation we must be content to draw out of obscurity some more or less relevant aspects.

We shall concentrate mainly on the book of Proverbs. Of course, it would be desirable to include Job, Ecclesiastes and other literature as well. Particularly with regard to their date, however, the isagogical problems presented by these books are (*mutatis mutandis*) the same as with Proverbs. In other respects they raise special issues of their own which are rarely connected with wisdom. The intellectual and theological influence of Job and Ecclesiastes in the nineteenth century, on the other hand, is much too weighty a theme for even marginal coverage in the context of a chapter such as the present one.

Even in the case of Proverbs this study will not be able to give a fully adequate account of the work undertaken by the commentators. The reputation for having most furthered understanding in the eighteenth century was attributed to the commentary on Proverbs by Albert Schultens.[3] In the nineteenth century a like reputation was enjoyed by Franz Delitzsch, though the crown belongs to Crawford H. Toy's voluminous interpretation in the last year of the century.[4] As in other cases, Ferdinand Hitzig[5] was the *enfant terrible* among the commentators; boldness and wit prompted H. J. Holtzmann to state that a comparison of Hitzig's book with the 'pathetic' commentary of Zöckler[6] showed 'how

---

[2] T. K. Cheyne found the study of books about wisdom 'most refreshing after the incessant and exciting battles of Pentateuchal-criticism'; see *Job and Solomon or The Wisdom of the Old Testament* (London, 1887), p. viii.
[3] *Proverbia Salomonis* (Leiden, 1748).
[4] *Salomonisches Spruchbuch* (Leipzig, 1873); cf. H. L. Strack, *Die Sprüche Salomo's* (Nördlingen, 1888), p. 310; C. H. Toy, *A Critical and Exegetical Commentary on the Book of Proverbs* (Edinburgh, 1899).
[5] *Die Sprüche Salomos, übersetzt und ausgelegt* (Zürich, 1858).
[6] *Die Sprüche Salomos* (Bielefeld and Leipzig, 1867).

massively our theology is deteriorating'.[7] Since Delitzsch's commentary was published shortly after this statement, however, such pessimism seems unjustified, and one is inclined to see rather, if not constant progress, at least a wave-like pattern in this theological field.

2 Date

Until the first decades of the nineteenth century, wisdom, as represented by the book of Proverbs, was widely held to be genuinely old. In 1803 the representative textbook of the time, J. G. Eichhorn's *Einleitung*, stated: 'All the proverbs of the entire book are old; at least, I find no convincing trace of their later date either in grammar or vocabulary.'[8] In some respects this is a cautious remark, and this caution prompts Eichhorn to add some further reservations. First, 'Even if something has escaped my notice and some proverb or other bears the hallmark of a later era, I am still confident that these must be isolated instances, and that these few would surely not be able to undermine the antiquity of the remainder.' The second reservation concerns Solomonic authorship. Eichhorn doubts whether *all* proverbs are by Solomon, because 'even a godly genius is hardly sufficient for such a wealth of sharp aphorism and witty invention'. For instance, Solomon may have written the whole introduction (i–ix) on his own, and also quite a few of the following proverbs.[9] But Eichhorn's caution increases further: 'Should someone claim that the first part, the present introduction, is not the work of Solomon but that of an old wise man who wrote his commendations of wisdom under the name of Solomon as being that of the most famous sage of the whole orient, I, for one, would not be able comprehensively to refute it.'[10]

Eichhorn's words show that in 1800 the antiquity and Solomonic authorship of Proverbs were no longer firmly grounded – nor, for that matter, the antiquity and Mosaic authorship of the Pentateuch, which Eichhorn defended in a similar way. As with the Pentateuch, though with less public attention, the late dating of wisdom gained acceptance during the course of the century. The Hegelian Wilhelm Vatke is generally held to be the first and, at the same time, a particularly resolute advocate of it, just as he is known to have promoted Pentateuchal criticism. In 1835 he dated Proverbs and Job in the fifth century BC and Qoheleth even later. His arguments arose less from philologico-historical criticism narrowly defined

---

[7] In C. C. J. Bunsen, *Vollständiges Bibelwerk* 6/2/2 (Leipzig, 1879). The author may not have been Holtzmann but his assistant Adolf Kamphausen.
[8] *Einleitung in das Alte Testament* (3rd edn, Leipzig, 1803), p. 518.   [9] *Ibid.*, p. 521.
[10] *Ibid.*, p. 522.

as from broad reflection in the context of 'Geistesgeschichte'. He claimed that the overall viewpoint of the ethical mind which is to be detected in these writings ('Totalstandpunkt des sittlichen Geistes') would have been incomprehensible at an earlier time. He found the prophetic mind still enduring here but freed now from particularist Jewish elements to a greater extent than at the time of the prophets.[11]

For philological aspects of this subject Vatke referred to a predecessor, Anton Theodor Hartmann, professor of theology at the University of Rostock, who in 1828 had reviewed the commentary on Proverbs by the Heidelberg orientalist Friedrich Wilhelm Carl Umbreit (Heidelberg, 1826). He replied to Umbreit's statement that Solomon was the collector of the book at least up to ch. xxv by saying that it 'had revealed just the contrary' to him. He thought that the written collection of proverbs was as loosely attached to Solomon as were the Song of Songs and Qoheleth. They were all bound 'to attain higher value if written by an illustrious sage of antiquity'. Not only is Solomon not the collector of the book of Proverbs, as claimed by Umbreit, but in fact not a single collection contained in the book is to be dated earlier than the period of the last Hebrew kings, 'from which our book's Aramaicizing character becomes understandable as it reveals itself in spelling, forms, compounds, construction and meanings'. Hartmann refers to several places where the reader may observe these linguistic peculiarities: i 17, iv 21, v 2, 22, vi 13, 30, vii 16, 20, 25, viii 3, ix 3, xi 12, 31, xii 26, xiii 4, 13, xiv 3, xvi 17, xvii 5, 26, xx 22, xxi 11, 12, 14, 24, xxii 6, 16, 19, xxiii 2, 7, 9, xxv 10, 13, xxvii 7, 15, xxviii 4, xxix 21, xxx 17, xxxi 3.[12]

The extent to which this criticism was convincing and effective is shown by the acerbity with which Franz Delitzsch – who was regarded as a conservative – refuted Solomonic authorship a generation later. 'Even today there are still some who, like Stier,[13] hold the whole of the book of Proverbs from first to last to be as old as Solomon . . . But since historical criticism has gained acceptance in the biblical field, this blind adherence to a (misunderstood!) tradition appears as an "uncriticism" which is scarcely worthy of being mentioned.' This negative statement is immediately followed by a positive summary of Delitzsch's own position: 'The book of Proverbs presents itself as a composition of varyingly shaped and differently dated elements. Critical analysis resolves it into a colourful market of the most manifold intellectual products of at least three epochs of proverbial poetry.'[14]

---

[11] *Die biblische Theologie* 1/1 (Berlin, 1835), pp. 563–4. An even closer connection between prophecy and wisdom is observed by B. Duhm, *Die Theologie der Propheten* (Bonn, 1875), pp. 244–5.

[12] *Theologisches Literaturblatt zur Allgemeinen Kirchenzeitung* 7 (Darmstadt, 1828), cols. 735–6.

[13] R. Stier, *Der Weise ein König* (Barmen, 1849); *Die Politik der Weisheit* (Barmen, 1850).

[14] F. Delitzsch, *Salomonisches Spruchbuch* (Leipzig, 1873), p. 3.

On the 'colourful market' we see the exegetes of the nineteenth century playing about and trying out most of the possibilities which are familiar in the twentieth century. The starting point and main focus of attention are the collections as singled out by the headings. Complicated literary criticism as necessitated by the Pentateuch therefore seems redundant, and the problem of dating can be addressed directly. The means for this are not only language in the sense that Hartmann used it but also poetic form. For instance, Delitzsch opposes the interpretation of Proverbs as simple folk sayings by drawing a detailed picture of the development of 'artificial "Mashal"-poetry'. Its basic form is the couplet, with different ways of relating its elements (synonymously, antithetically, synthetically, expressing a single thought, parabolically); it is able to reproduce itself to form four-, six- or eight-line units but also to expand to have three, five and seven lines; its boundaries are extended by the Mashal-song, of which there are fifteen examples in Prov. i 7–ix; finally, there are numerical proverbs and the Mashal-chain.[15] In this classification, as well as in the use of the history of its development for dating the collections, Delitzsch follows Ewald, but he wishes to proceed with greater flexibility. For instance, he calls Ewald's postulate that Solomon wrote exclusively antithetic couplets a 'really fatuous claim'.[16]

When grouping the collections according to their age, a degree of consensus is reached, starting with the 'proverbs of Solomon' (x 1–xxii 16) and assuming that by comparison the 'proverbs of Solomon collected by the men of Hezekiah, the king of Judah' (xxv–xxix) are more recent. In each case the passages following are thought to be supplements to the original collections.[17] In fact, differing views are also to be found, such as that of A. B. Davidson (with the cautious approval of S. R. Driver), who, on stylistic grounds, regards xxv–xxix as older than x 1–xxii 16.[18]

A special position was held by the beginning of the book, i–ix, which Davidson regarded as 'one of the most remarkable and beautiful things in Hebrew literature'.[19] Known for his unconventional opinions, Ferdinand Hitzig is practically the only one who assumes that it is the oldest part.[20] The *opinio communis* points in the opposite direction. While Ernst Bertheau[21] denies the unity of these chapters on the basis of content and structure, Delitzsch thinks that there exists no 'Old Testament piece of similar size with more systematic internal unity, nor one which bears

[15] *Ibid.*, pp. 7–13.   [16] *Ibid.*, p. 19.
[17] H. Ewald, *Die Dichter des Alten Bundes*, 2 (3rd edn, Göttingen, 1867), pp. 4ff., 41ff., as well as Delitzsch, *Salomonisches Spruchbuch*, pp. 20ff., 30.
[18] A. B. Davidson, 'Proverbs', *Enc. Brit.* 19 (9th edn, 1885), pp. 882–3; S. R. Driver, *An Introduction to the Literature of the Old Testament* (2nd edn, Edinburgh, 1891), p. 381, n. 2.
[19] Davidson, 'Proverbs', p. 879.   [20] *Die Sprüche Salomos* (Zürich, 1858), p. 4.
[21] *Die Sprüche Salomos* (Leipzig, 1847), pp. xxi–xxiii.

throughout a like formal impress'.[22] He considers the chapters to be an introduction to 'the older book of Proverbs' (x 1–xxii 16, with the addition of xxii 17–xxiv 22) by an editor who must have lived after Solomon but before Hezekiah, that is to say, more precisely, at the time of Jehoshaphat. But there is one even more specific connection: 'The whole flavour of this didactic poem is Deuteronomic. The admonitory addresses in i 7–ix are to the book of Proverbs what Deuteronomy is to the Pentateuch. Just as Deuteronomy seeks to spiritualize the *tôrâ* of the Mosaic law and to seal it upon the heart of the next generation, so do they with the *tôrâ* of Solomon's proverbs.'[23]

Before Delitzsch, Abraham Kuenen had had the same impression, but because of his later dating of Deuteronomy (following de Wette) this meant a postponement of more than two centuries: 'Proverbial poetry in the 7th century also had its Deuteronomist, the author of Prov. i 7–ix 18.'[24] This dating became prevalent at that time, and in 1887 it was still upheld by T. K. Cheyne in his major survey of wisdom.[25] Shortly afterwards, however, Cheyne gave it up (and with it the pre-exilic dating of the book of Proverbs as a whole), having been impressed by the arguments of Reuss, Stade and others, some of whom went so far as to date the book to Hellenistic times.[26] Regardless of the merits of this last suggestion, Cheyne formulated in 1893 what has been the consensus in biblical scholarship ever since: 'Indeed, however much allowance is made for the tenacity of the life of proverbs, and for the tendency to recast old gnomic material, one must maintain that in its present form the Book of Proverbs is a source of information, not for the pre-Exilic, but for various parts of the post-Exilic period.'[27]

The question of what 'old gnomic material' the book is commonly thought to contain is left open. A fixed point is provided by the comment about the collection of Solomon's proverbs by the men of Hezekiah. In the words of Wilhelm Nowack,[28] there is no reason to doubt the authenticity of

---

[22] Delitzsch, *Salomonisches Spruchbuch*, p. 14.   [23] *Ibid.*, p. 29; cf. pp. 25–6, 30.

[24] *De Godsdienst van Israël*, 1 (Haarlem, 1869), p. 456.

[25] *Job and Solomon or The Wisdom of the Old Testament*, pp. 168–9.

[26] Cf. E. Reuss, *Die Geschichte der Heiligen Schriften Alten Testaments* (2nd edn, Braunschweig, 1890), pp. 513–22, and, for the Greek origin of Prov. i–ix, B. Stade, *Geschichte des Volkes Israel*, 2 (Berlin, 1888), p. 216; he was followed by O. Holtzmann, in Bunsen, *Vollständiges Bibelwerk*, pp. 296–7, and extensively by W. Frankenberg, 'Ueber Abfassungs-Ort und -Zeit, sowie Art und Inhalt von Prov. I–IX', *ZAW* 15 (1895), pp. 104–32; compare also H. Oort, 'Spreuken 1–9', *ThT* 19 (1885), pp. 379–425. Opposition to Greek influence was expressed by A. Kuenen, *Historisch-critisch onderzoek naar het ontstaan an de verzameling van de boeken des ouden verbonds*, 3/1 (2nd edn, Amsterdam, 1892), pp. 98–9.

[27] *Founders of Old Testament Criticism* (London, 1893), p. 340; similarly *Jewish Religious Life after the Exile* (New York and London, 1898), p. 128.

[28] E. Bertheau and W. Nowack, *Die Sprüche Salomo's* (2nd edn, Leipzig, 1883), p. xxvii.

this comment. In saying this, he stands in a degree of opposition to his predecessor in the *Kurzgefasstes exegetisches Handbuch*, Ernst Bertheau, who, with almost Eichhorn-like caution, had observed of Prov. xxv 1 that 'we must take this comment to be strictly historical and maintain it as a fixed position which we may not weaken by doubt or abandon, even though we may be overcome by the temptation to do so quite often'. The temptation which he resisted so bravely confronted him for three reasons: (1) There is virtually no reference to Proverbs in the prophetic books. (2) In contrast with these, Proverbs implies the uncontested supremacy of Yahwism in Israel. (3) In some respects Proverbs is noticeably similar to the book of Sirach.[29] Bertheau's reluctance to draw the inevitable consequences from these circumstances may be partly due to the influence of his older Göttingen colleague Heinrich Ewald, who stressed over and over again that it was next to impossible 'to overestimate the extent to which the quest for wisdom (philosophy) had been cultivated in the centuries after David'.[30] Thus, despite all his merits, Ewald's authority may have been a delaying factor in the study of wisdom as much as in Pentateuchal criticism.

The consequences of this for the image of Solomon have been pointed out particularly vividly by Ernest Renan: 'Now not only do we have none of Solomon's own poetry but it is very likely that he never wrote at all. I imagine him rather more as a kind of caliph of Baghdad who amuses himself by watching scholars who have to work according to his orders; like a Harun al-Rashid, surrounded by singers, story-tellers and "gens d'esprit" to whom he speaks like an expert colleague.'[31]

3   Internationality

When one reads today the literature of the nineteenth century about wisdom in Israel, the first thing one notices is the lack of other oriental material. The discovery and investigation of this has in fact made the sharpest break in the history of the study of wisdom. As Walter Baumgartner states in retrospect, it has entailed 'two big surprises: first, the discovery that an essentially similar literature of wisdom existed and was cultivated from the Nile to the Tigris... The other surprise resulted from the fact that the wisdom of Israel fitted perfectly into that of the ancient orient just like a link in a chain, and this in all kinds of ways from the simple

---

[29] *Die Sprüche Salomo's*, pp. xli–xliii; cf. the well-balanced explanations by C. G. Montefiore in his great survey, 'Notes upon the Date and Religious Value of the Proverbs', *JQR* 2 (1890), pp. 430–53, especially 432ff.

[30] *Jahrbücher der Biblischen wissenschaft* 1 (1848), p. 96; cf. *Geschichte des Volkes Israel*, 3 (3rd edn, Göttingen, 1866), pp. 388–92.   [31] *Histoire du peuple d'Israël*, 2 (Paris, 1923), p. 176.

relation of subjects and ideas to identical wording and literary dependence.'[32] The two texts which contributed most to this caesura became available only in the twentieth century: the Aramaic fragments of Ahiqar in 1906 and the teaching of Amenemope in 1923.[33] As a result, the accounts of (Ewald and) Delitzsch mentioned above regarding the forms of proverbs were put back on the agenda, though now in the context of form criticism and with a more basic and methodical impetus.[34]

Though spectacular for contemporary scholarship, these findings were compatible with assumptions which were already quite possible in the nineteenth century. Thus Renan gives some credence to the thesis 'that among the monuments of Hebrew wisdom there is more than one piece which was created in one of the neighbouring tribes, even though not all the elements could ever be identical with their use in Israel, especially with regard to parallelism'.[35] Of course, the international character of wisdom had never been hidden from scholarship. The Old Testament itself speaks about it and in many respects it is evident to an observant reader, even if he does not know the ancient oriental material and might happen to know something about only Greek, Arabic or other proverbial writing. The scholars of the nineteenth century tackled the problem with the tools at their disposal, often on quite a large scale. At the beginning of his commentary, for instance, Umbreit devotes thirty pages to 'Oriental wisdom as a whole'.[36] It is not surprising, however, that in his review Hartmann characterizes this section as 'darkness which never completely recedes',[37] since at that time the subject could be dealt with only in a more or less speculative way; Umbreit does this extensively by constant reference to contemporary philosophers like Kant, Herder, Schleiermacher, Creuzer and F. Schlegel.

It was possible, however, to characterize the problem very briefly and without speculation as J. Wellhausen did when he wrote: 'The Proverbs of Solomon would not be worth considering if they had grown on Greek or Arabic soil; in their dim generality they are noteworthy only because they are of Jewish origin.'[38] Inevitably, this raises the question of the specific character of wisdom in Israel.

[32] *Israelitische und altorientalische Weisheit* (Tübingen, 1933), pp. 19, 23.
[33] Of course, some were already known in the nineteenth century and received the attention of Old Testament scholars; cf., e.g., the rules for behaviour in A. Erman, *Ägypten und ägyptisches Leben im Altertum* (Tübingen, 1885), p. 237; taken up by R. Smend, *Lehrbuch der alttestamentlichen Religionsgeschichte* (2nd edn, Freiburg, 1899), pp. 483–4, n. 2.
[34] Cf. H. Gressmann, 'Die neugefundene Lehre des Amen-em-ope und die vorexilische Spruchdichtung Israels', *ZAW* 42 (1924), pp. 272–96.
[35] *Histoire du peuple d'Israël*, 3 (Paris, 1924), p. 76.
[36] *Commentar über die Sprüche Salomos* (Heidelberg, 1826), pp. iii–xxxii.
[37] Cf. *Theologisches Literaturblatt zur Allgemeinen Kirchenzeitung* 7, col. 735.
[38] *Skizzen und Vorarbeiten*, 1 (Berlin, 1884), p. 89.

4   Characteristics

For quite a long time it was popular to characterize wisdom in terms of European 'Geistesgeschichte'. The most famous attempt in recent times was G. von Rad's thesis about the 'Solomonic enlightenment', which was not only aimed at wisdom but included it as a decisive element.[39] The oldest designation within this long tradition is 'philosophy'. In the Old Testament part of the *Introductio ad historiam philosophiae Hebraeorum* by J. F. Buddeus, which begins with Adam, Solomon figures as 'regum sapientissimus'.[40] Ewald's identification of wisdom and philosophy has already been cited.[41] Before him, Eichhorn had called proverbial wisdom literature 'philosophical poetry',[42] while as far as Israel was concerned W. M. L. de Wette had equated 'practical philosophy' with 'proverbial wisdom' and had separated them both from 'speculative philosophy', since at that time theology consisted of mythology, symbolics and poetry and was scientifically completely undeveloped.[43] Towards the end of the century, the wisdom literature was included under the heading 'religious and moral philosophy of the Hebrews' in E. Reuss's translation of the Old Testament.[44] Even as late as 1914 Karl Kautzsch could still entitle a small book *Die Philosophie des Alten Testaments*; its main sections are 'man and his duty' (Proverbs), 'man and his suffering' (Job), and 'man and his purpose' (Ecclesiastes).

Franz Delitzsch commended the Strasbourg theologian J. F. Bruch for having been 'the first to call attention to *Chokma* or humanism as a distinctive intellectual tendency in Israel' in his *Weisheits-Lehre der Hebräer* (Strasbourg, 1851).[45] In fact, humanism[46] is not the key word for Bruch, but philosophy. Bruch's book, subtitled 'A contribution to the history of philosophy', undertakes a broad reflection on the applicability of the term 'philosophy' to Old Testament wisdom, in contrast with other authors who simply make use of it without reflection. Bruch concedes that wisdom is 'more like philosophizing than philosophy', and also that it 'never works

---

[39] *Theologie des Alten Testaments*, 1 (Munich, 1957), p. 63 (E. tr., *Old Testament Theology*, 1 [Edinburgh and London, 1962], p. 55).   [40] Ed. nova (Halle, 1720), p. 52.
[41] See p. 263. It is most explicit in *Geschichte des Volkes Israel*, 3 (3rd edn), p. 391.
[42] *Litterärgeschichte*, 1 (Göttingen, 1812), p. 42. He was anticipated by Robert Lowth in his 24th 'Praelectio', who named them 'Carmina didactica' (*De sacra poesi Hebraeorum* [Oxford, 1753], pp. 324ff.).
[43] *Lehrbuch der Hebräisch-Jüdischen Archäologie* (Leipzig, 1814), p. 332.
[44] 6 (Braunschweig, 1894). Of course, Reuss does not use the terms naively; cf. his *Geschichte der Heiligen Schriften Alten Testaments* (2nd edn, Braunschweig, 1890), p. 524.
[45] *Salomonisches Spruchbuch*, p. 38.
[46] This appears in an especially emphasized form in Cheyne, *Job and Solomon*, p. 119, where it is said of the 'wise men': 'If a modern equivalent must be found, it would be best to call them the humanists, to indicate their freedom from national prejudice [...] and their tendency to base a sound morality on its adaptation to human nature'; cf. also Driver, *Introduction*, p. 369.

methodically',[47] but he advocates the thesis that 'speculative needs existed among the Hebrews as well as among several nations of antiquity, and these had to be given a place in the history of philosophy'.[48] As it was developed in Solomon's time, 'wisdom' is 'actually a speculative term in which a rich ethical and religious conception of the world is enclosed, far above the normal consciousness of the Hebrews'.[49] But this term cannot be detached from 'the whole complex of loftier conceptions to which the spirit of the Hebrews was raised on the way to a mode of speculative thinking', and thus Bruch undertakes 'a rendering of all the philosophical thinking of the Hebrews according to its origin, its pre-eminent characters, its different tendencies and its results, up until the time when Jewish Alexandrianism was eventually shaped'.[50] Especially regarding wisdom's central book, Proverbs, 'the fundamental ideas' are not loosely placed one beside the other but are 'profoundly connected and form a complete whole. Although at no point does it present itself in its full extent, it can be approximately reconstructed from its constituent elements, with varying degrees of dimness or clarity, as it probably once existed in the mind of the Hebrew wise men.' Taken together, all this adds up to a 'theory' which, despite its Hebrew character and without overpressing the similarity, 'recalls certain features of Greek philosophy', especially of Stoic ethics.[51] There is a fundamental difference, however, namely that the Greek wise men are searching for the world's absolute principle, whereas the Hebrew has already found it 'from the beginning in the sublime concept of God as formed by the religion of his ancestors'; in this respect his philosophy means 'religious philosophy on a supernatural foundation'.[52] As 'free reflection', however, it is 'more or less separated from the theocratic institutions and the legal cult of the nation, treating its historical traditions with a certain indifference'.[53]

Bruch's reflections met with broad approval,[54] though the final point was repeatedly attacked from the conservative quarter: in no way was wisdom opposed to law, priests and prophets; it was never independent of revelation; in Israel philosophy was completely absorbed by religion.[55] After all, even Davidson, who is opposed to the use of such terms as 'humanistic' or 'naturalistic', nevertheless finds in wisdom 'a line different from the main line of thought in Israel'.[56]

---

[47] J. F. Bruch, *Weisheits-Lehre der Hebräer* (Strasbourg, 1851), p. 381.

[48] *Ibid.*, pp. xiii–xiv.   [49] *Ibid.*, p. x.   [50] *Ibid.*, p. xii.   [51] *Ibid.*, pp. 152–3.

[52] *Ibid.*, pp. 60–1.   [53] *Ibid.*, p. 49.

[54] F. Hitzig is an exception in wishing to restrict the term philosophy to Ecclesiastes (*Der Prediger Salomo* [Leipzig, 1847], pp. 126–7).

[55] Delitzsch, *Salomonisches Spruchbuch*, p. 38; G. F. Oehler in several publications, lastly in *Theologie des Alten Testaments* (3rd edn, Stuttgart, 1891), pp. 862–4; E. Bertheau and W. Nowack, *Die Sprüche Salomo's*, p. xxxvii; cf. Umbreit, *Commentar*, p. l.

[56] *Enc. Brit.* 19, pp. 881–2.

In these debates, the theological position of the respective authors is quite often involved. This is inevitable when such a close connection of religious, philosophical and ethical questions is being treated (as is the case with wisdom), or at least when such a connection quickly develops in the course of its interpretation. In particular, what has been called the 'utilitarianism' of wisdom[57] has evoked much criticism from the theologians – naturally more from Protestants than from Catholics and from Germans more than from Anglo-Saxons. The first rallying-point for this criticism was Johannes Meinhold's *Die Weisheit Israels* (Leipzig, 1908), a comprehensive survey aimed at a wide public which tried to view wisdom as a perspective on the whole of Israelite religion. In this it differed decisively from the more concentrated and scholarly summary which T. K. Cheyne had presented two decades earlier, a summary which in a measure continued in the earlier tradition of Buddeus, though now at a new level of scholarship.[58] Meinhold has recently been credited with having been the first to recognize the separate existence of wisdom.[59] Although this is hardly accurate, Meinhold certainly introduced an acerbity into the discussion which was unusual up until that time. As a résumé of his runs, 'Wisdom offers us the thoughts of a typically middle-class morality whose only goal is one's own happiness, one's own welfare, one's own contentedness – as if there were nothing superior to that, as if to make others happy did not far exceed being happy oneself, as if the great characters in world history ... had not brought much happiness to others simply by denying themselves a certain degree of happiness and sense of well-being.'[60]

In the light of the newly-won knowledge of ancient oriental wisdom and especially on the ground of a better theology, Walther Zimmerli[61] renewed this criticism a quarter of a century later and so initiated the extremely fruitful modern discussion of wisdom. Often unawares, this debate has repeated much of that of the nineteenth century, not all of which could be covered in the present survey (for example, whether there were schools in ancient Israel or not,[62] and whether the proverbs which have reached us were shaped more by folk-tradition or by artistry[63]). Sometimes the

---

[57] Cf., e.g., Driver, *Introduction*, p. 369.   [58] See p. 258, n. 2.
[59] J. L. Crenshaw, in J. L. Crenshaw (ed.), *Studies in Ancient Israelite Wisdom* (New York, 1976), p. 3.   [60] Meinhold, *Die Weisheit Israels*, pp. 138–9.
[61] 'Zur Struktur der alttestamentlichen Weisheit', *ZAW* 51 (1933), pp. 177–204.
[62] A positive position on this issue was adopted by, e.g., H. Ewald, *Jahrbücher der Biblischen wissenschaft* 1 (1848), p. 97, followed by Delitzsch, *Salomonisches Spruchbuch* (above, p. 260, n. 14), pp. 33–4, and a negative one by Bruch, *Weisheits-Lehre*, pp. 57–8.
[63] Two more randomly selected opinions, which concern Prov. x 1–xxii 16 and xxv–xxix, are that they are 'folk sayings in their most original form' (so K. Budde, *Geschichte der althebräischen Litteratur* [2nd edn, Leipzig, 1909], p. 295) and that they are 'not folk sayings [...] but artistic poetry with a pedagogical aim' (so R. Smend, *Lehrbuch der alttestamentlichen Religionsgeschichte*, p. 483, n. 2).

positions adopted have been maintained even more rigidly than in the nineteenth century, whereas at other times it has turned out that the state of our sources does not allow us to go beyond an *Ignoramus* and that things are not always so polarized as they were initially believed to be; this applies to the subject of the theological criticism, on which even W. Zimmerli did not maintain his 1933 position unchanged. Thus the great Abraham Kuenen's statement remains true: 'How strongly does such a phenomenon as the *chokmah* confirm the truth of Renan's remark: "la vérité est dans les nuances"!'[64]

[64] A. Kuenen, *De Godsdienst van Israël*, 1 (Haarlem, 1869), p. 390 (E. tr., *The Religion of Israel* [London and Edinburgh, 1882], p. 389).

23   Wisdom and Old Testament theology

R. E. Clements

It is a significant feature of the influential work of Gerhard von Rad that his attention to the role of wisdom in the growth of the biblical tradition emerged after the completion of his *magnum opus* on Old Testament theology.[1] This phenomenon reflects a wider characteristic of the manner in which the many and varied attempts to construct an Old Testament theology have developed during the twentieth century, usually with relatively minor attention being given to the wisdom tradition. Since 1970, however, when von Rad published a stimulating study of the Israelite wisdom tradition,[2] the interest in it among scholars has grown immeasurably. This has not simply been a direct consequence of von Rad's attention to the subject, but is a reflection of the profound change of perception regarding the origin and nature of the wisdom tradition which was already in process. From being regarded as an aberrant offshoot of the mainstream of Israelite-Jewish religious life, it has increasingly been claimed as its most profoundly intellectual dimension, and consequently one that has primary interest for Old Testament and biblical theology.

Wisdom and the structure of Old Testament theology

Clearly part of the difficulty lies with the lack of any agreement on the question where the centre, and consequently the structural shape, of an Old Testament theology is to be found.[3] From a rigidly canonical perspective it might appear that since all the wisdom literature is to be found in the third, and consequently least authoritative, division of the Hebrew canon, its role

[1] G. von Rad, *Theologie des Alten Testaments*, 1–2 (Munich, 1957, 1960) (E. tr., *Old Testament Theology*, 1–2 [Edinburgh, 1962, 1965]).
[2] G. von Rad, *Weisheit in Israel* (Neukirchen-Vluyn, 1970) (E. tr., *Wisdom in Israel* [London, 1972]).
[3] G. F. Hasel, *Old Testament Theology. Basic Issues in the Current Debate* (4th edn, Grand Rapids, 1991); H. Graf Reventlow, *Problems of Old Testament Theology in the Twentieth Century* (London, 1985); cf. also G. F. Hasel, in B. C. Ollenburger, E. A. Martens, G. F. Hasel (eds.), *The Flowering of Old Testament Theology* (Winona Lake, 1992), pp. 373–83.

269

within a theology must inevitably be a minor one. If the structure of the canon is therefore made into a formative consideration of how an Old Testament theology should be presented,[4] then necessarily wisdom would appear to lie at its margins.

Similarly, von Rad's emphasis upon the *heilsgeschichtliche* nature of Israelite theological thinking[5] would appear to require that wisdom should be regarded more as a response to perceptions of the divine saving activity than as belonging to the central thrust of Israelite religious thought. W. Eichrodt's earlier use of the idea of covenant to provide a centre for an Old Testament theology[6] inevitably led to a similar result, although by a somewhat different route. So whether canon, saving history or covenant is taken as the central structuring concept for Old Testament theology,[7] wisdom is forced to appear at the periphery rather than at the centre. Probably very much the same result would accrue if the idea of God were given the central role; nor would the situation be significantly different if the concept of *torah* were placed at the heart of such a theology, as would seem to be essential for the idea of a *Tanakh* theology.[8] All such approaches which tend towards the theological marginalizing of wisdom result from the fact that the wisdom tradition appears to have been highly distinctive within the development of Israelite-Jewish religion and to have given rise to writings that inevitably retain the marks of this distinctiveness.

The would-be biblical theologian is then left to pursue a rather defensive line over the wisdom writings in order to explain their presence in the canon, or to suggest, with considerable plausibility, that the actual influence of wisdom was more pervasive and widespread than at first appears. So, not only in formal wisdom teaching, but in the historical

---

[4] B. S. Childs, *Old Testament Theology in a Canonical Context* (London, 1985), pp. 204–21, and *Biblical Theology in a Canonical Context* (London, 1992); A. H. J. Gunneweg, *Vom Verstehen des Alten Testaments. Eine Hermeneutik* (Göttingen, 1977) (E. tr., *Understanding the Old Testament* [London, 1978]); M. Oeming, *Gesamt biblische Theologien der Gegenwart* (2nd edn, Stuttgart, 1987).   [5] G. von Rad, *Theologie des Alten Testaments*, 1, *passim*.
[6] W. Eichrodt, *Theologie des Alten Testaments*, 1–2 (5th edn, Göttingen, 1960, 1964) (E. tr., *Theology of the Old Testament* [London, 1961, 1967]).
[7] Reventlow, *Problems of Old Testament Theology in the Twentieth Century*, pp. 187–9; Hasel, *Old Testament Theology*, p. 65; cf. also J. Høgenhaven, *Problems and Prospects of Old Testament Theology* (Sheffield, 1988), pp. 98–102.
[8] Gunneweg, *Vom Verstehen des AT*, pp. 42–84 (E. tr., pp. 43–95); cf. O. Kaiser, 'The Law as the Center of the Hebrew Bible', in M. Fishbane *et al.* (eds.), *Sha'arei Talmon. Studies in the Bible, Qumran and the Ancient Near East Presented to S. Talmon* (Winona Lake, 1992), pp. 93–103; R. E. Clements, 'Wisdom', in D. A. Carson and H. G. M. Williamson (eds.), *It is Written: Scripture Citing Scripture* (Cambridge, 1988), pp. 67–83; J. Levenson, 'Why Jews Are Not Interested in Biblical Theology', in J. Neusner *et al.* (eds.), *Judaic Perspectives on Ancient Israel* (Philadelphia, 1987), pp. 281–307.

literature,[9] certain of the prophets[10] and the developing concept of *torah*,[11] the subtle influence of wisdom methods and concepts has been traced.

However, over against such apologetic approaches markedly contrary conclusions have been argued,[12] based on the contention that the notion of God as Creator must be the formative, and co-ordinating, idea that holds together a biblical theology. Of all sections of the biblical literature it is the wisdom writings that give pride of place to the presupposition of a world shaped and governed by a single all-wise, all-seeing and all-powerful Creator.[13] If a religious universalism is placed in the central position, then a similar conclusion should probably obtain, since wisdom addresses its appeal to human beings as such, without regard for ethnic, political or social affiliation. Other possibilities can also be entertained, for instance if theodicy is given a central place as a concern to integrate religious thinking with the realities of the experienced world.

Most of these aspects concerning the problem of achieving a satisfactory understanding of the place that should be allocated to wisdom in an Old Testament theology have been carefully discussed, but without leading to any very widely recognized consensus. Scholars most directly concerned with the structure of an Old Testament theology find wisdom to be a rather errant child.[14] On the other side those most directly interested with the ideas of Israelite-Jewish wisdom find within it exciting, and previously unrecognized, riches which have a strong theological relevance.[15] Most especially they find it to be a tradition which endeavoured to grapple intellectually with the problems of religion, with its institutional structures

[9] D. F. Morgan, *Wisdom in the Old Testament Traditions* (Oxford, 1981) pp. 45–62; cf. J. L. Crenshaw, 'Method in Determining Wisdom Influence upon Historical Literature', *JBL* 88 (1969), pp. 129–42 (reprinted in J. L. Crenshaw [ed.], *Studies in Ancient Israelite Wisdom* [New York, 1976], pp. 481–94); R. N. Whybray, *The Succession Narrative* (London, 1968).

[10] H. W. Wolff, *Amos' geistige Heimat* (Neukirchen-Vluyn, 1964) (E. tr., *Amos the Prophet* [Philadelphia, 1973]); J. W. Whedbee, *Isaiah and Wisdom* (Nashville, 1971); cf. also D. F. Morgan, *Wisdom in the Old Testament Traditions*, pp. 63–93.

[11] M. Weinfeld, *Deuteronomy and the Deuteronomic School* (Oxford, 1972), pp. 244–319; H. Gese, 'Das Gesetz', *Zur biblischen Theologie: Alttestamentliche Vorträge* (2nd edn, Tübingen, 1982), pp. 55–84.

[12] H. H. Schmid, 'Schöpfung, Gerechtigkeit und Heil', *ZThK* 70 (1973), pp. 1–19 (= *Altorientalische Welt in der Alttestamentlichen Theologie* [Zürich, 1974], pp. 9–30; E. tr., 'Creation, Righteousness and Salvation: "Creation Theology" as the Broad Horizon of Biblical Theology', in B. W. Anderson [ed.], *Creation in the Old Testament* [London, 1984], pp. 102–17); J. J. Collins, 'The Biblical Precedent for Natural Theology', *JAAR* 45 (Supplement B; 1977), pp. 35–67; J. Barr, *Biblical Faith and Natural Theology* (Oxford, 1993), pp. 81–101.

[13] C. Westermann, *Theologie des Alten Testaments in Grundzügen* (Göttingen, 1978), pp. 85–6.

[14] Cf. R. K. Johnston, 'Images for Today: Learning from Old Testament Wisdom', in R. L. Hubbard *et al.* (eds.), *Studies in Old Testament Theology* (Dallas, 1992), pp. 223–39.

[15] L. Boström, *The God of the Sages. The Portrayal of God in the Book of Proverbs* (Stockholm, 1990); cf. R. E. Clements, *Wisdom in Theology* (Grand Rapids, 1993), p. 15.

and strange complex symbolism, and to submit this to serious critical examination.

The most significant point would appear to be that the diversity of current opinions about the place of wisdom in an Old Testament theology reflects in the first instance the undoubted fact that a great variety of answers exist to the question of what constitutes such an Old Testament, or biblical, theology. These varied answers have made the subject a controversial, and often very confusing, one. It seems to be a construction from the Hebrew Bible that we cannot do without, even though it has enjoyed only very limited acceptance within Judaism, and yet one where it is openly debated what exactly its methods are, and even whether it should properly exist at all.[16]

Simply surveying the options that exist for the enquiring mind to consider, or choosing to defend one standpoint to the exclusion of others, would appear at the current state of research to offer no real advance. Nor should we be deterred, or discouraged, by the lack of clearly defined conclusions, since theology itself is not an exact science. In many respects the fundamental dilemma that has persistently beset all attempts to construct an Old Testament theology is that of choosing between a rigidly historical and descriptive approach and one that is more evaluative, more open to an awareness of the hermeneutical uses to which the Hebrew Bible has been put in Jewish and Christian tradition, and one which views theology itself as a reflective and monitoring discipline. Religion, as a human phenomenon, is very much more than the sum of its ideas. Although these may give shape and direction to religious developments, they do not do so in a historical and social vacuum.

Viewed against such a background, we may argue for the creative theological importance of wisdom as a feature of ancient Israelite and Jewish life, without insisting that, from a historical point of view, this was consistently maintained in biblical times or that it received well-defined official approbation. Wisdom appears to have risen in influence at a particular time and then to have fallen from favour, leaving its mark only on the fringes of the canonical literature, whether viewed as *Tanakh*, or as a Christian *Old* Testament. Its strongly marked presence in the Old Testament Apocrypha further endorses the sense that an ambivalent attitude existed towards wisdom in the historical development of the biblical canon.

---

[16] Cf. R. N. Whybray, 'Old Testament Theology – a Non-existent Beast?', in B. P. Thompson (ed.), *Scripture: Meaning and Method. Essays Presented to A. T. Hanson* (Hull, 1987), pp. 168–80.

Wisdom and a comprehensive world-view

It may be helpful to reiterate and summarize conclusions about the rise and development of the Israelite wisdom tradition already published in my book *Wisdom in Theology*.[17] These are that wisdom entered into Israel at an early period in a relatively restricted role as an intellectual tradition encouraged and fostered at the royal court. Consequently it had close links to ideas of monarchy and the state, possessed a functional usefulness in promoting education for administration and made full use of the skills of literacy. That an even older tradition of folk wisdom existed, and that elements from this came to be drawn into the more sophisticated world of the royal court, need not be doubted. With the weakening of Israelite central government after 587 BC, the ending of the monarchy and the growth of a Jewish life in dispersion, the wisdom tradition enjoyed a new popularity and usefulness. Two factors contributed greatly to this: in the first place its original educational role was further enhanced by the increased need for instruction in the basic attitudes and demands made by belonging to a Jewish community in a predominantly Gentile world and worshipping the Lord as sole deity. Secondly, wisdom's lack of national covenantal presuppositions enabled it to serve as an internal apologetic to Jews and as a non-national basis for religiously motivated moral teaching of a high order. The fear of the Lord became readily identified with the way of wisdom!

We may give our attention to a number of the features which have made wisdom appear to be a difficult, and largely aberrant, tradition within the mainstream of Israelite and Jewish religious development. Right at the heart of these difficulties we must place consideration of the very nature of religion itself and, in particular, of the role that conceptual and ideological factors occupy in it. It belongs to the legacy of the strongly idealist interpretations of religion in the nineteenth century that theological expositions of the Old Testament have leaned heavily upon assumptions that religious rites, institutions and mythology stem from ideological attempts to conceptualize the nature of reality. On such an understanding ideas lie at the heart of religion and need to be looked for underneath its surface. Yet is this really so? More functional anthropological approaches have doubted this, and the remarkable facility with which old religious rites and institutions may be revitalized by the incorporation of new ideas fully bears out the rightness of such doubts. Ideas seem often to fulfil a monitoring, apologetic and systematizing rôle in the growth of religion.

[17] R. E. Clements, *Wisdom in Theology*, pp. 13–39.

Attempts to combine aspects of both older idealist and more recent functionalist approaches, by focussing on experience of the divine as an 'Elusive Presence'[18] are valuable, but end up lumping together too many disparate features and ideas under the umbrella of a very loosely defined abstraction. The use by scholars of the notion of 'Providence' to affirm a divine purpose giving shape and meaning to human experience and history has fared little better. All such abstractions remain too remote from the realities of the religion to which they are applied, and are too all-inclusive to help in understanding the sharp antipathies and conflicts which characterize the actual historical development of biblical religion. Nonetheless they do draw attention to the fact that ancient Israelite religion not only conveyed implicit ideological positions in its narrative traditions, but was built up around a complex symbolism of sanctuaries, rituals and mythology, which it inherited from the ancient near east and shaped in a highly distinctive way.

It is on this front that the contribution of wisdom would appear to have been particularly important, since, in spite of diverse, and originally extra-Israelite, origins, wisdom exercised a critical, monitoring and redefining rôle on the Israelite religious tradition. When the older cultic world-view, centred on the Jerusalem temple cultus, was challenged and partly discredited by the disastrous events of the temple's destruction by the Babylonians, then wisdom appeared as a useful tool to assist in the construction of a new one. This was less directly tied up to priestly institutions, and more open to a wider non-sacramental understanding of religion. In terms of a Weberian sociology of religion it contributed to its demystification.[19]

Against such a background of religious and intellectual development we can best understand the creative rôle fulfilled by wisdom in the formation of biblical theological ideas. Wisdom helped to 'theologize' the religious inheritance of ancient Israel by promoting the rationalizing and systematizing of cult symbolism and mythology and by spiritualizing many of its concepts.[20] The worshipper's attitude of mind and intention came to be accounted more important than actual performance of ritual. Fundamental abstract notions such as 'the fear of the Lord' and 'the way of wisdom' were used to co-ordinate and integrate a variety of inherited traditions. All of this took place under the broad conviction that a wise order prevailed throughout the experienced universe. Human beings therefore had to understand this order, relate their own activities to it and seek to uphold

---

[18] S. Terrien, *The Elusive Presence. Toward a New Biblical Theology* (San Francisco, 1978); cf. also, 'Presence in Absence', in B. C. Ollenburger, E. A. Martens, G. F. Hasel (eds.), *The Flowering of Old Testament Theology* (Winona Lake, 1992), pp. 254–76.

[19] Cf. M. Albrow, *Max Weber's Construction of Social Theory* (Basingstoke, 1990), pp. 60, 112.

[20] H.-J. Hermisson, *Sprache und Ritus im altisraelitischen Kult: zur 'Spiritualisierung' der Kultbegriffe im Alten Testament* (Neukirchen-Vluyn, 1965).

and preserve it. The 'natural' order of life was taken to reveal the mind of a single beneficent Creator.

Accordingly, notions of 'design' and 'purpose' obtrude prominently in the literature left by the sapientialists, demonstrating their intense concern with the cause and consequences of all life's activities. They could ultimately ask the most comprehensive of questions about what was the 'purpose' (Heb. *yitrôn* = gain, advantage, accrued benefit) of any person's life (Eccles. i 3, ii 11, 13, etc.).[21] Because of the high place accorded to human beings in the scheme of things, the need to see each individual human life as part of the much wider context of the natural world occupies a significant place in the wisdom tradition. Consequently it is this tradition that has contributed extensively to the Bible's doctrine of creation, displacing the inherent dualism of the older, cultically rooted, mythology of creation through conflict.[22]

Important as this doctrine of creation is, it needs to be linked to the process of humanizing and rationalizing the understanding of the world as a place of beneficent forces with which human beings can co-operate. Creation, as understood by the wise, implies a friendly, and truly providential, world order. In this the broad concepts of space and time, which had been given fundamental shape through the mythology of the cult, were also plucked from their cultic setting and refashioned in a non-sacramental form. The further repercussions of this altered world-view made wisdom a serious challenge to the magical, and quasi-magical, ideas which constantly hovered around the cult. Wisdom encouraged religion to be less mysterious, less prone to relapse into magic, less submissive to the fear of mysterious powers and forces which lay beyond the range of human control. In other words, the fundamental thrust of wisdom was to make Israelite religion more rational, and less dominated by fears of demonic powers, non-moral uncleanness and even of a holiness that could kill. On this front of the creation of a biblical world-view wisdom played a major rôle in shaping the prevailing features of Israelite-Jewish religious thinking.

Wisdom and the Hebrew canon

More negatively we need to recognize that, in shaping the fundamental literary form of the Old Testament canon, the contribution made by wisdom appears to have been very much more limited and constrained. This is inseparable from the fact that the characteristic literary form of this

---

[21] Cf. G. S. Ogden, *Qoheleth* (Sheffield, 1987), pp. 22–6.
[22] Cf. M. K. Wakeman, *God's Battle with the Monster. A Study in Biblical Imagery* (Leiden, 1973); J. Day, *God's Conflict with the Dragon and the Sea: Echoes of a Canaanite Myth in the Old Testament* (Cambridge, 1985).

literature is that of narrative, usually with a distinctly historical content. Somewhat surprisingly this historical narrative prevails even in the promulgation of codes of civil law and lists of cultic regulations. As a consequence biblical theology has felt compelled, if it is to be true to the nature of the biblical literature, to be a narrative theology. With few exceptions, the major legal, cultic and didactic lists of ancient Israel are given a historical setting by being placed within such a narrative context. It is especially noteworthy that more than a century of biblical theological enterprise sought to make use of this narrative form by interpreting its theology as a 'History of Salvation'.[23] The work of G. von Rad, in particular, represents a culmination of a range of attempts to come to terms with this 'History of Salvation' form.[24] Virtually an entire generation of efforts to prepare an Old Testament theology bounced to and fro between commitment to the actual history that is believed to undergird this, and concentration instead on the narrative form, as expressive merely of a history-like reality.

Yet the wisdom tradition displays only a very limited use of narrative form, usually in the shape of parables, allegories, or short didactic tales. The longer connected histories, which form the structural core of both the Pentateuchal and the Prophetic literature, are not narrowly sapiential in character, even though they were originally themselves dependent on a courtly scribal tradition. These histories, some of them based on official chronicles and others built around a thematic 'plot', have established their own literary and theological conventions.

In a contrasting manner, the teaching of wisdom is often anonymous and usually lacks specific historical context. It aims to teach timeless truths. Similarly, it is seldom made specific in its applicability to differing classes, or levels, of the human community. It is addressed to human beings in their wide ethnic, social and personal variety, living together in households, cities and nations. These are the significant social contexts in which the individual is assumed to encounter life's demands most directly and responsibly. Seen against this background of the narrative form of the major part of the Hebrew Bible, wisdom's rôle can only be adjudged to have been marginal, and contrasting, in its character. It served to shape and illuminate the component elements of the biblical narrative texts, without being able to dominate any of them.

In any concern to relate the theology of the Hebrew Bible closely to its canonical shape, then, it must necessarily seem that the contribution made

---

[23] Cf. J. Barr, *Old and New in Interpretation. A Study of the Two Testaments* (London, 1966), pp. 65–102.

[24] Cf. J. W. Groves, *Actualization and Interpretation in the Old Testament* (Atlanta, 1987), pp. 7–62.

by wisdom was secondary and derivative, rather than fundamental. However, the situation on this front begins to look rather different once we turn our attention away from the origins of the biblical literature to consider its final shape. G. T. Sheppard has shown how very significant was the rôle played by wisdom in the provision of hermeneutical techniques by means of which biblical traditions could be harmonized and new interpretations devised.[25] In a number of ways wisdom served to circumvent the limitations imposed by the biblical literature's literary and historical specificity. The truths of God's actions towards Israel could be raised to the level of examples and paradigms. Israel's heroes could be made into examples of faith and virtue, as in the celebrated hymn of Ben Sira in praise of many of the central figures of the narrative traditions (Ecclus xliv 1–xlix 16). Nor should we leave out of reckoning the extent to which wisdom's techniques of listing, comparison and classifying provided a means whereby many of the most influential characteristics of inner-biblical exegesis were formed.

It is not surprising that this should have been the case in regard to legal formulations and historical chronicles. Yet, in many respects it becomes most marked when we look closely at the way in which a prophetic literature has been formed out of a large, and originally essentially shapeless, series of anthologies of prophetic utterances. By techniques of what M. Fishbane has called 'mantological exegesis' a complex corpus of prophetic books was formed.[26] It is true that these could still be interpreted simply as collections of individual 'oracles',[27] yet increasingly it has become clear that all four of the major prophetic scrolls of the Hebrew Bible were edited into skilfully planned wholes. In these final scroll forms the poetic and interpretative skills which served to link together what were often isolated and distinct utterances have drawn heavily from the well of wisdom. The transition from spoken prophecy to written prophetic scrolls certainly owes much to the techniques and classifying skills of wisdom.

So we may argue that wisdom furnished the canon of the Hebrew Bible with an important hermeneutical device by means of which diverse, and sometimes conflicting, traditions could be harmonized.

If we carry this recognition a stage further to ask about the rôle of the Old Testament in a more comprehensive biblical theology, then it would seem that wisdom was quite exceptionally important. The way in which the New Testament develops, criticizes and uses the Hebrew Bible which it inherited

---

[25] G. T. Sheppard, *Wisdom as a Hermeneutical Construct* (Berlin and New York, 1974).

[26] M. Fishbane, *Biblical Interpretation in Ancient Israel* (Oxford, 1985), pp. 458–99.

[27] Cf. J. Barton, *Oracles of God: Perceptions of Ancient Prophecy in Israel after the Exile* (London, 1986), pp. 179–213.

from Judaism has occasioned an ongoing debate.[28] Whether to dismiss it as an outdated, and essentially flawed, form of apologetic, or whether to see it as an indispensable and constitutive part of both New Testament and Biblical theology, are two contrasting conclusions that may be drawn. Whichever side we favour there can be no doubt that it is the hermeneutical techniques nurtured by the wisdom tradition that have contributed substantially to the patterns of interpretation by which the New Testament appropriates the Old. It is even arguable that the comprehensive, if inconclusive, evaluation of the Hebrew Scriptures as constituting an 'Old' Testament reflects both the strength and the weakness of wisdom's hermeneutical usefulness. It could update, modify and reshape the Hebrew tradition, but only within certain limitations which were established by the wider parameters of early Christian understanding of the centrality of Jesus Christ.

Wisdom, causation and retribution

The felt need to co-ordinate and explain the varied phenomena of life, as they were actually perceived and experienced, led the wise to a preoccupation with questions of causation. It was an inevitable question to be asked on the basis of belief in a single all-wise Creator: 'Why are things the way they are?' Everything may be assumed to have a purpose and therefore to fulfil some specific rôle, or function, in the divinely planned scheme of things. Such assumptions could even be employed with a slightly cynical touch of humour. Even the wicked are created for their appropriate punishment (cf. Prov. xvi 4). It is in the light of this interest in the causes of things that we can understand how ideas of retribution drew the special attention of the sages.[29] Just as the exertion of physical pressure upon an object achieves a result, so, similarly, the exercise of will in the field of conduct achieves a good or bad result. It is this belief in a connected world of causation, prevailing everywhere, that lends special interest to the celebrated application

---

[28] The literature is extensive, but useful summary treatments are to be found in D. Moody Smith, 'The Use of the Old Testament in the New', in J. M. Efird (ed.), *The Use of the Old Testament in the New and Other Essays. Studies in Honor of William Franklin Stinespring* (Durham, N.C., 1972), pp. 3–65; R. Longenecker, *Biblical Exegesis in the Apostolic Period* (Grand Rapids, 1975); D. A. Carson and H. G. M. Williamson (eds.), *It is Written: Scripture Citing Scripture*, pp. 193–336. Broader issues concerning the relationship between the two Testaments are discussed in B. W. Anderson (ed.), *The Old Testament and Christian Faith. A Theological Discussion* (New York, 1969); D. L. Baker, *Two Testaments, One Bible* (2nd edn, Leicester, 1991).

[29] Cf. K. Koch, 'Gibt es ein Vergeltungsdogma im Alten Testament?', *ZThK* 52 (1955), pp. 1–42 (reprinted in *Um das Prinzip der Vergeltung in Religion und Recht des Alten Testaments* [Darmstadt, 1972], pp. 130–80; E. tr., 'Is There a Doctrine of Retribution in the Old Testament?', in J. L. Crenshaw [ed.], *Theodicy in the Old Testament* [London, 1983], pp. 57–87); H. Graf Reventlow, *Rechtfertigung im Horizont des Alten Testaments* (Munich, 1971), pp. 41–66; L. Boström, *The God of the Sages*, pp. 90–135.

by the wise of the laws of motion to the moral realm (Prov. xxvi 27).

Yet here we find the greatest level of inconsistency, since such sayings leave too much unsaid about the nature of moral evil. Will the result come about automatically? Will God intervene to bring it about? Will some human agency (? the elders of the community) have to step in in order to bring the wrongdoer to book? By drawing upon related sayings we could find support for believing that any, or all, of these three possibilities could be regarded as necessary in different circumstances.

From a general review of the evidence it becomes clear that 'making the punishment fit the crime' is very much a theoretical and ideal state of affairs. It is asserted by the proponents of wisdom, seemingly with bland over-confidence, that wrongdoing always gets its deserts and that the wicked come to a deservedly bad end. Several sayings of the wise make such affirmations sound as though the certainty of such desirable consequences were the outworking of a natural law.

The moral order is assumed to have been divinely planned, unchanging and divinely preserved by whatever temporary adjustments may prove to be necessary. Yet it is usually left unclear how this desirable state of affairs in the preservation of a just order is to be brought about. Sometimes God is said to intervene directly to ensure that it happens; at other times it is made to appear as though wickedness unleashes destructive forces which inevitably bring retribution on the wrongdoer. Quite often it is simply left indeterminate how it will come about. This makes it something of a puzzle to know how far the wise intended to encourage direct human action, either with or without appeal to public legal support, in order to execute redress for wrongs suffered. Something of an unresolved tension remains, since the wise insist upon the given, inescapable nature of the moral realm, yet do so with a deep sense of urgency in exhorting popular implementation of its rules and demands by training and punishment when necessary.

All these considerations raise the question of the extent to which the biblical wisdom tradition was concerned to promote a humanistic, not to say secular, interpretation of life. Yet Boström[30] argues convincingly that the Israelite wisdom tradition cannot properly be described as secular. It presumes too heavily upon the reality and interrelationships of a divine order for such terminology to be appropriate. At most it could be claimed that the wisdom assumptions concerning a natural and moral order to the world have interposed a certain distance between it and God. Certainly, too, wisdom stands at some distance from the more formal world of the cult. It appears often to recast and reshape cultic terminology and ideas, as though in a conscious desire to offer an alternative interpretation of God's

[30] L. Boström, *The God of the Sages*, pp. 37, 136.

actions in the world from the mythological world-view of the cult. So we find that cultic language concerning holiness appears only in a very restrained manner, although the cult is taken unquestioningly to be a proper part of the order of life (so especially in Eccles. iv 17–v 4 [v 1–5]). Certainly, the belief that bad consequences stem from bad actions is uppermost in wisdom's armoury of hortatory devices. Even this, however, can best be phrased more accurately to affirm a character-consequence relationship,[31] since wisdom is concerned to demonstrate that it is the nurturing of bad attitudes to form bad characters which leads to inevitable evil actions and ultimate ruin.

Wisdom's rôle in theology

The fact that there are still significant disagreements among scholars about the rôle played by wisdom in Israelite life, even as to whether it was a major, and broadly based, one, or one that was restricted to a small section of the community, has added to the difficulties in determining its theological importance. Furthermore, it is not clear to what extent the book of Job can properly be classified as a wisdom document at all, nor how far the little book of Ecclesiastes represents an idiosyncratic and highly personal achievement deriving from a single author, or whether it reflects more enduring trends of the mainstream wisdom tradition.

Yet all this points us to recognize that wisdom, both in its earlier and later forms, did not possess any wholly rounded body of doctrines. Rather, it points us to see it as a method of enquiry, a use of particular forms of teaching, and a desire to compare and co-ordinate phenomena, instead of a formally stated set of propositions. It may be classified basically as a passion for education, originally rather limited and élitist in its scope, but later broadening out to become a more popular, and largely domesticated, concern for instruction.

It appears to have depended heavily on certain basic assumptions regarding the existence of an order that needs to be observed, and which sought to integrate varying spheres of human activity – economic, social and political – into a comprehensive picture of a realm of a created design. It perceives moral demands to be founded on natural 'laws', which its proponents believe will quickly approve themselves to the honestly enquiring mind. Yet at the same time it appears to recognize that such 'laws' will not be recognized where the fundamental disposition provided by the 'fear of the Lord' is lacking. Where 'folly' prevails, human beings will fail to see the truth of wisdom's teaching. Good didactic intentions appear

[31] Cf. *ibid.*, p. 138.

to become mixed in with honest empirical observations which do not always support the original aim. Where persons align themselves with violence and wickedness, then all the teachings of wisdom will not evoke compliance and conviction.

In this setting it is evident that wisdom attached the greatest importance to the need to adopt a right attitude to life in general, based on a religious commitment. This needed to be backed up by a willingness to listen to, and heed, the teaching of the individual's parents, who are assumed to recognize and approve of this religious respect. Over against this fundamental religious regard all other teaching could have only a secondary impact. In line with this, even very basic moral duties are traced back to the adoption of such a right fundamental attitude, which alone can result in a positive and responsible outlook on life. So character formation through education is a primary concern of the wisdom tradition. When such considerations are pressed yet further, Ecclesiastes, in particular, ventures into the territory of calculating concepts of human happiness and contentment. This builds on the older wisdom concern to note the destructive consequences for an individual's wellbeing of psychological stress and suspicion, especially when it occurred directly within the individual's own household.[32]

Taken in a larger context, some useful observations may be made which have a bearing upon the role of wisdom in a biblical theology. The most obvious is that, in the post-exilic period, wisdom appears to have flourished as part of a programme of education carried out with the approval of, and probably within the location of, the individual household. Begin early, be persistent and, if necessary, do not shun physical punishment, in order to achieve results. These are seriously repeated maxims for instruction, aimed at parents, instructors and pupils. The very roots of religion and virtue are seen to rest within the relatively small household context of family life. The rewards of adherence to the dictates of wisdom are claimed to include security, prosperity and ultimately happiness. All of this indicates that religion is taken out of its cultic setting and is markedly domesticated. Parents, rather than priests, hold the key to its seriousness and success! Yet it is never secular in the formal sense, since it recognizes that, deprived of its religious foundations, it cannot succeed and will lack its indispensable starting-point.

Seen from this perspective wisdom contributed a great deal to the rise of the Jewish and Christian commitment to a sacred canon of scripture. This commitment functioned formatively by establishing the notion of a religious community built upon a sacred literature. 'The People of the

---

[32] Cf. R. E. Clements, *Wisdom in Theology*, p. 144.

Book' became the characteristic identifying feature of Jewish life, and this concept of a canon of scripture ensured that an appeal to the authority of its sacred writings became basic to early Christian apologetic. Yet this literary foundation for the formation and definition of religious communities was dependent upon notions of education and a universally applicable body of instruction which was nurtured outside the cultus and which wisdom helped to shape. Nor was its contribution in this direction a minor one, since wisdom directed the belief that a corpus of sacred writings provided an indispensable teaching tool in moulding the body of demands implicit in worshipping the Lord as God.

The assertion that 'the fear of the Lord' is the beginning of wisdom had important repercussions for cultic, economic and political life. Since it was the wisdom tradition which placed instruction in the home as fundamental to the upholding of a religion built upon *torah* (Deut. vi 7), the cultus was itself made subject to this more absolute authority of scripture. Neither priest nor prophet could usurp the authority of the *torah* which provided a given datum of belief. Furthermore, this written authority was something with which the individual was expected to be familiar from his, or her, earliest years. It encompassed the most basic, and elementary, of human duties and responsibilities.

So wisdom functioned formatively in shaping the literary dimension of Jewish faith. If theology is concerned to be truly biblical, therefore, it cannot ignore the extent to which wisdom contributed towards the elevation of what we can best describe as 'the scripture principle'. It served to make the Jewish sacred literature a basis for education. If, as I argued in a short study, the idea of the canon finds its earliest expression in Deuteronomy and the deuteronomic writings, then the combination of legal, prophetic and sapiential traditions which are woven into this must all be adequately recognized.[33]

If wisdom left an indelible mark on Judaism by making the educational rôle of literature a formative factor of its life, then a consequence of this must be seen in the way it has contributed to the understanding of the nature of *torah*. This feature of wisdom's contribution is especially significant when we examine the role of *torah* as the guiding component of the biblical tradition. In this area we no doubt enter the little-charted territory of biblical semiotics. Nevertheless, there are substantial reasons for accepting that the original roots of the concept of *torah*, as also the most basic understanding of the practice of 'the fear of the Lord', must be traced back to the ancient Israelite cultus.

The *torah* of the worship of the God Yahweh, as the practical definition

[33] R. E. Clements, *God's Chosen People* (London, 1968), pp. 89–105.

of how allegiance to this deity could be maintained, was originally an aspect of the cultus devoted to this end. The 'How?' and the 'Why?' of worshipping the Lord as God were originally traditions known exclusively to the priests who were its custodians and guardians. Yet this foundational cultic centre to the faith of Israel, and the world-view which it enshrined, came to be greatly modified in the course of Israelite-Jewish history. That it was so, owed a great deal to the influence of the wisdom tradition. If *torah* was initially a teaching relating to cultic activity, then wisdom broadened the understanding and functioning of it very greatly. *Torah* became education for a way of life, and no longer a narrow set of rules on how to worship the Lord as God.

The tensions, contrasts and interconnections between wisdom and cultus would therefore appear to be a major subject deserving of close attention. Valuable work has already been done in this field,[34] yet the full extent of the interplay between what were originally very distinct Israelite traditions has still not been adequately explored. Whenever we try to reconstruct an Israelite-Jewish 'world-view' we are faced with the differing assumptions and aims presented by the conflicting traditions of cult and wisdom. The sage takes a place alongside priest and prophet as a servant of religion, even though no priestly garb or cultic apprenticeship was demanded for the accomplishment of such a teaching rôle.

Wisdom, the origins of which lay outside the cultus, imposed major shifts of interpretation upon the priorities of religion. It served to establish a wider, and more open, context for the preservation, codification and teaching of *torah*. In its extant written form, as the central core of the Old Testament tradition, *torah* can most adequately be understood as a form of instruction. That it became so, and that it was open to be taught by lay persons in the home, would seem to have been especially a consequence of the degree to which the wisdom teachers encouraged a fundamentally altered understanding of it. The memorable axiom 'the fear of the Lord is the beginning of wisdom' became a remarkable two-sided programme. It altered the inherited variability and 'this-worldliness' of conventional wisdom axioms. At the same time it also altered irreversibly the ritualistic and priest-bound notions of religious *torah*. Had the Old Testament remained a purely cultically focussed religion, inseparable from the Jerusalem temple which formed its central home, it could never have developed into the Judaism which emerged among a people spread through

---

[34] Cf. G. von Rad, *Weisheit in Israel*, pp. 189–92 (E. tr., pp. 186–89); L. Perdue, *Wisdom and Cult. A Critical Analysis of the Views of Cult in the Wisdom Literatures of Israel and the Ancient Near East* (Missoula, 1977); R. Murphy, 'Religious Dimensions of Israelite Wisdom', in P. D. Miller, P. D. Hanson and S. D. McBride (eds.), *Ancient Israelite Religion. Essays in Honor of F. M. Cross, Jr.* (Philadelphia, 1987), pp. 449–58.

the Persian and Hellenistic worlds. Certainly it could not have given birth to the Christian tradition of the Roman era. The extent of wisdom's impact on the origin of the Christian tradition is now richly explored in A. E. Harvey's examination of the nature of the earliest Christian ethic.[35]

We may press this point somewhat further, since it is a striking feature of the later Jewish and Christian interpretation of *torah* that it was understood in some circles as a form of law (Greek *nomos*). Yet the educational context in which the written forms of *torah* first appeared with the deuteronomistic circle of authors and traditionists shows it clearly to have been understood as a collection of laws only in a very extended and much modified form. It was not a code of law, as Hammurabi's famous stone tablet existed as a code of law. Its legal and juridical content was only one aspect of a much wider-ranging presentation of guidance on what constituted the true knowledge of the Lord as God and the indispensable rules of life by which true worship could be expressed. From the perspective of the understanding of the nature of *torah*, therefore, it is arguable that the contribution made by the Israelite wisdom tradition was very influential. *Torah* could be understood as a corpus of wisdom and, conversely, there could be no true apprehension of wisdom without the religious dimension contributed by *torah*.

Wisdom and virtue

If we are correct in arguing that wisdom contributed a good deal towards showing how *torah* could be preserved and taught, then we may proceed further to claim that it also helped to shape the essential inwardness and moral intensity of Jewish piety. From earliest times it would appear that the biblical tradition was conscious of the confusion inherent in the wide number of concepts by which problems of conduct were controlled. Cultic notions of holiness were inseparable from concerns with hygiene. Adherence to the Lord as God also entailed the avoidance of contact with idolatry in daily life, thereby bringing concepts of taboo into considerations of daily conduct. Consequently the written *torah* was coloured by a vocabulary which sought to distinguish good from bad, clean from unclean, holy from profane, whole from imperfect. When to these complex ideas further concerns with legal concepts of justice were added, as well as social commitments to loyalty and faithfulness, we can see how confused was the mix of ideas which defined the nature of goodness. Both post-biblical Jewish writings, as well as the early Christian literature, are replete with examples and definitions which show how important was the need to

[35] A. E. Harvey, *Strenuous Commands. The Ethic of Jesus* (London, 1993).

establish priorities and to achieve some degree of harmonization over these issues.

From the perspective of a modern anthropologist it would appear that this was an inevitable legacy which Judaism and Christianity inherited from the ancient world in which their roots were planted. How could these varied concepts, each of which possessed its own world of emotional and intellectual responses, be harmonized and reconciled one to another? How could health be separated from morality, or food hygiene accommodated to the avoidance of idolatry? In some measure it was no doubt the existence of a written *torah*, whose pronouncements needed to be upheld, which generated the pressure for such harmonizations and evaluations. Yet it seems that it was especially the insights and reasonings of the wisdom teachers which provided the strongest level of guidance on such questions. In defining the nature of virtue and goodness, wisdom appears to have made possible so many of the conclusions which ultimately prevailed within Judaism and which were important to the beginnings of Christianity. The broad educational function of *torah* overruled the older cultic, and taboo-ridden, assumptions of the cultus.

Both in Jewish and Christian tradition, even with all their many divergences and distinctions, the close interlocking of religion and morality has become a paramount feature of the legacy of the Hebrew Bible. That this was so, must surely be credited in no small degree to the way in which the Jewish wisdom tradition sought out reasonings and arguments by which disparate features of life could be harmonized and seen as part of a larger world order. The integration of rules of behaviour and the demythologizing of the concept of evil, divesting it of its demonic and arbitrary elements, were no small achievements on the part of Jewish sages.

In the pursuit of adequate and consistent interpretations of the nature of good behaviour, it is significant that it appears to have been especially a feature of the wisdom movement to have focussed on the issue of intentionality. Even though Hebrew anthropology lacks any very exact counterpart to the concept of the 'will', the idea that it expresses is certainly strongly present. Probably the notion of the 'spirit' (Heb. *rûaḥ*) comes closest to it.[36] In view of the extent to which such a notion came to dominate mediaeval ideas of conduct and wrongdoing, it is worthwhile reflecting upon the emphasis which the sages placed upon it. The condemnation of evil plans and schemes, the dangers of human dissimulation and deceit, and the virtue of good intentions, are strongly present in proverbial instruction. Human beings are to be judged by the quality and sincerity of their intentions.

[36] H. W. Wolff, *Anthropologie des Alten Testaments* (Munich, 1973), pp. 57–67 (E. tr., *Anthropology of the Old Testament* [London, 1974], pp. 32–9).

All this suggests that, even if it is exceeding the evidence to claim that it was the wisdom movement which originated the strongly ethical concerns of Israelite-Jewish religious faith, nevertheless it was this movement which served prominently to work out its ramifications. Wisdom provided an agenda for reflection and rational apprehension of a wide range of behavioural issues. It demanded that priorities be established, if confusion and uncertainty were not to prevail. It pressed for harmonizations and concessions where conflicts of tradition emerged. It looked for larger goals than the mere implementation of conventional rules and the reinforcement of established prejudices.

This led it to raise questions about the rôle of goodness in promoting human happiness; it prompted questions about the ultimate meaning and goal of life. It investigated and questioned assumptions about the goodness of the world order and the design and purpose of its Creator. Although there remained a noteworthy speculative side to some features of the wisdom tradition, it remains its shunning of over-speculative imagery and ideas that marks its most enduring contribution to theology.

In the present day there has been a notable resurgence of irrationality in religion, with a resort to a new fundamentalism in many Protestant circles. Alongside this, and rather oddly coupled to it, has appeared a powerful emphasis upon charismatic phenomena and forms of worship. Although Jewish thought never produced a proper classification of rationality, as was to emerge in Greek philosophy, yet wisdom encouraged a staunchly rationalizing critique of religion. By embracing goals of explanation, harmonization and a focussing of attention upon cause-consequence relationships, it sought to draw religious activity under the umbrella of a wider social and conceptual framework. Without resorting to a narrow secularism, it nevertheless promoted a healthy humanizing and practicality to the intellectual aspects of religious faith. In the contemporary scene where the boundaries between theology, ethics and sociology are constantly being crossed, the Israelite-Jewish wisdom tradition provides a valuable reminder that the Bible itself offers important foundations for this intellectual adventure.

Biographical note: John Adney Emerton

1928	5th June. Born in Winchmore Hill, North London.
1939–46	Educated at Minchenden Grammar School, Southgate.
1947	Admitted to Corpus Christi College, Oxford.
1950	BA (Oxon.), First Class, Theology.
	Canon Hall Junior Greek Testament Prize.
	Liddon Student.
	Admitted to Wycliffe Hall, Oxford.
1951	Hall-Houghton Junior Septuagint Prize.
1952	First Class, Oriental Studies.
	Kennicott Hebrew Fellow.
	Deacon.
1952–3	Assistant Lecturer in Theology, Birmingham University, and Curate of Birmingham Cathedral.
1953	Houghton Syriac Prize.
	Priest.
1953–5	Lecturer in Hebrew and Aramaic, Durham University.
1954	Hall-Houghton Senior Septuagint Prize.
	MA (Oxon.).
1955	MA (Cantab.) by Incorporation, Corpus Christi College, Cambridge.
1955–62	Lecturer in Divinity, Cambridge University.
1960	BD (Cantab.).
	Visiting Professor of Old Testament and Near Eastern Studies, Trinity College, Toronto University.
1962	Select Preacher before University of Cambridge.
1962–8	Reader in Semitic Philology, Oxford University, and Fellow of St Peter's College, Oxford.
1968–95	Regius Professor of Hebrew, Cambridge University.
1970–	Fellow of St John's College, Cambridge.
1971	Select Preacher before University of Cambridge.
1971–89	Secretary, International Organization for the Study of the Old Testament.
1973	DD (Cantab.).
1977	Hon. DD (Edinburgh).
1979	President, Society for Old Testament Study.
	Fellow of the British Academy.

1982–3	Fellow, Institute for Advanced Studies, Hebrew University of Jerusalem.
1984–	Honorary Canon, St George's Cathedral, Jerusalem.
1986	Visiting Professor of Old Testament, United Theological College, Bangalore.
	Select Preacher before University of Cambridge.
1990	Corresponding Member, Akademie der Wissenschaften, Göttingen.
1991	Burkitt Medal for Biblical Studies, British Academy.
1992–5	President, International Organization for the Study of the Old Testament.

Bibliography of the works of John Adney Emerton

Karen K. Maticich

Note: Book reviews of less than one page have not been included.

1955

'The Aramaic Underlying τὸ αἷμά μου τῆς διαθήκης in Mk. XIV. 24', *JTS* ns 6 (1955), pp. 238–40.

1956

'The Purpose of the Second Column of the Hexapla', *JTS* ns 7 (1956), pp. 79–87.

1958

'The Hundred and Fifty-Three Fishes in John XXI. 11', *JTS* ns 9 (1958), pp. 86–9.
'The Origin of the Son of Man Imagery', *JTS* ns 9 (1958), pp. 225–42.

1959

The Peshitta of the Wisdom of Solomon (Leiden, 1959).

1960

'Commentaries on the Book of the Prophet Jeremiah', *Theology* 63 (1960), pp. 319–23.
'Some New Testament Notes', *JTS* ns 11 (1960), pp. 329–36.
'The Participles in Daniel v. 12', *ZAW* 72 (1960), pp. 262–3.

1961

'Did Jesus Speak Hebrew?', *JTS* ns 12 (1961), pp. 189–202.
Reprint of 'The Origin of the Son of Man Imagery' (*JTS* ns 9 [1958], pp. 225–42), in A. Farrer, C. F. Evans, J. A. Emerton *et al.*, *The Communication of the Gospel in New Testament Times* (London, 1961), pp. 35–56.

1962

'Appendix on the Numerals', in W. B. Stevenson, *Grammar of Palestinian Jewish Aramaic* (2nd edn, Oxford, 1962), pp. 97–107.

'Binding and Loosing – Forgiving and Retaining', *JTS* ns 13 (1962), pp. 325–31.

'Old Testament Scholarship and the Church – A Century after Colenso', *The Modern Churchman*, ns 5 (1962), pp. 266–71.

'Priests and Levites in Deuteronomy: An Examination of Dr. G. E. Wright's Theory', *VT* 12 (1962), pp. 129–38.

'*TO AIMA MOY THΣ ΔIAΘHKHΣ*: The Evidence of the Syriac Versions', *JTS* ns 13 (1962), pp. 111–17.

'Unclean Birds and the Origin of the Peshitta', *JSS* 7 (1962), pp. 204–11.

Review of E. M. Sidebottom, *The Christ of the Fourth Gospel in the Light of First-Century Thought* (London, 1961), in *JTS* ns 13 (1962), pp. 146–9.

1963

'Commentaries on Exodus', *Theology* 66 (1963), pp. 453–6.

'Notes on Three Passages in Psalms Book III', *JTS* ns 14 (1963), pp. 374–81.

Review of W. D. Davies, *Christian Origins and Judaism* (London, 1962), in *JTS* ns 14 (1963), pp. 133–6.

Review of P. Lamarche, *Zacharie IX–XIV: structure littéraire et messianisme* (Paris, 1961), in *JTS* ns 14 (1963), pp. 113–16.

1964

'A Note on Proverbs xii. 26', *ZAW* 76 (1964), pp. 191–3.

'Mark XIV. 24 and the Targum to the Psalter', *JTS* ns 15 (1964), pp. 58–9.

Review of D. W. Thomas and W. D. McHardy (eds.), *Hebrew and Semitic Studies Presented to Godfrey Rolles Driver in Celebration of His Seventieth Birthday 20 August 1962* (Oxford, 1963), in *JTS* ns 15 (1964), pp. 92–5.

1965

'Commentaries on the Wisdom of Solomon', *Theology* 68 (1965), pp. 376–80.

'Ugaritic Notes', *JTS* ns 16 (1965), pp. 438–43.

1966

Song of Songs, in *Song of Songs – Tobit – 4 Ezra. The Old Testament in Syriac According to the Peshiṭta Version* (Leiden, 1966).

'Did Ezra Go to Jerusalem in 428 B.C.?', *JTS* ns 17 (1966), pp. 1–19.

'Melchizedek and the Gods: Fresh Evidence for the Jewish Background of John X.34–36', *JTS* ns 17 (1966), pp. 399–401.

'"Spring and torrent" in Psalm lxxiv 15', in *Volume du Congrès: Genève 1965* (*SVT* 15, 1966), pp. 122–33.

1967

'Beth-shemesh', in D. W. Thomas (ed.), *Archaeology and Old Testament Study: Jubilee Volume of the Society for Old Testament Study 1917–1967* (Oxford, 1967), pp. 197–206.

'*Maranatha* and *Ephphatha*', *JTS* ns 18 (1967), pp. 427–31.

'Some Problems of Text and Language in the Odes of Solomon', *JTS* ns 18 (1967), pp. 376–402.

'The Meaning of אַבְנֵי־קֹדֶשׁ in Lamentations 4 1', *ZAW* 79 (1967), pp. 233–6.

'The Printed Editions of the Song of Songs in the Peshiṭta Version', *VT* 17 (1967), pp. 416–29.

The Textual Problems of Isaiah v 14', *VT* 17 (1967), pp. 135–42.

Review of K. Elliger, *Leviticus* (Tübingen, 1966), in *VT* 17 (1967), pp. 488–93.

Review of E. Kutsch, *Salbung als Rechtsakt im Alten Testament und im alten Orient* (Berlin, 1963), in *JSS* 12 (1967), pp. 122–8.

Review of H. C. M. Vogt, *Studie zum nachexilischen Gemeinde in Esra-Nehemia* (Werl, 1966), in *JTS* ns 18 (1967), pp. 169–75.

1968

'A Note on the Hebrew Text of Proverbs I. 22–3', *JTS* ns 19 (1968), pp. 609–14.

'Some Difficult Words in Genesis 49', in P. R. Ackroyd and B. Lindars (eds.), *Words and Meanings: Essays Presented to David Winton Thomas* (Cambridge, 1968), pp. 81–93.

'The Syntactical Problem of Psalm XLV. 7', *JSS* 13 (1968), pp. 58–63.

Review of M. Wilcox, *The Semitisms of Acts* (Oxford, 1965), in *JSS* 13 (1968), pp. 282–97.

Review of H. J. Zobel, *Stammesspruch und Geschichte: Die Angaben der Stammes-sprüche von Gen 49, Dtn 33, und Jdc 5 über die politischen und kultischen Zustände im damaligen 'Israel'* (Berlin, 1965), in *JTS* ns 19 (1968), pp. 245–51.

1969

'Notes on Jeremiah 12 9 and on Some Suggestions of J. D. Michaelis about the Hebrew Words *naḥā, 'æbrā,* and *jadă*', *ZAW* 81 (1969), pp. 182–91.

'Notes on Some Passages in the Book of Proverbs', *JTS* ns 20 (1969), pp. 202–20.

'Some Linguistic and Historical Problems in Isaiah VIII. 23', *JSS* 14 (1969), pp. 151–75.

'The Meaning of the Root "MZL" in Ugaritic', *JSS* 14 (1969), pp. 22–33.

1970

'A Consideration of Some Alleged Meanings of ידע in Hebrew', *JSS* 15 (1970), pp. 145–80.

'David Winton Thomas', *ZAW* 82 (1970), pp. v–vi.

With M. Masterman *et al.*, 'Dialogue: Translating the Bible', *Theoria to Theory* 4, 2

(1970), pp. 4–18.
'Were Greek Transliterations of the Hebrew Old Testament Used by Jews before the Time of Origen?', *JTS* ns 21 (1970), pp. 17–31.

1971

'A Further Consideration of the Purpose of the Second Column of the Hexapla', *JTS* ns 22 (1971), pp. 15–28.
'Some False Clues in the Study of Genesis xiv', *VT* 21 (1971), pp. 24–47.
'The Riddle of Genesis xiv', *VT* 21 (1971), pp. 403–39.

1972

'A Difficult Part of Mot's Message to Baal in the Ugaritic Texts (CTA 5. i. 4–6)', *The Australian Journal of Biblical Archaeology* 2, 1 (1972), pp. 50–71.
'A Problem in the Hebrew Text of Jeremiah VI. 23 and L. 42', *JTS* ns 23 (1972), pp. 106–13.
Review of H. Cazelles *et al.*, *Donum Natalicium Iosepho Coppens Septuagesimum Annum Complenti D. D. D. Collegae et Amici, I: De Mari à Qumrân: L'Ancien Testament. Son milieu. Ses écrits. Ses relectures juives* (Gembloux and Paris, 1969), in *JTS* ns 23 (1972), pp. 462–5.
Review of U. Kellermann, *Nehemia: Quellen, Überlieferung und Geschichte* (Berlin, 1967), in *JTS* ns 23 (1972), pp. 171–85.
Review of L. Koehler and W. Baumgartner, *Hebräisches und aramäisches Lexikon zum Alten Testament*, I (3rd edn, Leiden, 1967), in *VT* 22 (1972), pp. 502–11.

1973

'Notes on Two Proposed Emendations in the Book of Judges (11 24 and 16 28)', *ZAW* 85 (1973), pp. 220–3.
'The Problem of Vernacular Hebrew in the First Century A.D. and the Language of Jesus', *JTS* ns 24 (1973), pp. 1–23.
Review of K. Elliger and W. Rudolph (eds.), *Biblia Hebraica Stuttgartensia* (Stuttgart, 1969–71), in *ThLZ* 98 (1973), cols. 514–17.

1974

'A Neglected Solution of a Problem in Psalm lxxvi 11', *VT* 24 (1974), pp. 136–46.
'The Meaning of *šēnā'* in Psalm cxxvii 2', *VT* 24 (1974), pp. 15–31.
Reprint of 'The Purpose of the Second Column of the Hexapla' (*JTS* ns 7 [1956], pp. 79–87), in S. Jellicoe (ed.), *Studies in the Septuagint: Origins, Recensions, and Interpretations* (New York, 1974), pp. 347–55.
Review of W. A. van der Weiden, *Le Livre des Proverbes: Notes philologiques* (Rome, 1970), in *JTS* ns 25 (1974), pp. 476–81.

1975

(Ed.) *Congress Volume: Edinburgh 1974* (*SVT* 28, 1975).
'Some Problems in Genesis xxxviii', *VT* 25 (1975), pp. 338–61.
Review of L. Koehler and W. Baumgartner, *Hebräisches und aramäisches Lexikon zum Alten Testament*, 2 (3rd edn, Leiden, 1974), in *VT* 25 (1975), pp. 810–16.
Review of W. McKane, *Proverbs: A New Approach* (London, 1970), in *JTS* ns 26 (1975), pp. 128–35.

1976

'An Examination of a Recent Structuralist Interpretation of Genesis xxxviii', *VT* 26 (1976), pp. 79–98.
'Gideon and Jerubbaal', *JTS* ns 27 (1976), pp. 289–312.
'The Root *'aṣah* and Some Uses of *'eṣah* and *mo'eṣah* in Hebrew', in W. C. van Wyk (ed.), *Studies in Wisdom Literature, Outestamentiese Werkgemeenskap in Suid-Afrika* 15/16 (Pretoria, 1976), pp. 13–26.
'The Translation of Psalm LXIV. 4', *JTS* ns 27 (1976), pp. 391–2.
Review of T. L. Thompson, *The Historicity of the Patriarchal Narratives: The Quest for the Historical Abraham* (Berlin, 1974), in *JTS* ns 27 (1976), pp. 155–8.

1977

The Psalms: a New Translation for Worship (London, 1977) (with D. L. Frost, A. A. Macintosh *et al.*).
'A Note on Isaiah xxxv 9–10', *VT* 27 (1977), pp. 488–9.
'A Textual Problem in Isaiah 25 2', *ZAW* 89 (1977), pp. 64–73.
'Godfrey Rolles Driver 1892–1975', *Proceedings of the British Academy* 63 (1977), pp. 345–62.
'Notes on Some Passages in the Odes of Solomon', *JTS* ns 28 (1977), pp. 507–19.
'The Etymology of *hištaḥᵃwāh*', *OTS* 20 (1977), pp. 41–55.
'The Textual and Linguistic Problems of Habakkuk II. 4–5', *JTS* ns 28 (1977), pp. 1–18.

1978

(Ed.) *Congress Volume: Göttingen 1977* (*SVT* 29, 1978).
'A Further Note on CTA 5 I 4–6', *UF* 10 (1978), pp. 73–7.
'The "Second Bull" in Judges 6:25–28', *Eretz-Israel* 14 (1978), pp. 52*–5.*
'The Translation of the Verbs in the Imperfect in Psalm II. 9', *JTS* ns 29 (1978), pp. 499–503.

1979

(Ed.) *Wisdom of Solomon; Song of Songs* (with D. J. Lane), in *The Old Testament in Syriac According to the Peshiṭta Version*, II, 5 (Leiden, 1979).

(Ed.) *Studies in the Historical Books of the Old Testament* (*SVT* 30, 1979).
'A Note on Proverbs II. 18', *JTS* ns 30 (1979), pp. 153–8.
'Judah and Tamar', *VT* 29 (1979), pp. 403–15.
'Wisdom', in G. W. Anderson (ed.), *Tradition and Interpretation: Essays by Members of the Society for Old Testament Study* (Oxford, 1979), pp. 214–37.
Review of H. Gese and H. P. Rüger (eds.), *Wort und Geschichte: Festschrift für Karl Elliger zum 70. Geburtstag* (Kevelaer and Neukirchen-Vluyn, 1973), in *BO* 36 (1979), pp. 77–8.

1980

(Ed.) *Prophecy: Essays Presented to Georg Fohrer on His Sixty-Fifth Birthday 6 September 1980* (Berlin and New York, 1980).
'Notes on Two Verses in Isaiah (26 16 and 66 17)', *ibid.*, pp. 12–25.
(Ed.) *Old Testament Studies in Honour of P. A. H. de Boer* (=*VT* 30 [1980], pp. 385–533).
'Notes on the Text and Translation of Isaiah xxii 8–11 and lxv 5', *ibid.*, pp. 437–51.
'A List of G. R. Driver's Publications since 1962', *VT* 30 (1980), pp. 185–91.

1981

(Ed.) *Congress Volume: Vienna 1980* (*SVT* 32, 1981).
'A Problem in the Odes of Solomon XXIII. 20', *JTS* ns 32 (1981), pp. 443–7 (with R. P. Gordon).
'A Textual Problem in Isaiah XXX. 5', *JTS* ns 32 (1981), pp. 125–8.
'Notes on Some Problems in Jeremiah v 26', in A. Caquot and M. Delcor (eds.), *Mélanges Bibliques et Orientaux en l'Honneur de M. Henri Cazelles* (Neukirchen-Vluyn, 1981), pp. 125–33.
Review of E. Würthwein, *The Text of the Old Testament: An Introduction to the Biblia Hebraica* (E. tr., London, 1980), in *VT* 31 (1981), pp. 248–51.

1982

(Ed.) *Interpreting the Hebrew Bible: Essays in Honour of E. I. J. Rosenthal* (Cambridge, 1982) (with S. C. Reif).
'The Translation and Interpretation of Isaiah vi. 13', *ibid.*, pp. 85–118.
(Ed.) *Old Testament Studies Dedicated to G. W. Anderson* (=*VT* 32 [1982], pp. 1–128).
'A Further Note on Isaiah XXX. 5', *JTS* ns 33 (1982), p. 161.
'A Note on the Alleged Septuagintal Evidence for the Restoration of the Hebrew Text of Isaiah 34:11–12', *Eretz-Israel* 16 (1982), pp. 34*–6.*
'Leviathan and *ltn*: The Vocalization of the Ugaritic Word for the Dragon', *VT* 32 (1982), pp. 327–31.
'New Light on Israelite Religion: The Implications of the Inscriptions from Kuntillet 'Ajrud', *ZAW* 94 (1982), pp. 2–20.
'Some Notes on the Ugaritic Counterpart of the Arabic *GHAIN*', in G. E. Kadish

and G. E. Freeman (eds.), *Studies in Philology in Honour of Ronald James Williams* (Toronto, 1982), pp. 31–50.

'The Meaning of the Ammonite Inscription from Tell Siran', in W. C. Delsman *et al.* (eds.), *Von Kanaan bis Kerala: Festschrift für Prof. Mag. Dr. Dr. J. P. M. van der Ploeg O.P. zur Vollendung des siebzigsten Lebensjahres am 4. Juli 1979* (Neukirchen-Vluyn, 1982), pp. 367–77.

'The Origin of the Promises to the Patriarchs in the Older Sources of the Book of Genesis', *VT* 32 (1982), pp. 14–32.

1983

'How Does the Lord Regard the Death of his Saints in Psalm CXVI. 15?', *JTS* ns 34 (1983), pp. 146–56.

Review of L. R. Fisher (ed.), *Ras Shamra Parallels: The Texts from Ugarit and the Hebrew Bible*, I, II (Rome, 1972, 1975), in *JSS* 28 (1983), pp. 359–61.

1984

'The Meaning of Proverbs XIII. 2', *JTS* ns 35 (1984), pp. 91–5.

'The Odes of Solomon' (introduction and translation), in H. F. D. Sparks (ed.), *The Apocryphal Old Testament* (Oxford and New York, 1984), pp. 683–731.

Review of A. F. L. Beeston *et al.*, *Sabaic Dictionary (English-French-Arabic)* (Louvain-la-Neuve and Beirut, 1982), and J. C. Biella, *Dictionary of Old South Arabic: Sabaean Dialect* (Chico, 1982), in *VT* 34 (1984), pp. 489–93.

Review of D. J. Clark and N. Mundhenk, *A Translator's Handbook on the Books of Obadiah and Micah* (London, New York and Stuttgart, 1982), in *VT* 34 (1984), pp. 125–6.

Review of W. W. Hallo, J. C. Moyer and L. G. Perdue (eds.), *Scripture in Context II. More Essays on the Comparative Method* (Winona Lake, 1983), in *VT* 34 (1984), pp. 253–4.

Review of E. J. Hamlin, *Inheriting the Land: A Commentary on the Book of Joshua* (Grand Rapids and Edinburgh, 1983), in *VT* 34 (1984), pp. 254–5.

Review of H. B. Huffmon, F. A. Spina and A. R. W. Green (eds.), *The Quest for the Kingdom of God: Studies in Honor of George E. Mendenhall* (Winona Lake, 1983), in *VT* 34 (1984), pp. 371–2.

Review of L. Koehler and W. Baumgartner, *Hebräisches und aramäisches Lexikon zum Alten Testaments*, III (3rd edn, Leiden, 1983), in *VT* 34 (1984), pp. 500–6.

1985

(Ed.) *Congress Volume: Salamanca 1983* (*SVT* 36, 1985).

'Some Comments on the Shibboleth Incident (Judges XII 6)', in A. Caquot, S. Légasse and M. Tardieu (eds.), *Mélanges bibliques et orientaux en l'honneur de M. Mathias Delcor* (Neukirchen-Vluyn, 1985), pp. 149–57.

Review of A. F. L. Beeston, *Sabaic Grammar* (Manchester, 1984), in *VT* 35 (1985), pp. 118–19.

Review of E. Leach and D. A. Aycock, *Structuralist Interpretations of Biblical Myth* (Cambridge, 1984), in *VT* 35 (1985), pp. 250–2.

1986

Review of B. S. Childs, *Old Testament Theology in a Canonical Context* (London, 1985), in *VT* 36 (1986), pp. 376–8.
Review of N. K. Gottwald, *The Hebrew Bible. A Socio-Literary Introduction* (Philadelphia, 1985), in *VT* 36 (1986), pp. 504–6.
Review of J. A. Hackett, *The Balaam Text from Deir 'Allā* (Chico, 1984), in *JTS* ns 37 (1986), pp. 476–8.

1987

'An Examination of Some Attempts to Defend the Unity of the Flood Narrative in Genesis: Part I', *VT* 37 (1987), pp. 401–20.
'Sheol and the Sons of Belial', *VT* 37 (1987), pp. 214–18.
Review of C. L. Meyers and M. O'Connor (eds.), *The Word of the Lord Shall Go Forth: Essays in Honor of David Noel Freedman in Celebration of His Sixtieth Birthday* (Winona Lake, 1983), in *VT* 37 (1987), pp. 246–9.
Review of J. M. Miller and J. H. Hayes, *A History of Ancient Israel and Judah* (London, 1986), in *VT* 37 (1987), pp. 250–1.
Review of P. D. Miscall, *The Workings of Old Testament Narrative* (Philadelphia and Chico, 1983), in *VT* 37 (1987), pp. 251–2.

1988

(Ed.) *Congress Volume: Jerusalem 1986* (*SVT* 40, 1988).
'A Consideration of Two Recent Theories About Bethso in Josephus's Description of Jerusalem and a Passage in the Temple Scroll', in W. Claassen (ed.), *Text and Context: Old Testament and Semitic Studies for F. C. Fensham* (Sheffield, 1988), pp. 93–104.
'An Examination of Some Attempts to Defend the Unity of the Flood Narrative in Genesis: Part II', *VT* 38 (1988), pp. 1–21.
'The Interpretation of Proverbs 21,28', *ZAW* 100 (Supplement) (1988), pp. 161–70.
'The Priestly Writer in Genesis', *JTS* ns 39 (1988), pp. 381–400.
Review of A. Aejmelaeus, *The Traditional Prayer in the Psalms*, and L. Schmidt, *Literarische Studien zur Josephsgeschichte* (Berlin and New York, 1986), in *VT* 38 (1988), pp. 369–70.
Review of G. W. Ahlström, *Who Were the Israelites?* (Winona Lake, 1986), in *VT* 38 (1988), pp. 372–3.
Review of G. A. Anderson, *Sacrifices and Offerings in Ancient Israel: Studies in their Social and Political Importance* (Atlanta, 1987), in *VT* 38 (1988), pp. 377–8.
Review of D. Barthélemy (ed.), *Critique textuelle de l'Ancien Testament 2: Isaïe, Jérémie, Lamentations* (Fribourg and Göttingen, 1986), in *VT* 38 (1988), pp. 382–3.

Review of R. B. Coote and K. W. Whitelam, *The Emergence of Israel in Historical Perspective* (Sheffield, 1987), in *VT* 38 (1988), pp. 509–10.
Review of H.-P. Müller (ed.), *Bibel und Alter Orient: Altorientalische Beiträge zum Alten Testament von Wolfram von Soden* (Berlin and New York, 1985), in *JTS* ns 39 (1988), pp. 550–2.
Review of J. Van Seters, *In Search of History. Historiography in the Ancient World and the Origins of Biblical History* (New Haven, Conn., and London, 1983), in *VT* 38 (1988), pp. 250–1.
Review of J. D. W. Watts, *Isaiah 1–33* and *Isaiah 34–66* (Waco, 1985, 1987), in *VT* 38 (1988), pp. 124–5.

1989

'The Meaning of the Verb *ḥāmas* in Jeremiah 13,22', in V. Fritz, K.-F. Pohlmann and H.-C. Schmitt (eds.), *Prophet und Prophetenbuch: Festschrift für Otto Kaiser zum 65. Geburtstag* (Berlin and New York, 1989), pp. 19–28.
Review of J. H. Eaton, *Kingship and the Psalms* (2nd edn, Sheffield, 1986), in *VT* 39 (1989), pp. 123–4.
Review of J. D. Fowler, *Theophoric Personal Names in Ancient Hebrew: A Comparative Study* (Sheffield, 1988), in *VT* 39 (1989), pp. 246–8.
Review of W. Gesenius (ed. R. Meyer and H. Donner), *Hebräisches und Aramäisches Handwörterbuch über das Alte Testament*, 1 (18th edn, Berlin, 1987), in *VT* 39 (1989), pp. 104–10.
Review of C. Westermann, *Genesis 1–11; 12–36; 37–50: A Commentary* (E. tr., London, 1984, 1986, 1987), in *JTS* ns 40 (1989), pp. 146–51.
Review of R. N. Whybray, *The Making of the Pentateuch: A Methodological Study* (Sheffield, 1987), in *VT* 39 (1989), pp. 110–16.

1990

(Ed.) *Studies in the Pentateuch* (*SVT* 41, 1990).
'Some Problems in Genesis xiv', *ibid.*, pp. 73–102.
'The Site of Salem, the City of Melchizedek (Genesis xiv 18)', *ibid.*, pp. 45–71.
Review of G. J. Brooke (ed.), *Temple Scroll Studies* (Sheffield, 1989), in *VT* 40 (1990), pp. 502–3.
Review of R. E. Clements (ed.), *The World of Ancient Israel: Sociological, Anthropological and Political Perspectives: Essays by Members of the Society for Old Testament Study* (Cambridge, 1989), in *VT* 40 (1990), pp. 506–7.
Review of T. R. Hobbs, *2 Kings* (Waco, 1985), in *VT* 40 (1990), pp. 242–3.
Review of N. P. Lemche, *Ancient Israel: A New History of Israelite Society* (Sheffield, 1988), in *VT* 40 (1990), pp. 247–9.
Review of P. D. Miller, P. D. Hanson and D. McBride (eds.), *Ancient Israelite Religion: Essays in Honor of Frank Moore Cross* (Philadelphia, 1987), in *VT* 40 (1990), pp. 253–4.

1991

(Ed.) *Congress Volume: Leuven 1989* (*SVT* 43, 1991).
'A Further Consideration of D. W. Thomas's Theories about *yāda'*, *VT* 41 (1991), pp. 145–63.
'The Work of David Winton Thomas as a Hebrew Scholar', *VT* 41 (1991), pp. 287–303.
Review of T. N. D. Mettinger, *A Farewell to the Servant Songs. A Critical Examination of an Exegetical Axiom* (Lund, 1983), in *BO* 48 (1991), cols. 626–32.

1992

'The Source Analysis of Genesis xi 27–32', *VT* 42 (1992), pp. 37–46.
'The Translation of Isaiah 5,1', in F. García Martínez, A Hilhorst and C. J. Labuschagne (eds.), *The Scriptures and the Scrolls: Studies in Honour of A. S. van der Woude on the Occasion of His 65th Birthday* (Leiden, 1992), pp. 18–30.
Review of T. L. Thompson, *The Origin Tradition of Ancient Israel: I. The Literary Formation of Genesis and Exodus 1–23* (Sheffield, 1987), in *VT* 42 (1992), pp. 286–8.

1993

'Abraham Kuenen and the Early Religion of Ancient Israel', in P. B. Dirksen and A. van der Kooij (eds.), *Abraham Kuenen (1828–1891): His Major Contributions to the Study of the Old Testament* (*OTS* 29: Leiden, 1993), pp. 8–28.
'Lice or a Veil in the Song of Songs 1.7?', in A. G. Auld (ed.), *Understanding Poets and Prophets: Essays in Honour of George Wishart Anderson* (Sheffield, 1993), pp. 127–40.
'The Historical Background of Isaiah 1:4–9', in *Eretz-Israel* 24 (1993) (Avraham Malamat Volume), pp. 34*–40.*
'The "Mountain of God" in Psalm 68:16', in A. Lemaire and B. Otzen (eds.), *History and Traditions of Early Israel: Studies Presented to Eduard Nielsen* (*SVT* 50, 1993), pp. 24–37.
Articles on 'Aramaic', 'Hebrew', 'Names of God in the Hebrew Bible', and 'Tetragrammaton', in B. M. Metzger and M. D. Coogan (eds.), *The Oxford Companion to the Bible* (New York and Oxford, 1993), pp. 45–6, 271–3, 548–9, 738.
Review of R. B. Coote, *Early Israel: A New Horizon* (Minneapolis, 1990), in *VT* 43 (1993), pp. 140–1.
Review of I. Drazin, *Targum Onkelos to Exodus: An English Translation of the Text with Analysis and Commentary* (Hoboken, New Jersey, etc., 1990), in *VT* 43 (1993), pp. 280–1.

1994

'The Text of Psalm lxxvii 11', *VT* 44 (1994), pp. 183–94.
'New Evidence for the Use of *Waw* Consecutive in Aramaic', *VT* 44 (1994), pp. 255–8.

'When did Terah die (Genesis 11: 32)?', in S. E. Balentine and J. Barton (eds.), *Language, Theology, and the Bible: Essays in Honour of James Barr* (Oxford, 1994), pp. 170–81.

'What Light Has Ugaritic Shed on Hebrew?', in G. J. Brooke, A. H. W. Curtis and J. F. Healey (eds.), *Ugarit and the Bible. Proceedings of the International Symposium on Ugarit and the Bible, Manchester, September 1992* (Münster, 1994), pp. 53–69.

'"The high places of the gates" in 2 Kings xxiii 8', *VT* 44 (1994), pp. 455–67.

Review of N. P. Lemche, *The Canaanites and their Land: The Tradition of the Canaanites* (Sheffield, 1991), in *VT* 44 (1994), pp. 130–1.

In Press

'Are There Examples of Enclitic *mem* in the Hebrew Bible?', in Festschrift for M. Haran.

Editing and translating

From 1960: Member of the Old Testament panel for *The New English Bible* (1st edn, 1961; 2nd edn, 1970).

1967–74: Editor, *Society for Old Testament Study Monograph Series.*

1973–7: Chairman of the committee which prepared 'The Liturgical Psalter', in *The Alternative Service Book 1980* (Cambridge and London, 1980), pp. 1095–1289.

1964– : Editor of *The International Critical Commentary* (Old Testament).

1970– : Member of the Editorial Board of *ZAW.*

1971– : Member of the Editorial Board of *VT.*

1975– : Editor, *Vetus Testamentum.*

Index of authors

Compiled by Carol Smith

300

Principal biblical and apocryphal references